The *politics of* Clientelism

The politics of Clientelism

DEMOCRACY & THE STATE IN COLOMBIA

John D. *Martz*

TRANSACTION PUBLISHERS
New Brunswick (U.S.A.) and London (U.K.)

Library of Congress Catalog Number: 96-21482
ISBN: 1-56000-264-6
Printed in the United States of America

Library of Congress Cataloging-in-Publication Data

Martz, John D.
    The politics of clientelism : democracy and the state in Colombia / John
D. Martz.
        p. cm.
    Includes bibliographical references and index.
    ISBN 1-56000-264-6 (alk. paper)
    1. Patronage, Political—Colombia. 2. Patron and client—Colombia.
3. Colombia—Politics and government—1946–   . 4. Democracy—
Colombia. 5. State, The. I. Title.
JL2881.M37   1996
302.9861—dc20   96-21482
                                                                                CIP

To a remarkable pair of grandparents,
with love and the warmest of memories:
John D. and Carolyn Martz
Harry L. and Ada Sipe

Contents

Preface: A Personal Commentary   ix

Introduction: The Plan of the Book   1

Part I: Conceptualizing Colombian Politics

1. The Individual, the State, and Clientelism   7
2. Colombia: Clientelism and the Patrimonial State   35
3. Colombia: The Breakdown and Renewal of Clientelism   57

Part II: The Reimposition of Traditional Controls

4. Setting the Foundations: Lleras Camargo (1958–62)   75
5. Crises and Legitimation: Valencia (1962–66)   99
6. Reformist Developmentalism: Lleras Restrepo (1966–70)   119
7. The Drive for Consolidation: Pastrana (1970–74)   143
8. The Quest for Redistribution: López Michelsen (1974–78)   161
9. Traditionalism and Repression: Turbay (1978–82)   185

Part III: Modernization and Restructuring

10. "Apertura" and the Reformist Impulse:
    Betancur (1982–86)   209
11. The Shift from Biparty Government: Barco (1986–90)   243
12. Modernization and Restructuring: Gaviria (1990–94)   265

Conclusions: Corporate Clientelism and the
Political Future   291

Bibliography   325

Index   351

Preface: A Personal Commentary

A young North American exchange student first set foot in Colombia during the penultimate year of the Rojas Pinilla dictatorship. If a somewhat quixotic memory is not playing tricks on me, it was the eve of Bastille Day, no less. Consequently, even the least quantitatively oriented scholar will calculate that I have been observing and studying Colombian politics and society for four decades. Notwithstanding any possible protestations that I was uncommonly precocious when I first arrived in Colombia, my contemporaries today recognize me as a veteran of Latin American social studies who is literally as well as figuratively a graybeard. At the same time, the passing of years may well enhance one's intellectual experience while nourishing that historical perspective that the social sciences sometimes denigrate or forget in their search for empirical truths. In my own case, the early years led to a thesis on the Rojas dictatorship and then to the 1962 publication of *Colombia: A Contemporary Political Survey* (Chapel Hill: The University of North Carolina Press, 1962). The latter concentrated attention on the deterioration of elitist democracy and coalition government from the 1930s forward, punctuated by the rise of rural violence, the traumatizing *bogotazo* in 1948, and the breakdown of coalition governmental traditions that led to civilian authoritarianism under Laureano Gómez at the start of the 1950s. This culminated in military rule and the vicissitudes of General Gustavo Rojas Pinilla as he sought to build his own personalistic regime. His ultimate failure was chronicled, along with the introduction of the Frente Nacional—the National Front system designed for biparty control of a renewed democracy, one in which traditional elites would reestablish their customary domination of Colombian life and society. The book was later translated and published in Bogotá by the Universidad Nacional de Colombia (1969), and the original was republished by Greenwood Press in 1975. In the meantime, my own intellectual and regional research interests were relatively undisciplined. Thus, my publications touched on a rather broad variety of topics. That is irrelevant here, except to note that I maintained a keen interest and curiosity about the National Front, and hence the course of political events in Colombia. Occasional essays, reviews, and varied short pieces were forthcoming. With the gradual move away from the National Front, initially in constitutional terms but only more recently as a shift in political dynamics, my research activities responded in kind. This has led during the past dozen years or so to more concentrated attention on both single-country and comparative studies focusing on Colombia, Ecuador, and Venezuela. Visits to all three have been frequent, including extended stays in Colombia for teaching as well as research in both 1986 and 1992, along with the most recent in the summer of 1995.

Those published works of mine that are most relevant to this book are cited where appropriate—selectively, not exhaustively. At the same time, I have been pursuing truly comparative work, and envisage extended work on the political parties of the three Grancolombian nations in the near future. Before any of this, however, came the realization that, as a Colombian student put it to me one evening after a seminar, "it is time to go back and update your earlier book." I shrugged off the idea casually, but the thought lingered. The fact that anyone even remembered a book written so many years earlier was striking. Furthermore, in reexamining the book carefully and rethinking my early research career along with commitments and interests over more recent and current agendas for investigation, other ideas also began to take hold. It soon became obvious that the appropriate effort should be much more than "updating." For that matter, how does one merely update some thirty years of politics? Absurd.

I leave to the Introduction a discussion of those theoretical and conceptual questions that have informed the book, as well as thematic political concerns that stand out during the decades of Colombian political experience which are the subject of the analytic narrative. They draw on the rich literature of political clientelism—so much a part of the Colombian tradition—as well as the more uncertain if currently thriving contemporary literature on democratization. In so doing, I acknowledge an extraordinary intellectual debt to a large and still growing contingent of Colombian and foreign social scientists. When I was first trying to untangle and understand the complexities of Colombian social and political life, the number of scholars similarly engaged was small. What a pleasure it is to survey the situation today.

Social science research in Colombia is not only alive and well, but represents some of the finest work anywhere in the western hemisphere. International cooperation and collaboration has also been extensive, thus rewarding a growing number of North Americans and Europeans. In Colombia and abroad, new contingents of talented graduate students are responding to quality education, and the results bode very well indeed for the future. It would otherwise be impossible to undertake a project as broad in scope as this book. For better or worse, I ultimately designed and structured a work that, if feasible by a foreigner, necessarily relies heavily on the investigations of many other scholars. The amount of literature that I have attempted to traverse is extensive and intensive, to understate the reality grossly. Others will have to judge the extent to which my undertaking has justified the effort.

Even granting the inevitably personal element that must accompany any modest effort to acknowledge one's intellectual and institutional debts, there are dangers of omission. With apologies in advance for those who I may be slighting, however, I cannot fail to extend special appreciation for some of those who were most generous of their time, energy, resources, and—most important of all—their ideas. Many have been affiliated with one or another of the institutional bases from which I have taught and conducted research. In 1986 these included the Pontificia Universidad Javeriana and the Universidad de los Andes in Bogotá, and also the Escuela Superior de Administración Pública. Lectures and conferences were conducted at the Universidad de Cartagena, the Universidad Tecnología del Magdalena in Santa Marta, the Universidad del Norte in Barranquilla, and the Universidad de Antioquia in Medellín. Six years later my affiliation was exclusively with the Facultad de Estudios Interdisciplinarios at the Javeriana, along with several weeks at the Universidad Antónoma de Bucaramanga.

Both of these visits were made possible through the Fulbright program, whose personnel were unfailingly cooperative. In 1986 Dr. Francisco Gnecco was a warmly hospitable executive director; six years later I found the same cordiality from Dr. Agustín Lombana. Program coordinator Consuelo Valdivieso Camacho has shepherded Fulbrighters through Colombia with exceptional facility and efficiency for many years. Other members of the Fulbright staff, although shifting over time, have earned my gratitude in countless ways.

Beyond Fulbright, personal indebtedness extends further than can be acknowledged adequately. Javier Sanín, S.J., has been in charge of the program at the Javeriana while providing untiring support and friendship. Gabriel Murillo headed the political science faculty at Los Andes, where he and his colleagues have been collaborative, as many other foreign scholars can testify. Rodrigo Losada Lora has been a friend and colleague for many years, as is also true of Francisco Leal Buitrago. Vicente Torrijos Rivera at Javeriana also merits acknowledgment here. My intellectual debt to many other Colombian scholars and investigators is profound, as is true for North American *colombianistas*. Here too the list of names is prohibitively lengthy, although a particular word of appreciation is due Harvey F. Kline for both personal and professional favors.

My gratitude, then, goes to these and a host of friends, colleagues, and scholars. Would that they could have minimized the errors of omission or commission that follow—but these remain my responsibility exclusively.

John D. Martz
September 1995

Introduction: The Plan of the Book

There are certain themes—which some might prefer to designate as "characteristics," "historical trends," or simply treat as a conjuncture of important events and influences—that have dominated the reality of politics and society in twentieth-century Colombia. They have also provided the bases for the thinking and analyses of scholars and practitioners alike, leading to discussions and debates reflecting a variety of analytic perspectives and political experiences. While leaving serious consideration to the body of the book, a cursory summary would include: domination of politics and society by traditional elites in control of the historic Liberal and Conservative parties; solidification of a classically powerful clientelistic heritage; extensive rural violence from mid-century, both predating and surviving the breakdown of rule and an interregnum under military government; reestablishment of elitist control under an unprecedented constitutional system dividing power equally between the two major parties, while excluding all other participants; a gradual loosening of legal provisions while attempting to withstand growing participatory pressures; an inexorable process of modernization and urbanization; political maneuvering designed to redefine and restructure the state without altering fundamentally the exclusionary character of democracy; and prolonged domestic violence predicated on guerrilla activism as well as a flourishing drug industry.

To put this into even more terse if lucid shorthand, consider the resultant preoccupations as I undertook the project: traditional elitist rule; clientelism; democracy; the state; social and political controls; modernization and change. These required extended reconsideration of Colombian politics and of the literature extant—many times greater than that when I had written the 1962 book. They also demanded a probing of the theoretical literature on such topics as clientelism, democracy—both exclusionary and inclusionary—and the like. All of this led to organizational and conceptual priorities that have shaped the presentation from

1

beginning to end. At the risk of merely reciting the table of contents, let me nonetheless alert the reader to the path that I have laid down.

My thinking about a conceptualization of Colombian politics is set forth in the three chapters of Part I. Particular attention is devoted to clientelism, to that rich and powerfully suggestive general theorizing that others before me have presented as fundamental to an understanding of Colombian politics. The first chapter reexamines this literature and the role of the state. It also permits me to differentiate stages of clientelistic evolution, from traditional forms of feudalism and patrimonialism to modern forms that might be termed *corporate* or *bureaucratic* clientelism. These are applied in chapter 2 to the historical experience in Colombia. The subsequent breakdown of civilian government, a four-year interval of military rule, and a return to constitutionality are examined in the third chapter, as well as exceptional if ingenious institutional tinkering on the part of the political elites to restore a system in which clientelist mechanisms would be renewed.

Moving at this juncture more fully into the Colombian experience, Part II—"The Reimposition of Traditional Controls"—brings us into the period of the Frente Nacional and covers the years from 1958 to 1982. Consistent with my 1962 book and, more significantly, as a means of tracing the evolution of events and of political forces in detail, I have chosen to pursue a chronological approach, devoting individual chapters to the succession of four-year administrations. The Frente Nacional was originally intended as a sixteen-year experiment but, before having run its course, further reforms as well as practical political considerations further sustained its life. Rather than engage in debate at this point, let it merely be observed that I see the alleged *desmonte* or reshaping of the Frente system as having remained effectively functional through both the López Michelsen and Turbay governments.

There are certainly those who might insist that it was prolonged even beyond 1982. However, I will argue that a process of restructuring, in both institutional and behavioral terms, emerged with irresistible force during the Betancur government. As such, Part III pursues what are viewed as important redefinitions of clientelism and of the role of the state in its examination of the three administrations from 1982 through 1994.

In moving progressively through the nine successive governments from 1958 to 1994, comparability of analysis and of organization was deemed important. Thus, allowing for some adjustments in chapters 11 and 12, the basic structure of presentation is unchanged. Chapters are divided into "Policies of Governance" and "Politics of the National Front" (or after). The former opens with "The National Environment," which permits an overview of population, demographic shifts, and the unimpeded trend toward urbanization and its consequences, which have tested successive administrations and produced a gradual evolution of clientelistic practices. This is followed by "Policies of the Administration," wherein systemic and regime responses and initiatives are cited and evaluation. Closing the first half of these chapters brings us to "Social and Political Controls," with particular emphasis to the ongoing struggle with guerrilla and with drug-related violence, accompanied by unrest and upheaval.

The second half of these chapters is preeminently political in the strictest sense of the term. "The Party Competition" deals with the incoming president and his team; with interparty relations; and generally carries through the midterm congressional elections (and local elections as appropriate in recent years). More is added to earlier discussions of presidential style, policy orientations, and the general course of political relationships. "Candidate Selection" continues the narrative, as does the subsequent section on "Campaign and Elections." As the chapters come to a close, it is within the framework suggested heuristically by the titles of each part of the book, as well as chapter titles. Having eventually traversed the chapters of Part III, in which the impact of continuing modernization registers ever more powerfully and leads toward redefinitions of modern clientelism and the modern state, we then turn finally to the concluding chapter.

This opens with a broad consideration of the Constitution of 1991, which continues to develop and to be progressively incorporated into the prevailing state system as successor to the document that had endured more than a century. The individual who undertook responsibility for the reshaping of the Colombian state in 1994, President Ernesto Samper Pizano, was subsequently plunged into a Watergate-style morass of rumor and scandal that was threatening his administration as these words are written in September of 1995. Whatever the outcome, the corporate character of contemporary clientelism remains writ large in Colombia. This permits a further assessment of those themes already alluded to: a reform of democracy and its public manifestations, and the continuing challenges to the system of both drug-related and guerrilla-inspired violence. In coming full circle from both the original conceptual concerns and the cycle of political events covering virtually a half-century or more, we will hopefully have answered a few questions while raising many more for criticism, commentary, and future study. That is as it should be.

I

Conceptualizing Colombian Politics

1

The Individual, the State, and Clientelism

At the core of all theorizing about the character of Latin American politics are fundamental issues concerning the individual, his place in society, and the role of the state in overseeing the conduct of public affairs. Those who would delineate a heuristic framework for the politics of the region are directly engaged in theorizing about central and universal concepts. The vitality of recent intellectual currents constitutes a recognition of the pervasive impact of ideas. As Johnson wrote, political theory for Latin America constitutes "a body of prescriptive beliefs about how the body politic and the government *ought* to function, what should be the optimal preferred set of relationships between man and the State, and what values and goals ought to be organically central to the system."[1] Certainly the individual is linked symbiotically to the state, which in turn exerts an inexorably powerful influence on the members of the polity.

The state bears the responsibility for the realization of civic needs, providing goods and services to each citizen. To do so requires the exercise and maintenance of social and political control. Certainly in Latin America the role of political and social governance is crucial, and the state has historically played an influential role. It stands as the prime regulator, coordinator, and pacesetter of the entire national system, the apex of the Latin American pyramid from which patronage, wealth, power, and programs flow. As a consequence, the nature and extent of controls are dependent upon the regime and its impact on policy. Until recently, scholarship on Latin America has been inhibited by the absence of well-developed theory linking regime and governmental process to policy formulation and performance.

While this condition has been gradually changing, it nonetheless remains incumbent upon us to bear in mind individual values, especially as these are linked to the clientelist impulse.

7

It will be our contention that the theoretical formulations about Latin American politics in recent years, notwithstanding many unquestionably valuable insights, have so concentrated upon the role of the state as to blur and perhaps minimize the significance of the individual. Whatever the semantic distinctions between "state" and "regime"—about which there is still little real consensus—it is clear that the individual is most often treated as the dependent variable. Presumably, if there may be significance of regime type in terms of policy outputs, this ought not be viewed as unaffected by social customs, morays, and the attitudes of the individual. Thus, the latter becomes one of our central concerns throughout the pages to follow, with power and political leadership developed and elaborated within the parameters of clientelism.

In treating of patron-client (P-C) relations, we are at one with Eisenstadt and Roniger when they state that from a topic of relatively marginal concern, its study "has become a central one, closely connected to basic theoretical problems and controversies in all the social sciences." There has been a change from limited dyadic interpersonal relations to a broad array of more institutionalized social relations and organizations. This is also directly germane to our Colombian study, given "the growing recognition that the phenomena subsumed under the umbrella of patron-client or clientelistic relations...may constitute, as they seemingly do in many Mediterranean, Latin America, and Southeast Asian societies, a central aspect of the institutional patterns of these societies."[2] Clientelism, in short, lies at the very core of our inquiry.

The Universality of Clientelism

We would insist that clientelism and its relationships have been manifest in Latin America from colonial times to the very present. Indeed, the concept is universal in character and, as J. F. Medard has written, is indispensable in understanding politics both inside and outside the Third World. In his words, "It is necessary to admit that modern political societies are penetrated by phenomena of this order [e.g., clientelism] to various degrees and in different forms."[3] Consequently, our analysis throughout is one in which clientelism plays a central role, and serves as a basic element in the effort of each and every political system to exercise and maintain social and political order.

Not all observers agree on the presence of clientelism in those nations regarded as most fully developed. At the least, however, there is close to a consensus about the existence of the phenomenon as a state evolves and progresses from its early primitive condition. Gamer, who is generally critical of clientelistic politics, traces patron-client relationships through a developmental process, arguing that they exist to some extent in all societies. He declares that "developed nations still contain some patron-clientism but have moved beyond it; *the developing nations are ruled by patron-clientism and cannot move beyond it.*"[4] Other scholars also view clientelism as existing not only in the traditionalistic rural setting in which it was most customarily identified in earlier years, but in more advanced developmental stages.

Robert Clark, for one, describes P-C systems as

important features of urban politics in Third World countries.... In large cities throughout the Third World, such as Lima or Caracas, the festering slums and impoverished neighborhoods have produced squatters' associations...under the jurisdiction or control of local patrons who defend the interests of their clients and receive deference and respect (as well as more material rewards) from them in return.[5]

Clearly, developing nations today have moved beyond the stage in which clientelism existed solely in the countryside and the village. Over time, clientelistic systems have become crucial as links between national, urban-based modernizing elites and the masses in both urban and rural settings. Under present conditions most systems exist at both the levels of the rural village and of urban neighborhoods.

True to fundamental P-C relationships, there will be large numbers of individuals of low status, interacting with the powerful patron who defends their interests in return for deference or material rewards. The rural patron has increasingly become a member of the higher clientelistic system as well. He stands as an intermediary dependent on a patron who operates at the national level. This enables urban elites to mobilize low status clients for such acts as mass demonstrations of political loyalty to the regime. In one fashion or another, patron-client relationships and the mechanisms by which they operate are present at diverse stages of the long modernizing process. To repeat, at the core of our analysis is the contention that political clientelism is found in societies that have existed alternatively under feudal, patrimonial, or modernizing bureaucratic conditions.

While basic definitions of clientelism are not always universally accepted, there is substantial acceptance of the way in which John Duncan Powell has depicted the classic *traditional* P-C relationship:

First, the patron-client tie develops between two parties *unequal* in status, wealth, and influence.... Second, the formation and maintenance of the relationship depends on *reciprocity* in the exchange of goods and services.... Third, the development and maintenance of a patron-client relationship rests heavily on *face-to-face* contact between the two parties.[6]

A more recent definitional treatment by Scott Mainwaring is similar in citing four major features of P-C relations: (1) their unequal character; (2) uneven reciprocity; (3) their noninstitutionalized nature; and (4) their face-to-face character.[7] He derived these characteristics from Weingrod, Scott, Graziano, and Archer, accepting the first three points while qualifying the fourth. Other sources essentially confirm the overall qualities of clientelism as defined by these scholars, especially in terms of traditional clientelism, as further elaborated later.

All of this strongly suggests that patron-clientelism at its most basic level "involves sets of patrons and clients cooperating with one another to retain maximum benefit for themselves from all assets which any of them handle *by personally exchanging these assets among themselves*."[8] An articulate French scholar effectively sums up these elements with the observation that the clientelistic relationship "is one of personal dependence...which links two persons who control unequal resources, the patron and the client, for a reciprocal exchange of favors."[9]

Qualities of dependence, unequal status, reciprocity, and personalization are consequently fundamental to the patron-client relationship. They remain relevant factors even as the process of modernization progressively transforms societies and political systems. More broadly, *clientelism* is viewed as an enduring mechanism of internal control in society. If it is true that each and every political regime is pressed to offer identifiable goods and services in meeting citizen needs, then it must also find mechanisms to assure the maintenance of social and political control. This suggests that the unfailing presence of clientelism, identifiable in all times and settings, underlines the fundamental character of the concept for an understanding of Latin American social and political life. Although the forms of clientelism change over time, they constitute decisive factors in analysis of the nature of society, the state, and the political order. Such is the basis for the elitist exercise of power.

Consequently, another of our central themes becomes the omnipresence of clientelism as manifested in the long historical evolution from its traditional forms (feudalism and patrimonialism) to modernizing bureaucratic forms (labelled "corporate" by some scholars). The forms of clientelism, altered and reshaped over time, in recent years have been transformed into modern organizational form. We will sketch important ways in which the classical patron-client relationship, despite its relative transformation, has in no sense been diminished as a relevant political force. Indeed, the bureaucratization of clientelism serves as further evidence of the vitality of the concept as a central factor for political analysis.

A dissection of writings on clientelism and patron-client linkages will provide the background from which to look more closely at the Latin American experience. This in turn will be directed toward Colombia in the subsequent analysis. It will be argued that the clientelism that emerged in traditional form has been modified through a process of evolutionary response to the phenomena of modernization. The functioning of clientelism was embodied in the traditionally rural and peasantry-based forms of patron-client relationships during both feudal and patrimonial eras. With the advent of urbanization, technology, and rampant statism in more recent years, the clientelistic phenomena has been reshaped as a means of extending political and social controls under conditions of bureaucratic centralism.

To repeat, P-C relationships have been found in Latin America from colonial times down to the present. Systems imbued respectively with feudal, patrimonial, or bureaucratic characteristics have shared the basic necessity of providing services, responding to the needs of the populace, and to securing and maintaining social and political control. As the progression toward the modernizing bureaucratic state has unfolded, there has similarly been a shifting in many of the clientelistic relationships. Yet in one form or another, political clientelism has remained central to the functioning of the polity. And this in turn has continued to be writ large by the persistence of traditional attitudes toward the state and its role in society and everyday life.

John Sloan, in the course of discussions over regime types and policy performance, has put it well in reminding us that Latin Americans have never been attracted to a state that merely plays "the role of referee among the competing interests of society and...provides law and order and a minimum level of public services."[10] In fact, the modern state has come to be seen as the ultimate *patron*. The ideal arrangement is presumably one in which the state is the dominant institution in society. Given a mounting drive for modernization and development, the functions requisite for governance have expanded, in some cases exponentially. The advent of the bureaucratic state has brought genuine centralization of the system; pronounced statism; urbanization; the weakening of regional and local allegiances; industrialization; infrastructural improvements in such areas as transportation and communications; and economic diversification.

All of this necessitated the elaboration of new mechanisms for an exercise of authority, for a processing of demands without forfeiting social and political authority. Corporate forms of clientelism have taken shape, and on their effectiveness rests the fate of those who would govern. Equally significant is the impact on the populace, for to speak of the state, and of the *patron,* is also to treat with the citizenry—the individuals who are systemic clients. This underlines the innate conceptual relevance of clientelism historically. Governance has been effectuated through a broad array of society-wide linkages. The establishment and defense, or collapse and renewal of the ability to exercise social and political control, has been dependent upon the mechanisms of clientelism.

These took root and were nourished under the conditions of feudalism and then patrimonialism, only to move more recently toward bureaucratic centralism. The concept of clientelism is therefore basic to our theoretical formulations. The next two chapters will discuss the clientelist tradition in Colombia during the premodern era. This will lead to the more extended discussions in Part II, where the contemporary experience of Colombia's National Front (Frente Nacional) provides the framework for bureaucratic rather than traditional clientelist controls. This is further affected by the array of both institutional and noninstitutional changes that have been unfolding since the formal conclusion of the National Front. Most immediate, however, is a closer consideration of the literature on clientelism, after which this may be employed to inform our study of the Colombian experience.

The Traditional Concept of Clientelism

The Genesis

Originally the preserve of social anthropologists, notions of clientelage and patronage have gradually reached into allied disciplines while producing profound implications for Latin American studies. The seminal work serving as a point of departure for investigation of P-C relationships was the 1950 study of *compadrazgo* by Mintz and Wolf.[11] This helped to stimulate further study—derived predominantly from the Mediterranean and Latin America—which led to increasing dissection of the patron-client relationship. Foster's series of articles in the early 1960s, drawn from his research in Tzintzuntzan, Mexico, developed and elaborated social relations between pairs—the dyadic contractual linkage.[12] Along with Mintz and Wolf, he saw that vertical *compadrazgo* symbolized patron-client contracts between parties of unequal status.[13]

A broader concept of clientelism was gradually developed to designate a particular kind of interpersonal relationship. It stressed a reciprocal need of individuals engaged in a dyadic exchange of resources and services. Its preoccupation was the analysis of how persons with mutual interests but unequal authority conduct relationships in order to achieve their objectives. Such linkages between so-called patrons and clients deal variously in patronage, influence, goods, allegiances and benefits; while the literature applies these and other terms of reference, the concentration on the character of the relationships is virtually universal. For political scientists, it is the existence of "patronage," in terms of politics as well as society, which has come to attract a degree of attention during the last two to three decades. Moreover, clientelism constitutes "a concept that generally interests political scientists because the patron everywhere occupies a preeminent place and plays the role of the principal intermediary between the center and the periphery. He is an important actor in most political processes."[14]

This has been most notable in discussions of political clientelism in the Third World. Clientelism can no longer be regarded as the exclusive preserve of anthropologists and, to a lesser degree, sociologists.[15] Rather, it has emerged in the literature as a form of personalized reciprocal relationship that constitutes a generic element of all political systems, most particularly those in the process of development and modernization. Political clientelism per se provides an analytic alternative to the group and class analyses so heavily employed by the discipline. While there is no denying the contributions of Bentleyan group theory, for example, let alone either Marxist or non-Marxist class analysis, not all political behavior can so be illuminated. Particularly for the polities of the Third World, as well as the less developed European states, it can be argued that the horizontal, class-based model of conflict has its limitations.

The clientelistic model, especially as applied to Latin America, has often been described as distinctive from either group or class analysis. Given the vertical polyclass linkages of clientelism, it can be argued that considerations of class are irrelevant. Clientelist ties are viewed as curbing or discouraging class mobilization, thus rendering class analysis largely irrelevant. On closer examination, however, this total dismissal of class as a determining variable appears unwise; there may well be grounds for a reconciliation of clientelistic and class-based characteristics. Certainly the manipulation of class and clientelistic interests may coincide, while the mechanisms of control and coercion may readily exist in either model. As Flinn has contended, class consciousness and class formation may very well be found in a society typified by strong clientelist relations.[16]

Clientelism, then, does not constitute a totally separate and unique model. It does possess features and characteristics, however, which may well be ignored or minimized in other models. For a time there was a tendency among scholars to argue that clientelism was an artifact of the past, or at the very most, an anachronistic reminder of times better gone and forgotten. However, it is now more prevalent to acknowledge the renewed interest in clientelistic analysis as a means of enriching the study of politics, especially in societies undergoing socioeconomic change under the influence of modernizing forces. It also restores the relevance of cultural factors that are too often forgotten in the construction of other models. The result may well be a more sensitized understanding of younger societies undergoing unprecedentedly abrupt transitions, thereby bridging in some part the intellectual and theoretical gap between the more and less advanced nations.

Scott, for one, has written that in typical nonindustrial circumstances, political groupings cut across class lines vertically. Consequently, a patron-client model of association bears a particular relevance to political action. Drawing on his studies of Southeast Asian bureaucracies and political parties at the local level, he contends that an emphasis on primordial sentiments—ethnicity, language, and religion—brings the analyst closer to the "real" categories of those being studied.[17] Other comparativists have concurred on the relevance of devoting attention, even if preliminary and tentative, to this approach. Political clientelism is therefore among the few genuinely cross-cultural concepts available for the comparative study of systems in transition. Cutting across both "traditional" and "modern" referents, it possesses a heuristic value that recommends serious efforts to employ it as a tool.

Feudal Clientelism

Some observations on historical experience and on further definitional matters is in order here. Recall our previous concern about differentiating between two stages of traditional clientelism—first feudal, and then patrimonial. The former can be traced back at least to the rise of feudalism in Western Europe and Japan. P-C ties at this early point displayed such classic characteristics as dyadic reciprocity, in which authority and the exercise of power are unequal. These linkages became basic to the system of land tenure and agricultural production. They developed most notably in rural areas marked by a concentration of wealth, power, education, and control of the land in the hands of a small elite. In the feudal polity, the basic method of governance centered on the lord and his dealings with the vassal. Feudal dependency created a formalized and legally sanctioned hierarchical relationship. The system became effective when it was institutionalized, and contributed to the solidification of legitimacy and the wielding of political power. As clientelage gradually evolved from feudalism in the direction of true patrimonialism, specialized administrative officials were named by the ruler as a type of intermediary between patrimonial ruler and the vassal. Although the relationships thus became somewhat more complex, they did not alter the basic character of clientelism.

In time, the Mediterranean and Latin American regions became notable laboratories for the nurturing of clientelism under conditions of patrimonialism. The Spanish and Portuguese colonizers of the New World recognized the utility of the system in terms of an indentured and subservient labor force. On large plantations and landed properties, the costs of production were minimized. Catholicism, in preaching the helplessness of mankind and the need for benefactors, provided otherworldly justification for the acceptance of traditional values and practices. This also seemingly excused, or at least explained, the practice of repression when employed by the patron. The coercive nature of the patron-client linkage was omnipresent, with the latter entrapped in a vicious circle of obedience, subservience, and impoverishment.

This is not to suggest that the patron-client relationship was necessarily an automatic expression of evil by the former or certain harsh oppression for the latter. The client under conditions of patrimonialism could secure such arrangements as kinship systems and extended family and clan organizations. Moreover, the inequality of the relationship with the patron did not deny the presence of a form of reciprocity, the maintenance of which was crucial for both individuals. Yet on the economic level, peasants living in rural societies possessed only their own labor, not land. Such clients also lacked the opportunity to employ better tools or equipment, while intellectually ill-equipped or unprepared to understand or even know the law. Often unaware of rights and obligations, the client grew accustomed to endure arbitrary injustices. Therefore, his only recourse was to seek out the patron as a means of coping with problems.

For the vast majority of peasants and rural dwellers, life took place under conditions of scarcity, where the major source of productive wealth was the land owned and controlled by others. The environment was rife with violence, disease, and death; injustice could be met at any juncture, often without prior warning. Coercive elements were inevitable, thereby aggravating the evident power asymmetry between superior and subordinate, between patron and client. The former would normally enjoy a relative monopoly of agricultural resources, with clientelism the mechanism of internal control. In political terms the clientelistic structure went beyond the unequal distribution of resources within society to include levers of systemic control. Governance and rule as well as commercial domination emerged from clientelism, while as subjects the clients could terminate the relationship only with difficulty, unlike the patron. In the words of a student of Peruvian politics,

> The clientelistic structure is a political structure because all types of material and non-material resources needed and desired by the members of a society are acquired and distributed, and conflicts over distribution resolved through the dynamics of the structure. The clientelistic structure includes both the government and commercial sectors of the society, and therefore is the basic political structure of the society.[18]

In much of Latin America this would become the reality to flow naturally out of evolving patrimonial clientelism. In its purest and most basic form, clientelism embraced a true dyadic relationship, definitionally composed of only two individuals. On this micro level, there was a voluntary agreement between them to exchange favors and, in time of need, to assist one another. The dyadic alliance revolved about the terms on which favors are given and received. The two members of the alliance were customarily of unequal status or power.

As Wolfe put it, when instrumental friendship "reaches a maximum point of imbalance so that one partner is clearly superior to the other in his capacity to grant goods and services, we approach the critical point where friendships give way to the patron-client tie."[19] The result, in the felicitous description of Pitt-Rivers, is a "lopsided friendship."[20] Patrons and clients have different resources at their respective disposal, and the asymmetrical character of the linkage is a virtual certainty. Should the status of the two persons become equalized, both the asymmetry and the affective nature of the relationship are altered. At the rural level, then, despite a degree of reciprocity, feudal clientelism is commonly marked by a relationship in which a single patron defends the interests of large numbers of persons of lower status.

Brokerage and Patrimonial Clientelism

For colonial Latin America, the original dyadic relationship involved an economically and politically dependent client, and a patron. The latter, identified by the Spanish *patron* and the Portuguese *patrão,* explicitly designated an individual with status and authority. It was for the patron to dole out favors or indulgences selectively as a reward for loyalty, allegiance, and services from the dependent client. The two parties to the contract (whether or not a formal pact, its strength would be mutually recognized and accepted) would exchange goods and services on an increasingly nonequivalent basic. The offerings of the patron included protection against both legal and illegal exactions of authority, while some degree of economic recompense was also probable. The client, in turn, would offer both material and intangible assets. The first most commonly constituted labor and physical service, while the latter—by no means less important—would embrace loyalty and respect, along with supportive tasks that could well include directly political action.

The theoretical definition is perhaps nowhere better expressed than in Scott's words, drawn from his observations of Southeast Asian models of association:

> The patron-client relationship—an exchange relationship between roles—may be defined as a special case of dyadic (two-person) ties involving a largely instrumental friendship in which an individual of higher socioeconomic status (patron)

uses his own influence and resources to provide protection or benefits, or both, for a person of lower status (client) who, for his part, reciprocates, by offering general support and assistance, including personal services, to the patron.[21]

Thus, the bonds that tie the system together are vertical and, although in theory the patron and client demonstrate equitably a special concern for one another's welfare, the inequality of status and power is a given. Furthermore, the patron customarily enjoys alliances with a large number of clients, although the reverse is rarely the case. At the same time, face-to-face contact between the two persons will accompany the actions and exchanges of the "lop-sided friendship."

This helps to introduce a leadership-followership system that is less group-centered than it is dominated by the patron. It also may lead to the emergence of a more complex arrangement, one in which there are in effect several tiers of followers. The clients of a patron may in turn have their own personal clients, and the emerging system becomes increasingly composed of chains of vertical dyads linking the highest leaders to those at the bottom of the pyramid through a series of subleaders. This multitiered structure, seen as a historical process, moves political clientelism to a higher level of development, one in which intermediaries become critical to the linkages. As developed in Boissevain's classic discussion of brokerage in Sicily, these persons act as systemic middlemen or, simply, as what he termed *social brokers*. Given an increasingly complicated system, it becomes the task of the broker to bridge gaps in communication.[22]

The gradual passage from historical feudalism not only creates new social demands and pressures, then, but requires an extension of clientelism beyond the original lord-vassal pattern. A growing societal complexity, further propelled by a greater variety in the "goods" basic to the P-C relationship, leads to systemic necessities that are to be embodied by brokers. This in turn complicates what had originally been a simple and direct role for the feudal patron. As Boissevain saw it, postfeudal society was characterized by competition for scarce resources. Competition inevitably emerged between rival entrepreneurs. While it was still possible to exert direct control over what he termed *first order resources* (land, jobs, and low-level personalistic favors), the *second order resources* consisted of strategic contacts with individuals who either controlled directly or enjoyed access to those with authority to control the distribution of resources. Persons dispensing first order resources were patrons, while those managing second order resources were brokers. The fundamental brokerage role became that of placing people in touch with one another, bridging gaps in communication. For Boissevain, then, the broker was a "professional manipulator of people and information who brings about communication for profit. He thus occupies a strategic place in a network of social relations viewed as a communications network."[23] In time, with the further evolution of political forms and structures, brokerage functions provide means for bureaucratic directives to reach even the most remote peripheries of the state. There is a gradual shift away from kinship and family linkages to those performed by brokers in communication with patrons operating at the national level. Thus, the initial dyadic context of clientelism, having passed from the feudal to the patrimonial stage as a natural and uncomplicated adjustment, confronts greater pressures and demands with the growing complexity of society and the approach of the modernizing bureaucratic stage. At this point, the question is raised about the possibility of corporate clientelism. That is, must the clientelist model be restricted to relationships between individuals, or can groups and corporate entities act as patrons or clients?

We recall that with both of the traditional stages—the feudal and the patrimonial—clientelism was characterized by an inequality of participants; the reciprocal nature of exchanges; and the proximity of face-to-face actions. Society was agrarian, with the population dispersed across broad extensions of land and territory. Economic survival was based on local and regional, rather than centralized resources. Political authority was most often exercised meaningfully at the local rather than national level. Social mobility was scant, forms of mobilization primitive or nonexistent, educational levels depressed, and communications infrastructures extremely limited. As modernizing changes began to emerge, the structures and dynamics of patrimonial society and politics were questioned and challenged. Furthermore, although the term *patrimonial* could be used for traditional, historical political systems, its implications were becoming more far-reaching.

S. N. Eisenstadt was among those who argued along these lines, further insisting that patrimonialism might be applied not so much to a particular level of development, but rather to a way of coping with major problems of political life. It was on this basis that he sought to differentiate neopatrimonial from traditional patrimonial regimes. He saw them as sharing such common characteristics as "the basic modes of coping with political problems; the relations between center and periphery; the major types of policies developed by their rulers; and the general format of political struggle and process."[24] And while some of his terminology differs from ours, he anticipated the subsequent contention that questions of legitimacy and efficacy of rule would display similarities between the more traditional and the contemporary contexts.

Certainly social and political controls could no longer be assumed to operate as in the past. And so it was that clientelism, so crucial for generations, seemed for some to have sunk into uninterrupted decline, perhaps to become an anachronism with the progressive unfolding of the twentieth century. Yet others still viewed it as providing a malleable and very real tool for the maintenance and defense of the political system, accompanied by its myriad socioeconomic interests. At the very least, one needed to ask if clientelism was becoming an artifact of the past or whether, alternatively, it might be transformed into new shapes and forms of continuing relevance to the political system.

The Bureaucratization of Clientelism

The Impact of Societal Change

As societies have gradually progressed from those simpler times that nurtured the old traditionalistic structures of feudal and patrimonial clientelism, the process of emergent modernization has led in turn to a progressive transformation of political clientelism. A powerful demographic shift from predominantly rural to urbanized societies; a recasting of the economy; the strengthening of the state; a centralization of political power and authority; these and a host of related socioeconomic factors came together to influence the course of politics, and the very character of systemic clientelism. This was noted earlier with the gradual shift from the original dyadic relationships of feudalism to the spread of brokerage networks and the patrimonial condition. While traditional landowners and local patrons were essentially community-oriented, in time the very community had to be linked more effectively to leaders at the national level. This stimulated patrons to become brokers, as socioeconomic and political forces were required to operate in progressively more centralized fashion.

The patterning of patron-client relationships therefore rose toward a higher organizational level, where the loyalties of the latter were tied increasingly to predominantly material incentives. An increasingly complex form of political clientelism thus sought to meet the needs and demands of modernizing and urbanizing social and political life. This produced what Carl H. Lande termed *corporate clientelism,* which he described as a historical stage in the transition from personal clientelism to modern, supra-local politics. Thus, "It can be said...that the clientelist model can operate at any level ranging from the relationships between individual persons through that between sub-national groups to that between nation states."[25]

Gamer's analysis, if more simple, specified the existence of what he termed *minor* and *major networks.*[26] The former operates at the lowest level, serving the needs of the rural peasantry. Its patron, however, simultaneously acts as a broker through membership in a patron-client system on a higher plane. There, the role of intermediary becomes dependent upon a national patron belonging to the modernizing urban elite. The consequent function of the "major" network then serves as the primary source for the exercise of political authority and influence. The role of the state is enlarged. Gamer therefore concurs in the view that clientelistic relationships exist on different levels and operate in varied ways. A more telling statement comes from the sociologist Helio Jaguaribe in the Brazilian case:

> The essence of this system consisted in a bargain whereby patronage was accorded in return for the promise of support. The state served to foster and protect the existing regime, and at the same time provided the necessary number of sinecures to ensure the political support which the ruling class...needed in order to preserve its economic and political control of the country.[27]

When clientelistic activity extends beyond personalistic patrimonialism, it becomes largely dependent on the activities of interest groups and political parties. Where the rural social component remains sizeable, clientelism may turn organizationally to some form of collective peasant activity. Basic interpersonal clientelistic patterns become transformed into peasant organizations, with the capacity to link local, regional, and national interests. Such networks, consistent with the elitist characteristics derived from the patron, are themselves organized from above in purposive fashion and are intended as permanent institutionalized structures. Where they first take shape as peasant movements or federations, these in turn become linked to national political parties. The result is an urban-based form of clientelism, corporatist in fashion, which attempts to meet the demands of the emergent national system and its increasingly bureaucratized processes.

This nationalizing of local, peasant-based clientelist organization was sharply etched in Powell's study of the Italian and Venezuelan cases, where patterns of behavior were maintained through the development of modernizing organizational forms. Too often, he contended, there may be "insufficient appreciation of the fact that such behavior may survive, quite functionally, very late into the developmental process."[28] In practice, however, a more elaborate patron-broker-client network develops, one that helps the national electoral process to penetrate to the very peasant village itself. National or regional political leaders recruit local leaders from among patrons and brokers. These latter in turn recruit subleaders or political workers who themselves assemble a larger following from among friends, family, and clan.

Patron-client ties thereby exist within the context of a national structure in which, however, state activity remains limited and authority is significantly localized. A separation still divides villages from one another, from the region, and especially the state. Heavy reliance is placed upon traditional networks, even where they embrace a host of brokers and intermediaries. As the countryside is gradually drawn from traditional toward mass society over time, the rural areas become more fully integrated into the larger system, even if the process is incomplete. This transitional process was well illustrated in Venezuela's recent past. While its peasant leagues operated on the basis of traditional patron-client practices—unequal status, reciprocity, deference and loyalty, and face-to-face communications—at the same time they became oriented to national party politics via mass mobilization and electoral participation.[29]

Under conditions generally found in transitions toward the modern bureaucratized state, there is an enlarged social and economic role for the state, one requiring additional clientelist mechanisms. And whatever the degree of integration achieved, both the bureaucracy and the political parties are located at or very near the center of state functions. As developmental processes of modernization drive a nation toward a more urbanized existence, it is inevitable that state activities grow in concentration and intensity. The previous separation of town, region, and nation is altered as dividing lines are blurred and in some cases erased. Granted the broad bureaucratization of the state, patron-client linkages become collectivized more than personalized.

As Weingrod sees it, *"party-directed patronage...is associated with the expanding scope and general proliferation of state activities, and also with the growing integration of village, city, and state."*[30] The conditions of rural society become largely displaced, both in environmental setting and in the context of the former dyadic personal relationships. There is also some shift in the character of rewards and benefits for the clients and, once again, organizational rather than individual patrons become ever more powerful. While the evolutionary process moves further toward a concentration on urban dwellers and their politics, clientelistic mechanisms retain their basic importance. Influence, material rewards, and benefits—often conveyed simply by the word "patronage"—come into play as manifestations of so-called corporate clientelism in the modernizing, urbanizing setting.

In the broadest and most generic political sense, the term has been commonly employed by students of politics within the context of traditional big city politics in the United States. Thus, "patronage" has been virtually synonymous with the distribution of public jobs and the dispensation of special favors in exchange for political loyalty and electoral support. It has also been treated in many cases as a form of systemic corruption that taints the body politic. But the notion should not be this simplistic. The writings of political scientists have placed particular stress on the urban electoral process in dealing with patronage. For V. O. Key, this meant "the response of government to the demands of an interest group—the party machinery—that desires a particular policy in the distribution of public jobs."[31] To Frank Sorauf, patronage was an incentive system, a form of "political currency" with which to purchase political activity and responses. An active organization is to be maintained as a means of attracting and retaining loyalists in general and voters in particular. The conditions of rural society have been largely displaced, both in environmental setting and in the context of the former dyadic personal relationships.

To recapitulate, the early experience of feudal and of patrimonial clientelism is characterized by attitudes and actions structured about a personalized P-C relationship. The dyadic leadership-followership system is dynamic and susceptible to swift change. The personality, the charisma, and the general position of superiority enables the patron to exercise his own preferences. The reciprocity between patron and client is asymmetrical; the first seeks prestige and power, the latter largesse and protection. In view of the stark dependence on face-to-face communications at this stage of clientelism, agreements are necessarily private and informal. Political dimensions may well be modest, and there is little contact between those who are high and low in the hierarchy. What is described as political clientelism constitutes an affective, highly personalized relationship in which the participants engage in mutually beneficial transactions from positions of vastly unequal resources.

As already described, sociopolitical urbanization and the transition toward an industrializing, city-based society requires the growth of the state; this in turn provokes the necessary evolution of more complex and modernizing political clientelism. "Corporate clientelism," as Lande put it, moves beyond traditional dyadic clientelism and brokerage networks. With the enlargement of the state and its assumption of greater authority and responsibility for social controls and the distribution of wealth comes the ever more pervasive role of the bureaucracy. Public office proffers greater social mobility and enhanced personal status for the individual. At the collective level, the political parties provide the organizational sources for both economic and political rewards that may be bestowed through the brokers upon the ultimate clients. They offer a means to mobilize broad popular support and to meet the demands coming from society. If these latter demand major social change, the bureaucratizing response may well be resistant. It is often conservative in nature, and there is an inclination to maintain social and political controls—to manage conflict with a minimum of violence. The concomitant tendency favors policies and actions emphasizing short-run gains rather than long-range transformations, and the forces favoring the status quo remain powerful. This is generally consistent with the inherent systemic conservatism of P-C relationships, which labors to reinforce those already enjoying positions of strength.

Emergence of the modernizing bureaucratic state consequently requires new forms of P-C relationships. Old traditional forms will no longer suffice. To repeat, with this bureaucratization comes a nationalizing of the economic system; the process of industrial growth; a dilution of regionalism and localism by expanded networks for communication and transportation; the very urbanization of the population; and the impact of technological change and innovation. These and related circumstances render weak and insignificant the old clientelistic forms whereby social and political controls could be maintained. Whether or not national leaders have the capacity to develop and incorporate new forms and interpretations of political clientelism therefore becomes a basic question, answers to which may help determine the future contours of a modernizing political system. The effectiveness of a modernizing form of clientelism in exercising social and political control thus becomes an empirical question. Our central task here is to pursue this analysis with the case of Colombia. Before turning to these specifics, however, a broader discussion of the Latin American experience may well be in order.

Political Clientelism in Latin America

The Iberian Heritage and Traditional Clientelism

The implantation of patterns derived from the Iberian Peninsula of the sixteenth and seventeenth centuries began to shape traditional Latin American clientelism from the moment of discovery and conquest. Aristocratic forms introduced from Spain and Portugal swiftly produced a rigid two-class system. Colonial rule brought with it a landowning aristocracy claiming descent from the conquistadores and often from the Iberian landed gentry. The lower class was composed of peasants and servants. As racial intermingling took place, much of the region saw the emergence of the mestizo. While regarded less unfavorably than pureblooded Indians, the mestizo only rarely found it possible to enter the self-protective aristocracy in the colonies. In fact, with the passing of generations the latter tended to place particular pride upon its claims of *abolengo*—inheritance of racial and class purity from ancestors in the distant colonial past.

At least three sets of controlling attitudes or values took hold—all of them consistent with Iberian patterns.[32] One revolved about personalism, viewed as the unique character of every individual. The inner soul, the essence of the person was crucial to all human interrelationships. Consequently, friendship and family ties were of inestimable importance. To accomplish a task, one relied upon those closest to him. This in turn encouraged a second basic trait, that of strong kinship. Extended relationships of kin and clan were honored, based on marriage as well as direct blood ties. The practice of *compadrazgo* or co-godparenthood rested upon these ties, with a wide circle of relatives involved. Respect for the authority of the eldest in the family was included, thus lending a patriarchal quality to this set of values.

A third significant characteristic, closely linked with personalism and family ties, was that of hierarchy. It was believed that society was organized by strata, with everything placed on a vertical scale. The traditional pattern of class and caste lent itself to stratification in both social and political terms. From birth, the individual bore a rank or status in society—whether relatively superior or inferior—which was at best difficult to alter. This notion carried weight in religious, social, and political realms. The structure that would permit domination of colonial rule for three centuries from the Iberian peninsula superimposed a hierarchical system that withstood many challenges. Political, social, and religious structures were all rigorously stratified; so it was that hierarchy stood as a controlling concept. In this sense there was no escaping the Hispanic cultural heritage. Its impact was destined to survive long after the revolutionary wars of independence brought about the withdrawal of the Spanish and the Portuguese. For, as Wagley once observed,

> Any set of ideal patterns derived from historical experience and institutionalized in the religion, the family structure, the relations between socio-economic classes, and in the educational system of a society, will affect the behavior of future generations, even after such patterns have become out-moded.[33]

Society in Latin America, then, came to reflect powerful and durable vertical ties, with parallel hierarchies representing diffuse interests. Structured as it was in accordance with diverse pyramids of status and authority, society faithfully mirrored prevailing cultural values and behavior. A consequence of these persisting vertical structures was the importance of governmental institutions in the creation of wealth and status. Douglas Chalmers in a seminal article on Latin American political parties wrote in this regard that "[t]he intertwining of the social and political structures is, like the diffuse vertical character of the social structures, not a modern or traditional characteristic but one which has existed throughout Latin American history."[34] With the notion of hierarchy at the very core of such structures as well as attitudes, it was only natural that the patron-client system became a constant throughout much of the region.

This first took on the characteristics of feudal clientelism, with dyadic relationships reflecting uneven reciprocal obligations between members of different social strata. The patron was typically the owner of a hacienda or plantation, on which he acted as his clients' protector in disputes with colonial authorities. Housing, food, equipment, and specific usage of land were provided. Often serving as the godfather to the children of faithful servants and workers, the patron thereby demonstrated a personal interest that constituted in effect a linkage of ceremonial kinship. In return, the clients—workers, tenants, and retainers—owed the patron labor, service, and general allegiance. Loyalty in times of land disputes, civil strife, or other challenges to the interests and properties of the patron was also a part of the putative clientelistic bargain. In terms of the personalistic orientation toward politics, a description of pre-revolutionary Cuba demonstrates the importance of the patron:

> The patron...provides protection and special favors in exchange for loyalty and service. This relationship is founded upon mutual trust, not on legally defined obligations; in fact, it normally operates outside of, and to a great extent in conflict with, formally regulated social and economic (and political) structures. The benefits bestown by the patron are expected but not specifically required of him, and are looked upon as demonstrations of his generosity and magnanimity.[35]

Consistent with such attitudes was the spirit of *caudillaje* as it arose from the Renaissance tradition. For Glen Caudill Dealy, this embraced "a concept of man personified as a leader in a public setting." There developed a cultural ethos propelling the individual in a quest for influence, one that came to draw upon an elitist mode of behavior. Linked to this was the inclination for life to be organically rather than atomistically organized. "In other words, caudillaje cultures are ordered, hierarchical, and 'proper' in the sense of conveying deference to whom deference is due."[36] All of this endured through such core values as authority and personal relationships, carrying with them a conviction in the uniqueness of the individual. Furthermore, it was consistent with the character of the patron-client relationship. Traditional authority, true to Weberian theory, dovetailed neatly with the patrimonial characteristics of ancestry, heritage, and personality.

The original feudal form of clientelism established at the onset of the discovery and conquest was gradually restructured into less simplistic patrimonialism with the unfolding of the colonial era. In the century that followed the wars of independence, the broader traditions of the patrimonial framework retained their identity in much of the region, even while sporadically adjusting to changes in society at large. While the winning of independence from European imperialism—at least in the political realm—brought about some revisions in the structure of the ruling class, certainly the basic clientelistic system prevailed. Its networks gradually developed more extensive use of brokers, which eventually led toward the incorporation of party and labor leaders as well as government bureaucrats. This was a long and slow process, to be sure, and one whose course and timing varied somewhat from one to another country or region. It took place at a time when a formal political centralism masked the fact that until the twentieth century, social and political controls in much of Latin America were operated by regional foci of power.

True to clientelistic traits, central governments ruled through local political chiefs as much as through direct controls of their own. In his discussion of government and power, Richard Adams described the situation thusly:

> Most typically there was general oligarchic agreement that those who controlled the land were responsible for local government. Hacienda owners were really political bosses as well as economic controllers of the local scene. The church served as the bureaucratic scribe for many local tasks...and provincial centers evolved their own strong leaders and families of importance. A "central government" did exist under these circumstances, but it was a government that was generally weak and that ruled through the local power of the regional rulers.[37]

Latin America, then, was organized far more by vertical functional categories than by horizontal class categories.

Malloy has vividly depicted how a small elite exercised social and political controls through reliance upon patron-client networks. These vertically organized networks fanned out from the national center to the localities, cutting across class, caste, and regional lines. The hegemonic national elites exercised control by means of clientelistic nets descending to intermediary and thence to local subelites. It was, for all practical purposes, a patron-client relationship writ large on an increasingly collectivist rather than individualized basis, while at the bottom of the hierarchy communications and contacts were carried out by the clients with brokers and low-level patrons or their representatives.[38]

Modernization and Bureaucratic Clientelism

It was not until the 1920s, by and large, that the encroachments of industrialization and urbanization in the more developed countries presaged the arrival of delayed dependent capitalist development. Continuing economic growth and diversification, population migration from countryside to city, and the gradual elaboration of more complex institutions of governance nourished further reshaping of clientelistic relationships. The state was viewed increasingly as the patrimonial source of privileges—the collective patron, as it were. The political inclination was therefore directed toward capturing sources of state benefits in terms of patronage and privilege. Periodic efforts to introduce Weberian-style rational-legal systems of governance were opposed, delayed, or blocked by the vertical hierarchies of patron-client networks. The attachment to patrimonial systems of authority remained powerful, as were the values that still honored personal relationships and hierarchy.

When Latin America's experience with modernizing industrialization began to assume importance, the state undertook a redirection of national resources on behalf of altered economic priorities. State initiatives grew as a means of promoting industrial activity: capital was provided to the private sector for development; redistributive decisions were assumed; and semiautonomous public corporations grew up to supplement existing state agencies. The burgeoning labor movement itself assumed a clientelistic profile while accepting the primacy of the state. And as the latter encouraged and prodded the private sector in an enlarging area of economic activity, the power of the central state concomitantly expanded. For those devoted to populistic policies and to a broad commitment to social justice, the constant incorporation of more people into the state apparatus was mandatory. A concentric system of clientelism and patronage reached toward the periphery of the nation, guided by the ethos of the modern bureaucratic state.

Businesses, bureaucracies, and political parties developed their own networks of patrons, brokers, and clients. The last of these, in the form of employees, sought protection from higher levels; brokers and patrons in turn reached for their own larger, more powerful patrons. Personalized relationships had to be altered, for in large organizations it was not feasible to maintain these in traditional fashion. At the same time, however, the hierarchical perspective still held sway, including the expectation that services and obligations were durable. The extent to which the state itself attempted to fill this role came to be symbolized by social security, public housing, labor codes, and an expanding system of welfare services. Ever-expanding bureaucracy, first providing clients the benefits of employment and a degree of job security, also sought to develop and extend its own state-related networks throughout the citizenry.

In recent and contemporary times this has lent impetus to the evolution of a better-trained, more professionalized corps of *técnicos*. Specialists have become central to the functioning of ministries, independent state corporations, banking and financial institutions, and other assorted public entities. In theory this was expected to produce politically independent, responsibly expert, and professionally experienced decision makers. Agendas for action and national policy priorities would be worthy of the proudest and most unrepentant champion of Weberian legal-rational principles. As a practical matter, however, experience has often given the lie to such rosy expectations.[39] Without for the moment engaging further in questions concerning the relative efficacy of governance this is merely to stress once more the clientelistic impulses of the modernizing bureaucratic state in Latin America.

In cases where political parties also developed over time, they gradually sought to represent a host of different vertical hierarchies. In traditional form the parties found themselves dominated by their own patrimonial elites, dealing more with brokering intermediaries than directly with the mass base of clients. Parties that achieved some degree of national rather than regional or local status first did so through the leadership of traditional hierarchies. Thus, the earlier parties—some of which have endured to the present—historically tied themselves to a network of regional and local bosses. They tended to deal in goods and services, but on an ad hoc or incremental rather than programmatic basis. In some instances present-day parties still retain these qualities. Others, in contrast, have created independent nationwide networks in which the representative function is in evidence, diverse socioeconomic groupings have a voice, and there is the prospect for the true exercise of political power and authority if elections can be won.

Nonetheless, there are strong clientelistic characteristics in the functioning of even the most broad-based parties. Personalism may be exercised through charismatic leadership; decision making is centered in small elitist groups such as central committees; rewards and penalties are meted out to the rank-and-file, as well as to local patrons and brokers; the national patrons decide such important matters in response to the loyalty and allegiance of the clients. Programmatic and ideological tendencies may range from rightwing fascism to revolutionary radicalism of the left. Be that as it may, the mass-based parties may sometimes constitute superb examples of elitist entities operating on the basis of political clientelism.

All of this returns us once more to the question of social and political controls. If it may be argued that the relationship of the individual to the state has been that of client to patron under both patrimonial and now, under modernizing bureaucratized conditions or corporate clientelism, the question of its adequacy is writ large for an understanding of contemporary politics. To examine the matter in detail for the republic of Colombia becomes our central objective. The role of traditionalistic clientelism under patrimonialism requires an overview of Colombian political history. And as the modern bureaucratized period is reached, it becomes especially noteworthy to consider whether or not contemporary forms of clientelism have the capacity to provide the responses necessary for the maintenance of the system through the corporate exercise of political and social controls.

What we are insisting upon here is the fundamental merit in adopting an overarching analytic perspective that takes into account the individual as more than a mere dependent variable. We are also urging the necessity of examining the interrelationship of the individual and the state within the context of political and social controls. In so doing, it may be possible to give fuller recognition to the centrality of *political* elements, rather than relegating them to a subordinate position. In order to proceed with this undertaking, particular stress is being given to the concept of clientelism as a tool of notable force. The historic role of patrimonial clientelism has been part and parcel of the Latin American experience, and the socioeconomic forces of roughly the past half-century have dictated the reshaping or progressive bureaucratization of clientelism.

For Colombia, we will necessarily go beyond a discussion of patrimonial clientelism in analyzing and evaluating recent and contemporary political life. The challenges to the maintenance of social and political control will draw particular attention to the Frente Nacional arrangement adopted in the 1950s. The efforts of national elites to defend and solidify their rule—attempting in the process to develop mechanisms of bureaucratic clientelism in lieu of more traditional patrimonial tools— will be explored in some detail. From this there may emerge theoretical insights relevant to the study of other Latin American political systems. Our focus, then, turns to the Colombian experience, one of the richest and most complex in twentieth-century Latin America.

Notes

1. Kenneth C. Johnson, "Latin American Political Thought: Some Literary Foundations," in Ben Burnett and Kenneth C. Johnson, eds., *Political Forces in Latin America: Dimensions of the Quest for Stability* (Belmont, MA: Wadsworth Publishing Company, 1968), 479.
2. S. N. Eisenstadt and Louis Roniger, "Patron-Client Relations as a Model of Structuring Social Exchange," *Comparative Studies in Society and History* 22, no. 1 (1980): 49.
3. Jean Francois Medard, "Le rapport de clientele," *Revue Francaise de Science Politique* 26, no. 1 (February 1976): 104.
4. Robert E. Gamer, *The Developing Nations: A Comparative Perspective*, 2d ed. (Boston: Allyn and Bacon, Inc., 1982), 108.
5. Robert P. Clark, *Power and Policy in the Third World*, 3d ed. (New York: John Wiley & Sons, 1986), 102.
6. John Duncan Powell, "Peasant Society and Clientelistic Politics," *American Political Science Review* 64, no. 2 (April 1970): 412-13.
7. Scott Mainwaring, "Clientelism, Patrimonialism, and Economic Crisis: Brazil since 1979," Paper presented to Latin American Studies Association meeting, 4-7 April 1991, p. 4.
8. Gamer, *Developing Nations*, 104.
9. Medard, "Le rapport," 103.
10. John W. Sloan, *Public Policy in Latin America: A Comparative Survey* (Pittsburgh: University of Pittsburgh Press, 1984), 128.
11. Sidney W. Mintz and Eric R. Wolf, "An Analysis of Ritual Co-Parenthood (Compadrazgo)," *Southwestern Journal of Anthropology* VI (1950), 341-68.
12. For his broad overview, see George M. Foster, *Tzintzunzan: Mexican Peasants in a Changing World* (Boston: Little, Brown & Company, 1967).
13. For a brief overview of anthropological trends that marked the two decades following Mintz and Wolf's influential study, see Arnold Strickon and Sidney M. Greenfield, "The Analysis of Patron-Client Relationships: An Introduction," in Arnold Strickon and Sidney M. Greenfield, eds., *Structure and Process in Latin America: Patronage, Clientage and Power Systems* (Albuquerque: University of New Mexico Press, 1972), 1-19.
14. Mattei Dogan and Dominique Pleassy, *How to Compare Nations: Strategies in Comparative Politics* (Chatham, NJ: Chatham House Publishers, Inc., 1984), 76.
15. For a rich theoretical statement that stresses potential disciplinary breadth, see William T. Stuart, "The Explanation of Patron-Client Systems: Some Structural and Ecological Perspectives," in Strickon and Greenfield, *Structure*, 19-43.
16. Peter Flinn, "Class, Clientelism, and Coercion: Some Mechanisms of Internal Dependency and Control," *The Journal of Commonwealth and Comparative Studies* 12, no. 2 (July 1974): 157.
17. James C. Scott, "Patron-Client Politics and Political Change in Southeast Asia," *American Political Science Review* 66, no. 1 (March 1972): 91-114.
18. Laura Guasti, "Peru: Clientelism and Internal Control," in Steffen W. Schmidt, James C. Scott, Carl Lande, and Laura Guasti, eds., *Friends, Followers and Factions: A Reader in Political Clientelism* (Berkeley: University of California Press, 1977), 424.

19. Eric A. Wolf, "Kinship, Friendship, and Patron-Client Relations in Complex Societies," in Michael Banton, ed., *The Social Anthropology of Complex Societies* (London: Tabistock Publications, 1966), 16.
20. J. A. Pitt-Rivers, *The People of the Sierra* (New York: Criterion Books, 1954), 140.
21. Scott, "Patron-Client Politics," 92. His emphasis.
22. Jeremy Boissevain, *Friends of Friends: Networks, Manipulators, and Coalitions* (New York: Oxford University Press, 1974).
23. S. N. Eisenstadt, *Traditional Patrimonialism and Modern Neopatrimonialism* (Beverly Hills: Sage Publications, 1973), 60. Also see Boissevain, *Friends of Friends*, 147–48.
24. Wolf, "Kinship," 17–18.
25. Carl H. Lande, "The Diadic Basis of Clientelism," in Schmidt et al., *Friends, Followers*, xxx.
26. Gamer, *Developing Nations*, 101 ff.
27. Helio Jaguaribe, "The Dynamics of Brazilian Nationalism," in Claudio Veliz, ed., *Obstacles to Change in Latin America* (London: Oxford University Press, 1965), 168, as noted in ibid., 103.
28. Powell, "Peasant Society and Clientelistic Politics," 425.
29. See extended discussions, notably in the Introduction and Conclusion, in Powell, *Political Mobilization of the Venezuelan Peasant* (Cambridge: Harvard University Press, 1971).
30. Alex Weingrod, "Patrons, Patronage, and Political Parties," in Schmidt et al., *Friends, Followers*, 325. The original publication was in *Comparative Studies in Society and History* 10 (July 1968), 377–400. His emphasis.
31. V. O. Key, *Politics, Parties and Pressure Groups* (New York: Crowell, 1964), 348.
32. See the extended statement of John Gillin in his "Some Signposts for Policy," *Social Change in Latin America Today* (New York: Council on Foreign Relations, 1960), 14–63. An earlier statement worthy of attention is Gillin, "Ethos Components in Modern Latin American Culture," *American Anthropologist* 57 (1955): 488–500.
33. Charles Wagley, *The Latin American Tradition* (New York: Columbia University Press, 1968), 7.
34. Douglas A. Chalmers, "Parties and Society in Latin America," *Studies in Comparative International Development* 7, no. 2 (Summer 1972): 108.
35. Wyatt MacGaffey and Clifford R. Barnett, *Cuba* (New Haven: Human Relations Area File Press, 1962), 97.
36. Glen Caudill Dealy, *The Public Man; An Interpretation of Latin American and Other Catholic Countries* (Amherst: University of Massachusetts Press, 1977), 15.
37. Richard N. Adams, *The Second Sowing* (San Francisco: Chandler Publishers), 183.
38. James M. Malloy, "Authoritarianism and Corporatism in Latin America: The Modal Pattern," in Malloy, ed., *Authoritarianism and Corporatism in Latin America* (Pittsburgh: University of Pittsburgh Press, 1977), 5–12.
39. A recent work that delves into these matters from the perspective of public administration and political leadership is Barbara Geddes, *Politician's Dilemma: Building State Capacity in Latin America* (Berkeley: University of California Press, 1994).

2

Colombia: Clientelism and
the Patrimonial State

In few Latin American nations has the condition of recent and contemporary politics so confounded students and observers. In similar fashion, the institutional arrangements created in 1958 have constituted among the more unique in the three decades that have followed. For practitioners and theorists alike, both intuitive understanding and empirical findings have proven difficult to achieve, while consensus has been elusive at best. As a consequence, there are diverse explanations of post-1958 politics, just as debates over the near and mid-range future are both contentious and inconclusive. There is, at least, general agreement that Colombia has undergone significant changes in the last thirty years. Urbanization, industrialization, transportation and communications infrastructures, an expanded educational system—these are among many forces that have influenced life, society, and politics in the nation. The implications for the populace, for the governance of a modernizing Colombia, and for the exercise of social and political controls are less certain.

Characterizing Colombian Politics

At the most general level, it is true that Colombia has experienced a degree of formal democracy during much of the twentieth century. Following an atypical military interregnum, furthermore, the nation in 1958 constructed an idiosyncratic institutional framework that has proven durable. Enshrined by constitutional provisions adopted overwhelmingly in a nationwide plebiscite, the *Frente Nacional* or National Front constituted a bipartisan agreement between the two great historic parties, the Liberals and the Conservatives. Heralded by its exponents as a means of

35

restoring and nurturing democracy after its self-inflicted demise at the close of the 1940s and the early 1950s, the Frente Nacional envisaged an exclusionary sharing of power controlled by the two major parties.

There were three major provisions to serve this goal: *alternación* provided for the alternation of four-year presidential terms between Liberals and Conservatives for sixteen years. *Paridad* dictated an equal division of elective and appointive posts between the two parties. In addition, a two-thirds majority was necessary to pass legislation, both at the national and local levels. Presumably the savagery of party politics that had torn apart the earlier democratic system would be eradicated, with the spirit of compromise and accommodation leading the way to a full-blown competitive democracy beginning in 1974. If it was also true, as critics have argued ever since 1958, that the Frente would constitute a more effective and efficient means of preserving the historic hegemony of national elites, that was presumably the price that would have to be paid.

During the intervening years the Frente has, at one level, achieved its objectives. Formal democracy has been maintained and stabilized. In many other ways, however, its record has been spotty at best. As will be seen, the measures adopted at the close of the sixteen-year experience in 1974—the so-called *desmonte* or dismantling of the Frente—were hedged with qualifications. These will be detailed later, accompanied by our contention that the Frente remained, if in a de facto fashion, well into the 1980s. Only in 1982 did the Conservatives win a competitive election against the Liberals, and it was not until 1986, in the wake of a massive Liberal victory, that a government was established that did not share its positions, power, and patronage with members of the other party. From 1974 through 1986, the process of *desmonte* had left many institutional arrangements intact, while the informal dynamics of the operating system certifiably maintained the configuration and political dynamics of the original National Front. The impulse toward a redefinition of national politics, so strong today, did not attract major attention until the 1982–86 administration, after which momentum would mount (see Part III).

Whatever else might be said, the system adopted in 1958 was unique to the Latin American experience. For those given to broad comparative generalization, there were elements of consociational democracy. As described by Arend Lijphart in a lengthy series of publications,[1] this is a form of democracy wherein "the centrifugal tendencies inherent in a plural society are counteracted by the cooperative attitudes and behavior of the leaders of the different segments of the population."[2] Such antimajoritarian devices as grand coalitions, proportional rule, and mutual vetoes are employed by leaders of several subcultures to "bring stability to an otherwise badly divided society." Robert H. Dix, the dean of North American political scientists who specialize in the study of Colombia, explored at length the case for consociational democracy in the country. In the end, he concluded that Lijphart's conditions were only selectively relevant in explaining the Colombian case.[3]

While consociational features could be found at least as far back as 1910, this was not tantamount to accepting the applicability of the Lijphart thesis. For Dix, the major contribution of "consociational democracy" was its having stressed the availability of choices "as a more likely version of democracy (or something approaching it) for the Third World's plural societies than could be achieved in a replication of the majoritarian democracy of most of the Western world."[4] In a more recent work he has described the political system of the Frente as a paradox: "clearly democratic in form and in much of its practice, the resources of politics are nevertheless highly concentrated in a relatively few hands and rather frequent, albeit selective, use is made of repressive instruments and practices."[5] His analysis identifies characteristics of polyarchy, democracy, and oligarchy, accompanied by a dependent capitalist relationship to the outside world.

Other experienced observers have applied an ever-lengthening set of terms and concepts to the post-1958 system. A convenient bibliographic listing by Bruce Bagley noted that the social science literature "has been replete with adjectives used to modify the term *democracy,* such as restricted, controlled, limited, oligarchical, elitist, elitist-pluralist, and consociational."[6] Writing in the early 1980s, Bagley himself supported a thesis described as contradicting conventional wisdom of the day. Rather than a functioning democracy, the Colombian regime then appeared to him as inclusionary authoritarianism:

Colombia's economic growth and political stability have been achieved at the cost of severe restrictions on democratic political participation.... the absence of effective channels of participation produced a growing crisis of political legitimacy over the decade of the 1970s, which in the 1980s could threaten the regime's stability.[7]

Bagley described the system as having become increasingly restrictive and repressive during the decade of the 1970s. While directing the reader to Susan Kaufman Purcell's 1977 discussion of inclusionary authoritarianism in Mexico,[8] he set forth five characteristics to justify his application of the "inclusionary authoritarian" rubric.[9]

However, it might be argued, as we do, that Colombia has customarily been exclusionary, whether or not qualifying as authoritarian or democratic. Given the formalistic democracy and the presence of institutional structures consistent with orthodox definitions of such a system, it seems more appropriate to consider the National Front arrangement as exclusionary. Indeed, the five traits outlined by Bagley would justify the terminology. Low subject mobilization, restricted or limited pluralism, executive predominance, a patrimonial style of rulership, and the absence of any well-defined ideology; all of these features, unquestionably present under the Front, combine with democratic forms in what we prefer to term *exclusionary democracy*. Indeed, the desire to open up the system became critical in recent years, as will be described at some length. For the moment, the closed, elitist dominated political process under the National Front was to endure well after the formal conclusion of the Front in 1974.

The determination of Colombian elites to maintain power and assure an orderly society necessarily required the identification and elaboration of new and modern forms of clientelism. The question became whether or not the national patrons would be capable of moving from patrimonial mechanisms toward those of corporate clientelism and the modern bureaucratic state. That its traditions are clientelistic is not in question; these have been widely accepted as lying at the core of authority and control during the patrimonial era. A sizeable literature outlines the historical impact and innate characteristics of political clientelism. Much of this focuses on the biparty system, which has characterized Colombia in a region where multiparty systems are far more common. Some give an emphasis to political culture and to attitudinal traits. Whatever the thrust of P-C analysis, however, there is no doubt of its relevance to the Colombian political experience.

Colombians and foreigners alike, while not necessarily at one concerning specifics, agree on the fact that political clientelism has been part and parcel of the nation's history. Before we move to a chronological overview, some general commentaries might be illuminating. Fernando Cepeda Ulloa, founder of the prestigious political science program at Bogotá's Universidad de los Andes, has stressed the personalistic relationships, regional loyalties, and sectarian factionalism of what he terms biparty *caciquismo*.[10] For Francisco Leal Buitrago, the long and singular history of Colombian bipartyism has been characterized by clientelism, the recent weakening of which demonstrates the failing of the National Front.[11] Rodrigo Losada writes of the extent to which clientelism is accepted as the explanatory variable in Colombia.[12] In the view of Díaz Uribe, clientelism is a historical form of social domination in Colombia, one which has provided the spine of the biparty political regime and the basis for an administrative system opposed to socioeconomic progress.[13]

Non-Colombians also underline the fundamental impact of political clientelism in the nation. Harvey Kline speaks of a sectarian democracy taking hold after the winning of independence from Spanish rule, one in which patrimonial rule meant party hegemony. In his view, clientelism was largely political, with the two national parties engaged in machine-oriented payoffs until recent times.[14] While Kline feels that Colombia's transition from rural to urban society has produced significant changes, others believe that clientelism has remained essential to the functioning of the system. For Steffen Schmidt, the activities of patrons, brokers, and clients have been basic to the politics of the nation. Furthermore, he believes that patron-client networks remain alive and well, even as other aspects of national life and society evolve.[15] There is substantial agreement from Bagley, who describes the political parties as rooted in clientelism and patronage. This means that in both rural and urban areas, society is organized into "overlapping vertical chains of patron-client relations." Clientelistic relations had their origins in the rural hacienda society of the colonial and early independence period, but were subsequently "adapted to the contemporary urban environments."[16]

Once again, Robert Dix's analysis effectively summarizes the views that dot the available literature.[17] He sees clientelism as both cultural and political in character. In the sense of the former, he sketches a classic picture of the patron-client relationship as deeply rooted in Colombia. There is an emphasis "on hierarchy, deference, and paternalism." The tendency is for the citizen "to be born into a rank or status that makes them rather clearly superior or subordinate to those born to other social positions, positions that [are] difficult, though not impossible, to alter during one's lifetime."[18] This means that the culture is one in which a reciprocity is expected between government, with its policy outputs, and the presumably respectful acquiescence of the loyal "subject" citizen.

Official paternalism is expected, with the patron the political manifestation of the boss.

If this is indeed true, then status considerations constitute powerful incentives for Colombians seeking political office. Furthermore, they explain much about the political system and about the nonprogrammatic character of the two national parties. Ultimately, Dix provides an excellent summation of views about the centrality of clientelist characteristics to Colombian politics. The pattern of patron-clientism that pervades the parties and society generally, and has the effect of distributing the public largesse particularistically to persons and localities, has worked to a similar end. It might well be argued that Colombia's traditional party survives essentially because of its regionally distributive policy-making style—that is, its ability to allocate jobs, goods, and services to regional elites and supporters in a reasonably equitable manner.[19] Whether or not Colombia is, as we will argue, in the process of moving beyond the era of patrimonialism, the influence of the P-C relationship in national history was scarcely arguable. It had operated historically as a tool of elite domination, its interactions laced with policy-making pragmatism, programmatic flexibility, and a personal, sometimes charismatic form of leadership.

The patrimonial state in Colombia evolved as a highly malleable system committed to the maintenance of a responsive but ultimately personalistic public order, one dedicated most fundamentally to its own preservation and the unity of the state. Patrimonialism required a system of decision making based on the exchange of legal privilege, substantive rewards, and protection from external authority—to wit, political clientelism. Historically, it germinated and saw the light of day in a profoundly rural society. The level of national integration was modest at best and, in point of fact, there was no truly national identity shared by the citizens of Colombia. Geographic barriers were intimidating in appearance and decisive in impact. There was no national community as such, and this was not to develop until the middle of the twentieth century. Political clientelism was dominant with regard to group activity, but at the same time sought the ultimate objective of insuring the survival and political omnipresence of established national elites. This was, in the final analysis, the preeminent preoccupation of Colombian governance during the prolonged period of patrimonial politics.

The Patrimonial State and Society

In many regards, the colonial experience of what would become the independent republic of Colombia was less than unique for Spain's imperial holdings on the South American continent. Ultimate authority resided in the monarch as the personification of divine law. The system of governance and administration that the Spanish developed over the course of three centuries' rule was centralized, authoritarian, and hierarchical. The Casa de Contratación (Board of Trade) and the Consejo de los Indios (Council of the Indies) provided mechanisms to support mercantilist economic policies and maintain social and political controls. An extensive network of royal offices and officials extended from the monarch through the viceroys and down to the local level. For what would become Colombia, the first major settlement was Cartagena, dating from 1533, destined to become a major shipping facility throughout the colonial era. Two years later Santa Fe de Bogotá was founded, the city that in 1717 became the capital for the viceroyalty of Nueva Granada. The future Colombia, Venezuela, Panama, and Ecuador were to come from Nueva Granada.

Spanish rule constituted an authoritarian system in which power flowed from the top and allegiance was expected from all its subjects. Conquest and conversion were the objectives of the conquistadores, as was the amassing of wealth, power, and perquisites. A feudal pattern of social relationships was set in place, one that was basically exploitative; social class and race were important, and there was a hierarchical dependency of the many on the few.[20] Furthermore, despite the theoretically centralized character of the Spanish colonial system, there was a contrary decentralizing influence produced by diverse economic production in different parts of the viceroyalty. Regional interests and necessities grew up, encouraging the deepening of patron-client relationships. The characteristics of patrimonial rule had been implanted, then, by the time that the independence movement broke out.

The gathering force of pro-independence sentiment was powerfully propelled to the fore by circumstances of European politics. When Napoleon's troops swept across the Iberian Peninsula in 1808, deposing the Spanish and Portuguese kings in the process, leaders in the colonies first responded by declaring their loyalty to the ousted monarchs. The passing of time stimulated further pressures that eventually led to outright declarations of independence. Bogotá issued its proclamation on 20 July 1810; Cartagena followed on 11 November 1811. Fighting raged intermittently for more than a decade, until independence was assured by Simón Bolívar's defeat of the Spanish on 7 August 1819 in the Battle of Boyacá. It was further sealed when his forces triumphed in what became Peru at the Battle of Ayacucho five years later.

Bolívar's efforts at establishing the federation of Gran Colombia— embracing the territories of the former viceroyalty foundered in 1830 with the separate independence of Colombia, Venezuela, and Ecuador. Order was not soon to be found in any of the three, while the legitimacy vacuum left by the departure of Spanish authority further encouraged regionalism.[21] In the Colombian instance, the rugged topography added to the sense of isolation and localism that mitigated against the meaning-ful creation of a nation-state with universal loyalties and allegiances. Conflict became the order of the day from the very outset, embodied in a "raw struggle for power among *caudillos,* families, cliques, and regions, in a society from which the guarantor and mediator of a hierarchical social order had been eliminated."[22]

As Colombia entered the independence era, it displayed a precarious exporting economy that varied by product and by locality, presenting a regional political geography with a crazy quilt diversity of elites, econo-mies, cultural attitudes, social customs, and folklore. Tirado Mejía has written that contrary to most of Latin America, Colombia did not have one single urban center, but a number of such cities, dispersed through-out the national territory. From its inception the country was divided into regions with their own characteristics and with a relatively equal weight: the central, southern, and eastern Andean regions; the Atlantic and the Pacific coasts; the eastern llanos, and even the underpopulated Amazon. Each possessed its own social, political, and economic traits.[23] It was inevitable that efforts to project central authority would run counter to the interests of individual regions, thereby encouraging the strife and divisiveness that ensued.

Even those whose perceptions extended beyond narrow local or re-gional boundaries found themselves at odds with one another. Those dedi-cated to trade and commerce saw Colombia as an exporter of agricultural commodities; others, in contrast, championed economic production des-tined for domestic consumption. These broad perspectives gradually sharpened, and by mid-century marked the early partisan divisions that identified respectively the Liberals and Conservatives. The actual founding of the two parties is customarily attributed to 1848-49, when rudimentary organizations and programmatic fragments first appeared. More fundamental distinctions developed from the struggle over institutional forms and the role of the Catholic church in society. The constitutions of 1853, 1858, and especially the Rionegro constitution of 1863 gave increasing authority to the Colombian states, and along with political decentralization came the Liberals' insistence on the separation of Church and state.

The bitterness of the dispute over such fundamental issues contributed mightily to the sowing of Colombia's "odios heredados," or hereditary hatreds. These also fueled the rapidly deepening rift between Liberals and Conservatives. The partisan positions of traditional patrons reinforced the attachments of peasants who constituted the armies engaged in periodic outbursts of civil violence. By mid-century Colombia was traversing a postindependence historical watershed, accompanied by "the origin, or at least the strong reinforcement, of loyalties, hatreds, doctrines, issues, and alignments that have persisted...to the present day and have become embodied in two 'historic collectivities.'"[24] Clientelism under conditions of patrimonialism could therefore be expected to thrive, as indeed it did. For Guillén Martínez, the very history of Colombia "since 1828 has been this: a mass of public employees, arms in hand, facing a mass of armed aspirants to public office."[25] Partisan allegiances became of crucial importance, an element that continued for over a century.

"The genesis of clientelism," according to Díaz Uribe, "is inscribed in the political history of the country, which fundamentally is the history of the traditional parties, the Liberal and the Conservative and also, among other things, in the eight general civil wars, 14 local civil wars, and three barracks coups in the XIX century."[25] The patron-client relationship, oriented by political loyalties, dealt more in intangibles than in material rewards, for it was a time in which a weak state had notably modest resources at its disposal. As Leal Buitrago wrote,

> The exercise of what today is called clientelism, with material gifts on the part of professional politicians, was limited. Nevertheless, this lack of benefits to divide did not constitute a crucial problem, for it was well compensated by the ideological implications of party triumphs and defeats, supported by the nearly-religious feeling of belonging to the collectivities. This situation was part of the organization of a backward, rustic, agrarian society where servitude was a fundamental component of relations of economic production.... When the political parties be-

came an integral part of daily life, clientelism was converted into the political articulator *par excellence* of social classes and groups.[27]

With the succession of civil wars between the two groupings, intensity over the religious issue heightened partisan sentiment. Fals Borda called the religious struggle "emotional, bitter, and personal," one that assured that the political parties would become "simple agglomerations in which there coexisted both members of the elite and of the lower classes."[28] The repeated outbreak of armed violence thus provided an outlet for basic passions and loyalties, ones that strengthened clientelism and often emphasized the intangibles. Consequently, out of P-C and the heritage of personal, patrimonial rule came Colombia's two-party hegemonic politics. The taking up of arms in defense of one's party and its local or regional chiefs—or the occasional casting of a ballot—constituted the outlet for the expression of clientelist loyalties. The act of voting was itself more a matter of traditional allegiance than programmatic preferences or direct economic compensation.

As the differentiation of identifications and loyalties between the Liberals and Conservative grew from the 1850s forward, each organization stressed its own alleged legitimacy in the endless succession of power struggles, pitting its strength and resources against the opponent. Agrarian patrimonialism in Colombia was reinforced by the intensified competition of national elites, supported by their loyal followers. The intermittent outbursts of political wars—and wars indeed were often involved in the most literal sense—furthered the politicization of society, with masses of peasants drawn into the struggle. As this process unfolded in the years leading to 1886 another historical watershed—the progressive elaboration of the clientelistic system brought with it a less simplistic network than that found during the quasi-feudal conditions under Spanish colonial rule. Thus, traditional clientelism in Colombia increasingly took on the characteristics of patrimonialism in lieu of feudalism.

There were *jefes naturales* (natural chiefs), as they were commonly known, who operated at the national level on the basis of linkages to the regional and local levels. The latter were very often the owners of haciendas, and the landowning system was strengthened by a series of laws adopted in the 1850s and 1860s.[29] In time, local leaders achieved power without necessarily being landed proprietors in their own right. These were the so-called *gamonales,* whose presence further reinforced clientelism in Colombia. The eminent sociologist Orlando Fals Borda was direct and to the point:

> *Gamonales* were petty political leaders whose position in society permitted them to exert influence over rural voters. Public officials, hacienda owners and overseers, and some priests were counted among them. The machine organized by these leaders was designed to perpetuate them and the higher ranking *caudillos* in power. They saw that their friends, employees, and followers went to the polls and voted "right," paid for the liquor consumed as a reward, and acted as protectors of the constituents.[30]

The *gamonales,* customarily operating at the local level, were frequently the most active figures in the expanded clientage network. Certainly they were closest to the basic dyadic relationship on which clientelism is ultimately based.

Political clientelism for the *gamonal* found him operating as the patron in direct dyadic ties with a client. The interchange would typically be reciprocal, as the theoretical model would dictate. The patron might, for example, offer a client the support necessary for the son of the latter to travel to Bogotá for his education. The client would pledge to proselytize during the next campaign or—perhaps more typically in the nineteenth century—promise his labors on the lands of the patron, and if necessary would take up arms on behalf of the patron. As the system evolved to a higher level, the intermediaries or brokers assumed a more active role. This encouraged the formation of more extensive networks. In time, the clientelist pyramid in effect incorporated a "super-patron" at the top, whose direct personal communications would be with regional patrons. They would interact in turn with local patrons, the *gamonales* ultimately dealing with the clients at the bottom of the pyramid.[31] From the *gamonal,* then, the system reached up vertically toward the pinnacles of power.

In the final stage of clientelistic striving for power and authority, a *jefe natural* with the presumed approval or acquiescence of fellow patrons in the dominant party of the moment would reach for national power. Notwithstanding the limitations already ascribed to relatively poorly endowed national governments, there were still some rewards that could be dispensed. Often more oriented to politics and influence than to economics and wealth, the benefits nonetheless were scarcely negligible. For Peeler, an individual backed by an armed coalition of allied patrons and their clients would seize control of national government. At that juncture,

> He would then place supporters in all significant positions of power or patronage, from which vantage points they could control violent resistance and determine the outcome of elections. Then a docile constituent assembly could be elected to draft a new constitution along lines desired by the new leader. The leader could then assure an alternation in the presidency between himself and his supporters.[32]

The form of exchange, then, incorporated party loyalty and occasional electoral rewards, this latter enhanced by the absence of a meaningful civil service.

The predominant style of governance was sturdily infused with patrimonialism as Colombia moved toward 1886. In both rural and urban areas, society was characterized by interlocking vertical chains of patron-client linkages. The two traditional parties became ever more deeply rooted in the politics of clientelism, with national political and economic elites providing diverse forms of patronage in exchange for loyalty, political support, information, and a willingness to bear arms on the part of the clients. Moreover, they gradually came to represent somewhat differing views on the affairs of state, even in addition to the classic issues of centralism vs. federalism and clericalism vs. anticlericalism. The Liberals reflected an inclination toward change and reforms, while the Conservatives presented a commitment to the permanence of the established order. All of this was transpiring within the context of an ever more regionalized Colombian society, one in which no province dominated and a backward agrarian society mitigated against true economic progress.

The years immediately preceding 1886 were decisive for the parties in etching more vividly their differences from one another. The civil wars of 1876 and 1885 helped to solidify diverse socioeconomic groupings and interests. They also provided a symbiotic relationship with Rafael Nuñez, the onetime Liberal whose leadership brought the federalist era to a close via the centralist 1886 constitution. This document marked an important point of departure in constitutional terms, as well as introducing a period of Conservative domination that extended until 1930. In addition, it contributed to an enhancing of bipartyism, notwithstanding the frequency with which quasi-military *caudillos* assumed the banners of one or the other party and postured as soldier-politicians. As Mario Latorre wrote, the bipartyism that would characterize the nineteenth-century experience of independent rule exhibited personalism, regionalism, caciquismo, policlasismo, and a lack of formal organization.[33] It was also heavily reliant upon political clientelism to provide the dynamism for political action.

In addition, the system of governance enshrined by the Constitution of 1886 replaced the previous federalism with a sturdy centralism conducive to clientelism. The primacy of the national state in Bogotá was proclaimed, with presidential powers giving the chief executive the opportunity to function as national patron. He was empowered to appoint the governors of the *departamentos,* or states. The governors in turn named such officials as the mayors in their state, which obviously assured choices acceptable to the president. Local and state police officers were also selected by either mayors or governors. All of this inevitably contributed to a further binding of leader and follower that fully accorded with classic clientelist relationships. It also provided the basis for a strengthening of the two parties and a slow but perceptible extension of national networks by both Conservatives and Liberals.

At the same time, the putative reversal of direction from pronounced regional autonomy to systemic centralization following the 1886 constitution and the determined efforts of Rafael Nuñez could not be fully realized overnight. As a consequence, the *gamonales* serving as municipal leaders, mayors, or presidents of local councils, contributed their share to the continuing importance of PC relationships at lower levels. This meant that especially in the post-1886 period, the regional component was of major importance to the two parties. The character of clientelistic forms of political domination by national elites was heavily dependent upon the purely local and provincial level of activity. The *jefes naturales* could impose their nominal authority and unifying influence only with the backing of subpatrons serving as political brokers.

The two parties after 1886 assumed the guise, then, of regional federations of Conservatism and Liberalism. Hereditary hatreds inevitably grew deeper, political conflict degenerated into violence, and for many clientelistic followers the allegiance to party and patron was more basic than identification with an amorphous national entity known as Colombia. The resolution of disputes by armed contest grew even as the two parties were active in the national congress and sought to win electoral advantage whenever possible. For the masses of citizens following respectively the banners of one or the other political party, partisan socialization was omnipresent. The sociologist Eduardo Santa was perceptive in remarking that Colombians were born "with party identifications attached to their umbilical cords."[34]

As the century drew to a close, Colombia plunged once more into civil strife. In the civil wars that raged between 1839 and 1902, fully eleven years were stained by death and destruction. As Kline put it, the masses "participated" in these struggles; in most instances, "the mass participation was originally because of their adscription to a *patrón*, who instructed them to fight."[35] The longest and cruelest of these conflicts was the so-called War of the Thousand Days (1899–1902). By its conclusion, more than 100,000 lay dead, the economy was moribund, commerce and communications disrupted, and the treasury depleted.[36] This traumatic upheaval was followed barely a year later by the loss of the department of Panama to the Colossus of the North, yet another source of civic dismay and discontent.

General Rafael Reyes, a Conservative who reached the presidency in 1904, extended cabinet representation to the Liberals and sought to restore a modicum of partisan conciliation. Electoral engineering assured the Liberals minority representation in congress, and in 1909 a coalition government was formed. The authoritarian Reyes was soon ousted, but a constitutional reform in 1910 further diluted the degree of single-party hegemony. This permitted a succession of coalition governments, with Liberals receiving some patronage and material benefits while the Conservatives retained for themselves the lion's share of power and privilege. The Conservative domination of national power survived until 1930 when the party, harassed by the impact of the world depression and denounced for the bloody suppression of striking banana workers along the Atlantic in December 1928, fragmented over the choice of a presidential candidate and saw the Liberals return to power with Enrique Olaya Herrera.

During the long period of Conservative domination running from 1886 to 1930, the patrimonial state had extended its roots ever more deeply into the soil. At the same time, Colombia had undergone significant changes. Perhaps most consequential to the economy was the rise of coffee as the mainstay of agricultural production, which also buttressed the clientelistic quality of landholding. With coffee grown on small and medium-size farms, this also carried importance for rural bases of political support and involvement. It enhanced the significance of Antioquia—a classic Conservative stronghold—while subordinating the more Liberal areas to the east. Colombia's export-import trade grew enormously in magnitude, effectively moving the country away from older patterns of subsistence agriculture. In short, to cite Bernstein, although these years leading to 1930 showed additional economic and political pressure created by a Creole-capitalist textile industry and a foreign-owned oil production, "the emergence of coffee as the economic basis to Conservative agriculture and landowning...best explains the era of material and orderly progress during the Conservative epoch."[37]

If coffee was king, industry was beginning to emerge from its incipient stage and the manufacturing sector was also on the rise. While Colombia was predominantly agricultural, it is not irrelevant to note that the growing diversification of economic activities was tied to an increasing pace of urbanization. Moreover, economic elites were unified in many of their goals, and conflicts were less profound than those noted in the Conservative-Liberal political competition. And even with a nascent labor movement flexing its muscles, there were many sources of consensus, or at least of harmonious interchange. Colombian economic leaders believed that those economic elites "favoring policies to promote industrial development did not clash fundamentally with landowners, especially those tied to the all-important export trade in coffee." This meant that an "alliance between the new industrialists and the workers to push aside the landowners...did not emerge."[38]

The years from 1915 to 1930 provide incontrovertible evidence that the winds of change were blowing. Population rose from roughly 5 to 8 million, accompanied by urban growth and the shift toward cash crop farming of coffee (and bananas) from a more inward, subsistence-type agriculture. Politics grew in importance, even at local levels, while community partisanship increased. Political leaders on both sides sought to build their strength through favors consistent with clientelism and its customary personalized informality. The need to build contacts and relationships as a means of enhancing *palanca,* or leverage, was greater than ever. Patronage remained central to the functioning of the system, both before and after the replacement of the Conservatives by the forthcoming period of Liberal hegemony.[39]

As Enrique Olaya Herrera recognized, his victory by plurality in 1930 had been achieved only as a consequence of the Conservative division. He had won but 44.9 percent of the vote against Guillermo Valencia and Alfredo Vásques Cobo, while two-thirds of congress was controlled by the opposition. The new chief executive therefore named four Conservatives to his cabinet and chose six as state governors. At the same time, the Liberals moved to establish firm control through the exercise of patronage. During the next four years the "Liberalization" of Colombia meant the maximum control of patronage. The party directorate in Medellín made the point when it informed a Liberal mayor in an overwhelmingly Conservative town in Antioquia that "when the Governor's office names a Liberal mayor to administer a community with a Conservative majority, it is for the exclusive purpose that he Liberalize said community."[40] Such efforts reflected the party's determination to strengthen its own *gamonales,* that the workings of clientelism would produce a Liberal majority at the grass roots.

Furthermore, there were few scruples about the methods to be employed. Soon after taking office the Liberals concluded that electoral realities precluded their securing of legislative majorities; they consequently applied force in such Conservative strongholds as Boyacá and Norte de Santander. Local brokers destroyed ballot boxes, intimidated Conservative voters, or baldly rigged the count. The Liberal determination to retain power required electoral fraud and armed violence on a massive scale. When Alfonso López Pumarejo won the presidency in 1934, it was an uncontested race, yet one in which he received more votes than all three candidates four years earlier (938,934 to 823,787). As Schmidt wrote, the dependent status of the bulk of the population necessarily inhibited periodic bursts of electoral reformism.

> The importance of patronage in political competition tempted marginal men to struggle for its rewards without undue regard for legal procedures. *Gamonalismo,* the intertwining of human relationships on the basis of clientelistic connections,... allowed for a relatively systematic, and not always legitimate, penetration of the national political structures into the countryside.[41]

During the Liberal hegemony that ran from 1930 to 1946, the level of violence and conflict escalated. Again citing Schmidt, it was a time in which struggles for local preeminence led both brokers and *jefes naturales* at the national level to precipitate disputes. "The leadership during this period of violence was at least in part congruent with the functions of brokers, that is, to mediate between a clientele and the outside world and to provide reciprocally beneficial resources covering a wide range of needs and situations."[42] Moreover, as the Liberals gradually eroded the position of the Conservatives to establish their own primacy, clientelistic mechanisms were employed increasingly in the factional struggles that raged among Liberals throughout the period. Standing at the center of the controversy was Alfonso López Pumarejo, president from 1934 to 1938 and from 1942 to 1945, the architect of reformism from above.

With the launching of his vaunted *revolución en marcha* in 1934, López recognized that stability could well be endangered by incipient social and economic change. He pledged labor reform, social legislation, and an explicit commitment of the state to expand dramatically its duties and responsibilities. In the face of bitter opposition on all sides, he secured a series of constitutional amendments in 1936 that recognized the importance of the state in economic affairs. Article 19 proclaimed public assistance as the function of the state, to be provided all citizens lacking the means of self-support. Article 20 declared that property had a social function; expropriation with indemnification was therefore permissible. The rights of labor were extended through the constitutional recognition of the right to strike, and the state "for the first time had the power, indeed the duty, to intervene by legislation...to protect the worker from abuses."[43]

Although many aspects of the *revolución en marcha* were paper reforms that were not effectively implemented, it was nonetheless true that in balance they constituted "a significant departure in public policy and in government's role in the social order. In a real sense, 1934 marks the beginning of the modern Colombian state."[44] It also served to intensify party factionalism and the ferocity of partisan competition. Alfonso López, the scion of a distinguished banking family, found himself the focus for extreme political passions. His elite-directed effort at reforms, consistent with Colombia's rising commercial bourgeoisie, nonetheless provoked a major split among the Liberals. His so-called Radical Liberals were challenged not only by warring factions of the Conservative party, but by the Moderate Liberals headed by Eduardo Santos, owner-editor of Bogotá's *El Tiempo*. Divisions in the off-year congressional elections drove López to threaten resignation in May of 1937, and the following year he was succeeded in office by none other than Santos. Although López was to win reelection in 1942, the heady times of the *revolución en marcha* were in the past; he would resign a year before the close of his second term, which became characterized as "the reform of the reformer."

The youthful Alberto Lleras Camargo, not yet out of his thirties, headed an interim coalition that included Conservative representation until the

1946 national elections. Three members of the Moderates held cabinet posts, although the Historical Conservatives under the leonine *falangista* Laureano Gómez denounced the government without quarter. As Lleras explained at the close of his term, "my political perspective had to be conditioned strictly to the necessity of preserving national political stability."[45] Throughout his speeches during this period, he reiterated his view that democracy with a loyal opposition was not feasible for Colombia, and that political competition would provoke violence. Thus, a coalition had been a necessity. This same attitude, as Kline noted, marked Lleras's political philosophy a decade later when he was instrumental in creating the Frente Nacional.[46]

As the 1946 elections neared the Liberals, while still the dominant member of the hegemonic two-party system, were more divided than ever before. With the retirement of López, the Radical grouping formed about the controversial figure of Jorge Eliécer Gaitán.[47] As we once described him elsewhere,

> To his enemies Gaitán was a rabble-rousing, madly ambitious power-seeker; to his friends he was an inspiring leader, champion of the people, leader of the underprivileged, and opponent of oligarchy.... His eloquence was not too intellectual for his audiences, and what appeared to be tremendous power of conviction lay behind his basic simplicity of reason. Dramatic, belligerent, implacably anticonformist, Gaitán was guided by a *mystique* of personal destiny that shaped his words as a champion of the little man, voicing predictions of doom for the "reactionaries."[48]

Denouncing the "oligarchy" and issuing vague populist promises that were sometimes directed at the party system in general, Gaitán was by no means the revolutionary feared and hated by traditional political elites. Yet he did represent a potential challenge to customary patterns of governance, as well as the usual time-tested means of exercising social and political controls.

It was unsurprising that Moderate Liberals opted for their own candidate, Gabriel Turbay. When efforts at negotiation between the contending forces foundered, a disruptive struggle broke forth for the otherwise uncontested election. Six weeks before election day, however, the Conservatives unexpectedly presented a candidate of their own, Mariano Ospina Pérez. Another typical representative of Colombian elites—with former presidents and cabinet ministers dotting the family genealogy—he symbolized the moderate wing of his party and pledged a continuation of the National Union coalition. With the Liberals unable to resolve their internecine differences, Ospina Pérez won election on 5 May 1946 with 565,894 votes; Turbay and Gaitán trailed with 437,089 and 363,849 respectively. The new president honored his campaign pledge while extending the coalition further than that of Lleras, with six Liberals and six Conservatives in his cabinet.

In the effort to strengthen his government's legitimacy and soften somewhat the bitter partisanship that marked the clientelist system, Ospina also introduced a cross-over system at the departmental level. Under this arrangement, the governor and the secretary in each state came from different parties. In less rigid fashion, he attempted to broaden the bases for patronage at both regional and municipal levels. Later in his term, Ospina even went so far as to suggest that during the next government, the president would change annually, alternating between a pair of Conservatives and of Liberals. While never adopted, this too gave some hint of the terms that would later be incorporated into the Frente Nacional— all of this within the context of elite doubts over a democratic opposition and the possibility of dialogue and accommodation between the two dominant parties.

The effectiveness of the National Union was doomed from the outset, especially in light of its rejection by both Gaitán and Gómez. The former, no longer the perennial outsider, had seized control of the Liberal party and was the obvious candidate—and expected winner—in the 1950 race. For the Conservatives, Laureano Gómez also insisted on building his party's hegemonic control, and he proclaimed with exceptional and uncompromising oratory the need to save Colombia through a resurrection of hispanic Catholic values.[49] The result was spreading violence, which in the wake of the 1946 elections began to recur with growing frequency, most notably in the states of Boyacá, Santander, and Norte de Santander. Whatever the preferences of Mariano Ospina Pérez, it was inevitable that the return to power of the Conservatives would provoke offensive measures from the followers of both parties.

Local and regional positions, despite the government's cross-over scheme, in most cases fell into the hands of Conservatives. These officials were consequently sympathetic when peasants loyal to the party moved against local Liberals who had previously enjoyed their own period of aggressive domination. While security forces favored the followers of Conservative subpatrons and brokers, the latter in some cases moved to reclaim properties that the Liberals had seized back in 1930-31 when party domination had last changed hands. All of this produced heightened tensions throughout the countryside, with the functioning of clientelism ever more colored by party loyalties. If this were not enough, Conservative leaders across the nation sought to diminish if not decimate the prevailing Liberal congressional majority by employing any and all means to triumph in 1947 elections. As that contest unfolded in March, the Liberals again won with a majority of 151,888 (805,874 to 653,986). Even so, judicious control of the process by the Conservatives cut the Liberal margin in the Chamber from 80–47 to 73–58.

This further weakened Ospina's National Union, with Gaitán preaching a hard line and Gómez demanding the hispanization of the entire political system. Rural violence continued to grow, with the police ever more partisan for the Conservatives while bands of dispossessed Liberals took to the mountains. In January of 1948 Ospina decreed a state of siege in Norte de Santander, and the next month Gaitán drew a crowd of 100,000 in Bogotá to protest the breakdown of order and security. In a fiercely partisan appeal, which at the same time responded to the growing desperation over the conditions that prevailed, he directed his rhetoric to Ospina Pérez:

> Mr. President, we are not here to present economic or political demands. All we ask is that our country desist from a line of conduct that puts us to shame.... We ask that this persecution on the part of the authorities come to an end.... Put a halt, Mr. President, to violence. All we ask of you is the guarantee of human life, which is the least a country can ask.[50]

By this time, however, the level of violence and the inability of the system to assure peace and order were incontrovertible. And then, on 9 April 1948, came the assassination of Jorge Eliécer Gaitán in the streets of Bogotá.

Notes

1. Among the more significant are Arend Lijphart, "Typologies of Democratic Systems," *Comparative Political Studies* 1, no. 1 (April 1968): 3–44; "Consociational Democracy," *World Politics* 221, no. 1 (January 1969); and *Democracy in Plural Societies: A Comparative Perspective* (New Haven: Yale University Press, 1977).
2. Lijphart, *Democracy in Plural Societies*, 1.
3. Robert H. Dix, "Consociational Democracy: The Case of Colombia," *Comparative Politics* 13, no. 3 (April 1980): 303–21.

4. Ibid., 319.
5. Robert H. Dix, *The Politics of Colombia* (New York: Praeger Publishers, 1987), 206.
6. Bruce Michael Bagley, "Colombia: National Front and Economic Development," in Robert Wesson, ed., *Politics, Policies, and Economic Development in Latin America* (Stanford: Hoover Institution Press, 1984), 125.
7. Ibid.
8. Susan Kaufman Purcell, *The Mexican Profit-Sharing Decision: Politics in an Authoritarian Regime* (Berkeley: University of California Press, 1977).
9. Bagley, "Colombia," 129.
10. Fernando Cepeda Ulloa, "Factores que Contribuyen al Mantenimiento del Sistema Político Colombiano," Trabajo preparado para el 45 Congreso Internacional de Americanistas (Work prepared for the 45th International Congress of Americanists), Bogotá, julio de 1985.
11. Francisco Leal Buitrago, "Colombia: un Bipartidismo en Crisis," mimeo, 1985. Also see extended discussions in Leal's *Estado y política en Colombia* (Bogotá: Siglo Veintiuno Editores, 1984).
12. Rodrigo Losada Lora, *Clientelismo and elecciones* (Bogotá: Pontificia Universidad Javeriana, Programa de Estudios Políticos, 1984).
13. Eduardo Díaz Uribe, *El clientelismo en Colombia; un estudio exploratorio* (Bogotá: El Ancora Editores, 1986), 12–13.
14. Harvey F. Kline, "From Rural to Urban Society: The Transformation of Colombian Democracy," Paper for XII International Congress of the Latin American Studies Association, April 1985.
15. See the discussion in Steffen W. Schmidt, "Bureaucrats as Modernizing Brokers?" *Comparative Politics* 6, no. 3 (April 1974), 425–50.
16. Bagley, "Colombia," 135.
17. Dix, *Politics of Colombia*, 75–82.
18. Ibid., 76.
19. Ibid., 217.
20. For a provocative interpretation of European feudalism as contrasted with Latin American colonial society, see Claudio Veliz, *The Centralist Tradition of Latin America* (Princeton: Princeton University Press, 1980), especially the Introduction, 3–16.
21. The notion of the "legitimacy vacuum" was elaborated by Martin C. Needler. Among his many treatments of Latin American politics that are particularly germane to this discussion, see his *Latin American Politics in Perspective* (New York: D. Van Nostrand, 1963). A short piece that still merits rereading today is his "Putting Latin American Politics in Perspective," *Inter-American Economic Affairs* 16, no. 2 (Autumn 1962).
22. Dix, *Politics of Colombia*, 18.
23. See the analysis by Alvaro Tirado Mejía, *Descentralización y centralismo en Colombia* (Bogotá: Editorial La Oveja Negra, Fundación Friedrich Naumann, 1983), 41–60.
24. Dix, *Politics of Colombia*, 19.
25. Fernando Guillén Martínez, *El poder político en Colombia* (Bogotá: Punta de Lanza, 1979), as quoted in Kline, "From Rural to Urban Society."
26. Díaz Uribe, *El clientelismo*, 19.
27. Leal Buitrago, *Estado y política*, 159.

28. Orlando Fals Borda, *Subversion y cambio social* (Bogotá: Ediciones Tercer Mundo, 1968), 101–102.

29. Among the more influential were the expropriation of Church properties and the right of the Indians to sell their lands. Such measures undergirded what Dix calls "a significant reordering of agrarian property relations" (*Politics of Colombia*, 21).

30. Orlando Fals Borda, *Peasant Society in the Colombian Andes* (Gainesville: University of Florida Press, 1969), 241.

31. Rodrigo Losada Lora, *Clientelismo & elecciones* (Bogotá: Pontificia Universidad Javeriana, Programa de Estudios Políticos, 1984), 97 ff.

32. John A. Peeler, *Latin American Democracies; Colombia, Costa Rica, Venezuela* (Chapel Hill: University of North Carolina Press, 1985), 50.

33. For a detailed treatment that weaves these characteristics into the lengthy evolution of the party system, see Mario Latorre, *Elecciones y partidos políticos en Colombia* (Bogotá: Uniandes, 1974).

34. Eduardo Santa, *Sociología política de Colombia* (Bogotá: Ediciones Tercer Mundo, 1964), 37.

35. Harvey F. Kline, *Colombia: Portrait of Unity and Diversity* (Boulder: Westview Press, 1983), 38.

36. Jesús María Henao and Gerardo Arrubla, *Historia de Colombia*, 8th ed. (Bogotá: Talleres Editoriales de la Librería Voluntad, 1967), 814–15.

37. Harry Bernstein, *Venezuela and Colombia* (Englewood Cliffs: Prentice-Hall, 1964), 116–18.

38. Dix, *Politics of Colombia*, 32.

39. See the comments of Edwin G. Corr, *The Political Process in Colombia* (Denver: Monograph Series in World Affairs, nos. 1–2, 1971–72), 10–13.

40. Abel Carbonell, *La quincena política* (Bogotá: Ministerio de Educación Nacional, 1952), 47.

41. Steffen Schmidt, "Patrons, Brokers, and Clients: Party Linkages in the Colombian System," in Kay Lawson, ed., *Political Parties and Linkage: A Comparative Perspective* (New Haven: Yale University Press, 1980), 275.

42. Ibid., 276.

43. See Samuel Guy Inman, *Latin America: Its Place in World Life*, rev. ed. (New York: Harcourt, Brace and Company, 1942), 233.

44. Dix, *Politics of Colombia*, 34.

45. Alberto Lleras Camargo, *Sus mejores págines* (Bogotá: n.p., n.d.), 104.

46. Harvey F. Kline, "The National Front: Historical Perspective and Overview," in R. Albert Berry, Ronald G. Hellman, and Mauricio Solaun, eds., *Politics of Compromise: Coalition Government in Colombia* (New Brunswick, NJ: Transaction Publishers, 1980), 67.

47. For an insightful treatment, see Richard E. Sharpless, *Gaitán of Colombia: A Political Biography* (Pittsburgh: University of Pittsburgh Press, 1978).

48. John D. Martz, *Colombia: A Contemporary Political Survey* (Chapel Hill: University of North Carolina Press, 1962), 42–43.

49. See the forthcoming study of Gómez's political thought by James Henderson; also consult that author's *Cuando Colombia se desangró* (Bogotá: El Ancora Editores, 1984).

50. Quoted in Germán Arciniegas, *The State of Latin America*, trans. by Harriet de Onís (New York: Alfred A. Knopf, Inc., 1952), 161.

3

Colombia: The Breakdown and Renewal of Clientelism

La Violencia: The Collapse of Social and Political Controls

The violent death of Gaitán sparked "the crazed, fleeting passions of the crowd that took to the streets...to avenge his murder. In a few hours downtown Bogotá was in flames, its public buildings bombed and ransacked, its stores looted."[1] "Black Friday" demonstrated the society-wide ailments that had accumulated. Contrary to the myth of idyllic and enlightened democracy that Colombians had proffered, the incredible outburst recorded in history as the *bogotazo* had stripped away the veneer of civilization. As a British scholar was to write, "Even the wildest demagogue must have been alarmed to see...the appalling savagery of a mob whose feelings had been constantly exacerbated...by the preaching of doctrines above its standard of political education against a background of unsatisfactory standards of living."[2]

Several days' violence followed in Bogotá and other urban centers, while the unimagined outburst in the capital city left scars on the national psyche. Yet it was the continuing bloodletting in the countryside that extended *la violencia* for years to come. Essentially a rural phenomenon, it would run from 1946 to 1957 before undergoing a substantive shift from partisan-based violence to sheer criminality and lawlessness. Based solely on a calculation of numbers of annual deaths, one authoritative source later argued that *la violencia* ran a full twenty years, until 1966.[3] By that time, conservative estimates placed the number of deaths at no fewer than 200,000 Colombians, while economic losses and property damage were incalculable. The sociological costs of brutality, savagery, and inhumanity were also profound, as investigators were to recount in grisly detail.[4]

For Hobsbawm, writing in 1963, *la violencia* was "probably the greatest armed mobilization of peasants...in the recent history of the western hemisphere, with the possible exception of some periods during the Mexican Revolution."[5] Over time, it was localized rather than national—with the locus of fighting shifting periodically. Rival bands of peasants took the measure of other such groups, as Conservatives and Liberals often battled along party lines. Revenge, retribution, personal animus, and a host of highly personalized motives were prevalent. Where there was a dominant interparty component, local clients were struggling on behalf of longstanding loyalties to brokers and subpatrons. On other occasions, partisanship was reflected in the predominance of Conservative government forces, contending with embattled antigovernment Liberals over the question of local or provincial power. Even before the *bogotazo,* but especially in its wake, both the national police and the army had increased their activity on behalf of the Conservatives, thereby aggravating *"odios herederos"* in many rural areas.

Furthermore, the military itself had been drawn increasingly into the attempted suppression of armed protest. The Bogotá police had largely deserted the government on April 1948's "Black Friday," and the role of the army grew perceptibly. The national police were placed under the command of an army officer, while other soldiers were appointed governors in departments where pro-Liberal bands of insurgents were challenging Conservative authority. As President Ospina found it increasingly difficult to maintain his coalition and work with the Liberal-controlled congress, he progressively brought the armed forces more directly into the political struggle, sometimes in conjunction with a growing number of Conservative irregulars who were active in some parts of the country. Polarization between the parties grew, with the government seeking its own survival as well as future electoral victories, while the opposition—still traumatized by the murder of Gaitán—reinforced its own determination to assert what it believed was majoritarian support from the citizenry.

In April of 1949 the Conservatives demonstrated their insistent drive for partisan hegemony by naming as their presidential candidate Laureano Gómez—clearly the dominant ideologue and caudillo in the party, but also the most polarizing figure in Colombian politics. A month later, on 21 May, President Ospina dismissed remaining Liberal governors, decreed further powers to the military, and accepted the inevitable resignation of the six Liberal cabinet ministers. His Unión Nacional coalition was dead. And with attention directed increasingly toward new elections, the climate of party competition grew even warmer. It was inevitable that the president would ultimately declare a state of siege, and in November of the year the Liberal-dominated congress was closed down. That party announced that its anticipated candidate, Darío Echandía, would not participate in presidential elections.

As testimony to the temper of the times, Echandía and a group of associates were attacked shortly thereafter on a Bogotá street in full daylight. When the firing had ended, Echandía's brother Vicente and four others lay dead; the government regretted the episode but declared that its police had first been attacked, although the Echandía party was unarmed and, moreover, Vicente was not politically active. The incident further underlined the breakdown of civility in the political process, and symbolically paved the way for yet another uncontested presidential election—as we have seen, scarcely a rarity in Colombian experience. As it was, Laureano Gómez was announced the presidential victor with all but 14 of 1,140,634 votes. On 29 November 1949, Gómez consecrated his victory to God in a public statement that underlined not only his own brilliant personal victory in his lengthy quest for power, but at the same time dramatized the progressive decay of traditionalistic politics under the patrimonial state.

I praise God because He has permitted me to walk through the fires of hatred without allowing my heart to become contaminated by it, and has kept it happy, free from the dark shadows of vengeance, pure, without the dregs of bitterness.[6]

With Laureano Gómez's assumption of power, the partisan bitterness of *la violencia* progressively intensified. Prosecution of the campaign to assert government control throughout the nation led to partisan persecution by security forces. The army was relied upon more heavily than ever before, while the military establishment consequently enjoyed increasingly preferential budgetary and managerial treatment. President Gómez insisted upon an increasingly partisan role from the Armed Forces, although it periodically lodged uncomfortable objections. Rural violence endured, notwithstanding the most earnest and determined efforts to eradicate armed opposition. The military found itself sandwiched between the Conservative government's determination to solidify its political controls, and the angry, sometimes apolitical but always defiant actions of antigovernment forces. Meanwhile, the level of violence and disruption of public order continued.

Gómez suffered a heart attack in 1951 and passed the presidency to fellow Conservative Roberto Urdaneta Arbeláez. His authority nonetheless remained, and Gómez insisted upon continuing attention to the fighting in the countryside. By this time the level of conflict, with its admixture of partisan, localized, and clan-related animosities, was at its peak. Moreover, there was frequently an anomic quality that was attached to bursts of conflict. Violence and bloodletting was increasingly beyond the control of Colombia's national elites, while the quirks or idiosyncrasies of clientelism at lower levels took their toll. By way of illustration, an account that the author reproduced more than a quarter-century ago, still bears an agonizing flavor that justifies lengthy quotation. It comes from a firsthand report by a correspondent for *Time* magazine, and captures the dynamics of the strife in the early 1950s:

> Liberal guerrillas were in the neighborhood, and the stoutly Conservative residents of San Pedro de Jagua knew well that their homes might be struck next....
> At 4:30 one day recently, there was a dull boom in the east. The warning did not save San Pedro. Minutes later a uniformed column approached the village. "Don't shoot!" cried one marcher. "We're the Army." By the time San Pedro's garrison of 18 realized that the column was some 50 bandits in stolen army uniforms, it was too late. "Surrender or die!" the bandits roared, and with one brief volley they dispersed the defenders. Two hundred more bandits, not uniformed, poured into the city, shouting "Long live the Liberal Party!"
> The rising sun showed the villagers who their attackers were: mostly country boys, some as young as 14, every one with a good Mauser rifle (a few had automatic rifles), a revolver, 1 a machete, a knife. Commanding the bandits from San Pedro's central plaza was a lightly-built man of about 25, clad in a new *ruana*. This was the storied bandit chief, Tulio Bautista....
> The bandits found a single Liberal in the local jail, held on suspicion of aiding the bandits. Freed, this man showed Tulio's boys where there were two drums of oil fuel for the local power plant. "If only they hadn't found that fuel," mourned a San Pedro survivor later. Tulio ordered the homes of the town burned, to flush out any possible police ambush, but forbade his men to fire the church or the school....
> By mid-afternoon, the bandits were ready to leave. At the cemetery they buried their single casualty with military honors. Then they marched away in good order, leaving smoldering ruins and 24 bodies. The surviving people of San Pedro stayed long enough to bury their own dead, to disinter the bandit's body and throw it away to the buzzards. Then, the civil war's newest refugees, they straggled westward to seek shelter in the nearest towns.[7]

The repressive character of official attempts to end the strife and assert hegemonic control over society gradually heightened, but with no visible impact on the scope or frequency of violent actions. In July of 1952 acting president Urdaneta issued a decree granting arbitrary authority to departmental governors. This further assertion of clientelistic controls stripped from departmental legislatures their previous appointive powers; similar motivation also reached municipal level, where all elections were suspended indefinitely. In the meantime, the Conservative regime also sought to politicize further the military, as officers believed sympathetic to the Liberals were reassigned, shipped abroad, or sent into early retirement. With the government thus bent on converting the army into an instrument of party domination, the partisan element to *la violencia* further escalated. There was also an organizational strengthening of hierarchical control over the Armed Forces, with the creation of the post of commanding general immediately below the minister of war. This was filled by Gómez in the person of General Gustavo Rojas Pinilla.

As civil strife raged throughout these years, it became increasingly evident that the state was losing political control. Recognizing as much, Laureano Gómez sought a solution via drastic constitutional reform. With a change of regime "resembling that of Franco's Spain at the time, he sought to revive political control over society and brake the process of social mobilization with the prerevolutionary aspects being borne by *la violencia*."[8] For Gómez, the principles of *hispanidad* required a hierarchical state with a medieval vision of Catholicism. His perspective drew upon an exaggerated stereotypical conception of clientelism, with the emphasis upon the duties and responsibilities of society's elites—the systemic patrons. As he wrote in 1953,

> Universal suffrage contradicts the nature of society. The management of the State is by definition a product of intelligence.... Society resembles a pyramid whose apex is occupied by...an individual of very outstanding position by his intellectual condition. Below are found those with lesser capacities, who are more numerous. Thus continues a kind of stratification of social capabilities...abundant in inverse proportion to intelligence, until arriving at the base...which supports the entire pyramid and is composed of the obscure and inept multitude, where rationality scarcely appears to differentiate between human beings and brutes.[9]

The Conservative caudillo's vision was committed to a new constitution mitigating against the customary game of rotation inside the national political leadership. From the far right politically, it promised to revolutionize the very substance of national politics. Ospina Pérez was among those criticizing Gómez's plans on the grounds that it was necessary instead "for the bureaucratic exercise of traditional biparty management, to look for an alternative formula which would at the same time solve the weakening of institutionalized political control, the antidemocratic danger, and the prerevolutionary situation."[10] By 1953 the rift between Gómez and Ospina had deepened, with the latter anticipating a 1954 presidential re-election and Gómez determined to impose his own will through the mechanism of an Asamblea Nacional Constituyente (ANAC).

In the meantime, the *ospinista* wing under Gilberto Alzate Avendaño, with tacit Liberal approval, quietly stepped up its quiet proselytizing of the military. With public violence worsening, state institutions continuing to lose social control, and the *laureanista* constitutional reforms threatening political traditions, national elites sought a formula to deal with the evident weakening of institutionalized political control. As the political conflict deepened, the march of events progressively overwhelmed the nation's leaders. Amid mounting attacks and counterattacks between the two Conservative factions, exacerbated by alleged scandals involving ranking military officials, Laureano Gómez resumed the presidency from his *designado* on 13 June 1953, and peremptorily dismissed Lt. General Rojas Pinilla. The latter, at the moment disinterested in personal power, reluctantly assumed authority on behalf of the Armed Forces, with Gómez and his family sent abroad into exile. Responding to the perils of civil strife and the partisan excesses that had produced Colombia's first military dictatorship of the century, Rojas addressed the nation as spokesman of that institution:

> The Armed Forces call on all Colombians of good will to form a crusade that, faithful to the traditional mandate of the Country, puts this above the parties and puts the common good above the conveniences of castes and of groups.... No more bloodshed, no more depredations in the name of any political party, no more strife among sons of the same immortal Colombia. Peace, Law, Liberty, Justice for all, without differentiations or preference for the classes more or less favored. The country cannot live tranquilly while it has hungry and ill-clothed sons.[11]

As the new military government assumed power to the relief of virtually everyone but dyed-in-the-wool *laureanistas,* it therefore confronted the necessity of restoring peace and order by curbing or otherwise reducing fighting throughout Colombia. Surely there had been a failure of social and political controls, one that ultimately destroyed the institutional system long in place. It was important to recognize that the character of conflict was "above all one of peasant versus peasant, village versus village, Liberal versus Conservative, and not, in the main, class warfare. Second, *la violencia* was a complex phenomenon with varying motives and different manifestations at different times and in different localities or regions."[12] The sectarianism that had so marked Colombian politics for decades had ultimately spun out of control of its leaders, producing as its logical conclusion *la violencia,* while the system of bipartisan agreement had collapsed. In the process, patrimonial clientelism had been shredded.

Like the civil wars of the second half of the nineteenth century, the strife had served to reinforce the adherence of the masses to bipartyism. It underlined the progressive inability of the Liberals and Conservatives to play their customary role of channelling and controlling the accumulated socioeconomic problems of regions and localities. This had been accompanied by changing relationships of production in the agricultural sector, while the trend toward modernization carried with it a greater complexity and fragmentation of dominant elites. Overlapping industrial and commercial bourgeoisie were articulating their own interests and asserting their own demands for power and influence. All of this meant that the new military government had assumed power at a time when capitalist development was moving forward with dynamism. There was a great need, as Leal has discussed, for a change of economic organization and relationships. And in political terms, the new government meant less a drastic or fundamental change in the rules of the game, and more a pause for reorganization. For the civilian elites who had supported and stimulated military intervention, the intention was an interregnum in the exercise of formal democracy while bases might be created for a transformation in the role of bipartyism and the constitution of a state already defined in its capitalist nature.[13]

For General Rojas, the most immediate and obvious task was that of rural pacification. He issued amnesty to all those participating in the fighting, conditioned upon their agreement to surrender their weapons, foreswear further violence, and return to their homes and occupations. The immediate response was favorable; on 7 July, more than 600 surrendered in Medellín alone. By August Rojas told foreign newsmen that 90 percent of those who had fought the Gómez government had given up, and claimed that total pacification was at hand. Meanwhile, the longstanding state of siege decreed in 1949 by Mariano Ospina Pérez was maintained, as was partial press censorship. The initial climate approving military intervention gradually deteriorated as the Rojas government became clumsily tough-minded in its swing to open authoritarian rule. In mid-1954, what had first been designed as the *laureanista* Constituent Assembly met instead to rubber-stamp Rojas for a four-year presidential term. ANAC also ratified the state of siege, extended suffrage to women, outlawed the Communist party, and provided a sycophantic forum for the general.

Before the close of the year rural violence began to spread once again, especially in rural zones with long traditions of peasant activism and small bands of dedicated communist loyalists. The Conservative and Liberal parties had previously withdrawn support from their partisans, which led insurgent groups in the direction of outright banditry. With the sharp drop of coffee prices late in 1954, the military government's honeymoon period drew to a close. General Rojas also began to move toward a perpetuation of his own power. He sought to build a "third force" of his own, patterned vaguely after Peronist tactics in Argentina. There was even an attempt to model his young daughter María Eugenia along the lines of a Colombian Evita; she headed the newly created Secretariado Nacional de Asistencia Social (SENDAS), which dispensed with food and clothing to the urban poor. By this juncture, moreover, Conservatives and Liberals were reopening lines of communication, and the early glimmerings of what would become the Frente Nacional were on the horizon.

By 1957 opposition to General Rojas had expanded to include the Church, labor, and business. The party leaders were proceeding with plans for a coalition government, while the fighting in the countryside continued on the upswing. Rojas himself planned another Constituent Assembly to extend his rule for another term. His efforts were doomed, labor demonstrations added to urban turmoil, and ranking military officers forced his resignation. Rojas's flight led to the installation of a caretaker Junta Militar whose five members had been close collaborators of the dictator. They worked with Conservative and Liberal leaders for fifteen months, during which time the details of the Frente Nacional were thrashed out and ultimately approved by national plebiscite on 1 December 1957. Of the 4,397,090 total vote, 4,169,294 approved the reformed charter. There were only 206,864 nay votes, with the remainder null or blank. The die was cast for the inauguration of the Frente Nacional. It was to provide the maximum test of Colombia's elites in modifying clientelistic controls consistent with the needs and demands of the emergent bureaucratic state.

Bureaucratization and the Frente Nacional

The Frente Nacional, drawing on the ideas of Alfonso López Pumarejo and the coparticipatory experience of Mariano Ospina Pérez, was devised through a pair of meetings between Laureano Gómez and Alberto Lleras Camargo. Thus, the party elites were amply and appropriately represented as the institutional revisions were developed. At two towns in Spain—Benidorm in July 1956 and Sitges in July 1957—the pair of party leaders progressively shaped the foundations for the accord. In final form, the results of course constituted the unique set of agreements set forth elsewhere. They were without parallel in the Latin American experience, but broadly consistent with Colombia's periodic recurrence to coalition arrangements devised as a means of maintaining elitist social and political controls. They also presumed that even with the bureaucratization of the political system, the Frente Nacional would prove capable of molding new clientelistic forms appropriate to conditions under renewed biparty domination.

Fernando Cepeda Ulloa has observed that the capacity for political compromise has been a factor that has periodically contributed to the maintenance of the Colombian political system. There has been the willingness to create alliances between enemies "irreconcilable" to the death. Pacts, accords, amnesties, and pardons have repeatedly constituted the order of the day, rather than permit the violent rupture of the system. In the pre-Rojas period, of course, the system had indeed foundered, but the strange coexistence of violence and compromise resurfaced. Thus, for Cepeda, periods of virtual collapse have led to the resultant appearance of miraculous, eternal formulae for salvation couched in the language of *"el acuerdo nacional,"* or national agreement.[14] At least to a degree, history was therefore repeating itself in 1957 when the Conservatives and Liberals presumably left behind their old partisan disputes and mutual mistrust. A heavy popular participation in the plebiscite seemingly underwrote the strength of the new coalition form while the two parties would resume their domination of the political system.

The legal mechanism of the Frente, as explained previously, divided power equally between the two parties. In addition to the principles of *paridad* and *alternación,* major legislation would require passage by a two-thirds margin. Furthermore, additional provisions importantly included the provision that no new political parties could participate in elections during the life of the Frente. There were also fairly clearcut statements about the importance of a civil service system, whereby nonappointive bureaucrats at middle and lower levels would be selected on the basis of merit rather than partisanship—a rather dim hope, as the Frente experience would show. All such provisions sought a reinstitution of the process of political reunification for the dominant classes, reified by the constitutional character of the Frente Nacional.

The attitudes of the major Frente architects were a matter of public record. Kline provides an excellent recapitulation of both Lleras Camargo and Gómez, noting their reasons for enunciating and supporting the Frente. Beyond the ouster of Rojas and the restoration of civilian, party-based government, the two disparate party chieftains agreed on pacification of the countryside, resuscitation of the economy, modernizing development of the nation, and a humanizing quest for progress and justice. As a result, the system would be revived "if the *clase dirigente* (the ruling class) would dedicate itself for sixteen years to a gigantic effort of progress and justice, without pulling itself apart." The parties would become instruments of "democratic action" rather than arms of destruction, with political institutions consolidated.[15]

Alberto Lleras Camargo, a preeminent advocate of the Frente and eventually its first chief executive, was capable of considerable oratory on its behalf. Shortly after the plebiscite he told *Visión* that

> those of us who propose the thesis of government by joint responsibility of the two Colombian parties are sure that it will have to execute policy without stumbling and with great benefits for the Colombian political culture.... an infinite patience will be needed as well as a spirit of transition and of permanent agreement...so that a new generation can take advantage of that truce in preparing to administrate the country in correct form and without sectarianism.[16]

Certainly the Frente recognized the necessity of collaboration within the constitutionally adjusted two-party understanding in order to retain hegemonic sway while still worrying about the provisions for bureaucratic positions. Antimajoritarian devices assured that neither party could win—or lose.

This was designed to eliminate conflict over government powers and perquisites, thereby encouraging a diminution of partisan violence and fighting in the countryside. The prolonged and institutionalized period of power-sharing would "also afford Colombia's political and economic elites the opportunity to promote the country's economic development, and even to carry out certain reforms, while minimizing the dangers of counter-elite mobilization."[17] At the same time, the role of the traditional parties under the Frente Nacional was clearly crucial, along with the effort to construct new clientelistic mechanisms. All of this became fundamental to the systemic challenge of 1958 and—in a different sense—to our subsequent analysis. Certainly it raised questions about clientelism and, ultimately, about more basic theoretical concerns as Colombia moved from its longstanding patrimonialism toward the putative bureaucratization of a modernizing system.

The original feudal form of traditional clientelism had long since evolved into patrimonialism, as already discussed. The hacienda had provided the original context for the oft-irrational political loyalty stimulated by the dyadic P-C relationship. Highly personalized hierarchical structures had taken shape, in which reciprocity had been reflected in an exchange of client labor and loyalty for the protection of the patron. The spread of violence and terror through the wars of the nineteenth century had tied partisanship to land tenancy and an expanding latifundio system, encouraging the development of brokerage and an ever-expanding network of clientelistic relationships that were patrimonial rather than feudal. This endured until mid-century, while deeply rooted loyalties in the political parties encouraged the unprecedented national trauma of *la violencia* and suggested the inadequacy of prevailing attitudes and structures.

The so-called old clientelism, as Díaz Uribe put it—that which existed under the patrimonial system—had been widely accepted and rarely questioned even as the movement toward national modernization gradually built up momentum. There had been little occasion to question unconditional personal loyalties, emotional gratifications, and the hereditary character of loyalties; these had all served to enhance the unifying and homogenizing power of the *jefes naturales* who exercised authority at the national level.[18] The system was little changed in the countryside, notwithstanding the gradual introduction of large-scale commercial agriculture. In business and in politics the individual had still sought a patron. Secondary patrons had primary ones, and these latter had larger patrons. Hierarchical patterns of asymmetrical relationships ran from bottom to top of the social structure. The paternalistic sentiment had become deeply embedded in the clientelist system. This was a significant part of the individual sense of belonging that sprang forth from allegiance to either Conservative or Liberal groupings.

These loyalties had been engendered during the previous century by the nonexistence of an internal market, the topographical fragmentation of territory, regional heterogeneity, and the absence of one single nationally dominant class. Often as much personal as they were organizational, ties with one or the other party traditionally focused on the local *gamonales* and thence the regional patrons. The clientelistic element insured that while in one sense the parties would be multiclass in character, at the same time they would be controlled in hierarchical fashion, ultimately directed by a small national elite. Through the parties, resources, albeit sometimes modest in material terms, flowed down through the system via patronage and rewards, jobs, goods, and protection. The exchange that was basic to clientelism thus influenced political party competition, adding to the intensity of politicization. This extended deep roots during the long course of the patrimonial state.

Increasingly, it was the local *gamonal,* in the guise of political bosses, who was plugged into the national party system. They operated via a set of socioeconomic exchanges that had reinforced the party system for a century and more.

> Election controversies and conflicts...afflicted Colombian clientelist politics from the very start.... [I]n the struggles for local preeminence, both the brokers and their national party allies often precipitated quasi-insurgent conflicts. The leadership during this period of violence was at least in part congruent with the functions of brokers, that is, to mediate between a clientele and the outside world and to provide reciprocally beneficial resources covering a wide range of needs and situations.[19]

All of this had facilitated the development of both Conservatives and Liberals as parties of notables rather than masses, despite large numbers of supporters and sympathizers. It was the underlying patron-client relationship, rather than institutionalized organization, that provided the basis for the parties.

Not until the decade of the 1930s had organizational structures begin to evolve, including the networks of conventions, assemblies, and party officials at all levels. As we wrote more than twenty years ago, the organizational charts were impressive and the structures were carefully described in party documents, but in actual practice often existed only sporadically and infrequently.[20] At the pinnacle of each party apex was the national directorate, but this organ does not necessarily include the most influential leaders. As seen in the pages to follow, former presidents retain extensive power, whether or not enjoying a formal party position. Nominating conventions also typically rubber-stamp choices already decided among small elitist circles. When previous selections have not been worked out, the result may well be a stalemated convention, or the splintering of the party between rival contenders.

Throughout the long patrimonial period, and most strikingly in the quarter-century from the 1930s, the linkages between the individual Colombian and party regional and national structures were eminently clientelistic. Dix put it succinctly:

> The selection of candidates and of party directorates at the department levels tends to be self-perpetuating, and the "natural chiefs" play a major role behind the scenes at all levels of the party system. Yet they are hardly dictators; they must provide the appropriate favors in the form of jobs or regional benefits in order to retain the devotion of the *gamonales*. The "natural chiefs" would be lost without the ability and the willingness of local powerbrokers to mobilize the vote. Patron-client relationships are, after all, intrinsically two-directional, even if the exchange is between unequals in power and resources.[70]

Even in the decade of the 1950s, the characteristics of clientelistic patrimonialism remained basic to the system. Schmidt argued that structurally the central government still had, at best, limited control over much of the country:

> Local notables and peasant village leaders continued to mobilize themselves either on the offensive or the defensive. Guerrilla leaders were patrons (often literally speaking in the sense that they were local landlords or their sons). They offered leadership, protection, arms and food in exchange for the loyalty of peasant followers.[22]

By this time, however, the conditions of the patrimonial state were shifting with dramatic rapidity. The population explosion had burst upon the nation; the migration from countryside to city produced an equally powerful trend toward urbanization; this combined with industrialization to bring an enlarged proletariat; a large mass of mainly rural migrants inhabited the shantytowns of nearly a dozen cities; and in the meantime a rising middle sector issued demands in many cases contrary to the capacity of the state. Income disparities threatened to produce greater gaps between classes and subclasses; violence incorporated classic rural banditry with ideological clashes derived from assorted Marxist insurgents; and systemic problems in dealing with challenges to social and political controls multiplied. The constitutional provisions of the Frente also promised to provoke major shifts in the exercise of party loyalties when the payments and rewards were to be equally shared by Conservatives and Liberals alike.

All of these crucial socioeconomic and political factors, coming together at the same historical conjuncture, underlined the shift from traditional patrimonialism to the modernization inextricably linked to bureaucratization of the state. The mounting pressures demanding a truly national, centralized state meant that the authority of public order would be dependent upon an administrative apparatus unaccustomed to such responsibilities. Its duties in exercising authority, defending the legitimacy of the state, and bearing the demands for social and economic development were expansive rather than restrictive. The hegemonic role of the parties required substantial adjustments, the flexibility of which could only be questioned. Where the parties might be inadequate, the bureaucracy in the broadest definitional sense of the state apparatus would have to step in. Rather than the dominant party of the moment—or a bipartisan coalition—it would be the state that would monopolize public services in seeking the loyalty and support of the populace. This government sector would provide services in the best clientelistic tradition, with support presumably flowing throughout the formal hierarchical structure.

The avowed objectives of the newly instituted Frente were widely disseminated: (a) reestablishment of constitutional democracy; (b) replacement of military by civilian leaders; (c) the stimulation of cooperation between Liberals and Conservatives; (d) the restoration of two-party control; and (e) the promotion of modern, efficient, and responsive government. Less widely understood was the hidden agenda: (a) restoration of elitist control of politics and the state; (b) maintenance of traditional biparty hegemony; (c) protection of elite economic interests; and (d) the control of the popular sector and the lower class generally. As Peeler wrote, Colombia was still a strongly inegalitarian society, with the small propertied elite exercising control through the biparty monopoly:

The parties had been outstandingly successful as capstones of the old clientelistic system of political control,...but they could not maintain control as the increasingly urban populations were mobilized as citizens.... The National Front was a determined and successful effort to demobilize and control the citizenry without formally abandoning liberal democracy's commitment to universal suffrage and aliberal political system.[23]

As the nation undertook its constitutional experiment in 1958, the fundamental systemic question became the degree to which it might be capable of adapting modernizing clientelistic tools in order to exercise social and political controls under conditions of the modernizing bureaucratic state. While clientelism presumably would be transformed to parallel the changes in the larger society, both its altered forms and its capabilities remained to be tested. A Colombian-born political scientist etched the contours of unresolved questions to be confronted by the Frente Nacional in the following language:

> The most important determinant [for problems of under-development]...is the success with which the political parties can reestablish their clientelist links, among which will be the use of the bureaucracy as an important "currency" source in political transactions. How well the modern bureaucrat can adapt to these conditions...is a question of great importance for Colombian politics.... The brokerage and political functions of the bureaucracy in modernizing countries, in a broader sense, might be a focus of future attention by political scientists.[24]

As a manifestation of elitist compromise and negotiation, the Frente Nacional was unquestionably exclusionary in nature. The ban on new political parties exemplified the determination of Liberal and Conservative leaders to protect their own interests, maintaining social and political hegemony. It was evident that a few brisk brushes of the Frente Nacional broom would not sweep away political clientelism. Whatever new forms might emerge, the restriction of popular participation was still an enduring objective of Colombian elites; there was no serious thought of installing a truly inclusionary system.

Notes

1. Herbert Braun, *The Assassination of Gaitán: Public Life and Urban Violence in Colombia* (Madison: University of Wisconsin Press, 1985), 3.
2. W. O. Galbraith, *Colombia: A General Survey* (London: Royal Institute of International Affairs, 1953), 133.
3. Paul W. Oquist, *Violence, Conflict, and Politics in Colombia* (New York: Academic Press, 1982), 9.
4. The most extensive and heavily documented study is the two-volume work by Germán Guzmán Campos, Orlando Fals Borda, and Eduardo Umaña Luna, *La violencia en Colombia* (Bogotá: Ediciones Tercer Mundo, 1962 and 1964).
5. Eric J. Hobsbawm, "The Anatomy of Violence," *New Society* (11 April 1963): 16.
6. Quoted in Germán Arciniegas, *State of Latin America*, trans. by Harriet de Onis (New York: Alfred A. Knopf, Inc., 1952), 176.

7. "Death in the Countryside," *Time* (6 August 1959): 30–31.
8. Francisco Leal Buitrago, *Estado y política* (Bogotá: Siglo Veintiuno Editores, 1984), 141.
9. Laureano Gómez, "Yerros Constitucionales," *El Siglo* (21 May 1953): 1–4.
10. Leal, *Estado y política,* 141.
11. Colombia, Dirección de Información y Propaganda, *Seis meses de gobierno* (Bogotá: Imprenta Nacional, 1953), 10.
12. Robert H. Dix, *The Politics of Colombia* (New York: Praeger Publishers, 1987), 40.
13. Leal, *Estado y política,* 143.
14. Fernando Cepeda Ulloa, "Factores que contribuyen al Mantenimiento del Sistema Política Colombiano," Trabajo preparado para el 45 Congreso Internacional de Americanistas (work prepared for the 45th International Congress of Americanists), Bogotá, julio de 1985, p. 10.
15. Harvey F. Kline, "The National Front: Historical Perspective and Overview," in R. Albert Berry, Ronald G. Hellman, and Mauricio Solaun, eds. *Politics of Compromise: Coalition Government in Colombia* (New Brunswick, NJ: Transaction Publishers, 1980), 73.
16. Alberto Lleras Camargo, "Colombia Escoge su Destino," *Visión* (3 January 1958), 21.
17. Dix, *Politics of Colombia,* 42.
18. Eduardo Díaz Uribe, *El clientelismo en Colombia: un estudio exploratorio* (Bogotá: El Ancora Editores, 1986), 26–28.
19. Steffen Schmidt, "Patrons, Brokers, and Clients: Party Linkages in the Colombian System," in Kay Lawson, ed., *Political Parties and Linkage: A Comparative Perspective* (New Haven: Yale University Press, 1980), 276.
20. John D. Martz, "Political Parties in Colombia and Venezuela," *Western Political Quarterly* 2 (June 1965): 320–21.
21. Dix, *Politics of Colombia,* 90.
22. Steffen W. Schmidt, "*La Violencia* Revisited: The Clientelist Bases of Political Violence in Colombia," *Journal of Latin American Studies* (1974): 102.
23. John A. Peeler, *Latin American Democracies: Colombia, Costa Rica, Venezuela* (Chapel Hill: University of North Carolina Press, 1985), 59.
24. Steffen W. Schmidt, "Bureaucrats as Modernizing Brokers: Clientelism in Columbia," *Comparative Politics* 6 (April 1974): 449–50.

II

The Reimposition
of Traditional Controls

4

Setting the Foundations:
Lleras Camargo (1958–62)

The Policies of Governance

The National Environment

As the period of the National Front began, Colombia was an essentially agricultural country, with the bulk of the people living and working in the countryside. The population was estimated at 15,154,000, having virtually doubled during the last twenty-five years. This meant that Colombians were predominantly young, with 43 percent under the economically active age of fifteen. Urbanization was increasing, with 44 percent living in centers of 1500 or above. Bogotá, Medellín, and Cali had over one-half million in residents, while Barranquilla was nearing that mark. Another eight had arrived at 100,000, thus underlining Colombia's historic pattern of demographic regionalism and dispersion.

As befits an agricultural economy, the major sector contributing to the gross domestic product in 1958, at 36.7 percent, was agricultural. Manufacturing followed with 16.2 percent and commerce stood third at 12.1 percent. Coffee was Colombia's major export *par excellence* and bore a heavy responsibility for the cycles of boom or bust that had marked the country's economic history. Although the economy had been growing by as much as 5 percent annually since the close of World War II, it had not progressed in terms of equitable distribution throughout the citizenry. In the absence of detailed data for 1958, an extensive study based on 1964 figures is illustrative: the top 10 percent of income earners received some 48 percent of income, the bottom 50 percent about 13 percent, and the bottom 20 percent a bare 2.6 percent.[1]

Certainly economic power was concentrated in a small number of hands. Robert Dix reported that in 1954 Colombia's five largest banking institutions accounted for over three-quarters of the capital, reserves, and profits of all national banks. Furthermore, a 1960 survey of high executives in the firms listed on the Bogotá stock exchange reflected similar concentration. According to yet another study, 4.6 percent of the population earned 40.6 percent of national income.[2]

The condition of education had done little to alter existing inequalities. It was continuing to serve as a source of elite status in Colombia, for in the absence of education, upward social mobility is seriously restricted. Even secondary education was effectively denied to a majority of Colombians. In 1958 there were a total of 1,613,685 attending school, of whom 1,381,190 were enrolled in primary school. The total for secondary school, including vocational and trade institutes, stood at 169,959.[3] At the outset of the National Front, in the words of Robert Arnove,

> education was a social institution serving the interests of the dominant elite and middle class groups. It was by no means an agency promoting social mobility for children of the rural and urban poor.... On the contrary, the educational situation in 1958 was one of neglect of the most disadvantaged sectors, notably the rural area, and one of privilege for the economically powerful and politically articulate groups, who used education to certify their status and to guarantee the access to the modern sector of the economy.[4]

As the new administration prepared to take office, this array of problems and conditions, many of them structural in character, was also accompanied by a sagging economy. Although it was an exaggeration to speak of the 1957–58 "crisis," as did a number of contemporary observers, there was unfavorable news at hand. The relative vigor of the Rojas years had suddenly been sapped in 1957 with a precipitate decline of coffee prices. There was a sizeable short-term international debt, capital flight, growing inflationary pressures, and stagnating output. The military junta that replaced Rojas in May of 1957 moved to install a stabilization program the following month. It simplified the multiple exchange-rate structure, tightened controls over credit, and softened some of the immediate problems. The rate of inflation was pushing 20 percent, to be sure, and the growth of the GDP for 1957–58 fell below the rate of population increase. Even so, with the inauguration of Alberto Lleras Camargo on 7 August 1958, there was a sense of national hope, even optimism that the new and untried experiment in controlled democracy might prove successful.

Policies of the Administration

Sworn into office by Laureano Gómez, the new president needed to be, in Lleras's own words earlier, "a magician, prophet, redeemer, savoir and pacifier who can transform a ruined republic into a prosperous one."[5] The major architect of the National Front, Alberto Lleras was a natural choice to initiate the system and attempt to put its foundations in place. Born in 1906, he had entered political and diplomatic life as a young man, becoming foreign minister, then Liberal *designado,* and as such served as interim president in 1945–46 to complete the term of the re-signed Alfonso López Pumarejo. He had been a prime organizer of the Unión Nacional coalition government and then favored biparty coopera-tion under Conservative president Mariano Ospina Pérez. Serving as secretary-general of the Organization of American States from 1947 to 1954, he had then returned home and, as already described, became in-strumental in negotiating the National Front.

Alberto Lleras by social background and political outlook was pre-cisely the figure to whom Colombia's elite might most comfortably turn at this critical juncture. As Dix wrote,

> If the National Front was the construction of a modernizing elite, Alberto Lleras Camargo was a true son of such an elite; if it was a product of moderation, fair play, and an evolving tendency to give the opposition its due, Lleras epitomized that spirit;…insofar as it depended on one man it would rest with him whether the National Front would prove a solution to the problems of violence and partisan intransigence, and whether "modernization from above" could succeed in Colombia.[6]

The Lleras Camargo government—and that which followed—pursued an avowed policy of import substitution industrialization that would pre-sumably lead to national independence from an unpredictable world economy.[7] The Lleras administration thus elaborated an avowedly pro-tectionist policy of industrial development. It was felt that there was no better means of advancing economic development, and the first priority was increasing rather than redistributing national wealth. The order of the day, rather than reform, was recovery and growth. To strengthen and institutionalize the planning process, the president created the Comisión de Planeación (Planning Commission) and the Consejo Nacional de Política Económica y Planeación (National Council of Economic Policy and Planning). Law 19 of 1958, the original draft of which was prepared by the government's Carlos Lleras Restrepo, had later to be refined after early experience, but provided an important base for the policy-making process. Before the conclusion of Lleras's term, a new generation of bright young professionals were being attracted to government service.

An early major statement of economic policy was presented by Hernando Agudelo Villa, Lleras's minister of finance, on 4 September 1958. He outlined the necessity of protecting and encouraging investment while strengthening fiscal control. Austerity measures to restrict imports while curbing prices and wages were also announced. Initial results were positive. The economy produced a favorable balance of trade of $86 million for the year, the best in two decades. The rise in the cost of living stood at 8 percent at the close of 1958, and by the close of Lleras's first year in August 1959, Colombia's international credit had been restored. In the meantime, the government maintained a set of exchange controls and high external tariffs to control and direct investment and productivity levels.

Among the most notable policies was the 1961 agrarian reform presented in Law 135. Developed under the skillful direction of Liberal leader Carlos Lleras Restrepo, it was to become one of the most controversial elements in National Front policy-making. As discussed later, its divergent treatment by disparate governments was customarily linked with the degree of administration traditionalism, as well as prevailing political attitudes and elite influence. In its genesis, Law 135 was envisioned as a means of stimulating higher agricultural productivity through better land use, while politically it was intended as a means of responding to the rise of rural dissent and protest. This was not designed to encourage any drastic social changes in the countryside, however.

In keeping with usual institutional and political procedures, the bill was developed by a host of agricultural technicians and then altered and revised by representatives of landowning interests, to the exclusion of farm groups and peasant leaders. Carlos Lleras Restrepo was among the few who contended that a meaningful reform, including a revision of land tenure, was in the long run important to avoid a radicalization of the peasantry and finesse the possibility of a homegrown *fidelista* movement. With the increasingly Marxist tone of the Cuban Revolution by the early 1960s, coupled with the rural electoral support for the Colombian MRL in March 1960 (see below), the timing was propitious. Lleras Restrepo in particular worked earnestly and vigorously to achieve adoption of the measure.

A complete assessment was not possible for some years after Alberto Lleras's term, for the legislation was later reformed, and of course was treated variously by later governments. At the same time, the first National Front president was not disposed to discourage, let alone oppose Lleras Restrepo and others who wished to move ahead on the matter. There was a reasonable degree of approval for the idea of agrarian reform, although opinion as to contents of such a policy understandably varied. In September of 1960 the Catholic church publicly endorsed the notion, and there were few who denounced the official initiative.

According to Albert O. Hirschman, there were six major features. Among these were: eliminating inequitable land concentration or its subdivision into uneconomic units; promotion of economically rational use of lands; guarantees of security of tenure to small tenants and sharecroppers; and the defense, conservation, and utilization of natural resources.[8] The new law supported the distribution of large landholdings to peasants, starting first with publicly owned lands, and only afterwards moving to uncultivated or undercultivated private land. Related provisions, as noted, attempted to deal with the *minifundio*—both through consolidation of small holdings and an avoidance of creating new properties too tiny to be productive.

Critics saw the reform as a manifestation of shifting agricultural patterns. Certainly, as one analysis remarked, land was being seen less as an end in itself by Colombian landowners. Thus, the legislation was true to "the changing interests of the large landowners and the related decline in the importance of the traditional extensive *latifundios* vis-à-vis the more modern capitalist farmer."[9] A sharper and more political interpretation held that the law passed by congress was essentially "anti-land-reform legislation," which mirrored "the existing economic and political structure...in parliament."[10]

Among the most important aspects of the initial agrarian reform law was creation of the Instituto Colombiano de Reforma Agraria (INCORA), the Colombian Agrarian Reform Institute. With rather extensive powers to implement Law 135 and bills that were to follow, INCORA provided a significant focus for the attention of all those with interests in the agricultural sector. It also faced the responsibility of dealing with a group of great significance to the country at a time when the process of modernization was growing rapidly. From another viewpoint, moreover, it fit into requisite administrative adjustments consistent with provisions of the Alliance for Progress program being championed by the United States at the start of the decade.

When John F. Kennedy officially proclaimed the Alliance on 13 March 1961, he was following a course long advocated by both Lleras Camargo and Lleras Restrepo. Colombia was designated a showcase for the Alliance, in no small part because agrarian reform was in place. The unfolding of the Alliance also meant that Colombia needed to present the requisite development program. In fact, it was the first Latin American country to do so—although its document was largely a revision of the four-year plan drawn up by Lleras Camargo's advisors in 1960. This Plan General de Desarrollo, released in December 1961, set forth detailed and often ambitious objectives for an entire decade.[11]

The plan's stated objectives for 1961–70 were in many ways unrealistic from the very outset, although presenting a clear macroeconomic overview of Colombia's economy. It was to grow by 5.6 percent annually (2.5 percent per capita); the Colombian government was committed to greater investment and an enlarged role in developmental efforts. Lleras Camargo consistently sought to set out guidelines, develop a greater degree of economic expertise in the government, and present a picture of institutionalization to the entire nation. He was forced to do so at a time when the state was far from powerful. Indeed, its relative frailty was highly susceptible to Colombia's economically powerful groups. Despite Lleras's best efforts, the governmental apparatus was far from independent of society at large.[12]

The administration maintained its effort to apply austerity measures while stimulating import substitution industrialization. As the president remarked on one occasion, the campaign against inflation could not be relaxed. He stated that the country would progress by "working toward a stabilized level which will allow...[it] to grow without going into bankruptcy or falling prey to internal disruption and political turmoil."[13] In the meantime, the first National Front government altered the tariff structure in May 1959 while augmenting its financial and entrepreneurial input to the industrial sector.[14] The fight against inflation was difficult, and in Lleras's final year it reached 12 percent and was rising.

Most importantly, however, Lleras's commitment to the settling of basic National Front foundations had been accepted and implemented. He himself had symbolized and promoted the notion on the part of both Liberals and Conservatives that in the area of policy-making Colombia required a concerted drive toward national development and economic growth. Neither party could afford the luxury of attempting to exclude the other from the patronage inherent in government. In defending the interests of existing elites, it was important that economic development be nourished as a means of avoiding basic reforms, income redistribution, or outright social revolution. This was, after all, precisely what the National Front had explicitly identified as a major objective:

> stimulate economic development and forge the structure of a modern society...which offers to all its members remunerative employment, a decent standard of living, protection against risks,...and broad opportunities to rise to positions of leadership both in the sphere of private activity as well as in the field of public affairs.[15]

While both National Front leaders and members of the Colombian private sector were deeply concerned with administration policies and with economic growth, these were not initially the predominant considerations. If, as Laureano Gómez had written, the Front was born because the greatest enemy of a Conservative was not a Liberal (or vice versa) but a military dictator,[16] this highlighted the necessity of reestablishing legitimacy nationally:

> The first priorities of the National Front were political peace and the restoration of the constitutional order, taking precedence over any objectives of economic development or social reform. Hence, the accords between the party leaders were directed primarily at the political arena.[17]

The question of political peace—of the state of social and political controls by the first National Front government—therefore stood at the center of concerns for Alberto Lleras Camargo.

Social and Political Controls

The president had promised shortly after his May 1958 election to give high priority to securing "order, austerity, good administration, and the moderating and rational effect on the play of republican institutions, under which Colombia has had its most fortunate epochs." The nation, "and with it the parties and public parties, does not know all the causes of this extremely complex phenomenon, which certainly includes economic roots and motives.... [But] there must be more effective efforts in continuing the struggle against violence."[18] In his inaugural address Lleras

Camargo subsequently noted that a major objective was concluding the civil war, and therefore Colombia should prepare "for an intense campaign of pacification."[19]

The president in so speaking was honoring pledges incorporated into the very formation of the National Front itself. The July 1957 Pact of Sitges, signed by Lleras and Laureano Gómez, had committed the Liberal and Conservative parties to a two-pronged campaign of pacification: respective party leaderships were to curb those of their followers who would encourage violence and political sectarianism; this was to be accompanied by a program of national reconciliation. Similar objectives had already been partially institutionalized by the provisional military government through its creation of a special commission to investigate the causes of violence. Composed of representatives from the two traditional parties, the Church, and the military, it worked throughout the remainder of 1958 to collect documents, interview guerrillas, and work toward understanding between warring forces. Its recommendations included a call for an Office of Rehabilitation, which Lleras Camargo made the responsibility of a close confidante, José Gómez Pinzon.

With the government needing to repress, co-opt, or in some fashion to mollify dissident elements and discourage further rural violence, Lleras Camargo recognized the value of rehabilitation for victims of *la violencia* and sought to persuade guerrilla leaders to return to more normal civic life. He also believed that the wave of public affirmation that had greeted the restoration of civilian constitutional government and his own inauguration might provide leverage for the pacification effort. Thus, a major step became the lifting of the state of siege, which had been in effect since being decreed by Mariano Ospina Pérez on 9 November 1949. Lleras announced his intention on 18 August 1958, and on the twenty-seventh his Conservative minister of interior, Guillermo Amaya Ramírez, appeared before congress to read the official decree. At the same time, modified restrictions were applied to certain of the more troubled departments—notably Caldas, Cauca, Valle del Cauca, Huila, and Tolima.

While the administration could and did undertake programs of rehabilitation—especially in some of the more disruptive zones of violence—much of its effort rested in the hands of the military. After four years of dictatorship, the military rebellion against General Rojas, and the somewhat delicate relations between the Armed Forces and party leaders, this was to a degree ambiguous. While the military later developed close and generally supportive ties to leaders of the National Front, this was not the case in 1958. Pro-Rojas sentiment had driven members of the military and the national police to arrest Alberto Lleras Camargo and four members of the five-officer provisional junta barely forty-eight hours before the 4 May elections. While the attempted coup failed to generate the support necessary, it suggested the heterogeneity of military attitudes. And it may well have been that the undertaking would have succeeded but for the failure to capture the fifth junta member, and then by allowing Lleras to slip away and reach the presidential palace where he could address the nation by radio.[20]

Notwithstanding promises of rehabilitative programs and less than universal support from the military, the president necessarily relied upon continuing armed action against the guerrillas. Rural garrisons were reinforced, small mobile units were buttressed, and appropriations to the armed forces were increased. This led to a notable reduction in death and destruction during 1958–59. The number of victims of *la violencia* was reduced by almost one-third, and the administration reiterated its belief that there was no further political basis for guerrilla activity. Presumably a popularly elected government with public legitimacy was in power, and was attempting to deal with social and economic factors that had aggravated conditions.

The government was quite prepared to declare itself the victor and the violence at an end. In April 1959 the minister of war announced that internal peace was at hand, and on 1 May 1959, Lleras Camargo proclaimed the completion of pacification. Amaya Ramírez told the senate that the daily average of deaths had been reduced to four; in the first six months of 1958 the figure had been 15.2 a day. Soon, however, strife resurfaced in Caldas, Tolima, and Valle; in Tolima alone, 206 deaths had been recorded by the end of the month.[21] The burst of killings amply reminded the government of the severity of the problem, notwithstanding the unmistakable diminution in the level of violence in the earliest stages of the National Front. There were also early indications of potential inroads by the emerging anti-Front MRL faction of Alfonso López Michelsen, with its electoral strength most notable in zones where the violence continued unchecked.

It was still true, all denials by the National Front leaders to the contrary notwithstanding, that partisan sentiments were not irrelevant to *la violencia*. The phase of Colombian violence initiated with the National

Front in 1958 was to run until 1965. It was characterized by government forces opposing Liberal remnants primarily reduced to banditry, revenge, and extortion.[22] Political factors had not been expunged, national leaders could not always control local followers, and at least some pro-Rojas sentiment also played an occasional role. In fact, the presence of *rojistas* was not irrelevant to prevailing political passions, and these were fanned by the return of the general to defend his honor, present his views, and contest the effort of the National Front to terminate any possible political activity through a formal trial.

Shortly after taking office in 1958 the new government had announced that Rojas Pinilla might return home whenever he wished. The former dictator, who consistently maintained that he had relinquished power voluntarily, flew back to Colombia on Sunday 12 October 1958. He soon began issuing a series of so-called *communiques,* which defended past actions, and said that his return had been strictly to defend his honor. Although Rojas insisted that any effort to judge him should come from military courts, the senate proceeded to prepare a case. He was tried there on charges of malfeasance and of injuring the institution of the presidency. After lengthy proceedings that included forty hours of rambling discourse by the general himself, a final verdict was announced on 18 March 1959. By a vote of 62–4 he was condemned for acting "in violation of the national constitution" and, by a vote of 65–1, of "abuse of power by improper conduct in the exercise of the office of President."

The actual sentence was subsequently drafted by a senatorial committee, after which the full chamber reconvened for final action on 3 April. Rojas was stripped of all political rights, military honors, and monthly pensions as a former officer and president. The action also meant that he could not vote, hold public office, or return to military duty. In practice, not all of these prohibitions were to be observed. In 1961 Rojas founded his own political party, the Alianza Nacional Popular (ANAPO), and he later ran for the presidency with his Popular National Alliance. Certainly the senate action did not relegate the erstwhile self-styled populist to the political dustbin. It was more by way of a declaration of indignation over his exercise of power. As Francisco Leal wrote some years later, too many prominent Colombians had been too close to Rojas's government to permit more than somewhat ambiguous accusations. Rojas himself might have incriminated or embarrassed a number of former associates or supporters had the trial attempted to probe too deeply.[23]

Despite Rojas's gradual shift toward electoral efforts to topple the National Front, which reached its high point in his 1970 presidential bid, he constituted for the Lleras Camargo government a potential source for serious destabilization. Shortly after his 1958 return to the country a small band of supporters were linked to an intended conspiracy. The general was arrested on 3 December, and Lleras declared a state of siege in response to "a subversive plan to overthrow legitimate authority...under the personal direction of General Rojas Pinilla."[24] The general was placed on a navy frigate and held incommunicado in the Caribbean while troops went to the streets and some fifty suspects were rounded up. With the back of the plot broken, Lleras lifted the stage of siege on 13 January 1959 (excepting the five departments most seriously affected by continuing rural violence).

Pro-Rojas sentiment with the armed forces, while distinctly in the minority, nonetheless constituted another element that could threaten the government's social and political control. In October of 1961 General Rojas, in another of the provocative speeches that he periodically unleashed, issued a call for armed revolution as a means of achieving social justice. Shortly thereafter a mutiny led by two army lieutenants sparked short-lived rebellion in eastern Colombia. While loyalists quickly snuffed out the attempt, it was sufficient to cause reinstatement of a state of siege throughout Colombia. This was to prove the last such challenge under Lleras Camargo. It did not mean, however, that the military would unquestionably accept a role subordinate to civilian authority.

What did occur under the first National Front government was an effort to modernize the military and professionalize the service. From 1958 to 1970 the armed forces were to triple in size with a budget that was doubled in real terms. While the period of most rapid expansion would come from 1966 to 1970, the Lleras Camargo government recognized the necessity for modernization and gave its support to the effort. By 1962 the military was composed of 22,800 members while expenditures stood at $56 million, which was 15.9 percent of the budget.[25] With the shift of emphasis toward counterinsurgency, the assistance of the United States also exerted some influence. In 1961 U.S. policy channeled its military assistance toward a greater emphasis on internal security. In time, this too would augment the capacity of the National Front to employ coercive measures in the interest of social and political control. These would prove rather less benign with some later administrations than was true with Lleras Camargo.

The Politics of the National Front

The Party Competition

At the start of the first National Front government, its chance for success depended upon the enduring support of both Liberals and Conservatives. Yet the factionalism that had reared itself during the events leading to the Lleras nomination and election carried over into the new system. For the Liberals, who had chosen Carlos Lleras Restrepo as party director on 14 June 1958 in the wake of Lleras Camargo's election, it was believed that unity had been established. The party's congressional vote of 2,132,741 had all been cast for the official slates; thus, all 74 deputies and 40 senators were regarded as loyal to the constitutional arrangement. Lleras Restrepo, publicly committed to a strengthening of the Liberal organization at regional and local levels, worked assiduously until 1959 when he temporarily withdrew from politics, vacated his own senate seat, and left for an extended European trip.

At the Liberal party convention on 16 March 1959, he was replaced as director by the veteran Darío Echandía, who had been elected *designado* with bipartisan support the previous August. A distinguished party leader who had borne such a heavy burden for the Liberals in the late 1940s and early 1950s, Echandía viewed the priorities and responsibilities of the National Front in much the same light as Alberto Lleras. This, however, was not fully satisfactory for a vigorous party minority loyal to Alfonso López Michelsen, son of former president López Pumarejo. These so-called *alfonsistas* were anxious to correct social and economic disequilibriums, and believed that the system in general and the administration in particular were doing too little. Known initially as the Unión Popular Nacional (UPN), this National Popular Union fought for development and reform. It also believed that while party collaboration was important, the Liberals as a natural majority should accept the responsibility of governance without apology or qualification.

As a wing on the left of the Liberal party, this group soon assumed the official designation of Movimiento de Recuperación Liberal (MRL), or Movement of Liberal Recovery. This was later changed, without altering the acronym, to the Movimiento Revolucionario Liberal.[26] While the regular Liberal leadership attempted to ignore or minimize the MRL as long as possible, the fact remained that the more progressive, and often the younger Liberals found good reason to join the MRL, or at least to pursue its general direction. A further indication of this current of thought came in January 1960 when Gloria Gaitán de Valencia, daughter of the assassinated Liberal populist of an earlier era, left the party with a denunciation that it had turned its back on the principles of true liberalism. With her husband she undertook a separate movement, which, despite few successes, spoke further of the Liberals' internal problems.

All of this paled, however, when compared to the situation for the Conservatives. Recall the infighting and conflict that preceded the initiation of the first National Front government. In contrast to the Liberals, the Conservatives' 1958 congressional vote had also been fragmented. The party's total vote of 1,556,273 had produced forty-five *laureanistas,* seventeen *ospinistas,* and twelve independents/*alzatistas* in the Chamber. For the senate it was composed of twenty-six *laureanistas,* ten *ospinistas,* and four so-called independents/*alzatistas.* Before the first year of congressional sessions had been concluded, the factionalism extended to at least five separate groups. Those with Laureano Gómez were the officialists who backed the National Front, and they bore the brunt of Conservative participation in the Lleras government. Followers of Ospina spoke somewhat more of mild reform, but with their highest priority the winning of Conservative control from *laureanistas.* On the political right were the groups under Jorge Leyva and Gilberto Alzate Avendaño. The former totally opposed the National Front, while the latter hoped to gain further influence within the Conservative mainstream.

President Lleras had hoped initially to work with all of the factions represented in congress. This proved impossible, however, and he turned to the current majority which, based on the March 1958 race, was *laureanista.* The president's effort at balance and neutrality, symbolized by his naming of several *ospinistas* to his government early in 1959, was not satisfactory to warring Conservatives. In June of 1959 a party convention convened by the followers of Gómez asserted its domination of the party, and the aging Conservative caudillo mounted a vigorous public defense of the Front, of parity and alternation. As he and his followers remained adamant in their efforts to monopolize the party and its fortunes, an opportunistic understanding was reached between Mariano Ospina Pérez and Gilberto Alzate Avendaño. This *alza-ospinista* front, as it became known, gathered force in its challenge to the majority status inside the Conservative party of the *laureanistas.*

As it moved forward from late 1959, the group charged the government with having violated the original bipartisan agreement. First, quite naturally, was the selection of a Liberal rather than Conservative president. Second was a denunciation of the exclusion of minority representatives from the government. In this case, as already seen, Lleras Camargo had done his utmost to secure participation from Conservatives of diverse factions. The president attempted to act as moderator over the forthcoming 1960 congressional elections, inviting the participation of all factions while urging a thorough exposition of differing views and programs. The competitors responded with vigorous campaigning, although the presentation of their policies was often less than illuminating.

In December of 1959 the Conservative battle was launched when Alvaro Gómez Hurtado led a Bogotá demonstration on behalf of his father and in defense of the National Front. Among those to echo the *laureanista* position was Belisario Betancur, who contended that to vote against Gómez would mean a rejection of Lleras Camargo and the Front. Before long the *alza-ospinista* front was also in full swing, and former president Ospina, having stood somewhat apart from the political struggles of the day, enjoyed substantial personal prestige. His followers and those of Alzate reached for hardcore Conservatives who still saw the administration as but one more Liberal government. At the same time, Laureano Gómez himself was suffering from the ravages of age and ill health. Although defending collaboration with the National Front, he was far less vigorous at this stage of his long career.

Competition on the Liberal side was less intense, but nonetheless was relevant to the future of the National Front. Alfonso López Michelsen, who had entered national politics only in 1958 at the age of forty-five, proclaimed his opposition to alternation and sought to stir Liberal allegiances in behalf of another Liberal president rather than a Conservative in 1962. Returning to Colombian politics with a vigorous commitment following the death of his father in November 1959 in England, the younger López convened his followers in January. Adopting the motto of *salud, educación y techo,* the MRL convention recommended a virtual socialization of health, education, and housing. If López's proposals were less than revolutionary, they constituted reformist changes designed to modernize the state. As we wrote a quarter-century ago,

> The increasing impatience of the masses for reform found a ready outlet in *alfonsismo.* The faction was faced with a campaign task of overcoming suspicions

of political opportunism, and it is fair to say that the dissidents were, on the whole, sincerely and patriotically wedded to their declarations. Although Echandia and the National Liberal Directorate tended to underrate the new movement, it profited by a strong appeal to Liberal sympathies.[27]

For three months an active, sometimes angry campaign swept across Colombia. At stake were 152 seats in the Chamber and over 5000 seats in the collective councils and assemblies of 890 municipalities and sixteen departments. The Conservatives' rivalry centered on the struggle for leadership between Laureano Gómez and his *alza-ospinista* challengers, although it was generally expected that control by the former would prevail. As to the Liberal dissent, there was no question of the MRL faction gaining control, but the extent of its appeal remained to be tested. Preparations for election day fully occupied the attention of the government, which recognized that whatever the outcome, the legitimacy of the new system depended upon acceptance of the electoral process. In 1960, this was the single most important event in the process of institutionalizing the National Front.

The government consequently focused on the maintenance of public order and a defense of the individual right to enjoy suffrage. Alberto Lleras Camargo made but one speech during the course of the campaign, in which he spoke on behalf of the presumed sixteen-year commitment to shared bipartisan government:

> The Frente Nacional, constitutionally and politically, is not conceived as an adventure of four years, but as a long and glorious chapter in the history of Colombia.... Sectarianism of government parties, which has been eliminated as a pest to our political life...has the fault of creating the habit of trusting to persuasion or direct political action on the people, in support of the *official* machinery...calculated to destroy all possibility of free competence to its adversaries.... The country has resolved to end this form of slavery, but present political conduct nevertheless harkens back to its old antecedent.[28]

On 20 March 1960, congressional elections took part amidst a climate of public order and peace. The results forced a necessary reassessment and realignment inside the government. A total of 2,542,651 votes were cast, which represented 57.8 percent participation as compared with 68.9 percent in March of 1958. The Liberals outpolled the Conservatives by 1,478,403 (58.1 percent) to 1,059,370 (41.7 percent), which represented a minuscule advance during the two-year interval. More important, however, was the distribution of competing factions within both parties. For the Liberals, the MRL amassed some 300,000 votes—21.5 percent of the Liberal vote—which gave it twenty seats in the Chamber to fifty-six for the officialists. With the Conservatives, the *alza-ospinistas* polled some 53 percent to 42 percent for *laureanistas,* while Leyva secured the remainder. This left the former group with thirty-nine members of the Chamber to thirty-seven for the followers of Gómez. The application of proportional representation and adjustments of the quotient left the two delegations virtually equal, but the resounding defeat of Gómez by his opponents went well beyond the sheer division of seats.

In point of fact, there were three important results that reflected on the fate of the National Front. One was the victory of the *alza-ospinistas* over the *laureanistas* as the most recent chapter in the long-running feud for domination of the Conservative party. Second was the unexpectedly high level of abstention, which greatly troubled many observers. Third was the partial success of the MRL in winning one-fifth of the Liberal vote on its platform of Liberal control and a modernization of both party and program. For the government itself, a new set of operational guidelines was required in the wake of elections. The defeat of the *laureanistas* produced a wave of resignations by their cabinet ministers. On 22 March Gómez himself labelled the results a denunciation of his leadership and said that his group had no choice but to withdraw. He also announced his own formal retirement from politics. This removed any possible ambiguity over the party leadership, allowing Ospina Pérez and Alzate Avendaño to deal with Alberto Lleras Camargo as new defenders of the National Front. The president replaced the previous Conservative members of the administration with followers of the two factional leaders.

For Lleras Camargo, who was now forced to work with a congress in which the opposition was numerous—half the Conservatives and one-fourth of the Liberals (the MRL)—the parties' relationships were far more tenuous. Lamenting the fact that electoral factionalism had left the government "with the representation of everyone and without the power to influence anyone," he warned party leaders that in the worst of events, he would have no choice but to resign.[29] In November of 1960 he virtually forced four *alza-ospinistas* and two *laureanistas* to accept the six Conservative ministerial positions; however, congressional members of the latter group denied their colleagues permission to accept. A further complication came with the unexpected death of Gilberto Alzate Avendaño.

A prominent Conservative leader for more than a decade, and for years a figure who was at best restive under the power and authority of Laureano Gómez, Alzate at the age of fifty had shown some inclination to bypass the older and less vigorous Ospina Pérez. However, his death from complications following minor surgery left Ospina as the dominant Conservative of what had become the pro-Front wing. By early 1961, Laureano Gómez was emerging from his putative retirement to advance the interests of his own Conservative faction, and he thereby brought renewed uncertainty to his party's role, participation, and responsibility in the National Front. The picture for the Liberals was only marginally clearer.

In the wake of the elections, Darío Echandía announced his resignation as Liberal director. A party gathering in July 1960 attempted to return party leadership to Carlos Lleras Restrepo, who declined the post, recommending a seven-man directorate that was duly constituted. In the meantime he agreed to nomination as the *designado,* which placed him first in the line of presidential succession behind Lleras Camargo. When periodic rumors suggested that the president might be stepping down, this inevitably brought his cousin's political interests back to the national spotlight. In the meantime, Lleras Restrepo could temporize somewhat with regard to the MRL and Alfonso López Michelsen.

Unsurprisingly, Carlos Lleras Restrepo soon returned to the Liberal party leadership, formally accepting the post at a national convention on 24 February 1961. He opened private channels of communication with Alfonso López Michelsen, whose MRL had organized their own convention, repeating earlier criticisms of the "oligarchically dominated" National Front, and attacking the notion of a Conservative president of the republic in 1962. At the same time, López spoke favorably of Lleras Restrepo's progressive outlook. Denying that the MRL was a distinct political party of his own, he contended that it reflected a modernization and reorientation of Liberal party principles. The relationship between López and Lleras Restrepo was to have a profound impact on national politics during the next two decades. At this juncture, it dealt more with the orientation of the Liberal party than the policies of the National Front.

Candidate Selection

At this time it was still very early in the National Front experience, and Alberto Lleras Camargo continued to face the necessity of strengthening the new and unusual system. While attempting to press ahead with economic policies and a potential strengthening of government controls, he also labored both publicly and privately toward a solidification of the Front. Continually warning that it constituted the only defense against anarchy and extremism of both right and left, President Lleras worked assiduously toward a reuniting of diverse factions. Another leader fighting for the survival of the system was Carlos Lleras Restrepo, who in 1961 was working to promote a series of "unity conferences" designed to smooth factional differences while greasing the skids for the intended process of presidential candidate selection.

Already viewed as the presumed Liberal successor to Lleras Camargo when his party would next choose the National Front candidate, he had emerged as a dominant figure in the emergent bureaucratic centralist regime. A taunting cartoon in the *laureanista* daily in October 1960 had put it well: Lleras Restrepo held a handful of balloons showing his roles as *designado,* architect of agrarian reform, Liberal party director, president of the Celanese Company of Colombia, and the like. He was shown pointing a finger at Lleras Camargo who had but one balloon—the presidency of the republic.[30] Certainly Lleras Restrepo's position was in many ways second only to the president, and the latter would be leaving office in August of 1962. At the same time, both men were involved in the process of assuring the nomination, then the election and inauguration of the second National Front president.

National leaders most committed to continuation of the system gradually moved toward one another. In June of 1961 Carlos Lleras issued an invitation to the Conservatives, which was accepted by the followers of Ospina and rejected by the *laureanistas.* This led to installation of the so-called Committee of the 40 on 29 June 1961, which produced a policy document signed by Lleras and Ospina Pérez on behalf of the two party directorates. Subsequently reissued in the press on 19 February 1962, this provided a broad government program intended for the candidate of the National Front. Two days later the Liberals officially agreed on Guillermo León Valencia as presidential candidate. The Conservatives meanwhile retreated, ratifying neither the platform previously accepted, nor the Valencia nomination. Such actions were placed on hold until the convening of congressional and local elections in March of 1962.

The results produced general support for the National Front, although the degree of enthusiasm was unremarkable. The level of participation was scarcely changed, with 3,090,203 votes representing 57.9 percent of the eligible voters. The Liberal margin over the Conservatives was slightly if insignificantly shaved. The majority party won 1,685,531 for 54.5 percent against the Conservatives' 1,287,199 for 41.7 percent. ANAPO, contesting congressional elections for the first time, polled a scant 115,587, for 3.7 percent of the vote. Of particular interest, naturally enough, was the pattern of pro- and anti-Front forces.

On the Liberal side, the MRL vote reached 600,000, which represented 36 percent of the party vote. This meant that the new congress in 1962 would include twelve MRL representatives among the forty-nine Liberals; in the Chamber the *alfonsistas* won thirty-three of the ninety-two Liberal seats. In short, they had picked up twelve senate seats and an additional thirteen Chamber seats above previous totals. Across the aisle, the followers of Ospina Pérez improved their situation vis-à-vis the *laureanistas*. They amassed 57 percent of the vote to 35 for the supporters of Gómez, with the remaining 8 captured by the ANAPO lists. In terms of the congressional composition, this meant that of the forty-nine Conservative senators, thirty-one were *ospinistas,* sixteen were *laureanistas,* and two represented ANAPO. In the Chamber, fifty Conservative members were with Ospina, thirty-six with Gómez, and six with Rojas Pinilla.

In sum, all of this meant that the National Front had basically maintained its position since 1960. If antisystem Liberals seemed stronger, the reverse was true for the Conservatives. Moreover, in the latter instance the situation was rather more subtle, for the *laureanistas* were not rejecting the Front itself, but rather the government of Lleras Camargo. And all of this was sheer political opportunism on both sides, given the long rivalry between the two former Conservative presidents and their mutual desire to control their party to the exclusion of the other. With these congressional configurations as the product of March 1962 elections, it remained in May to choose a successor to Alberto Lleras Camargo. In light of events dating back to 1957, this realistically could be none other than the Conservatives' Guillermo Leon Valencia.

Campaign and Elections

As he hit the campaign trail following the March congressional races, Valencia was assured the backing of all pro-Front groups. At issue was not the formal continuation of the Front, but rather the extent to which antisystem sentiment might be expressed. Three presidential candidates carried opposition banners: López Michelsen, Jorge Leyva, and Gustavo Rojas Pinilla. Two of the three would have been ineligible to assume the office in the event of victory—López because he was not listed as a Conservative, which was mandatory in 1962, and Rojas in the absence of civic rights, which had been removed by his sentencing in the senate.

Clearly the strongest, and potentially the most disruptive opponent of the National Front was López Michelsen. His campaign, while not notably sharp or inflammatory, nonetheless suggested an expression of counterelites who felt that less traditional policies were necessary. The MRL, which had its genesis with young Liberal intellectuals in 1958 and had subsequently organized at its initial convention in February 1960, at no point went beyond reformist proposals, and this was certainly the case for its candidate in 1962. Sympathizing with the Cuban Revolution but rejecting the program of the latter; accepting the tacit backing of the Colombian Communists while maintaining their distance; advocating state interventionism in such areas as health, education, and housing; all of these were a part of the campaign, and of the overall MRL position during its 1960s activism.

Alfonso López Michelsen was himself less than a charismatic or spellbinding figure—he was no Gaitán. Moreover, his years as member of a wealthy and aristocratic family and past political inactivity marked him during the 1960s as something of a dilettante. While later events corrected this image, certainly during his MRL years López was sometimes seen as more the elitist amateur than a serious political organizer capable of organizing and stirring the masses on his behalf. As Liberal leader Julio César Turbay told an interviewer—at this juncture a sharp critic of the man with whom he would later develop a close political relationship—López "has the qualities suitable for a member of a planning council, but he lacks those indispensable for leading a mass movement."[31]

As to the others who opposed Valencia, less need be said. Jorge Leyva, at age fifty a one-time minister of public works for Laureano Gómez who was more adamantly anti-Front than his old mentor, drew unofficial support from those *laureanistas* most resistant to Valencia. Nonetheless, the Conservative factions were for the most part united. For ANAPO, which was still in its infancy, Rojas Pinilla did not conduct an active campaign. Thus, the stage was set for the presidential elections of May

1962, with the degree of participation and the level of support for the National Front the only real questions at issue. Neither proved capable of producing more than routine approval from the public.

The Registraduría Nacional del Estado Civil reported 5,404,765 potential voters for the May competition. When the counting had been completed, a total of 2,634,840 ballots had been cast; the abstention rate was therefore over half, at 51.2 percent. This was noticeably higher than the 1958 presidential abstention of some 42 percent, which had been virtually identical for the 1962 congressional race. It was not surprising that with the outcome foretold, the May participation was below that of the factional March competition. Similarly, the 1958 presidential vote had constituted another form of systemic plebiscite, and thus drew greater attention. This suggested both some normalization of the National Front system, as well as an absence of strong popular sentiment toward its continuation under Guillermo León Valencia.

As the officialist candidate, Valencia won 1,636,081 votes for 62.1 percent of the total. For the anti-Front candidates Alfonso López Michelsen received 625,630 or 23.7 percent; Jorge Leyva won 308,992 for 11.7 percent; Gustavo Rojas Pinilla drew barely 2.1 percent with 54,562; the few remaining votes were divided among several candidates of negligible relevance. For the MRL, the drop-off of one-third, from 36 to 24 percent, was something of a disappointment. At the same time, the unconstitutionality of a López Michelsen presidency in 1962 clearly affected the outcome. With the selection of Guillermo León Valencia as president-elect and the obvious continuation of the National Front into a second term, it also presented Colombia with the opportunity to move beyond the traditionalistic policies pursued by Alberto Lleras Camargo in attempting to assure the institutionalization of the National Front. It would be necessary to follow the leadership of someone other than the primary designer and builder of the system.

Notes

1. Miguel Urrutia and Albert Berry, *Income Distribution in Colombia* (New Haven: Yale University Press, 1976), as noted by Berry's "The National Front and Colombia's Economic Development," in R. Albert Berry, Ronald G. Hellman, and Mauricio Solaun, eds., *Politics of Compromise: Coalition Government in Colombia* (New Brunswick: Transaction Publishers, 1980), 2. For selective but illustrative data from early years, a readily accessible source is W. O. Galbraith, *Colombia: A General Survey,* 2d ed. (London: Oxford University Press, 1966).

2. Gustavo Pérez Ramírez, *El campesinado colombiano*, 2d ed. (Bogotá: Centro de Investigaciones Sociales, 1962), 89.

3. Drawn from OAS and UNESCO data appearing in Foreign Area Studies, *Area Handbook for Colombia* (Washington, D.C.: U.S. Government Printing Office, 1977), 163.

4. Robert F. Arnove, "Education Policies of the National Front," in Berry et al., *Politics of Compromise*, 381.

5. *Time* (5 May 1958): 30.

6. Robert H. Dix, *Colombia: The Political Dimensions of Change* (New Haven: Yale University Press, 1967), 159.

7. Bruce M. Bagley, "National Front and Economic Development," in Robert Wesson, ed., *Politics, Policies, and Economic Development in Latin America* (Stanford: Hoover Institution Press, 1984), 137. For both administrations, as Bagley wrote further, ISI was viewed as stressing "high external tariffs, prior import deposits, exchange controls, and a selective import-licensing system."

8. Eugene Havens, William L. Flinn, and Susana Lastarria Cornhill, "Agrarian Reform and the National Front: A Class Analysis," in Berry et al., *Politics of Compromise*, 355.

9. Ibid., 356.

10. Ernest Feder, "Counter Reform," in Rodolfo Stavenhagen, ed., *Agrarian Problems and Peasant Movements in Latin America* (New York: Penguin Books, 1970), 178, as cited in ibid.

11. Dix, *Colombia*, 148.

12. Edgar Reveiz and María José Pérez, "Colombia: Moderate Economic Growth, Political Stability, and Social Welfare," in Jonathan Hartlyn and Samuel A. Morley, eds., *Latin American Political Economy: Financial Crisis and Political Change* (Boulder: Westview Press, 1986), 269.

13. Quoted in "Colombia's Road to Recovery," *Latin American Report* (Stanford) (September 1959): 9.

14. Francisco E. Thoumi, "Industrial Development Policies during the National Front Years," in Berry et al., *Politics of Compromise*, 331.

15. República de Colombia, *Programa del Frente Nacional, 1962* (Bogotá: Editorial ARGRA, 1962), 4.

16. Quoted in Dix, *Colombia*, 164.

17. Ibid., 147.

18. "Renacimiento Colombiano," *Vision* (23 May 1958): 11.

19. *New York Times* (8 August 1958): 2.

20. For more details see John D. Martz, *Colombia: A Contemporary Political Study* (Chapel Hill: University of North Carolina Press, 1962), 270–71.

21. Ibid., 277.

22. Robert H. Dix, *The Politics of Colombia* (New York: Praeger, 1987), 37.

23. For details see the accounts in Martz, *Colombia*, 279–85; República de Colombia, *Rojas Pinilla ante el Senado: El gobierno militar ante la historia* (Bogotá: Editorial Excelsior, 1959); and Daniel Premo, "Alianza Nacional Popular: Populism and the Politics of Social Class in Colombia, 1961–1970." Ph.D. dissertation, 1972, pp. 27, 32.

24. Martz, *Colombia*, 281.

25. J. Mark Ruhl, "The Military," in Berry et al., *Politics of Compromise*, 187.

26. For a detailed treatment by a former member and activist, see Mauricio Botero Montoya, *El MRL* (Bogotá: Publicaciones Universidad Central, 1990).

27. Martz, *Colombia*, 304.
28. Quoted in *Semana* (18–24 February 1960): 42.
29. *New York Times* (4 July 1960): 2.
30. Reproduced in "Colombia," *Hispanic American Report* (December 1960): 666.
31. From interview quoted in Dix, *Colombia*, 259.

5

Crises and Legitimation: Valencia (1962–66)

The Policies of Governance

The National Environment

While the four years preceding the inauguration of President Valencia had not produced remarkable demographic changes, the important trends observable at the very beginning of the National Front were still very much in evidence. The population had grown by another two million persons, reaching some 17,226,000. Urbanization was estimated at half the total population; the 1964 national census recorded a figure of 52.8 percent. By that time 20.6 percent of all Colombians were living in the four largest cities. According to the first systematic study conducted in Bogotá, over half that city's residents were unemployed or underemployed.

The economic situation had not been fundamentally altered. The agricultural sector did not reflect a significant impact from the 1961 agrarian reform law, which had not yet been effectively implemented. As Valencia was inaugurated, the situation described in the 1960 agricultural census was largely unchanged. As it showed, 62.6 percent of the nation's farms were under five hectares in size, constituting a total of 4.5 percent of the farm area. Properties above 1000 hectares were but 0.2 percent of total farms, but amounted to 30.4 percent of the farm area.[1] Coffee exports in 1958 had totalled 5.4 million bags (at 132 pounds) and earned $391 million; in 1962 the figures were 6.6 million bags, which, however, produced but $332 million.[2] An anticipated boost from the production of crude oil had not materialized; although production rose from 46,878,000 to 51,908,000 barrels from 1958 to 1962, domestic consumption had also grown substantially, from 16,850,000 to 27,710,000 barrels.[3]

The industrial sector was beginning to provide a more significant component to the economy, although this was not necessarily a result of the National Front political arrangement. During the 1950s national industry had begun stressing the production of intermediate consumer durables and capital goods. Thus, by 1958 the bulk of domestic consumption of light industrial products came from Colombian sources, while heavy industry was also beginning to thrive. As Thoumi wrote, the Lleras administration had inherited a growing industrial sector and a changing industrial structure. The manufacturing value added as a percentage of GNP rose from 13.5 percent in 1958 to 16.8 in 1962. Colombia's expanding industrial output had outstripped GNP under the Lleras government, and during the Valencia years was further solidified.[4]

For Valencia, the basic task was to deepen the policies set by Lleras Camargo, improving processes while strengthening regime institutionalization. Economic clouds were gathering on the horizon in 1962 as the result of coffee prices' vertiginous descent (from 52 cents to 40 cents per pound on the international markets). Furthermore, the balance of payments was becoming a problem of serious proportions. Negotiations between Bogotá and Washington had taken place from December 1961 to April 1962, resulting in a balance of payments loan from the United States of $30 million, while Colombia began to restrict its imports in a reversal of the 1959–61 liberalization of licensing. The government had also begun to attack its growing budget deficit. This was not unrelated to the effort at systemic modernization, which was bringing the growing influence of the government into previously untouched areas of national life. The effort to structure a bureaucratic centralist state, at the same time, bore its own financial implications.

The central government, which had reported a budget surplus of 64 million pesos in 1960, had seen this become a deficit of 619 million pesos in 1961 and, in the last year under Lleras, a deficit of 212 million pesos. National budgets were reaching record highs. The necessity of equal treatment for Liberals and Conservatives at all levels of government—equality of patronage opportunity, as it were—was also nourishing an increasingly gluttonous bureaucracy. The economic perspective facing the new president was mixed.

If to this fiscal panorama one adds the concentration of income and of wealth, bounded by the traditional tendency of an economic structure supported by the policy of the State, and the increasing support of foreign investments during the first National

Front government, the operative mark of the State on the economy was made even more difficult by the great counterposition of [diverse] societal interests.[5]

Yet the new chief of state had remarked during his campaign that he lacked experience in administration and was expert "only in struggling for the people."[6] Put in less informal fashion, it could be truly said that with the inauguration of the new administration in August 1962, Colombians found as their new president "a remarkable man of talent and courage, but not particularly interested in economics, just at a time when the inherited situation called for a chief executive with an appetite for financial matters."[7]

Policies of the Administration

The successor to the austere, ascetic Lleras Camargo was strikingly different in background and personal style. Guillermo León Valencia had been born on 27 April 1908, the son of the modernist poet Guillermo Valencia, the famed "Maestro of Popayán" who had himself sought the presidency from the Conservative party in 1918 and 1930. Valencia the younger had been raised in the southwestern city of his family, where traditional values and the historic domination of the landed elites was deep-seated. After taking his law degree at the University of Cauca, he had founded Popayán's *La Claridad* in 1933. An early exponent of Hispanidad who favored the Spanish *falange* in the last 1930s and early 1940s, Valencia had participated in local politics before reaching the senate in 1939 as his father's alternate.

Upon his father's death in 1943 Guillermo León Valencia continued in the senate on his own, and during the Gómez government served as Colombian ambassador to Spain. A frequent if not constant member of the Conservative party directorate, Valencia had frequently outmaneuvered political opponents who underestimated what they scorned as merely a traditionalistic regional caudillo. Valencia built a long and honorable, if less than distinguished career. However, as a man of moral and physical courage—a major actor in the ousting of Gustavo Rojas Pinilla—Valencia could appeal to both the Right and Left, owing more to personal qualities than political initiatives.[8] One observer put it thusly:

[G]iven to flowery rhetoric,...his undisciplined oratory occasionally led him to commit unpolitic blunders. His appearance...added to the impression of a somewhat anachronistic personal and political style. The net effect was to present an image which suggested, in contrast to Lleras, the stereotyped picture of the classic Colombian politician of the nineteenth century rather than the president of a modernizing nation skilled in the ways of administration and attentive to the undramatic facts of the balance of payments and the annual rate of economic growth.[9]

During his campaign Valencia had addressed problems in terms of generalities more than specifics. While referring directly to the need for a "Christian social revolution," he praised the Alliance for Progress enthusiastically as symbolizing desirable developmental priorities. Calling with characteristic rhetoric for a "revolution of life, not of blood," he had not indicated any real conflict with Lleras Camargo in advocating growth and improvement within the existing social and economic structure of Colombia. Certainly he had been a supporter of the Lleras team's economic plans, and offered neither campaign criticisms nor proposed changes of direction. What seemed increasingly important for the continuation of the system, then, was the degree and manner in which the new president would deal with medium and short-run problems that could erode the National Front.

Once he assumed office the new president showed himself as an unsystematic administrator, fully capable of delay or procrastination, then at the last moment taking decisive if sometimes unpredictable action. This was demonstrated when Valencia was confronted with appointing his coalition cabinet. The major problem centered on the six Conservative seats, especially as the former followers of Alzate Avendaño demanded their own status in contrast with that of the *ospinistas*. Valencia eventually developed a practice known as *milimetría,* whereby each Conservative faction received two ministries apiece. This was maintained even after the *laureanistas* and *alzatistas* moved toward one another after the 1964 midterm elections.

At the beginning of the term, however, one of the by-products of initial presidential hesitation was delay in naming the crucial minister of finance. He eventually settled on Carlos Sanz de Santamaría, who had been ambassador to the United States under Alberto Lleras. Having done so, Valencia then reiterated his commitment to a renewed policy of austerity and, in effect, turned things over to Sanz. The latter, having been away from Bogotá, was better attuned to economic problems than to political ramifications when he moved to formulate answers to the more nagging problems.

It was evident that devaluation was necessary if the monetary system were to be stabilized. Official discussions inside the government were leaked, which encouraged premature speculation, distorted the exchange market, and was followed by prompt devaluation by the Banco de la República. As a largely private central bank, it had customarily shown independence from the executive branch. By so doing on this occasion, the monetary upheaval was unnecessarily pronounced. Sanz moved to lay the government's plans before congress early in November. In addition to devaluation, a package of new taxes anticipated the raising of an additional 400 million pesos.

With congress moving very slowly toward approval of presumably emergency measures in December, the finance minister negotiated a standby agreement of $57.5 million from the International Monetary Fund, and then a new balance-of-payments loan of $60 million from Washington. When legislation was passed regarding the devaluation, it was not accompanied by the proposed taxes. Instead, without discussions or communications between congress and the chief of state, the former passed a 40 percent increase in the minimum wage, along with increases of 30 percent in the public and 25 percent in the private sector. This irresponsible legislative action, all of it without the involvement of the executive branch, reversed a projected budget surplus, discouraged foreign investment, and spurred a renewal of inflation.

The latter, which had been averaging some 12 percent annually under the National Front, burst to a level of 25 percent within a few months, and was pushing 30 percent by the close of 1963. The 1963 budget had provided development plans with an intended investment of 1,100 million pesos, while a total of 1,900 million was required. A shortfall of at least 300 million pesos had been recognized even after Sanz's proposed new taxes were approved. The inflationary spiral contributed to a 29 percent rise in the cost-of-living index for 1963. Continuing inaction on tax increases left the government itself nearly bankrupt; some of its payments were months in arrears. Public protests and demonstrations sprung up during this period: business groups and agricultural producers struck; schoolteachers stayed home to protest nonpayment of wages; truck drivers demanded higher rates. Nearly all such actions produced government concessions, which further aggravated its own monetary difficulties.

Finally, in May of 1963 the Valencia government requested of congress a bill authorizing emergency powers. Congress was asked to delegate to the administration the authority to enact those measures that had been hung up in the legislative halls for months. It was a sign of the chaotic conditions of executive-legislative relations and the internal politicking of congressional party leaders that this request was actually approved in August of 1963. President Valencia, now moving decisively in the face of further strike action and growing lack of confidence in his ability to govern, decreed a 20 percent surtax on the income tax and its supplements for both 1962 and 1963, along with a 30 percent surtax on inheritance and gift taxes.

The severity of the accumulated fiscal deficit continued to be covered largely through inflationary measures, including an enlarged plan for external loans. Perhaps the only positive result from these months of controversy, crossed signals, and uneven presidential leadership was the reorganization of the Banco de la República. Its behavior in the devaluation crisis led to doubts that the board of governors, reflective of private sectors interests, should bear responsibility for government economic policies and prices. This led to creation in late 1963 of a Junta Monetaria or Monetary Board consisting solely of cabinet ministers. The action created a furor with major economic leaders of the private sector, who charged that the powers of the Junta would threaten both the economic development and the political system. That such an anti-laissez-faire measure would be introduced seemed unacceptable; however, the recent experience persuaded the government that its own forms of economic interventionism required such a policy-making instrument.

One of the administrative trends under the president, in fact, was something of a withdrawal from the emphasis under Lleras on greater and more expert economic planning. This responded both to Valencia's inclinations as well as to early problems with institutionalization of state activism. Recall that the original composition of the Consejo Nacional and the Comisión de Planeación had created both internal rivalries and cross-cutting authority patterns. These were renewed under Guillermo León Valencia, and efforts to resolve the conflict came via Decree 3242 in December 1963. This produced a reconstituted Consejo Nacional de Política Económica y Planeación, whose membership numbered the ministers of finance, development, agriculture, and public works, as well as heads of the Banco Central, the Comisión de Planeación, and the Federación Nacional de Cafeteros.[10]

Administrative structures were also adjusted by revising the 1958 law treating of central government budget planning. Decree 1675 of 1964 set forth in detail the role and participation of Planeación in the process, which in practice was "an important step along the road to more systematic and technical planning."[11] Such measures did prove constructive over time, although, under the administrative style of President Valencia, the impact was not immediately evident. Certainly professional and technical participation in economic decision making was regarded far more lightly by Valencia than by Lleras before him. As Leal Buitrago would write, this administration "took a backward step in the planning function of the State, such that the Planning Department fulfilled in the bureaucratic system a basically nominal role, while the Ministerio de Hacienda reasserted its own role of improvising on economic decisions of the state."[12]

The ongoing planning of the Valencia administration proceeded largely without the explicit approval of the president. However, a continuation of the National Front sharing of power meant that the decision-making levers still tended to be within the reach of officials chosen via patronage and partisan allegiances, not technical expertise. In some policy areas, the relative inactivity of Valencia had the effect of minimizing the best efforts of even those who were professionally committed to modernization of the state. This was especially true in agricultural policy where, after all, much of the allegedly progressive and forward-looking thrust of the National Front rested.

The 1961 reforms of Law 135 remained to be implemented by the Valencia government. INCORA itself had been very slow to get off the ground, and only in July 1962 were executive orders issued that would move INCORA into the normal bureaucratic flow. The agency itself became the central focus of both partisan and substantive debate for some years. Its initial staff of dedicated young professionals sought in particular a revision of Colombia's land tenure structure. In short order they recognized that the authorizing legislation did not deal in detail with such an alteration. With Guillermo León Valencia, moreover, Colombia had a chief executive who doubted the value of land redistribution and—only in a fairly vague and uncertain fashion—sought greater exploitation of the nation's rural patrimony.[13] The president, not persuaded by the importance of agrarian reform and INCORA, was at heart a true traditionalist and Conservative of the old school.

The Valencia administrative policies were typified by the events and actions of his first eighteen months. It was a difficult time, as Colombia experienced rampant inflation, rising prices, and food shortages. Many of these problems were laid exclusively at the feet of Valencia, although the blame was not his alone. It would be fairer to suggest, in Holt's words, "that the basis for Colombia's economic difficulties in late 1962 and early 1963 had been laid in earlier years, but that these difficulties had been compounded by some of the actions of the Valencia Administration and of congress—as well as by some actions congress failed to take."[14] In truth, the second National Front president was "likewise a victim of economic dislocation arising from policies which both he and Lleras followed in an attempt to right the country's balance of payments difficulties. On Valencia fell the popular dissatisfaction over the resulting devaluation and inflation."[15]

Economic policy-making under Valencia did not depart greatly from the National Front pattern that had been established under Alberto Lleras. While questions of administrative style and personal leadership are never irrelevant, in the broader sweep of recent and contemporary Colombian political history, they pale in significance when compared with basic political and economic currents. To be sure, there was reason to suggest that the "chaotic" economic policy of the State was consistent with the governmental inability to define and pursue a coherent economic line.[16] Yet even so, in a broad sense Valencia's economic policies did not diverge in fundamental fashion from the increasingly dominant National Front currents.

In light of President Valencia's traditionalistic background and experience, it was unsurprising that his attention was directed elsewhere. Vacillation on economic policy, periodically interrupted by dramatic pronouncements, mirrored this reality. While many saw him as a political anachronism, Valencia found it less complicated to deal with problems of internal peace and the challenge of the guerrillas.

Social and Political Controls

The continuing problem of rural violence had been seemingly contained, but by no means eradicated by the first National Front government. After more than fifteen years, *la violencia* had become increasingly institutionalized. What had long existed as relentless warfare between groups of partisan loyalists, now having passed to a second generation of participants, by 1962 constituted sheer *bandolerismo*. Banditry, criminality, and methods of extreme sadism and brutality were common. At the same time, there were also groups with revolutionary political ideals, and these were viewed with particular apprehension in the early period of the Cuban Revolution.

Of particular prominence were the zones of self-defense to the south—the self-styled "independent republics." Two of them, Viota and Sumapaz, dated back into the 1940s. By 1958 there were nearly a dozen of them, where guerrillas essentially exercised authority to the exclusion of the military. The concerted efforts of the military under Lleras Camargo had helped to pacify some of the rebellious region south of Tolima, but a number of the "republics" survived virtually untouched. Furthermore, the Marxist element was on the rise. In 1962 the Ejército de Liberación Nacional (ELN) was founded, an avowedly pro-Castro organization. A greater potential threat came from the Fuerzas Armadas Revolucionarias Colombianas (FARC), which emerged in 1964 as the informal armed wing of the Communist party.

In the light of generalized alarm over the course of events in Cuba and the *fidelista* pledge to convert the Andes into the Sierra Maestra of South America, press accounts helped to publicize, and in some cases to magnify the strength of Marxist guerrilla organizations. Britain's *The Economist,* for one, reported in August 1965 that five independent republics, five new guerrilla cells, and eight centers of peasant activists were in existence, all of them Marxist-dominated. It concluded, "It is doubtful whether a communist guerrilla movement can prosper at this time in a nation so sated with rural violence as Colombia. But a few well-aimed blows in this deepening political malaise could produce a popular convulsion to be felt throughout the hemisphere."[17]

The Colombian military moved to expand its professional capabilities, extend the scope of antiguerrilla activities, and seek a general institutional modernization. A central figure in both professional and political terms, was General Alberto Ruiz Novoa. Having first attracted attention while commanding the Colombian battalion in the Korean War, Ruiz had later served as Contralor General de la Nación during the military government, and in 1959 became army commander. In seeking a political and doctrinal as well as professional modernization of the military, he developed and elaborated an ideology in which a nonpartisan perspective would be buttressed by a vigorously aggressive nationalistic mission.

In 1960 his *La misión del ejército* called for constant vigilance in the defense of national sovereignty against challenges of anarchy and antinationalism. The armed forces, "of which the Army is a fundamental part, are the institution responsible for guaranteeing normality against external and internal enemies, and the only [force] capable of doing so in times of crisis."[18] Striving to awaken a sense of pride and of intellectual inquiry on the part of the officer corps, he promoted professional publications and broadened the curriculum of the Escuela Militar. Ruiz also contended that socioeconomic conditions helped spur revolt, and that the military therefore owed the nation its concern with ameliorating such problems. For Ruiz, the vision of a modern military establishment thereby required a sensitivity to a broad range of domestic problems.

Ruiz was still refining and expanding his views when the new president named him minister of war in 1962. Adopting a tactical approach that was consistent with the advice being proffered by the Pentagon to favored Latin American governments of the day, Ruiz and his colleagues developed Plan Lazo. A prototypical civic action program, the plan adopted a wide array of rural improvement projects in combination with more orthodox repression. Health care, adult literacy classes, public works construction, sanitation programs—these and similar activities sought to attract peasant support. The relative success of this campaign was suggested by the declining number of rural deaths. The average from 1959 to 1962 was 200 per month, but by 1965 the total for the entire year was 544. At the same time, there were important inroads toward the "independent republics." A massive deployment of troops overran Marquetalia. Others falling to the army in 1965 included Río Chiquito and El Pato.[19]

While the armed forces were achieving progressive successes, the growing visibility of the articulate Ruiz Novoa was gradually creating stresses in civil-military relations. As the general preached the relevance of socioeconomic conditions to popular discontent, he was elaborating undisguised criticisms of the administration itself. In his official ministerial report for 1964, for example, he spoke of "the need to eliminate the social and economic differences which Colombian society today suffers…the injustice in which a vast section of the population is buried, living in very different conditions, constituting an undeniable cauldron for disorder."[20] He was soon declaring publicly that structural changes in Colombian society were necessary, and criticisms of President Valencia's stewardship became ever less guarded. In September of 1964 he called for an openly autonomous role for the military in national development.

In Ruiz's words, the government should promote the integration of the armed forces into society "as an urgent evolution and in contrast to the traditional isolation of the military."[21] This constant prodding of the government and publicizing of military issues at first attracted support from fellow officers, but there were also misgivings over Ruiz's political ambitions. Memories of the experience in power under Rojas Pinilla, including the subsequent loss of face before the public, informed a strong anti-interventionist current within the military. Furthermore, there was a fear that the armed forces might be manipulated by socioeconomic elites for their own private purposes while publicly emphasizing the anticommunist struggle. Consequently, as General Ruiz was going public with growing frequency, his standing gradually deteriorated.

A crisis surfaced at the very close of 1964 when the government was threatened by a nationwide strike. General Ruiz held meetings with labor leaders, and on 23 January 1965, leaflets in the streets of Bogotá proclaimed Ruiz Novoa as Colombia's solution to order and progress. Four days later the general was called to the presidential palace and dismissed by Valencia. A new minister of war explained that the removal of Ruiz was necessary for the maintenance of military discipline and unity. He told the press that "theories about economic, political and social themes that General Ruiz Novoa was making could not continue in that way, because considering that the statements come from...an army officer and minister of war...puts in danger the unity of the institution."[22] The assertion of civilian authority by President Valencia was effective, and Ruiz Novoa faded into the background, despite his hopes for the 1966 presidential race.[23]

Valencia had thus responded firmly to the apparent challenge of civilian supremacy. At the same time, the military under Ruiz Novoa had become an increasingly effective weapon in the maintenance of systemic controls. In addition to a greater elaboration of security doctrine and greater movement toward modernization, the armed forces had also grown from some 23,000 in 1961 to 37,000 in 1965.[24] This was important as the character of rural violence began to take on new dimensions from 1965 forward. The emergence of the ELN began to attract new supporters—in many cases youths who had been unimpressed with the orthodoxy of the Communist party. The ELN followed Cuban ideology in speaking of the so-called subjective as well as objective conditions for revolution. It was the ELN to whom the rebel priest Camilo Torres would soon turn after seemingly exhausting all other channels of protest.

Without engaging in an extended treatment of Torres here,[25] suffice it to say that his concern for the condition of the average Colombian led Torres to advocate a change in the values of the elite. He pursued the effort in university and government positions, and in 1965 created a broad United Front movement that sought grass-roots organization in Colombia. By September of that year, however, the undertaking had foundered seriously, and Torres joined the ELN in armed insurrection the following month, only to be killed by army troops during a firefight in February 1966. His ultimate rejection of the Catholic church in Colombia helped to dramatize its internal disagreements of both a doctrinal and political nature. However, the Church as an institution basically supported the National Front in its exercise of authority, whatever the views of individual members.

If the Valencia administration saw a great enlargement and application of both civic action and coercive techniques by the armed forces in reducing the level of rural violence, it was also experiencing the closing of the traditional era of *la violencia* and the opening of the countryside to more ideological currents of thought and action. With the ELN and then the FARC attempting to capitalize on presumed lessons from the guerrilla warfare in Cuba, the character of the conflict was transformed. In addition, urban terrorism was on the rise. Recurrent kidnappings began to plague wealthy Colombians; ransom payments increased; and strike-related violence spread.

From 1965 the government also began to employ more widely the powers of state of siege; civilians were also subjected to military rather than civilian courts.[26] The armed forces continued its pursuit for greater professionalization, while a vague concern with social reformism—a response to General Ruiz's influence—blended with a strongly uncomplicated view of international communism. General Gerardo Ayerbe Chaux, who would become defense minister in the next government, typified the latter when he wrote in 1965 of the linkage between Marxism and internal unrest in Colombia:

> [Communism] is a palpitating reality which has for some years been manifesting itself by means of intense, copious and well-directed propaganda, by the methodical agitation of different social sectors, by various front organizations, by the infiltration into the university, the high schools and into different state and private organizations, and finally by the guerrilla movements in the country which have taken different names according to circumstances.[27]

During all of this Guillermo León Valencia had generally remained relatively uninvolved in the mechanics of social and political controls. He was much more at home with the party-based arena of politics.

The Politics of the National Front

The Party Competition

The second National Front government had entered office with a two-thirds margin in the senate and a somewhat smaller majority in the Chamber. This was little different from the situation under Alberto Lleras Camargo. However, Valencia's support broke down in short order over questions of devaluation and taxes. Where the parties were concerned, Guillermo León Valencia was better equipped to deal with internal Conservative factionalism than his predecessor, although the Liberals presented their own set of problems.

The incoming president was driven to *"milimetría,"* dividing the six Conservative ministries among the three factions. Once this was accomplished—accompanied by a similar division of party positions at lower levels—the latent Conservative factionalism did not prove unduly annoying. In March of 1963 the *ospinistas* (often called *unionistas*) and the *laureanistas* struck an agreement whereby they agreed on the division of congressional positions and coordinated their actions with one another. Although President Valencia generally tended to treat the congress haughtily, the Conservatives were able to benefit from his presence in the palace. What was less manageable for Valencia, and certainly more unpredictable, was the internal turmoil of the Liberals.

The apparent growth of the MRL in response to rural discontent helped to complicate the picture. The wave of irregular strikes and popular protests engendered by the inflationary explosion of early 1963 provided grist for the MRL mill. This also contributed to a growing differentiation between the MRL's *línea dura* and *línea blanda,* or hard- and soft-line. It became a matter of public record with the founding on 8 May 1963 of the hard-line group. Headed by Alvaro Uribe Rueda, a member of the *La Calle* intellectuals from which the MRL had originated, the *línea dura* rejected López Michelsen's apparent tendency to negotiation and talk with *oficialistas.* Its program was more radical than that of López and, rather than publicly calling for a takeover and streamlining of the Liberal party, proposed formation of a nationalistic bloc including members of the Colombian Left.

Facing this challenge to his leadership, López Michelsen and his colleagues founded their own newspaper *Izquierda* after losing control of *La Calle*. The *línea blanda* did not alter its basic political stance. As he had told the convention of the then-united MRL in November 1962, López was willing to accept support from the Communists and from other groups, but not at the price of advocating radical solutions. Neither was he willing to yield leadership to Uribe or other challengers, even in the face of widespread opinion that López's public persona lacked the qualities so outstanding in his father. Nor would he shift his perspective in the face of demands from the youth wing of the MRL. This would cause even further fragmentation, for the Juventudes del MRL (JMRL), praising the Cuban Revolution and accepting the possibility of violence to achieve political ends, spoke of radical solutions and progressively withdrew from the MRL.

In retrospect, López's MRL sought major change rather than outright revolution. In Dix's view, "Apart from a few individuals on its left wing, the MRL is not a revolutionary movement to depose the elite altogether; rather, it is an attempt to break the elite's *monopoly* on social, political and economic power."[28] Alfonso López Michelsen himself, ever the elitist scion of an aristocratic family with distinguished political credentials, was viewed as "a wealthy intellectual who talks of a social revolution but hopes for moderation."[29] For the short term, however, the question was the nature of the MRL dissension and its relationship to the traditional Liberal party. The latter was coming increasingly under the control of Carlos Lleras Restrepo, a progressive if far from radical critic of the system.

The Liberals had convened a gathering of legislators on 20 March 1963 that promulgated a new set of official party statutes—this the work of Lleras Restrepo. He attacked the Conservatives for sectarianism and President Valencia for failing to honor fully the biparty agreement. Resigning from the party directorate, he announced his own presidential candidacy in August. At the Liberal convention in February of 1964 he was officially selected as the party candidate for the next National Front presidency. Lleras Restrepo accepted the charge, called upon the Conservatives to accept his candidacy, and spurred the party to greater activity as the *mitaca* elections neared.

Abstention was high when Colombians voted on 15 March 1964. A total of 2,261,190 votes were cast, which constituted a bare 36.9 percent of eligible voters. This was the lowest figure yet in the history of the National Front. The Liberals retained their majority status, with 1,141,503 votes for 50.5 percent. The Conservatives received 802,282 votes for 35.5 percent, while the nascent *rojista* forces of ANAPO startled most observers with 309,678 votes and 13.7 percent—10 percent above their total in 1962. The division of Liberal votes gave the *oficialistas* a 2–1 margin over the MRL, while the *línea blanda* easily outstripped the *línea dura* by 3–1, at 284,952 to 96,895 votes. What this meant for the new Chamber of Deputies was the mandated division of 184 seats between Liberals and Conservatives. The former had fifty-nine officialist seats, thirty-one with the MRL (twenty-three soft-line, eight hard-line), and two others. On the Conservative side, there were sixty-five pro-Front deputies for the *ospinista-laureanista* alliance of the moment, twenty-six from ANAPO, and one other.

In the wake of elections, Guillermo León Valencia had his customary margin, the Liberals maintained their advantage over the Conservatives, the MRL division had weakened but not overcome Alfonso López Michelsen, and the challenge of ANAPO was no longer a laughing matter for the Colombian elites. The support for Rojas Pinilla was disturbing to Front leaders, while the general himself confidently issued thinly disguised suggestions that he might seek power by nonelectoral means. If the pro-Front margin remained solid at some 67.8 percent to 29.9 percent (for the two MRL factions and the ANAPO totals from both Conservative and Liberal ballots), it was based on a sharply reduced level of popular participation.

Candidate Selection

Support for Carlos Lleras Restrepo as next Frente president was accompanied by renewed partisanship and opportunistic maneuvering. The preelection Conservative reunification of March 1963, strongly influenced by Guillermo León Valencia, had created a united party directorate with Mariano Ospina Pérez in charge and Alvaro Gómez Hurtado, Laureano's son, as vice chairman. By the time midyear congressional sessions opened, however, there was growing backbiting over the presumed responsibility for losses to ANAPO. Furthermore, Ospina's acceptance of Lleras Restrepo, who had been so helpful in the choice and election of Valencia, was not shared by the *laureanistas*. They remembered all too well Lleras's sharp opposition to the Gómez administration years before. On 9 June the *ospinistas* withdrew from the Conservative directorate. The *laureanistas* denounced Lleras Restrepo while charging that the National Front had proven itself incapable of the restoration of social peace and order.

Meanwhile, Carlos Lleras continued his steady march toward eventual selection as nominee. In October of 1964 he met with López Michelsen to discuss possible collaboration, and on 4 December a Liberal convention ratified his candidacy, adopted statutory revisions that had been a product of *llerista* labors, and named three veteran leaders to the directorship: Darío Echandía, Julio César Turbay Ayala, and Victor Mosquera Chaux. Apparent party unity was also highlighted by the participation and approval of former president Lleras Camargo. All of this left Lleras Restrepo increasingly certain of his own party, but still without backing from the opposition party. In a tactic that he would repeat in later years to force a political issue, Carlos Lleras on 8 May 1965 resigned his candidacy in the face of renewed Conservative factionalism and the continuing public neutrality of President Valencia.

The latter, while already describing himself as a "first-rate" *llerista,* insisted upon his need to be institutionally noncommittal. "As an individual I can have whatever political sympathies I like, but as a ruler I have to be absolutely impartial. It is not true that *llerista* or anti-*llerista* machines are being established in the country."[30] While the president maintained this public posture, however, the Conservatives moved increasingly toward Lleras Restrepo. A prime mover was the senior architect of the entire system, Alberto Lleras Camargo.[31] In October he called a bipartisan group to the Hotel Tequendama, created a bipartisan committee with Misael Pastrana and Belisario Betancur as Conservative spokesmen, and invited Lleras Restrepo to resume his candidacy. The following month a mass meeting was held in Bogotá at which Carlos Lleras agreed to run and reaffirmed his agreement with the Conservatives. On 4 December 1965, a Conservative convention accepted the inevitable and recognized Lleras Restrepo as National Front candidate.

There had never been serious doubt about the choice, which had materialized much earlier in the process than that of Valencia four years earlier. While there had been occasional murmurs about Julio César

Turbay Ayala, he was content with reelection as party director at the February 1964 Liberal convention. López Michelsen did not contest the nomination, while Lleras Camargo made his own preferences obvious. Guillermo León Valencia, despite contradictory public statements, had been favorable almost from the beginning. The Liberals recognized Lleras Restrepo as their most capable and popular figure, while the Conservatives, mired in their own internecine disputes, had nowhere else to go.[31]

At the elections on 20 March 1966, the number of ballots cast totalled 2,939,222. This translated into an abstention rate of 55.5 percent, which was higher than presidential year totals in March 1958 and 1962 but lower than the rock-bottom figure in 1964. The total Liberal vote was 52.1 percent, with 1,529,746. This included 72 percent for the officialists and 23 percent for the MRL—this latter its weakest performance since 1960. The *lopistas* had regained factional control, as members of the *línea dura* had largely disappeared. The remaining 5 percent of Liberal votes went to ANAPO lists. For the Conservatives, two-thirds were backers of the National Front, with the *ospinistas* winning by a 3–2 margin. This left one-third of the Conservative vote to anti-Front ANAPO lists.

In terms of seats, this transferred itself to forty-six Liberal and seven MRL senators; there were twenty-one *ospinistas,* fourteen *laureanistas* (now becoming known as *alvaristas* following the death of the elder Gómez), and eighteen from ANAPO. In the Chamber the proportions were similar. There were seventy Liberal, twenty-one MRL, and four ANAPO members; the Conservatives included thirty-eight *ospinistas,* twenty-four *alvaristas,* thirty-two from ANAPO, and one independent. The most striking electoral gains belonged to ANAPO, with its combined Liberal and Conservative lists producing a total of eighteen senators and thirty-six deputies. Given the decline of the MRL—plus the harbingers of a possible accord between Lleras Restrepo and López Michelsen—ANAPO therefore stood as the major anti-Front movement. And with López having declined a presidential race after the March showing of his party, it also simplified the prospects for the presidential race set for 1 May 1966.

Campaign and Elections

Lleras Restrepo, his candidacy sanctioned by both coalition parties, had launched his campaign under the rubric Frente de Transformación

Nacional (FTN). This transformation was promised in reformist terms, with a series of study groups established to develop plans for a host of different policy areas. The activity had begun well before the convening of congressional elections, although the intensity grew as May neared. With López Michelsen having eschewed a candidacy, there was some talk of an anti-Front accord between the MRL and ANAPO. This proved too unusual a combination to bear fruit, and eventually the latter chose the little-known José Jaramillo Giraldo, fifty-one, a longtime Liberal congressman from Manizales who had been a cabinet minister under Rojas Pinilla and still remained loyal to the former strongman.

Campaigning only during the final month, Jaramillo was vigorous in his denunciations of the National Front and fulsome in praise of Rojas Pinilla. It was a time of considerable activity despite the certainty of the outcome. President Valencia saw fit not to lift the state of siege during the campaign, and there were a series of student protests and clashes with troops toward the close of April. On 1 May, with an electorate officially listed as 6,611,352, a total of 2,638,411 valid votes were cast. The abstention rate of 60.1 percent was the highest yet in presidential elections under the National Front. Carlos Lleras Restrepo received 1,891,175 votes, for 71.4 percent, to Jaramillo's 742,133 and 28 percent; the remaining 0.6 percent for minor candidates. The new president-elect busily conferred with supporters and opponents alike in preparing for what promised to be an activist administration. Meanwhile, President Valencia closed his terms with a final rash of conflicts and disagreements.

He maintained the state of siege with firm military support. There were additional strikes, and inflation was at its highest yet during the Front experience. More generally, the level of abstention not only became a major topic of daily speculation but, in more basic terms, underlined popular perceptions of the National Front after eight years. If the increasingly widespread decision to opt out of electoral participation suggested the existence of what Johnson called "the alienated non-involved"—thereby rejecting the possibility of a massive antisystem vote—it demonstrated the lack of popular support on which the government might draw.[32] It also raised the specter of increasing rural violence and guerrilla activity, while urban crime and kidnappings continued.

Guillermo León Valencia had regularly drawn public scorn and even mockery in response to both his temperament and administrative style.

Yet to be fair, many of the manifold problems lay at the doorstep of the Front system itself. As one contemporary account remarked,

> It is debatable...whether the prime responsibility for the faltering of the National Front after 1962 rested as much with President Valencia as with the system itself.... Valencia was likewise a victim of economic dislocation arising from policies which both he and Lleras followed in an attempt to right the country's balance of payments difficulties. On Valencia fell the popular dissatisfaction over the resulting devaluation and inflation. Most of all, the president was the captive of a system which favored accommodation over resolute action. Valencia's political skills were partly responsible for the temporary union of the major Conservative factions in 1963. But in essence the problems of intraparty factionalism continued unabated, and to these were added an increasing tendency for pressure groups to become assertive in their demands on the executive.[33]

It was with a determination to alter systemic processes, reshape national policies, and move toward a modernization of both Colombia and the Liberal party that Carlos Lleras Restrepo prepared for the third government of the National Front.

Notes

1. León Zamosc, *The Agrarian Question and the Peasant Movement in Colombia: Struggles of the National Peasant Association 1967–1981* (Cambridge: Cambridge University Press, 1986), 24.
2. W. O. Galbraith, *Colombia: A General Survey*, 2d ed. (London: Oxford University Press, 1966), 94.
3. Ibid., 110–11.
4. Francisco E. Thoumi, "Industrial Development Policies during the National Front Years," in R. Albert Berry, Ronald G. Hellman, and Mauricio Solaun, eds., *Politics of Compromise: Coalition Government in Colombia* (New Brunswick: Transaction Publishers, 1980), 330.

   For the results and analysis of a 1966–69 RAND project in conjunction with the Agency for International Development—which focussed on specific Colombian developmental issues with data concentrating on the 1951–64 years—see Richard R. Nelson, T. Paul Schultz, and Robert L. Slighton, *Structural Change in a Developing Economy: Colombia's Problems and Prospects* (Princeton: Princeton University Press, 1971).
5. Francisco Leal Buitrago, *Estudio del comportamiento legislativo en Colombia. Tomo I. Análisis histórico del desarrollo político nacional, 1930–1970* (Bogotá: Tercer Mundo, 1973), 133.
6. Pat M. Holt, *Colombia Today—and Tomorrow* (New York: Frederick A. Praeger, Publishers, 1964), 69.
7. Carlos F. Díaz-Alejandro, *Foreign Trade Regimes and Economic Development: Colombia* (New York: Columbia University Press, for the National Bureau of Economic Research, 1976), 25.
8. Holt, *Colombia Today,* 67–68.

9. Robert H. Dix, *Colombia: The Political Dimensions of Change* (New Haven: Yale University Press, 1967), 159.
10. R. Albert Berry, "The National Front and Colombia's Economic Development," in Berry et al., *Politics of Compromise*, 298.
11. Ibid.
12. Leal, *Estudio del comportamiento*, 134.
13. Holt, *Colombia Today*, 74–101.
14. Ibid., 183.
15. Dix, *Colombia*, 160.
16. Ibid.
17. *The Economist* (28 August 1965), as quoted in Galbraith, *Colombia: A General Survey*.
18. Leal, *Estudio del comportamiento*, 209.
19. For more detailed analysis see Richard L. Maullin, *Soldiers, Guerrillas and Politics in Colombia* (Lexington, MA: D.C. Heath & Co., 1973).
20. Alberto Ruiz Novoa, *Memoria del Ministro de Guerra* (Bogotá: Ministerio de Guerra, 1964), 5–6, as cited in J. Mark Ruhl, "The Military," in Berry et al., *Politics of Compromise*, 191.
21. Alberto Ruiz Novoa, "El Derecho de Opinión," *Revista del Ejercito 4* (September 1964): 3.
22. *El Tiempo* (28 January 1965).
23. For a fuller exposition of General Ruiz's thinking, see his *El gran desafío* (Bogotá: Tercer Mundo, 1965).
24. Pierre Gilhodes, "El Ejército colombiano analiza violencia," in Gonzalo Sanchez y Ricardo Penaranda, comps., *Pasado y presente de la violencia en Colombia* (Bogotá: Fondo Editorial Cerec, 1986), 306.
25. For an excellent biography see Walter J. Broderick, *Camilo Torres* (New York: 1975). Among the more accessible collections of Torres's writings, see Maurice Zeitlin, ed., *Revolutionary Priest* (New York: 1972).
26. An excellent survey is Gustavo Gallon Giraldo, *Quince años de estado de sitio en Colombia, 1958–1978* (Bogotá: Editorial America Latina, 1979).
27. Gerardo Ayerbe Chaux, "La amenaza comunista," *Revista del Ejército 5* (December 1965): 237.
28. Dix, *Colombia*, 269.
29. Tad Szulc, "Colombia Faces Political Crisis," *The New York Times* (26 March 1961): 31.
30. *El Espectador* (14 March 1965).
31. Laureano Gómez had died in July 1965.
32. Kenneth Johnson, "Political Radicalism in Colombia: Electoral Dynamics of 1962 and 1964," *Journal of Inter-American Studies* (January 1965), 15–16.
33. Dix, *Colombia*, 160–61.

6

Reformist Developmentalism: Lleras Restrepo (1966–70)

The Policies of Governance

The National Environment

With the August 1966 inauguration of Carlos Lleras Restrepo, the National Front reached the appointed midpoint of its projected sixteen-year life. The estimated population stood at 19,590,000—an increase of some four million since the beginning of the National Front. The annual rate of change during the eight years was 3.17 percent, the third highest for all Latin America. Urbanization was nearly 55 percent. Furthermore, from 1960 to 1965 the percentage of the urban population in the largest cities—those above one-half million had risen precipitately from 24.3 percent to 38.8 percent. This had been drawn in considerable part from communities in the 100,000–500,000 range, where the 25.1 percent of 1960 had declined to 15.6 percent by 1965.[1] Colombian urbanization was therefore reaching new and unparalleled dimensions as Carlos Lleras Restrepo took office. Dix described the situation tellingly:

> The consequences of urbanization for the Colombian economy, society, and polity are incalculable. Economically, the prospective market for manufactured goods is increased and made more accessible while the tertiary sector of the economy expands to meet urban needs.... Many of the new arrivals to the city are unemployed or underemployed, yet their proximity to urban amenities and urban communications raises their aspirations. Politically, potential discontent is more concentrated as a result of urbanization, while at the same time the poor are released from some of the old forms of domination and control by the *patrón* and the cacique.[2]

In the largest cities, then, overtaxed and inadequate facilities stirred popular aspirations but provided scant sustenance for newly arrived mi-

119

grants. The flood from countryside to town and city also underlay a gradual decline in economic importance for the agricultural sector. Where it had provided an annual average of 36.5 percent of the GDP from 1950 to 1954, this fell below 30 percent for the four years beginning in 1965. And although agricultural products remained the dominant element in total exports, this had dropped from 85.3 percent to 75.7 percent. Even coffee showed a declining value of exports; here, the annual 1950–54 average was $417.1 million, while for the later period it was down to $350.6 million.[3] Prices for Colombia's major export had been sagging throughout the life of the Front, thereby causing aggravated trade deficits. So-called minor exports—everything but petroleum and coffee—had received little attention, thereby underlining the need for a revitalization of the agricultural sector. It had also seen proposed Lleras land reforms first watered down, then largely ignored following the 1961 passage in congress.

Taken in national terms, the Colombian economy had continued to grow from 1958 at an average 5 percent annually; the 1962 growth rate of 6.2 percent was followed by only 3.6 percent the next year. This was an apt indicator of the unfavorable situation facing the new administration. The limits of early import substitution had virtually been reached, and per capita income increases were far too small to compensate for an average yearly inflation of 17 percent. The 1962 and 1965 devaluations had provided limited comfort through the exchange rates or balance of payments. As the World Bank later reported, the Valencia years had been marked by a chronically overvalued peso, which hindered export diversification. Stabilization efforts from devaluation were unsuccessful, and policies were too often uncoordinated:

> The use of selective administrative controls to manage scarce foreign exchange and financial resources resulted in their inefficient allocation, substantial excess industrial capacity and, ultimately, slow growth. Expansionary monetary and wage policies generated inflationary pressures which wiped out the beneficial effects of devaluations and actually worsened the real exchange rate.[4]

It was a time, then, when the National Front found itself ever more taxed by the demographic and economic pressures of a modernizing country. The bureaucratic centralization of the state was proceeding too slowly to respond adequately to civic needs. While the final vestiges of the original *violencia* were nearly eradicated, they were giving way to urban crime

plus guerrilla activism motivated by ideological conviction and a growing mass of both rural and urban citizens who felt alienated from the
system. It was a time of testing for the National Front, and it directed its
hopes to the action-oriented reformism of the new chief executive.

Policies of the Administration

Carlos Lleras Restrepo came to the presidency with impressive credentials. Born in 1908 and trained as an economist, he entered public life
at an early age. Serving as minister of finance to Liberal administrations
as early as 1938, he reached the Liberal directorate for the first time in
1943. Later serving on several occasions as its *jefe único*, he had achieved
greater authority and a more detailed knowledge of the party's inner
workings than any of his contemporaries. This had been buttressed through
years of service in both chambers of congress, where he had been elected
designado under Lleras Camargo in 1960.

Short, balding, and bespectacled, Lleras Restrepo was forceful, energetic, and abrasive when encountering those less intelligent or slower to
act. Arguably the best trained and professionally equipped National Front
president in terms of technical knowledge, he was a pragmatically oriented economist and businessman, relying on a group of young emerging
técnicos more than on career politicians, unlike his two predecessors.
Lleras Restrepo thus represented a break in presidential style, almost the
prototype of the "developmentalist" of the 1960s, as Dix put it. At the
same time, his Liberal party roots were great. Thus, the new president,
although "quintessentially the builder of industrial Colombia," had followed a career that was hardly that of pure technocrat.[5]

Carlos Lleras Restrepo had well-formed diagnoses of national problems and concomitant prescriptive policies well before taking office. A
prime example was the resuscitation and modernization of the agricultural sector, which he had sought through the 1961 legislation. There
were many other priorities on the immediate agenda when he took the
oath of office in August 1966. With the growth rate disappointing, it was
being argued that the time was ripe for a shift in development strategy;
this was to take the shape of reformist activism on the part of the new
chief executive. Lleras was committed to construction of a modern bourgeois state, one in which the government would institutionalize national
planning and serve as a veritable *patrón* of development. Such a mod-

ernizing transformation of traditional clientelism would presumably result in a centralized bureaucratic state wherein the elites could proceed with their traditional hegemonic control without having their interests seriously challenged.

For Lleras Restrepo, the time was ripe for a shift from the protectionist import-substitution economic model. He sought to reshape economic policy in favor of export-led growth, buttressed by reliance on state planning. This required further reform of the prevailing administrative system. The plethora of decentralized institutions, traditionally resistant to presidential control, had long been utilized for purposes of patronage. In many cases they had also been responsive to pressures from the economic sectors over which they were presumably responsible. Lleras selectively attacked a number of these agencies through such devices as slashing budgets and reorganizing economic policy-making. The result was a streamlining of state planning, which encouraged institutional modernization while facilitating presidential efforts to develop coherent long-term economic policy. It also implied further movement toward bureaucratized clientelism.

Far better than most of his political contemporaries, Carlos Lleras Restrepo understood that Colombia stood in need of structural and bureaucratic changes in the state. He consequently gave continual attention to the reorganization and modernization of the entire institutional structure of economic policy-making in Colombia. This represented a sharp departure from the Valencia administration, which had demonstrated its disinterest in ways such as permitting the Comisión de Planeación to operate for more than a year without an appointed director. Lleras Restrepo himself came to rely heavily on Planeación. Recruitment of personnel was based on technical competence while its organizational responsibility rapidly increased. During the Lleras administration Planeación was assigned dual tasks: first, to improve the process of project selection, evaluation, and presentation to international agencies for funding; and second, to advance sectoral planning, most particularly for electricity and transportation.[6]

With the Consejo Nacional de Política Económica y Planeación also reactivated and prodded to greater participation by the new government, Lleras firmly insisted that his key policymakers also make conscious efforts to oversee and coordinate economic policy.[7] The president labored with deliberate urgency to employ extensively a growing array of state planning institutions. Even before the important constitutional reforms of 1968 (see below), the impetus was undeniable. Edgar Reveiz and María José Pérez drew attention to this in a recent analysis of Colombian economic growth:

> During the Lleras presidency, numerous new state institutions and agencies for economic regulation and intervention were established.... This was a period of "state capitalism," though obviously "in transition to capitalism" in the sense of the state intervening not only by supplying credit but also by direct capital investments. The state supported efforts to build a more efficient capitalist structure in the country, one that was capable of competing in world markets, without changing the social structures of production.[8]

While making ample use of state regulatory agencies in the shaping of monetary, fiscal, and exchange policies, the government also nurtured other state institutions linked to credit and fiscal matters. Thus, the Instituto de Fomento Industrial (The Institute of Industrial Development, or IFI) acted as a source of government financing and oversight while directing credit toward selected industrial sectors. Another important agency was the Fondo de Promoción de Exportaciones (PROEXPO), or Export Promotion Fund, which was employed on behalf of nontraditional exports. A decentralized institute created by Decree-Law 444 on 22 March 1967, PROEXPO provided liberal credit to exporters, negotiated equity capital, and generally promoted nontraditional commodities. It even engaged in domestic advertising, sporting billboards insisting that "Exporting is the best business in Colombia" as a means of promoting an export mentality.[9]

The administration also set up an elaborate specialized bureaucracy to deal specifically with multinational corporations and the regulation of foreign private investment. Moving into an area where Colombia had customarily followed a noninterventionist pattern, the government incorporated extensive provisions into Decree-Law 444, based on the premise that all foreign investment should necessarily be consistent with the national interest. While the existing Departamento Nacional de Planeación (DNP) received new duties in reviewing and authorizing proposed foreign investments, an Oficina de Cambios, or Exchange Office, was made responsible for recording and approving capital outflow. Import licenses were to be authorized through the Instituto Colombiano de Comercio Exterior (INCOMEX), the Foreign Trade Institute, and still other government agencies were involved in different aspects of foreign investment. All of this testified to official recognition of expanding investment, which had outstripped that of most Latin American countries. It also gave Lleras Restrepo a further opportunity to strengthen the national government in his construction of a more powerful, and presumably more modernized form of state centralism.

It was only the presidency of Lleras Restrepo, then, which fully recognized the importance for the National Front of a strong state with a bureaucratic apparatus responsive to the political leadership. It is worth noting that much of the content of institutional innovations, including many elements of the 1968 reforms, had been planned by Lleras Restrepo prior to his inauguration. This was demonstrated through details incorporated into the 1968 constitutional reform, which sought to readjust the relations of the National Front before it reached what would presumably be the last of its four governments (1970–74).

The reform attempted to redefine the functions and composition of both the Consejo Nacional and the Comisión de Planeación. There were also provisions dealing with the respective responsibilities of the legislative and executive branches in the formulation and implementation of economic policy. The results strengthened the initiatory role of the executive, along with the congressional exercise of oversight during the consideration and ultimate the execution of plans. There were administrative adjustments to the Consejo Nacional and its duties, while Planeación received greater budgetary authority as well as its own powers of review concerning foreign technical assistance.[10]

Lleras Restrepo's attention to export income, and to the furtherance of nontraditional commodities as insurance against the vicissitudes of coffee prices on the international market, had been demonstrated most dramatically with Decree-Law 444 of 1967. Besides creating PROEXPO, as mentioned, it sought a full-blown institutional mechanism of export promotion via new trade and exchange regulations. That the president was deeply involved is the fact that for a good four months prior to the promulgation of 444, his daily schedule was dominated by meetings and discussions related to the matter. Officials concerned with noneconomic policy questions found access to the president very difficult. When the decree came into being, it effectively introduced an innovative foreign exchange system, incorporating the effort to promote exports, as a major element in Lleras Restrepo's own strategy of reformist developmentalism.

The move to shape and adopt what became Decree-Law 444, which Bagley correctly characterized as the centerpiece of *llerista* reforms to the national development strategy, had begun in the earliest weeks of the administration.[11] Coffee prices, which were 50 cents per pound in the first quarter of 1966, had dropped to 45 cents during the final quarter. This helped move the government to the decision on 29 November that free exchange market operations be suspended. The government rejected calls from foreign creditors to devalue, and price controls were imposed. On 27 January 1967, Lleras ordered an increase in import deposit rate requirements, and before the close of the following month Decree-Law 444 had been set in place.

The drive to encourage an export mentality and to nourish nontraditional exports constituted a deliberate effort by Carlos Lleras to shift from coffee export income or ISI to diversified exports as the motor of development. Tax credits for exporters of all products but coffee and petroleum were decreed. A general tax-credit certificate, the Certificado de Abono Tributario (CAT), set at 15 percent of export value, was provided for those dealing in minor commodities; it could be used for tax payments a year after being issued. Further incentives came from Plan Vallejo, which permitted exporters to bring into Colombia duty-free machinery necessary for their production process. PROEXPO, already described, represented an official attempt to help prod the general drive for increased and diversified exporting of manufactured products. All these efforts, it is important to note, were carried out as a means of furthering and diversifying national exports, but not to the detriment of coffee. That is, the government continued to be supportive of the coffee industry, and the customary close links between FEDECAFE and the government were maintained.

This was also true of import substitution industrialization, which remained important but with less emphasis than in the past. Decree-Law 444 had meanwhile incorporated provisions to encourage the economy generally, including exports and industrialization, through a new method of managing the exchange rate. Consequently, it issued trade and exchange provisions that established a crawling peg mechanism of small, frequent devaluations to accompany the system of incentives. These were designed to promote stability by keeping pace with inflation, thus avoiding the abrupt and discordant volatility of exchange rates and balance-of-payments crises changes that had marked National Front governments prior to Lleras Restrepo.

Lleras devoted greater attention than his two National Front predecessors to the agricultural sector. They had emphasized a reestablishment of rural peace and a reassertion of control by the dominant landowners in the wake of *la violencia* and civil strife. Thus, Law 135 of 1961 had reflected a consensus among the mainstream Liberals and Conservatives that favored policy measures designed to recreate the familiar patterns of the past. Notwithstanding much rhetoric and an impressive listing of specific goals, reform had been conceived by Colombian elites "as a social palliative rather than as a transformation of the rural economy."[12] Carlos Lleras Restrepo, without necessarily holding different views about pacification and class relationships, was more forward-looking in understanding the potential benefit of an agricultural sector experiencing both economic and social progress.

With the economy threatening serious recession as import substitution reached its limits and coffee prices stubbornly remained depressed, it was clear that greater agricultural productivity was desirable. From a political standpoint, the benefits of a peasant movement also emerged as a possible means of solidifying the system and, in point of fact, easing the pressures on the National Front being exerted from the countryside. Lleras's policies toward an emergent peasant movement constituted an important aspect of his effort to exert social and political controls. Regarding more explicitly economic measures, an orthodox but significant input came from greater budgetary support.

State expenditures by the agriculture ministry, for example, had averaged 3.6 percent under Lleras Camargo and 4.7 percent with Valencia; they rose to 6.1 percent under Lleras Restrepo, with the figure of 6.7 percent in 1970 the highest ever recorded.[13] New credits were directed toward commercial agriculture, infrastructure was expanded, and Law 1 of 1968 curbed many of the restrictions in Law 135 of 1961, which had held back the redistributive effect that Lleras had originally intended. While there was an evident rise in land expropriations toward the close of Carlos Lleras's years, land tenure had not been fundamentally altered. Of greater importance for the strength of the National Front system was the burgeoning peasant movement, and this was more directly a function of efforts to extend systemic legitimacy and better to penetrate the Colombian countryside.

The major administrative efforts to improve and to modernize the nation's economy, then, as developed by Lleras Restrepo and his advisors, clearly intended to promote reformist developmentalism well beyond that exercised previously in Colombia. In doing so, the government sought to create a level of bureaucratic competence and technical professionalism that would assure the best of public sector planning in the future. Here again, Lleras Restrepo was pursuing goals that went well beyond previous National Front administrations, and intended that the results would leave a permanent imprint of state centralism, certainly one that would long outlive his four years in office. Granted the systemic significance of such an undertaking, it was also true that even the most concerted rationalization of economic planning and procedures of governance transpired within the constricting boundaries of the political and social structures.

Certainly there were conditioning realities that impinged upon presidential and governmental actions. In the view of the Francisco Leal Buitrago, there were at least three dominating factors. First was the tradition of a deep-seated capitalist system within which limits on state intervention exercised a constraint on economic planning. In the second place Colombia's capitalist underdevelopment, linked to dominant international interests, could not disregard the influences that emanated from abroad and left their mark on Colombian reality. Third were the existing, long established internal controls traditionally guided or manipulated by elites accustomed to a concentration of political and economic privilege.[14]

In addition, at least two more might be added: one rested on the limitation of Colombian human resources, for an upper tier of well-trained professionals was poorly served by a mass of ill-trained bureaucrats and officials, often enjoying position only because of traditional clientelism and partisan patronage. The other was dependent upon the limitations of the existing economy, for even assuming a higher level of rationality and immunity from sociopolitical influences on the part of state planners, there was a decidedly finite character to the availability of known resources. It remained true that the evolving Colombian system, if moving beyond traditional patron-client relationships, still required means of responding to the needs of a mobile and urbanizing public. The extent to which this could not be accomplished produced assured greater pressures on systemic legitimacy. With Carlos Lleras in power, there was a greater realization of these pressures, as well as a characteristic impatience with obstruction and delay. What this meant was a concerted effort by the president to extend the authority of the state more fully into the countryside, and to build a higher level of legitimacy. This led him toward a more diverse array of control policies than the customary methods of coercion and repression.

Social and Political Controls

Carlos Lleras Restrepo was concerned with the succession of crises that had seriously sapped the vitality of government and the viability of social and political controls under President Valencia. He also believed that National Front governments had a mandate to do more than merely react to events. The incoming president envisioned the erection of a state capable of meeting popular needs and demands without pursuing radical solutions. This led him to go beyond orthodox counterinsurgency campaigns and patchwork civic action projects into such untraditional and sensitive areas as population growth and mobilization of the peasantry.

The former was especially sensitive. It had been a major event when former president Lleras Camargo told an international population conference at Cali in August of 1965 that the government should encourage slower population growth. Carlos Lleras had the temerity to echo this sentiment. It was an act of forthrightness for him to sign the United Nations Declaration on Population on 10 December 1966; no other Latin American chief of state did so. A few months before, Lleras's health ministry had contracted for a program of training and research that included family planning as an important component.[15] Under Lleras Restrepo, then, Colombia committed itself to a slowing of the rate of population growth. Extensive technical assistance was sought internationally, including such controversial sources as the Ford and Rockefeller Foundations.

Support for family planning gradually mounted. Even the Catholic church, while criticizing the underlying philosophy, at the same time quietly argued for responsible parenthood and small families. In addition, two influential groups of professionals added their own weight to government policy. For one, the medical profession was concerned with questions of public health. At the same time, economists and social scientists viewed matters within the context of balanced national development. Lleras Restrepo meanwhile remained the most vocal advocate for policies that might reduce population pressures on Colombia's limited resources and institutional structures. As he told a conference of bishops in February of 1967, the family planning program in no sense restricted parents' inalienable right to decide the number of their children. When a lengthy congressional inquiry concluded with an official report in October of 1969, its conclusions

> amounted to a resounding vote of confidence in the family planning program and supported "the conduct which the government has assumed in this important matter," expressing the hope "that the respective plans increase as a first procedure to better the conditions of Colombian society."[16]

On a different front, the administration sought to deal with problems of the peasantry as a means of linking rural conditions to national developmental patterns. Mobilization of the peasantry in responding to its needs and demands was justified on several grounds. Politically, Lleras was sensitive to the rising strength of ANAPO, as well as to the expanding activities of the FARC, ELN, and EPL. Economically, in his own words,

> urban demand of labor for industries and services will not surpass supply but, on the contrary, the latter will have excesses extremely difficult to absorb;...in such conditions, whatever contributes to bind the peasant population to the land can be considered as socially and economically useful, even though in some cases it may imply the prolongation of an economy of simply subsistence.[17]

Two months before his inauguration, the president had named a committee to consider organizing the peasantry into "users" of government services. This led to publication on 2 May 1967 of Decree 755, which created the National Association of Peasants (Asociación Nacional de Usuarios Campesinos, ANUC). In bypassing congress by this presidential action, Lleras "set the stage for peasant mobilization, using ANUC to spearhead the agrarian project of bourgeois reformism."[18] Organizational responsibility was given to the ministry of agriculture, which in turn mounted a hierarchy of agricultural institutions throughout Colombia. Although Lleras declared that the government had no desire to exercise authority over the *usuario* associations, in practice the ministry registered the peasant organizations and ANUC headquarters were located in the same Bogotá building.

With the prodding of the president, institutionalization of the peasant organization moved forward briskly. By 1970 nearly 5000 *usuarios* from 300 municipal associations had undergone leadership training; five departmental associations were active; and regional offices were also in operation. That year the First National congress of ANUC was convened, and Lleras addressed its members in calling for a bettering of the lot of the peasant. Nearly one million *campesinos* had become members and, despite bureaucratic rigidities imposed from above, the peasant movement had become a lively force. As Zamosc put it, ANUC "had not followed the typical clientelist pattern of downward links and intermediate brokers. The organization had started at the grass-roots levels and successive stages had been based on the principle of representation."[19]

While such measures were going forward, Carlos Lleras was also concerned with more orthodox means of applying systemic controls to combat violence and unrest. Rural *banderolismo* by the second half of the decade was giving way to the appeals of revolutionary ideology. As described elsewhere, the FARC had officially proclaimed its existence in mid-1966 and was increasingly active in Tolima. Affiliated with the Communist party, it was led by a near-legendary figure from the original *violencia,* Manuel Marulanda ("Tiro Fijo" or "Sure-Shot"). The ELN had first come to light in late 1964 in Santander under former student leaders, especially the brothers Vásquez Castaño. Drawing inspiration from Fidel Castro and Ché Guevara, the ELN aroused particular apprehension on the part of the government in the wake of the Tricontinental Conference at Havana, where Guevara renewed calls for guerrilla activism throughout Latin America. The EPL, while smaller and less menacing at the time, further underlined rural discontent in and around Antioquia and Cordoba.

Lleras Restrepo did not alter the basic tactics of the military and security forces. Early in 1967 the president issued an official declaration that effectively unleashed further coercive actions by the armed forces, ones were directed indiscriminately toward members or supposed sympathizers of not only the ELN and the FARC, but also López Michelsen's MRL. The military was also busily engaged in seeking to stem, indeed to dig out roots of urban protest and opposition. This included the invasion of the Universidad Nacional campus in Bogotá, and occasionally harsh methods to break up unauthorized demonstrations by workers. Such events were periodically interspersed by presidential efforts to demonstrate a softening of controls. In October 1967, for example, a temporary diminution of both antigovernment and official activism led Lleras to issue a call for national peace, pardon students previously jailed on assorted charges of subversion, and even make personal visits to a number of campuses—not, however, including the Universidad Nacional.

The character of civil-military relations generally remained unchanged. Adoption of Plan Andes in 1968 to eradicate subversion was not fundamentally dissimilar from the earlier Plan Lazo, and Lleras generally stood apart from military matters. However, when General Guillermo Pinzón Caicedo, the army commander, criticized the government's budgetary decisions in 1969, he was swiftly and unceremoniously sent on his way.[20] In the absence of any such challenge to his authority, the president was content to maintain the prevailing military efforts in combatting guerrilla violence.

The Politics of the National Front

The Party Competition

During his 1966 campaign Carlos Lleras had indicated that the strengthening of Colombian democracy required a modernization of the state. He undertook a reshaping of institutional and regulatory reforms from the very start of his administration; on 23 August 1966, a host of reform projects were introduced in congress, where interparty communication was critical for the maintenance and strengthening of the National Front system. The new so-called National Transformation government, faced with the continuing requirement for a two-thirds vote on major issues, only enjoyed some 62 percent in the senate and 55 percent in the lower house, leaving a vocal opposition composed of the MRL, members of ANAPO, and dissident Conservatives. Lleras focused his attention on the first of these, entering into negotiations with López Michelsen.[21]

The courtship was lengthy, having begun even before the president's inauguration. When the Liberals convened their national convention in early 1967 the party's collaboration with MRL congressmen was already taking shape. On 22 August 1967, Lleras Restrepo and López Michelsen signed an agreement that formalized their understanding. This in turn led to formation of a Comité Coordinador Parlamentario that drew up terms for programmatic cooperation in congress. On 20 October 1967, another Liberal convention convened to incorporate the MRL; it named as party directors Julio César Turbay Ayala, Alfonso López Michelsen, and Hernando Agudelo Villa. With the MRL thus linked to a Liberal party in the process of reunification, the new national directorate aimed for the 1968 *mitaca* elections. At the same time, *lauro-alzatista*

Conservatives and ANAPO formed an electoral coalition of unified congressional lists in several departments.

None of this increased public interest in the elections. On 17 March 1968, a total of 2,496,455 votes were cast—a mere 37.3 percent of eligible voters. The Liberal officialists strengthened their position, winning 988,540 votes; dissidents polled 196,457; remaining MRL at 55,984; ANAPO Liberals 82,294; and others 5351. Thus, pro-Front Liberals received 74.4 percent of the party vote. Conservatives won a total of 1,160,448. On the straight party division, then, the Liberals led by 53.2 percent to 46.8 percent. Of greater practical significance was the total of 578,485 for the *ospinistas* or *unionistas*. ANAPO Conservatives won 319,609; independents 199,330; and others 63,024. Proportions for the two relevant groups were 49.9 percent for *unionistas* and 27.6 percent for ANAPO. In terms of the government, a combination of officialist Liberals and *unionista* Conservatives produced 1,567,025 votes, or 62.8 percent. The addition of other lists that generally leaned toward the Front brought the vote total to 1,763,482, representing 70.6 percent of the vote backing the government coalition rather than the opposition.[22]

While the abstention rate had been great, the results otherwise marked a success for the Front and for Carlos Lleras. Of the 204 seats in the Chamber, officialists Liberals now held seventy-eight and *unionista* Conservatives fifty seats. With a number of other groups with a handful of deputies either backing the government or prepared to listen, Lleras Restrepo could reasonably anticipate a two-thirds margin when desired.[23] The senate of course was unaffected, and its 106 seats still numbered forty-six officialist Liberals and twenty *unionistas*. If the seven MRL senators joined them, and a few other semi-independents could be wooed, a two-thirds margin in the upper house was also a live possibility.

All of this strengthened the president's hand as he moved toward major systemic reforms. Balancing the more progressive interests of the MRL and modernizing Liberals against the more traditionalistic approach of Julio César Turbay Ayala and his followers, Lleras fought with his characteristic combination of energy and obstinacy. As discussions continued via ordinary congressional sessions in the second half of 1968, he ultimately achieved many of his goals but was forced to yield on others. The substance of the 1968 constitutional reform would be of critical importance for the future of the National Front in both legal and political terms. Some elements of the original accord were preserved, while others were extended beyond the original 1974 expiration date. The sum total centered on the eventual process of dismantling the National Front—the *desmonte,* as it became popularly known.

That label was something of a misnomer, for revisions assured a preservation and extension of elite control. A major element of the *desmonte* declared that ministries, governors, mayors, and other administrative positions not a part of the civil service would continue to be divided equally between Liberals and Conservatives until 7 August 1978. In addition, this four-year extension of Front provisions might effectively be continued even further. The reform specified that after 1978 these offices would be divided among the parties in such a way as to "provide *adequate and equitable participation* [my emphasis] for the major party other than that of the president." Only if that party withdrew from participation would the president be freed from naming representatives it would put forward. This provision would not be applied to elected bodies. In fact, local municipal councils and departmental assemblies were to become fully competitive in 1970 (rather than 1974). The reforms also permitted new parties to participate in those 1970 elections not controlled by *paridad,* thus incorporating all elections beginning in 1974. A further provision of particular practical importance was termination of the required two-thirds vote for congressional approval.

The 1968 reforms were inevitably controversial, and a mixture of motives had affected the process of negotiation and compromise. There were those who sought an indefinite extension of the National Front; something resembling the officialist hegemony of the PRI in Mexico was the intention. At the opposite end of the spectrum were those who criticized the artificiality of the Front and argued that Colombia was ready for a more direct and full-blown exercise of democracy, free from the constraints adopted in 1957–58. Ranging between these polar extremes were those who variously argued that the Front needed more time to fulfill its basic objectives; others who feared the potential consequences of a so-called participatory opening to democracy; and a wide array of political leaders, certainly including Carlos Lleras, who adopted positions reflecting both systemic and personal goals.

The provision effectively extending parity of high level executive positions until 1978, along with the "adequate and equitable" division after that date, clearly provided future presidents and party leaders with the opportunity to maintain their collaboration in the formulation and implementation of policy. Reforms at the legislative level permitted only the most gradualistic opening, for local and departmental competition was not highly significant so long as national congressional parity was maintained. This, however, would be phased out in 1974, which was consistent with the original conception of the National Front. Taken together, these were elements in the *desmonte* that permitted political elites further time to phase out the National Front or, alternatively, to adjust and refine the mechanism while maintaining a monopoly over the levers of power.

Reforms of a more instrumental nature dealt with legislative and executive processes. The removal of the two-thirds vote in congress certainly provided greater latitude for the executive branch and for any government, which could only overcome legislative immobilism with great difficulty under terms of the original National Front. In administrative procedures, as cited elsewhere, economic policy-making was enhanced by extension of technical planning procedures and a measured decentralization of the planning process by sector. Moreover, an addition to the more directly political changes in Article 120 was set forth with Article 121, which importantly allowed presidential declarations of a state of economic emergency. This was to prove, as Lleras had hoped, a highly useful mechanism for presidents in the formulation of economic development strategy.

Candidate Selection

The choice of the fourth Front candidate was far from automatic. The very process demonstrated the tradition of elitist political control, the personalism of national politics, and the internal problems of both parties. With the hard-driving pugnacity of Carlos Lleras Restrepo dominating the political landscape, it was left for the Conservatives to name his successor. At least in theory, their convention would provide a list of up to five names that would be submitted to the Liberals; the convention of the latter would in turn name the Conservative who was preferred by his own party. However, neither party was united, and the ensuing problems imperilled the very survival of the National Front.

The Liberals had to some extent drawn together, given the incorporation of López Michelsen into the government and the gradual absorption of the MRL into the officialist Liberal organization. The Conservatives, however, faced a more diffuse situation. The former *laureanista* faction, now known as *alvaristas,* was less formidable under Alvaro Gómez than it had been with his father, but nonetheless constituted a determined opponent for the *ospinistas.* The surviving pre-Front Conservative ex-president, while enjoying reasonable health, had been born in 1891 and by this juncture was far more interested in the exercise of power as a senior statesman and party leader than as an octogenarian president. If Ospina Pérez wielded behind-the-scenes influence, it was not without sporadic challenges by former president Guillermo León Valencia, then serving as ambassador to Spain, who was a strong critic of the *desmonte.*

There was no one single or obvious Conservative candidate for the 1970–74 period. Among those nursing presidential ambitions were Misael Pastrana Borrero, Evaristo Sourdís, Belisario Betancur, Hernán Jaramillo Ocampo, and José Elías del Hierro. By early 1969 Betancur had made progress in creating a group of local and departmental leaders supportive of his selection. Yet it was Misael Pastrana, more the organization man in contrast to Belisario Betancur, an independent-minded maverick, who gradually drew favorable glances from both Ospina Pérez and the Liberal party leadership, including Lleras Restrepo. On 7 November 1968, Pastrana had resigned as Lleras's minister of government and moved to Washington as Colombian ambassador. In his absence, many party leaders hoped to pave the way for his easy and uneventful nomination. However, the road toward a possible Pastrana candidacy was strewn with formidable obstacles.

On 16 April 1969, a group of Conservative congressmen produced a "Manifesto to the Party," which denounced Pastrana as being imposed on their party by the Lleras government. Doña Bertha de Ospina, herself an influential party leader as well as the wife of the former president, counterattacked the following day, but *unionista* cohesion had been brought into question. By August Lleras Restrepo began to insert himself more directly into the process. Calling for a political accord between Liberals and Conservatives over candidate selection, Lleras conducted serious talks with Mariano Ospina Pérez on 6 September; the next day the two met with Conservative ministers, Alvaro Gómez Hurtado, and a group of independents. The Liberal Directorate was also drawn into conversations, resulting in the 17 September signature of a bipartisan agreement over a mutually acceptable program of government. By this time Pastrana had resigned his ambassadorship to return home in quest of the nomination, and he was proclaimed by the *ospinista*-controlled Conservative machine in Medellín. However, another group of Conservatives, stimulated by former president Valencia, proclaimed Betancur their candidate. Evaristo Sourdís and Elías del Hierro were also increasing the intensity of their own pre-candidacies.

For Lleras, committed to building a noncontroversial selection process, the next step was the "Accord of the Casa de Moneda," signed in the palace on 28 October 1969 by the two party directorates, Ospina Pérez, and himself. Its policy thrust was modernizing in character, while the continuity of the Front was strongly advocated. This led to the convening of both party conventions in early November, from which the officialist candidate would emerge. However, the process was not to be simple or free from controversy. It began on 7 November when some 550 Conservative delegates met; Ospina Pérez presided while Alvaro Gómez served as vice president.

Only two men were officially nominated: Pastrana Borrero and Evaristo Sourdís, the latter a regional leader from the coast who enjoyed strong support from congressional Conservatives. Other would-be aspirants pulled out of the contest in order to maximize anti-Pastrana strength. The result was a narrow Sourdís victory of 276–272, a major defeat for Pastrana that nonetheless fell far short of the convention's required two-thirds margin. The vote reflected, perhaps for the first time, a blunt challenge to traditional clientelistic authority. A day later, following overnight conversations, an embattled Ospina Pérez called for a public vote. After angry debate his proposal was accepted, but it did not clarify the competition. Sourdís and Pastrana tied with 278 votes, hasty attempts to negotiate failed, and Ospina finally sent both names to the Liberals, whose own convention had been slated to open on 10 November. Guillermo Leon Valencia then submitted the name of Betancur as well.

By this time, as Leal later wrote, the nominating process was unmistakably demonstrating "the structural incompetence of dominant groups to achieve an organizational principle."[24] The National Liberal Directorate under Turbay, unwilling to permit an open convention in which the outcome was not predetermined, postponed it indefinitely. By the time the Liberals came back into session on 5 December, the issue had been settled in high level conversations. The officialist nominee was Misael Pastrana. Sourdís and Betancur both withdrew from consideration, with 82 of their followers walking out. The Liberals endorsed the elites' nominee with 512 votes; Betancur received ten, Sourdís received two, and there were twenty-two blank ballots. The "Accord of the Casa de Moneda" was confirmed with the convention's approval of its policy declarations. In the meantime, both Sourdís and Betancur announced their intentions of running independent campaigns for the presidency.

Interpretations of the systemic imposition were manifold. Many felt that the selection of Misael Pastrana Borrero offered stark testimony to the elitist character of national politics and the enduring role of dominant personalities. Mariano Ospina Pérez had been praising Pastrana in the pages of his *La República* as early as 1967, and had been something of a political godfather for some years. Carlos Lleras had also observed Pastrana as his key political minister for more than two years, and approved of him as a successor—or, as critics would contend, as a keeper of the faith until Lleras might return to the presidency in 1974. For Ospina Pérez, facing a serious internal party challenge some four years after his ancient antagonist Laureano Gómez had departed the scene, it had at least been possible to nullify the challenges of other candidates.

Beyond these individual interests, however, Pastrana's nomination basically reflected the imposition of the great party leaders, without concern for the interests and forces committed to such men as Sourdís and Betancur. The *jefes naturales* remained capable of asserting their authority, although without enjoying the former passivity of regional and local acceptance that had been so much a part of clientelism under the old patrimonial state. In choosing to do so, these "historic" leaders adopted a position that might properly assure continuation of the National Front. At the same time, it seriously jeopardized the very fate of the system. And the challenge was mounted by such figures as Sourdís and Betancur, not simply the resurgent Gustavo Rojas Pinilla and his ANAPO.

Campaign and Elections

Given the delay in the nomination and the subsequent year-end holidays, there were barely 100 days for the campaign. This was advantageous to Rojas Pinilla, who had been stumping the country for months with energetic attacks on the Front. An unqualified opponent of the existing system, he claimed a forthcoming victory and issued repeated promises that he would not sit still for fraud. Anti-Front criticism was also inflamed by the *Curas del Golconda,* a group of rebel priests who were actively urging their congregations to abstain as a means of protesting the unresponsiveness of the entire system. Enjoying the protection of Buenaventura bishop Gerardo Valencia Cano, they added to the unsettled atmosphere. Before long there were also outbursts of violence between backers of the other Conservative candidates. This encouraged such events as the February killing of a *pastranista* municipal councilman in Antioquia, and President Lleras ordered special police measures for the duration of the campaign.

By mid-March, as the contest entered its final month, it was evident that the choice lay between Pastrana and Rojas. Evaristo Sourdís, a traditional politician with his base on the Atlantic and extensive links to regional landowning interests, generated limited mass appeal. While Belisario Betancur was a more effective campaigner, his role in 1970 was that of a party rebel more liberal than conservative in orientation—who could only hope to build support for a potential future candidacy. Pastrana's own industrious campaigning failed to overcome his fundamentally lackluster image as candidate. Typical was a slogan—wisely dropped early in the race—of "I am not a man, I am a program." Other battle cries were scarcely better, and traditional campaign techniques failed to catch the public imagination. Pastrana's strategy was devised by a series of "bipartisan committees" that were diffuse and poorly coordinated. They also paid too little attention to the crucial task of bringing out the vote.[25]

In the end, it was President Lleras who brought fire and vigor to the cause of the National Front. While pledging his constitutionally mandated neutrality, Lleras argued that he had no responsibility to remain silent in the face of attacks on his government. When Rojas alleged government corruption, notably in the foreign trade institute, the president reacted sharply. He also charged the former dictator with having been "disrespectful" of the military during his time in power, while energizing what was otherwise an uninspired campaign on behalf of the Front. However, much of the initiative still remained in the hands of the opposition, as Rojas continued with a relentless combination of demagogic promises and anti-Front denunciations. Among his promises were the reduction of taxes and public transport fares; extensive nationalization of trade; and a lower cost of living.

As election day dawned on 19 April 1970, the race between Pastrana and Rojas appeared to be close. An interruption in the vote count late in the day lent credence to later allegations that the Front eventually counted out the retired strongman when he had actually been elected. Even before the voting had concluded, Rojas Pinilla charged the government with massive fraud and threatened both a general strike and urban guerrilla warfare. Lleras Restrepo, taking no chances, declared martial law and imposed a street curfew. The day after elections *rojista* crowds ran through the streets of Bogotá calling for revolution. A special bipartisan commission was also named by the president to validate the vote, and it was announced that at least two weeks would be required.

Rojas was placed under house arrest, partial censorship was imposed, and martial law was gradually relaxed. Lleras Restrepo swiftly took additional steps to assure that social and political control would not be shattered. *El Tiempo* launched a campaign to discredit General Rojas as covertly allied with leftist extremists, and the eventual Pastrana victory became a virtual certainty. When official results were finally released, they gave Pastrana 40.3 percent of the vote, with 1,625,025. Rojas Pinilla polled 38.7 percent with 1,561,468. Belisario Betancur received 11.7 percent (471,350) and Evaristo Sourdís 8.3 percent (336,286). A total of 4,028,259 votes (including blank and null votes) were cast, representing some 56 percent of eligible voters. Pastrana's announced victory as standard bearer of the National Front was underwhelming. He won an absolute majority in only three departments. He lost all but one major city as well as each of the four most populous urban centers. His defeat at the hands of Rojas in Bogotá was striking, where the margin was nearly 30,000 votes, at 44.9–39.8 percent. Subsequent electoral analysis not only underlined the weakness of the Front and its candidate, but also spoke to the characteristics of ANAPO in April 1970, which had been especially successful in tapping the discontent of the urban masses.[26]

Congressional results essentially confirmed the patterns of the presidential contest. A total of 3,980,201 votes were cast at this level, which was 51.9 percent of the total. Officialist Liberals received 1,470,928 votes (37.0 percent) to 1,083,024 pro-Front Conservatives (27.2 percent). For ANAPO, there were no less than 1,412,752 votes (35.5 percent). In terms of congressional representation, the margin for the Front was of course narrow. In the senate thirty-nine Liberals and eighteen Conservatives were committed to the National Front; there were thirty-eight opponents from ANAPO, while eleven followers of Sourdís and twelve of Betancur held seats. In the Chamber, with 210 seats in 1970, the Liberals secured sixty-three and the Conservatives thirty-one seats. ANAPO won seventy-two, leaving twenty with Sourdís and twenty-four with Betancur, which could conceivably hold the balance. Put in other terms, pro-Front Liberals and Conservatives led ANAPO in the senate by 48–32 percent and 45–34 percent in the Chamber, with the others basically pro-Front but also theoretically capable of overturning a majority for the government.[27]

By the time the dust began to settle, it was apparent that the National Front had barely survived the elections. General Rojas's populist promises and anti-establishment posture, as Corr wrote, spotlighted his capacity to exploit grievances and frustrations—the consequence of the failure of the governing elite to adjust adequately to the demands of the bureaucratic centralist state.[28] There was irony in the fact that Carlos Lleras Restrepo, the most energetic and genuinely reformist National Front leader, had presided over a government and system that may well have been honestly voted out of office. Results of the 1970 elections resurrected questions about the structural and institutional capacity of the Front to fulfill the demands of the masses, especially in the cities. They also dramatized the urgency of challenges to effective governance— this at a time when the legitimacy of the system was dependent upon a president-elect who lacked a strong popular mandate.

Notes

1. See the summary of data from the Economic Commission for Latin America in Robert H. Dix, *Colombia: The Political Dimensions of Change* (New Haven: Yale University Press, 1967), 39.
    A rich source of data with particular relevance to the Lleras Restrepo period is Colombia, Departamento Administrativo Nacional de Estadísticas (DANE), *Colombia política: estadísticas, 1935–1970* (Bogotá: DANE, 1972).
2. Colombia, Departamento Administrativo Nacional de Estadísticas (DANE), *Colombia política: estadísticas, 1935–1970* (Bogotá: DANE, 1972).
3. Leon Zamosc, *The Agrarian Question and the Peasant Movement in Colombia: Struggles of the National Peasant Association 1967–1981* (Cambridge: Cambridge University Press, 1986), 23.
4. See the figures in World Bank, *World Tables, 1988–89 Edition* (Baltimore: The Johns Hopkins University Press, 1989), 40–41. For a broader discussion, see Fernando Cepeda Ulloa and Christopher Mitchell, "The Trend towards Technocracy: The World Bank and the International Labor Organization in Colombian Politics," in R. Albert Berry, Ronald G. Hellman, and Mauricio Solaum, eds., *Politics of Compromise: Coalition Government in Colombia* (New Brunswick: Transaction Publishers, 1980), 237–57.

5. Robert H. Dix, "The Colombian Presidency: Continuities and Changes," in Thomas V. DiBacco, ed., *Presidential Power in Latin American Politics* (New York: Praeger, 1977), 91–92.
6. R. Albert Berry, "The National Front and Colombia's Economic Development," in Berry et al., *Politics of Compromise*, 299.
7. An excellent description of planning in Colombia is Augusto Cano M., *El proceso de la planeación en Colombia* (Bogotá: Fedesarollo, 1972).
8. Edgar Reveiz and María José Pérez, "Colombia: Moderate Economic Growth, Political Stability, and Social Welfare," in Jonathan Hartlyn and Samuel A. Morley, eds., *Latin American Political Economy: Financial Crisis and Political Change* (Boulder: Westview Press, 1986), 272–73.
9. Carlos F. Díaz-Alejandro, *Foreign Trade Regimes and Economic Development: Colombia* (New York: Columbia University Press, for National Bureau of Economic Research, 1976), 61.
10. Cano, *El proceso*, 23.
11. Bruce Michael Bagley, "Colombia: National Front and Economic Development," in Robert Wesson, ed., *Politics, Policies, and Economic Development in Latin America* (Stanford: Hoover Institution Press, 1984), 138.
12. Zamosc, *Agrarian Question*, 35.
13. See the compilation of data from Berry in *Politics of Compromise*, 294–95.
14. Francisco Leal Buitrago, *Estudio del comportamiento legislativo en Colombia. Tomo I. Análisis histórico del desarrollo político nacional, 1930–1970* (Bogotá: Tercer Mundo, 1973), 151–52.
15. A useful account is William Paul McGreevey, "Population Policy under the National Front," in Berry et al., *Politics of Compromise*, 413–33.
16. J. Mayone Stycos, *Ideology, Faith and Family Planning in Latin America: Studies in Public and Private Opinion on Fertility Control* (New York: 1971), 154.
17. Zamosc, *Agrarian Question*, 48.
18. Ibid., 51.
19. Ibid., 61.
20. Alvaro Valencia Tover, *Testimonio de una época* (Bogotá: Planeta Colombiana Editorial S.A., 1992), 538–41.
21. A treatment of the MRL from inception to demise by one of its important activists is Mauricio Botero Montoya, *El MRL* (Bogotá: Publicaciones Universidad Central, 1990). For a brief account of the progressive rupture of the MRL and Lleras Restrepo's successful negotiation of López Michelsen's return to the ranks of the Liberal party, see Rafael Ballén, *Liberalismo hoy: opción de cambio o agónica supervivencia* (Bogotá: n.p., 1985), 170–73. Among other sources, see Jorge Child, *López y el pensamiento liberal* (Bogotá: Editorial Tercer Mundo, 1974).
22. Mario Latorre Rueda, *Elecciones y partidos políticos en Colombia* (Bogotá: Uniandes, 1974), reviews the 1968 elections on pp. 199–221.
23. Rodrigo Losada Lora, *Clientelismo & elecciones* (Bogotá: Pontificia Universidad Javeriana, Programa de Estudios Politicos, 1984), provides a detailed analysis and related data.
24. Leal, *Estudio de comportamiento*, 173.
25. Selected speeches and declarations in the period immediately preceding his candidacy are found in Misael Pastrana Borrero, *Gran impulso: ideas y acción política para la nueva Colombia* (Bogotá: n.p., 1970).

26. A rigorous analytical dissection of the data is found in Judith Talbot de Campos and John McCamant, *Cleavage Shift in Colombia: Analysis of the 1970 Election* (Beverly Hills: Sage, 1972).
27. For an overview see Malcolm Deas, "Coalition in Colombia," *Current History* 60, no. 354 (February 1979): 90–94, 117–18.
28. An astute treatment of the contemporary scene is Edwin G. Corr, *The Political Process in Colombia* (Denver: Graduate School of International Studies, Monograph Series in World Affairs, nos. 1–2, 1972).

7

The Drive for Consolidation: Pastrana (1970–74)

The Policies of Governance

The National Environment

As Misael Pastrana Borrero took office, the population stood at an estimated 22 million, an increase of 7.8 percent from 1966. The rate of urbanization had risen above 55 percent as the influx from countryside to city continued. The rate of economic growth under Lleras Restrepo, which had been running at some 7 percent annually, had reflected a diversification of exports, while the coffee industry was thriving. However, his legacy included shaky balance of payments, and coffee prices began dropping just as Pastrana was being inaugurated. There were also harbingers of growing conflict with organized labor; for, although Lleras had managed to limit wage settlements while buying more time for macroeconomic growth, the prospects for a rapid increase in the cost of living were very real. In the meantime, the public external debt by 1970 was requiring an annual servicing of roughly $150 million, which nearly doubled the average payments of principal and interest made annually from 1968 to 1970.

The continuing growth of the labor force was a potentially troublesome problem. It had been accelerating since the mid-1950s, but had not been accompanied by a comparable increase in the national demand for labor. From 1966 to 1970 the annual growth in the labor force was estimated at 2.6 percent, reaching a total of 6,244,000.[1] This provided a growing reservoir of antisystem sentiment, as suggested in electoral terms by the 1970 contest. Centered in the poorer areas of the cities, this segment of opinion had not been moved by the reforms of the Lleras administration. Neither had its rather substantial macroeconomic accomplishments and institutional reforms produced an untapped pool of Colombians with deepening allegiance to the National Front. The positive elements of the Lleras developmental thrust then did not rest on solid foundation stones, and the broad task for Misael Pastrana was that of achieving further systemic consolidation.

The growing pressures from demographic forces, urbanization, maldistribution of income, and rapid changes in the needs and demands of the citizenry all continued to demand official action. As traditional clientelism was eroded through the declining importance of the rural sector, Pastrana was confronted with the responsibility of defending the National Front and assuring the nation's elites that their authority would be secured under conditions of heightened bureaucratic centralism. He did so from a position of relative weakness, having been neither the undisputed Conservative party leader nor the unchallenged victor in national elections. It was through the grace of Lleras Restrepo and other senior Liberal party leaders, further endorsed by Ospina Pérez, that he had arrived at the presidential palace. Neither could he rely extensively on more effective party organizations, for they had yet to respond to the slowly declining influence and effectiveness of traditional rural clientelism.

Policies of the Administration

Born in Neiva in 1923, Pastrana had studied law and economics at the Universidad Javeriana, receiving his doctorate in 1945 and beginning his diplomatic experience at Colombia's embassy in the Vatican. He soon returned home as general secretary to President Mariano Ospina Pérez, briefly filled this position for Laureano Gómez, and later occupied a variety of government and diplomatic posts. Under Lleras Camargo he served variously as minister of development, public works, and finance. In 1966 he was named minister of government for the Lleras Restrepo government, leaving in 1968 for the customary ambassadorship to the United States prior to launching his presidential candidacy. Pastrana was also an active industrialist, and for a time was president of Celanese Colombiana, one of the nation's largest textile enterprises. Over the years he built close ties with the business community in Antioquia, the effective heartland of Colombian entrepreneurship, a fact not unnoticed by Ospina Pérez.

During his campaign, Pastrana had promised to seek a "new equilibrium" in defense of the social and political order:

> There is no way we can continue to develop if three-fourths of the population is immersed in poverty and ignorance. Social differences demand immediate action.... A Colombia of national integration is the grand proposal and the first priority of my government.[2]

Similar preoccupations were outlined in Pastrana's inaugural address, which stressed the need for social equity while maintaining a strengthened management of the economy by the state. His *técnico*-dominated cabinet—its average age was only forty-three—was instructed that social reformism was a desirable goal, with improved distribution of national wealth both an acceptable and legitimate objective. The result was an economic development program based on the macroeconomic theories of the North American economist Lauchlin Currie.[3]

Known as the "Four Strategies," the program centered on the notion of a "leading sector," selected by the government, which would exercise a multiplier effect on the remainder of the economy. Currie recommended construction, especially in urban areas, as the trigger for economic development. In addition, agricultural exports were to receive particular emphasis. As elaborated by the administration, the "Four Strategies" were designed as a coherent approach to reinvigorated national development.[4] The four crucial "strategies" were: (a) stimulation of housing construction; (b) promotion of exports; (c) more agricultural production; and (d) improved income distribution. The emphasis on construction—largely in major urban areas—was expected to absorb greater numbers of the unskilled labor force, with their earnings being funnelled into the economy. Construction would help to solve the housing shortage while enlarging Colombia's internal market for domestic industrial production. While further industrialization would be encouraged, assistance to commercial agriculture would provide cheap food while earning foreign exchange via increased exports.

The "Four Strategies" plan was put into effect in 1972 as Pastrana's approach to the stimulation of national growth and urban employment. Presumably the national rate of savings would increase substantially by offering a secure interest rate above price inflation, thereby assuring a spurt in private construction. This was fully consistent with the administration plan's focus on urban construction and commercial agriculture.

Private investment in the former was encouraged through the introduction of the so-called units of constant buying power: Unidades de Poder Adquisitivo Constante (UPAC). The system created a constant-value investment, where an investor's deposit would be increased through interest and also via introduction of an inflation factor. Investments and mortgages would both be corrected for inflation. A real interest rate of at least 5 percent was guaranteed through the UPAC savings certificate. In addition, the UPAC concept was extended to new savings and loans assets, the *corporaciones de ahorro y vivienda,* which encouraged private financing of construction.

All of this, adopted under a Conservative president, extended the institutional protection of the state significantly. The Banco Central Hipotecario (Central Mortgage Bank-BCH) was strengthened by its coordinating role with a new group of savings and loan corporations— Corporaciones de Ahorro y Vivienda (CAVI). Colombians would refer to the many aspects of daily life as having been *"upaquizado,"* including construction investments, mortgages, insurance benefits and premiums, and the like.[5] The basic UPAC mechanism, the solid cornerstone of Misael Pastrana's development program, survived long after his term, continuing to produce controversy over its impact. The basic housing strategy created new jobs and injected capital into construction. Even so, unemployment in the large cities increased as salaries fell, and there was a notable decline in real terms of the minimum salary in the first half of the 1970s. The inevitable economic overheating produced by massive investment in construction stimulated an inflationary mentality among Colombians, and by 1974 the rate of inflation reached 27 percent, a major issue in the presidential campaign that year. The emphasis on urban construction also was affected by systemic bottlenecks and shortages of materials. Financial resources from industry and agriculture were predictably diverted, and the Pastrana administration shifted away substantially from the agricultural policies of Carlos Lleras.

If Pastrana's predecessor had focused substantial fiscal and monetary attention to the rural sector, then the new president preferred to concentrate on the construction sector. Pastrana was no convert to the notion of extensive land redistribution, and the new administration viewed further agrarian reform as unnecessary for development. Concentration on commercial agriculture was designed as economically effective and politically acceptable. Land redistribution was secondary to increased agricultural output. Such policy emphases were consistent with the views of Colombia's landowning elite, which has been nervous about Lleras Restrepo's initiatives. Pastrana and J. Emilio Valderrama, the new agriculture minister, found it difficult to deal with the ANUC. Its Comités Ejecutivos were controlled by independent-minded peasant leaders, some of whom encouraged land invasion. When ANUC supported a major urban work stoppage in March 1971, both the minister and the head of INCORA were unceremoniously sacked. A month later the government suppressed *Carta Campesina*, the ANUC newspaper, and by July Agriculture Minister Hernán Jaramillo Ocampo called for an interruption of agrarian reform. Protests by local ANUC leaders led to further government pressures, and by the midpoint in his term Misael Pastrana had effectively fragmented the peasant movement.

In both symbolic and practical terms, this was reflected by the so-called Chicorral Agreement in which the government, landowners, party representatives, and a handful of peasant leaders agreed to policies favorable to commercial agriculture and large landowners.[6] This further marginalized the Lleras-championed Asociación Nacional de Usuarios Campesinos, while Misael Pastrana had honored his own ties with *antioqueño* industrialists and modernizing commercial agriculturalists. By 1973 he had further reduced both INCORA's budget and functions. While the decline in rural living conditions continued to nourish the exodus of Colombians from countryside to city, the government's preoccupation centered on productivity. As Bagley wrote, the Pastrana government deliberately interrupted a decade of policies committed to modern land reform. This constituted a critical turning point in national developmental policies:

> At the economic level, it symbolized the adoption of a strategy of agricultural modernization without serious attempts at redistribution. At the political level, it revealed the resurgent political power of the large landowners and their allies within the ruling coalition and the deepening political impotence of the peasantry. The practical consequences of this shift in rural development strategies were significant increases in discontent in the countryside.[7]

When Pastrana entered office, it was with an expectation that moderate reformist sentiment might somewhat offset his political and class ties to dominant elites. In practice, however, he adopted the "Four Strategies" as a developmental approach largely breaking with his predecessor's policies. This allowed Pastrana to reflect the interests of the political and business class, and compensated in part for his fundamentally weak personal position. His basic concern was with economic growth rather than social changes. Systemic consolidation rather than political reformism constituted the prevailing philosophy of his administration. Growth rates were relatively high: 6.7 percent in 1970, 5.5 percent in 1971, 7 percent in 1972, and 7.1 percent in 1973. A gradual import liberalization trend and the promotion of minor exports were positive. With the concerted emphasis on urban construction, however, the domestic economy overheated and inflation rose in 1973 and 1974. The state of the economy thus would become a major source of partisan debate in the 1974 presidential race.

Social and Political Controls

Misael Pastrana inherited from Carlos Lleras a nation in which change and reform appeared to be promising further progress. Furthermore, the latter's efforts to build constituencies and encourage at least a modest increase of mass mobilization and participation suggested that social and political controls might be applied less harshly. However, within six months of his inauguration the new government reimposed a state of siege as a means of quelling disturbances in Cali. Students protesting new price increases were attacked by army troops, resulting in eight deaths. President Pastrana imposed a curfew in the city, banned all public demonstrations, and authorized the formation of special military courts. In a nationwide broadcast he referred to the situation as "extremely delicate" and charged the demonstrators with seeking to impose an antidemocratic system "totally alien to the interests of the Colombian people." At the same time, groups of peasants were carrying out land invasions in Córdoba, Huila, Sucre, and Tolima, all with the approval of ANUC. Requested by the administration to withdraw, the response was a refusal to return the land "to the selfish oligarchic exploiters. The people must defend it."[8]

University-related problems provided another arena for conflict. Late in April of 1972 the ninth rector in three years at Bogotá's Universidad Nacional resigned to protest government intervention. The situation had been triggered by clashes between students and police during incidents preceding local and regional elections. The aftermath led to exchanges of letters and public declarations between the rector, Jorge Arias de Grieff, and President Pastrana. The latter insisted that the state-funded university was in danger of becoming a center for subversion, at which point de Grieff resigned in protest of this threat to academic autonomy. A twenty-four-hour strike by some 12,000 students was followed by violent actions on May Day, with protests spreading to other universities.

The temperature gradually lowered and a new rector was named. Before the close of the year, however, confrontation was renewed, this time provoked by attempted reforms of university rules and regulations at the Universidad Nacional. Several student leaders were arrested by the Departamento Administrativo de Seguridad (DAS), which was joined by the army in exercising surveillance on campus. Although the Catholic universities customarily remained aloof from such clashes, the Church itself was not totally uninvolved. The senior hierarchy maintained its long heritage as among the most conservative in the hemisphere. However, there were ties—both real and imagined—which linked some younger priests with guerrilla movements.

Reports claiming mistreatment of selected parish priests by the armed forces continued to circulate. The military charged that the guerrillas were infiltrating the Church at the rural level, while priests retorted that they were merely trying to alleviate the living conditions of the peasants with whom they worked and lived. In one well-publicized case, a priest disappeared from Barrancabermeja after extended and well-known complaints that the armed forces were mistreating his parishioners. Late in 1972 three Spanish priests were expelled from Colombia on the grounds of constituting a national security threat. Another half-dozen were detained and their daily duties suspended on charges of alleged revolutionary activity. Similar episodes arose sporadically. The very possibility of links between priests and guerrillas fueled preoccupations about simmering rural violence.

At the beginning of the decade the two major guerrilla organizations were the ELN and the FARC. The Ejército de Liberación Nacional (ELN), or National Liberation Army, had first appeared in the early 1960s under the Vásquez Castaño brothers and fellow students from the Universidad Industrial in Santander. Attracted to the ideas and personality of Fidel Castro, the ELN operated primarily in Santander as well as rural Antioquia. Independent of the Conservative-Liberal sectarianism that had sparked *la violencia,* the ELN began to extend its operations somewhat further, following the Magdalena River almost to the coast. The Fuerzas Armadas

Revolucionarias Colombianas (FARC), or Colombian Revolutionary Armed Forces, had originated in a coalition of groups active in the south, notably the departments of Huila and Tolima. It enjoyed ties with the Colombian Communist party and advocated social revolution, although generally demonstrating less ideological sophistication than the ELN.

The initial assumption that both groups were in the process of deterioration was shaken by growing rural attacks on small military bands in 1971, and was shattered in October when the ELN attempted unsuccessfully to assassinate General Alvaro Valencia Tovar, commandant of the officers' training school. Within the week there were bombings at the Universidad Nacional and destruction of Sinclair's pipeline on the Atlantic. The fourth anniversary of Ché Guevara's death was marked by announcement of a new Frente Unido de Acción Guerrillera. Given the apparent shift to urban violence and apparent communications directly between the ELN and the FARC, the administration responded with an array of emergency security measures. The military also shifted to more vigorous rural activity, where it had previously been content simply to contain guerrilla movements.

Greater violence flared once more at the beginning of 1973 when the ELN kidnapped a half-dozen persons, all from wealthy families, to be held for ransom. This followed by only a month the seizure of former Antioquia University law dean Jaime Duque Pérez, who was released after payment of some $25,000. With the ELN approaching its own eighth anniversary, it hoped to accumulate resources adequate to support a more extensive program. Further outbursts in the early months of the year spread an attitude of official gloom, with Pastrana speaking of "shadows over the country" while the minister of defense conceded the difficulty of coping with the problem. One government response was a series of harsh legal penalties, but rural clashes continued unabated for months.[9]

The panorama of guerrilla movements was also marked increasingly by the presence of the Ejército Popular de Liberación (EPL), or Army of Popular Liberation. While operating in the mountains of Antioquia and Córdoba since 1967, it was so small as to have been largely ignored. Broadly Maoist in outlook, it too became more visible during the early 1970s. Also sharing occasional communications with the FARC and the ELN, this gave an increasingly extensive geographic arena for the guerrilla efforts to exploit rural discontent. It also stiffened the resolve of the military to move more decisively than in the past few years. Occasional killings of ransom victims spurred its efforts at the same time that public opinion was chilled.

The emergence of the M-19 further underlined the problems for the administration. As described later at greater length, it was manned by those who protested the alleged electoral fraud of 1970. First adopting the tactic of gaining domestic and international attention through highly visible acts in defiance of the National Front, the M-19 made a dramatic impact with its 1973 theft in Bogotá of Simón Bolívar's sword. It left behind a note proclaiming that the Liberator's sword "now begins new combats. Now it confronts the Yankee, the exploiter, those who deliver our country to sorrow, the landowner, the capitalist, the oligarch."[10] In time the M-19 would become a much more nettlesome thorn under the skin of National Front governments.

The Pastrana government was determined to bring the guerrilla movements to heel. Military initiatives in 1973 were the toughest in years. Several ELN leaders were captured or killed while the FARC for a time was thrown into a state of disorganization. Perhaps the most significant consequence of the Pastrana policies was the increasing involvement of the Colombian military in activities theoretically reserved for police and security forces. It was under Misael Pastrana that the National Front, perhaps inadvertently, converted the armed forces into an instrument for preservation of social and political control. As J. Mark Ruhl observed,

> The armed forces' role of keeping order, of course, extended beyond the rural guerrilla conflict. It frustrated ELN attempts to initiate an urban guerrilla movement and contained recurrent student rioting.... Various violent striking groups were also held in check, e.g., oil workers, teachers, bus drivers. Under the state-of-siege laws operative during most of the era, military courts were used to try most public order violations.[11]

The Politics of the National Front

The Party Competition

The forthcoming competitive presidential race in 1974 represented a special challenge to elitist perpetuation of systemic controls. Conservatives and Liberals consequently engaged in ferocious infighting over presumed internal party control as well as candidate selection. The former were relatively less fragmented as the fight over the 1970 nomination had temporarily papered over divisions between traditionalists and moderates. Even so, the rivalry continued to be played out during the first two years of the Pastrana administration, especially over issues of appointments and patronage. When Pastrana shook up his cabinet in June 1971, he labored intensively to reach a balance, and eventually named a majority of conservative leaders while appointing moderates to key ministries.

Alvaro Gómez Hurtado, leader of the traditionalists, hoped to move swiftly toward his own presidential nomination. However, neither Mariano Ospina Pérez nor Misael Pastrana were avid enthusiasts of Laureano's son. Given the elimination of midterm *mitaca* elections, the only electoral test came with April 1972 municipal contests. Some 8400 municipal councillors and 406 deputies to departmental assemblies were to be selected. While the Liberals would win, Gómez succeeded in organizing a vigorous campaign and in strengthening his own organizational power. Dissident followers of Belisario Betancur remained on the sidelines, and Gómez's presidential hopes soared. This clarification of the Conservatives' situation was in contrast to that of the Liberals.

Three factions contended for party control: those headed respectively by Carlos Lleras Restrepo, Alfonso López Michelsen, and Julio César Turbay Ayala. The first two—relatively more progressive and reformist in orientation—were in uneasy alliance, while the Turbay faction stood alone on the party's political right. Early efforts to convene a convention for April 1971 failed when first Lleras and then López refused to attend. The former declared that the party's organizational unity would not be served, while López attacked the Pastrana government and criticized Liberals who collaborated. The meeting was then rescheduled for 21 May. López promised a "leftist" thesis for official adoption, while Turbay prepared a resolution committing the party to collaboration with the government. Turbay managed to secure passage of his proposal, but only after followers of Lleras and López walked out of the Teatro Colombia. Lleras then announced that municipal elections offered little opportunity for partisan advantage, concluding that the national party would not take an active part. Supported by López, he ceded to local leaders the responsibility for their own campaigns.

The panorama was greatly complicated by ANAPO, which itself was suffering from internal contradictions and erratic leadership. Having polled 35.5 percent of the congressional vote, it enjoyed ample representation in congress and in many departmental councils; it also controlled the Bogotá city council. Even prior to its formal reconstitution as the "Gran Partido Nacional" in 1971, however, ANAPO was plagued by ideological impurity, a weakening of its posture as unqualified critic of the National Front, and the fragile health of Gustavo Rojas Pinilla. Ignacio Vives Echeverría, a onetime member of López's MRL and the leader of ANAPO Liberals, fought to move the party to the Left. He was summarily expelled, while angrily denouncing Rojas for betraying the movement's popular base as a prelude to imposing the candidacy of his daughter in 1974.

Despite the trappings of a modern mass party, ANAPO had remained dependent upon the personal leadership of the general and his daughter. Mass rallies had been less participatory than they were adulatory. The national command was largely limited to rubber-stamping the decision of Rojas, María Eugenia, and her husband. The Vives challenge underlined the deteriorating image of ANAPO's leadership, as well as stripping the party of five municipal councils that his group had controlled. A brief flirtation with Belisario Betancur over an electoral alliance came to naught, and the campaign for 1972 municipal offices drifted aimlessly.

The government took vigorous measures to assure a peaceful vote. Senior military and security officers worked with state governors to guarantee normality. At the last moment, Carlos Lleras reversed course and plunged actively into the campaign. López Michelsen followed suit, and even Alberto Lleras turned out to give political addresses. The result was a solid victory for the Liberals—especially for its more progressive elements—and a decisive defeat for ANAPO. Abstention was some 73 percent of the electorate, and ANAPO lost every department it had controlled and over 90 percent of its municipal councils, including Bogotá. This presumably improved the solidity of the National Front, as well as helping the Conservatives. Attention was redirected toward the selection of candidates for 1974.

Candidate Selection

For the Conservatives, Alvaro Gómez Hurtado represented a traditionalist advocacy of growth and development from above; he was also perceived as an effective candidate in appealing to rural voters.[12] Progressives who opposed him believed that the key to victory was the urban electorate, however, and thus put forward Agriculture Minister Hernán Jaramillo Ocampo. Mariano Ospina Pérez, as Conservative party president, sought to moderate the competition. This was interrupted in April 1973 by the so-called Carta de Bruselas, in which Lleras Restrepo proposed a joint Liberal-Conservative candidate for 1974. Gómez and Bertha Hernández de Ospina led the protests of the traditionalists, and the matter was dropped as Liberal rivals succeeded in thwarting Lleras at this point.

In September 1973 the Conservatives held one of their most united conventions since 1949. A new set of party statutes were adopted, replacing those formulated on 20 March 1948 by Laureano Gómez and Luis Navarro Ospina. In addition, with Bertha de Ospina presiding, 635 delegates on 4 September unanimously proclaimed Gómez the party candidate. This had been preceded by the withdrawals of Betancur, Jaramillo Ocampo, and J. Emilio Valderrama in the face of domination by party traditionalists.

The internal struggle for the Liberals was far more complicated, with the basic fight waged between reformist and traditionalist elements over the ambitions of three powerful pre-candidates. The reluctance of Lleras and López to cooperate with the Pastrana government, contrasted by the willingness of Turbay, further confused the situation. If this were not enough, Carlos Lleras maintained a flirtation with the notion of a joint two-party candidate in 1974. The most dynamic and controversial of the three aspirants, Lleras had seemed the most likely nominee following the strong showing of progressives in the municipal elections. On 15 October 1972, he was elected *jefe único* at a Liberal convention, thus gaining authority to draw up rules for candidate selection. López accepted the action, but Turbay opposed it until it was evident that Lleras had prevailed.

Lleras moved with characteristic energy, revising party statutes, reviving internal policy discussions, and reinvigorating the recruitment of new party members. However, he also shunted aside *lopistas* and, in a major misstep, proposed a single national candidate in his "Carta de Bruselas" on 13 April. Liberals who anticipated an easy victory in the 1974 presidential contest saw little purpose in a formal biparty accord, and found their discontent voiced by both Alfonso López and Julio César Turbay Ayala, the latter then serving as ambassador to the Court of St. James. Another national party convention was duly opened on 9 June, where López shared its presidency with the aging party statesman Darío Echandía. Lleras attended as the *jefe único* of the Liberal Directorate.

The 280 delegates heard Lleras deliver an impassioned defense of the theses proposed in the Brussels Letter, but were unpersuaded. *Lopistas* preferred a straight party competition, which they were confident of winning, while Turbay cautiously put forward the same argument in calls to his followers from London. Lleras angrily stalked out of the convention and proclaimed his resignation as director. The delegates then adjourned until 30 June while postponing candidate selection until a separate meeting in December. When they came back into session, however, Lleras precipitously urged immediate nomination of the candidate. At this juncture a tacit understanding between López and Turbay led to the nomination of the former. The son of former president Alfonso López Pumarejo received 162 votes to 88 for Lleras Restrepo. With López Michelsen the candidate, Turbay was named the new Liberal *jefe único.* Despite the series of party meetings, the Liberals had once again arrived at major decision through the relationships and negotiations of a handful of dominant politicians. In this instance, despite Lleras Restrepo's unmatched credentials, he was unable to prevail when his two rivals formed a pact against him. López Michelsen had completed his return from the political wilderness of early MRL days, while Turbay had gained control of the organizational machinery despite his colorless persona.

This set the scene for Colombia's first competitive presidential race in a quarter century. Elitist domination of public affairs was dramatized by a race in which three offspring of former presidents were in contention: Alfonso López Michelsen, Alvaro Gómez Hurtado, and, for the ANAPO, María Eugenia Rojas de Moreno. In addition, Senator Hernán Echaverry, a former Liberal who had moved to ANAPO, also entered the race with a small leftist coalition, the Unión Nacional de Oposicion (UNO).

Campaign and Elections

With both a competitive presidential race and a fight for control of congress at issue, the stakes for the 21 April elections were high. The gradual modernization of Colombian electoral techniques was marked by greater reliance upon media and public relations initiatives, as well as heavy expenditures:

Loud "slogans," based on modern techniques of image manipulation, were used to push each candidate. This publicity increment increased the superficiality of the message: the old rhetoric, which the people applauded without understanding, was replaced by the bombardment of [media] spots and the war of posters.[13]

For the Conservatives, Alvaro Gómez Hurtado hoped to avoid charges of inherited fascism and falangism while proposing a *desarrollista* program, one in which the economy was to be stimulated without a hint of reformism. Production was to be the key. In similar fashion, agrarian policy would stress output rather than ownership or class reconciliation. In harking back to the simpler ways of the old patrimonial state, Gómez also felt that the private sector, rather than the state, bore responsibility for both development. It remained for the state to assure favorable domestic conditions while defending nationalistic interests in a moderate fashion. "We will not hand our resources over to satisfy the pretentions of a colonialist economy, but neither are we going to immobilize ourselves to satisfy leftists who lack faith in the patriotism of Colombians."[14]

The well-financed Gómez campaign relied heavily on the media techniques designed by consultants from Chile, while drawing as well on the candidate's personal vigor. Gómez carried his banner throughout the country and, while not a spellbinding public orator, held his own with Alfonso López Michelsen in traditional campaign settings. The latter was not an especially persuasive messenger, but had an advantage in denouncing existing problems and promising in general terms an equitable redistribution of income. Attacking *desarrollismo* as responsible for greater concentration of wealth in the hands of the few, López called for an *economía concertada,* which would conciliate class interests while at the same time expand the economy. In contrast to his Conservative foe, López argued for an enlargement of state responsibilities.

Implicitly recognizing the necessity for a bureaucratic centralist state, he repeatedly stressed its developmental role:

The strong government which I propose is one which does not yield to the pressures of minorities. It means that the press, with all the power of its freedom, may not be stronger than the State; that economic forces may not be in a position to impose their points of view on the government; that civic and labor strikes may not determine decisions that correspond to the community's prevailing interests. In sum, there may not be anyone stronger than the State, since any lack of strength would be totally detrimental to the very essence of authority.[15]

López described the role of the government in *concertación* as seeking the views of all social and economic sectors in the formulation of policy.

Thus, a balance would be struck to assure equity for business, labor, the peasantry, landowners, and other groups. The evils of sectarianism were to be dissipated through rigorous adherence to constitutional and moral norms. López termed the campaign a civic contest that would produce a government dependent upon all parties and citizens. He insisted that the Liberals were not engaged in a partisan war to the death, but rather were seeking a mandate to assume responsibility for directing public affairs.

As the campaign unfolded, the sharp differences between Gómez and López gradually blurred. The former, burdened by his father's reputation, relied on media efforts to escape the past and soften his own personal image. At the same time, the latter was seeking to erase his earlier years as an antisystem heretic who had deserted the MRL when it became politically opportune to do so. This helped to explain his evident campaign strategy of soft-pedalling his original views and watering down reformist proposals. Meanwhile, María Eugenia Rojas de Moreno was conducting a vigorous campaign of her own, although presenting a programmatic message at odds with that of ANAPO four years earlier. Her platform spoke of nationalizing basic industries, initiating a massive agrarian reform, and imposing fundamental structural change. As detailed in the party's new *Bases de una nueva Colombia,* this was a departure from the fundamental traditionalism of General Rojas's 1970 "Decalogue."

When the voting was tabulated, Alfonso López Michelsen had won a victory of historic proportions. With 5,212,133 citizens casting a vote for president, the percentage of eligible voters who participated was 58.1 percent, higher than at any time during the National Front. The winner received 2,929,719 votes (56.2 percent) to 1,634,879 (31.4 percent) for Alvaro Gómez. María Eugenia Rojas de Moreno barely reached one-half million, effectively marking the end of the once-vigorous movement that had nearly won power only four years earlier.[16] The Liberal triumph included a comfortable majority in congress, winning both chambers by 55.6 percent to 32 percent for the Conservatives. ANAPO was slightly below 10 percent. The relative unpopularity of the Pastrana administration and the unavoidable evocation of the *laureanista* past for the Conservative candidate were factors that magnified the margin of victory for López Michelsen. Coming to office with a powerful popular mandate, he was positioned to push the bourgeois reformist nationalist of his earlier years; alternatively, he could serve as yet one more representative of the Colombian political elite, essentially extending the practices and procedures of the National Front. More than any of his predecessors for years, López Michelsen was essentially free to make the choice. And despite his years of antisystem activity, he proved a willing captive to the morays and customs of traditional Colombian politics. The imagination and initiative of early years had been cast aside in his personal quest for power.

Notes

1. R. Albert Berry, "The National Front and Colombia's Economic Development," in R. Albert Berry, Ronald G. Hellman, and Mauricio Solaun, eds., *Politics of Compromise: Coalition Government in Colombia* (New Brunswick: Transaction Books, 1980), 290.
2. As quoted in Edwin G. Corr, *The Political Process in Colombia* (Denver: Graduate School of International Studies, Monograph Series in World Affairs, no. 1–2, 1972), 118.
3. His views are presented in Lauchlin Currie, *Accelerating Economic Development* (New York: McGraw-Hill, 1965).
4. The official Pastrana plan is presented in Departamento Nacional de Planeación, *Las cuatro estrategias* (Bogotá: DNP, 1972).
5. An authoritative statement is Lauchlin Currie, *Ahorro, corrección monetaria y construcción* (Bogotá: Universidad de los Andes, 1974).
6. For a useful review see Merilee S. Grindle, *State and Countryside: Development Policy and Agrarian Politics in Latin America* (Baltimore: The Johns Hopkins University Press, 1986), 143–53. Another convenient source is Bruce Bagley and Matthew Edel, "Popular Mobilization Programs of the National Front: Cooperation and Radicalism," in Berry et al., *Politics of Compromise*, 270–80.
7. Bruce Michael Bagley, "Colombia: National Front and Economic Development," in Robert Wesson, ed., *Politics, Policies, and Economic Development in Latin America* (Stanford: Hoover Institution Press, 1984), 139.
8. "Colombia," *Latin American Report* (5 March 1971): 79.
9. "Colombia," *Latin American Report* (2 February 1973): 33.
10. For a succinct review of M-19 activities during this period see Jenny Pearce, *Colombia: Inside the Labyrinth* (London: Latin America Bureau, 1990), 170–82.
11. J. Mark Ruhl, "The Military," in Berry et al., *Politics of Compromise*, 197.
12. A penetrating overview of the party struggles over organizational control and especially the selection of the 1974 candidates is Rodrigo Losada Lora, *Realidades de la concentración/dispersión del poder político en Colombia 1966–1978* (Bogotá: Pontificia Universidad Javeriana y Banco de la República, 1983).
    There are also informative sections on organization and conventions in Jorge Ramírez Aljure, *Liberalismo: ideología y clientelismo 1957–1966* (Bogotá: Fotolito Inter 2000, 1986), 68–83; also Rodrigo Lara Bonilla, Rodrigo Losada Lora, and Humberto Uribe Toro, *Los partidos políticos colombianos: presente y futuro* (Bogotá: Pontificia Universidad Javeriana y Fundación Simón Bolívar, 1983), including party statutes on pp. 161–242.
    A convenient source of *llerista* opinions during this period is Carlos Lleras Restrepo, *El liberalismo colombiano, 1972* (Bogotá: Tercer Mundo, 1973). Campaign speeches of the eventual Liberal victor are compiled in Alfonso López Michelsen, *El mandato claro* (Bogotá: n.p., 1974).

13. Fernán Gonzalez G., *Colombia 1974: I. La política* (Bogotá: CINEP, 1975), 6.
14. Ibid., 22.
15. Ibid., 26.
16. Electoral data, as always, comes from the Registraduría Nacional del Estado Civil, *Estudios electorales 1962–1984* (Bogotá: DANE, 1986). An excellent source for detailed information on congressional seats can be found in Reza Rezazadeh and Joseph McKenzie, *Political Parties in Colombia: Continuity in Political Style* (Platteville, WI: University Microfilms International, 1978).

8

The Quest for Redistribution: López Michelsen (1974–78)

The Policies of Governance

The National Environment

The first official census in nine years was held in 1973. It reported a population of 22,571,000; a total of 13,430,000 were living in urban areas, bringing the percentage to 59.5. When the new government took office in mid-1974 the population had passed 24 million. The rate of change, which ran at 3.17 percent from 1958 to 1966, had declined only marginally during 1966–74 with a figure of 3.03 percent. The labor force had grown by some 700,000 during the past four years, and was rapidly approaching 7 million. These were trends that had continued without fundamental change during the Pastrana period. With the initiation of the first officially non-Front government, Colombia awaited the efforts of the new administration in its pledge to confront endemic economic problems and to alleviate social inequities.

Whatever the benefits of Pastrana's "Four Strategies," it had produced rampant inflation and urban unemployment. DANE reported that the October 1974 rate for the latter in seven big cities was 11.7 percent. This included 16.3 percent in Manizales and 16.2 percent in Barranquilla, with rates of 12.9 percent in Medellín and 12.5 percent in Cali.[1] Nationally the total had surpassed one-half million, while the number underemployed stood at three-quarters of a million. Other economic problems awaiting the attention of the new administration included a foreign debt that approached $4 billion, and a mounting budget deficit that was fueling the rising cost of living. Despite such difficulties, popular enthusiasm and optimism surrounded López's ascension to power, and he entered

161

office with far greater mass-based legitimacy than had been the case for Pastrana in 1970. He began with a much-publicized "Mandato Claro" or mandate for change, as his government was to build bridges from the National Front toward a more competitive system.[2]

Policies of the Administration

The son of Alfonso López Pumarejo, the reformist president of 1934–38 and 1942–45, Alfonso López Michelsen had devoted most of his adult life to public affairs. Born in 1913 and educated in law, his career was characteristic of the political elite. Service in the legislature, activism within the party, international postings abroad, and a stint as newspaper editor (*El Liberal*) were all a part of his experience. During the 1960s, to be sure, he had raised challenges to the National Front through the creation of the MRL. Yet these were designed less as a means of truly overturning the system than of breathing greater life and vitality into its corpus. The MRL years also permitted him to move out from the shadow of his widely admired father (who had died in 1959), and in due course to leapfrog ahead of others in his generation.

López's inevitable return to the ranks of the Liberal party, effectively deserting a number of his most dedicated MRL colleagues, was assiduously encouraged by Carlos Lleras Restrepo, who named him governor of César in 1967 and foreign minister the following year. From that moment forward, López took on the cloak of a Liberal *presidenciable,* and few doubted that candidacy was only a matter of time. His links to Carlos Lleras were strong politically, and they shared a belief that the modernization of Colombia required forceful intervention on the part of the state. When internal party rivalries and the fight for the 1974 nomination produced the break with Lleras, López was left in effective command of the Liberal party, organized and maintained by Julio César Turbay Ayala. He was also free to voice a cry for reform and for redistribution, as he did while moving toward office. By August of 1974, then, his long experience and his journey from ideological heretic to mainstream leadership of the Liberal party, seasoned by his prominence as a member of Colombia's systemic elite, encouraged the popular expectation that his administration promised better times for the ordinary citizen.

As president-elect, Alfonso López had already assembled an economic team to begin charting policy as early as May 1974. In sketching the outlines of the 1974–78 development plan, it assumed an expanding economy in terms of both output and employment. At the same time López's advisors recognized the perils of rapid inflation and the deteriorating balance of payments, and therefore gave a neoliberal twist to short-term policy. Measures were devised with the intention of curbing inflation and liberalizing the balance of payments. Basic redistribution—or at least an improvement of the distribution of income—would remain a major objective, but one to be achieved over the long run. This thinking was not fully consistent with the *lopista* campaign cry promising "El Mandato Claro," which had repeatedly insisted upon the need to improve the distribution of goods and income as a means of directly attacking poverty and inequality.

The government soon began to describe its development plans under the label "Para Cerrar la Brecha"—to close the gap.[3] The overriding theme remained that of erasing the gaps created by the traditional developmental model—"between country and city, the gap between rich and poor barrios, [and] the gap between those who have access to health services and education and the illiterate and undernourished."[4] In more concrete terms, the new administration promptly set aside the UPAC-based strategy. The president undertook a "100 days" blitz by declaring an economic emergency. The first president to use these powers since their incorporation into the 1968 constitutional reform, López was thereby empowered to rule by decree for sixty days.

Shortly after convoking the so-called Tripartite Commission on 17 September 1974 with representatives of business, management, and the state, López put the emergency machinery into motion. During the next forty-five days the president issued twenty-two legislative decrees, most of which focused on reforms of the tax structure. The short-term monetary and fiscal measures sought four major goals: increased progressiveness of the tax system, a more balanced allocation of resources, increased revenue to strengthen economic stability, and an administrative simplification that might enhance collection and reduce evasion. Related planks in the emergency economic package called for a liberalization of import restrictions and new credit lines for agriculture.[5]

With the effort to decree a more progressive tax structure, restrict export subsidies, and promote industrial production, López's administration had been launched in dramatically forceful fashion. In López, it appeared, Colombia could count on a man of action, drawing upon a situation of political strength, who could indeed lead the state toward a more just and efficacious exercise of national authority. The rhetoric of the government did nothing to belie this impression, and in his year-end address López spoke with optimistic vigor about the economic situation. Presumably the inflation was being controlled, growth encouraged, and redistribution nudged forward through an interventionist tax reform. Agricultural production for 1974 had grown by 5.6 percent compared with the 1973 rate of 4.7 percent. Nontraditional exports had increased over 1973, and while there seemed a lull for the industrial sector, it had nonetheless grown by 7.2 percent during 1974. The specter of inflation was downplayed by the president, who contended that it was no more than 25 percent for the year and was destined to fall below 20 percent during the next twelve months.

The official perspective was therefore rosy, but before the conclusion of López's first full year in office, the early bloom was fast fading. Prices continued to rise, inflation did not come down, and the domestic market predictably contracted in response. By mid-1975 the president had reimposed a state of siege to deal with widespread disturbances in protest of economic problems (see next section). Despite a costly and showy parade on 7 August 1975 to commemorate López's first year in office, the administration faced immediate problems, which the most judicious or far-reaching of tax reforms could scarcely dissolve. Furthermore, new difficulties—totally unanticipated by López's economic planners—shifted the focus of attention sharply.

The sudden vertiginous explosion of coffee prices on the world market stimulated a bonanza, which, in conjunction with the growing volume of drug trafficking, threatened to overwhelm the nation. Prices in 1975 ranged from $0.65 to $0.80 per pound, but a severe frost in Brazil in July of that year caused prices to rise swiftly. By April of 1976, with Colombia planning an exportable production of 7.5 million bags for the year, the price on the big board at the National Coffee Growers Federation went off the chart as it passed $1.20 per pound. Coffee export income for the year was projected at more than $1 billion compared with $800 million the previous year. The administration sought measures to control the money supply. Coffee taxes were raised, import restrictions relaxed and public investment slowed. Prices continued to rise, however, and went above $2.00 per pound in 1977. For the rest of López's term the money supply continued to expand from 20 to 30 percent per year.

There was no way realistically to reduce inflation under such conditions, while it was ironic that for the first time there was too much rather than too little foreign exchange. This was further aggravated by Colombia's increasing involvement in the drug industry, which by the close of the administration was estimated at more than $2 billion.

The López administration could not be faulted for inattention to the problem, and its responses were sound. In the eyes of the World Bank,

> For the period 1974-78 the administration achieved a qualified success in its stabilization objective by preventing inflation from rising, despite a substantial improvement in the terms of trade. Moreover, international reserves were built up by over US$2 billion and the official debt service position was strengthened by reducing public external debt.[6]

On the negative side, however, there was a slowdown in public investment and a decline in economic growth. Industrial production also slowed markedly. Overvaluation of the peso for noncoffee exports and for imports contributed to a shortage of capital. Production costs rose while the overprotected industrial sector languished. Technological backwardness was still prevalent, and the state was not inclined in this instance to play an interventionist role. Neither did it direct major initiatives toward the agricultural sector although commercial agriculture expanded moderately.[7]

In balance, López Michelsen's economic policies over the full presidential term were somewhat erratic, and observers differed in characterizing his record. For many, the approach reflected an eclectic neoliberalism: state subsidies were curbed and the government reduced its role in the financial markets. Early redistributive promises were set aside or ignored as time passed, especially after the coffee bonanza began to make an impact. At the same time, however, the tax reforms and related emergency economic measures of 1974 were scarcely the handiwork of a government that did not question the wisdom of state intervention. Neither were its later fiscal and monetary policies indicative of an administration committed to a shrinking of the state. It was also willing to undertake significant steps in dealing with energy-related questions revolving about petroleum and especially the development of coal.[8]

None of this indicates progress in redistribution of goods and services, nor does it suggest that the emergent bureaucratic centralist system was adequately meeting public needs and demands. Indeed, López

Michelsen tended to give free play to regional leaders' appetites for power, a move that dovetailed with *turbayista* political ambitions while resuscitating traditional aspects of clientelism. Furthermore, his own capacity to formulate and implement policy declined during the course of his administration, plagued by an increasingly assertive military establishment, an almost permanent reliance on a state of siege, and a policy outlook that gravitated with rising cynicism toward reliance upon short-term pragmatic replies to socioeconomic problems. None of this was conducive to effective or strengthened legitimacy in the process of governance. The early momentum of the "Mandato Claro" had been short-lived, while López was plagued by resurgent rural violence, a potentially insubordinate military, and rising leftist activism in the universities.

Social and Political Controls

Alfonso López Michelsen faced the test of demonstrating the extent to which systemic social and political controls might be affected under the first nominally post-National Front administration. While political debate over proposed constitutional revisions continued, it was crucial that the new government assert its authority. Although the new chief executive had arrived in office with a major electoral victory, it was uncertain how endemic national problems might be handled. One immediate response, to be sure, was López's swift adoption of emergency economic measures. Yet this was an indirect if important effort to deal with conditions on which social and political unrest fed.

Within three months of his inauguration López was faced with a wave of demonstrations to protest inflation, and in May of 1975 a more extensive round of disturbances broke out. Cement workers, employees of the Caja Agraria, and a quarter of a million school teachers went on strike. By June protests had spread to the universities, the rector of Bogotá's Universidad Nacional had been dismissed, and a clash with the military leadership had driven the president to fire army commander General Alvaro Valencia Tovar. A state of siege was declared, limited at first to three departments—Antioquia, Valle del Cauca, and Atlántico. On 25 June the state of siege was extended to the entire nation. In a televised address López blamed the disturbances largely on "mafias," by which he meant criminal organizations with international ties. He told an interviewer that "there is a mafia of drugs, of smugglers,...there is corruption within the government, officials of the government—in customs, taxes and law enforcement."[9]

Before the first anniversary of his inauguration, then, López had reinstituted the siege controls that had prevailed in all but two years since 1948. The protests spurred by social unrest were to become increasingly frequent. Before the close of 1975 there had been further outbursts, especially in Medellín and in Bucaramanga, as transport workers sought higher wages and demonstrated in the streets. Worsening living conditions in urban areas continued to plague the administration, while guerrilla activity also rose. Both the FARC and the ELN raised their visibility. In April 1975 the former attacked and occupied Puerto Rico, a city of some 25,000 in Caquetá, withdrawing only when regular forces approached. The ELN in the meantime sought to reestablish its own credentials under Fabio Vásquez Castaño, its dominant caudillo after the death of his two brothers in October 1973. He reopened communications with the FARC, declaring that revolution Cuban-style was the destiny of the republic.

Assurances from the armed forces that they would guarantee public tranquillity and democratic institutions were plagued by internal wrangling that resounded throughout the government. On 27 May 1975 the minister of defense, General Abraham Varón Valencia, publicly denied that a *golpe de estado* had been in the works. The following day the army commander, General Alvaro Valencia Tovar, and two other senior officers were summarily dismissed. Valencia Tovar, a ranking authority on counterinsurgency and guerrilla movements, had been representative of those officers influenced by the views of General Ruiz Novoa. Thus, they had continued to be critical of domestic social conditions while advocating extensive civic-action programs. However, the López government had little interest in such a definition of the military mission, and General Varón was also inclined toward a less sweeping view. Personnel changes following the dismissal of Valencia Tovar effectively heralded the disappearance of the developmentalist concept in military policy.

The existence of divisions within the military did little to enhance the campaign against the guerrillas, and a wave of kidnappings further violated any semblance of social peace. In January of 1975 Eric Leupin, a Canadian businessman and honorary Dutch consul in Cali, was abducted from the lumber camp he owned by the FARC. Greater embarrassment came in August when Donald E. Cooper, assistant manager of Sears Roebuck and Company in Colombia, became the first U.S. citizen to be abducted. Neither of these cases had been resolved when General José Ramón Rincón Quiñones, the army's inspector general, a noted counterinsurgency expert, and fifth-ranking officer on active duty, was gunned down in the Bogotá outskirts. The ELN promptly took credit for the killing, while the military under defense minister Varón Valencia was preoccupied with further forced resignations as a means of solidifying the control of hard-liners. Indeed, the military acted more vigorously in pursuing its own corporate interests than its constitutional duties against guerrilla violence. For one, it continued a war of words with the leftist criticisms from Gabriel García Márquez's weekly *Alternativa* and the daily *El Bogotano*. The defense minister threatened civil action against the weekly, and at the close of September the three service commanders requested that the president control the "defamation campaigns" against them.

The military was especially riled by allegations that the killing of General Rincón Quiñones had actually been the handiwork of right-wing paramilitary organizations rather than the guerrillas. There was an understandable determination to punish someone for the assassination, and this too was poorly managed. A military court martial of four accused attackers, conducted under provisions of the state of siege, resulted in a public outcry against illegalities, incompetence, and alleged military corruption. Defense charges that Rincón Quiñones had been killed because of his investigation into cases of embezzlement and ties with drug runners, among others, created a wave of journalistic sensationalism. There was a widespread belief in the legal community, and in the capital at large, that those responsibility for the killing had not been found. The retirement or reassignment of several senior officers left an especially bad taste in the aftermath of the proceedings.

During the time leading up to the 1976 *mitaca* elections, the frequency of both urban and rural violence increased. In mid-March the president authorized a tightening of security controls in the wake of outbursts in which an estimated 300 students and police had been injured. A new wave of wildcat strikes were also met with force from the government. There was a brief respite following the April elections and President López, anxious for a restoration of normality, unexpectedly lifted the state of siege on 22 June 1976. The military renewed its anti-guerrilla activities with greater commitment, and in October the Canadian-born Eric Leupin was released unharmed after 20 months of captivity, apparently after receiving an undisclosed ransom payment.

A new round of conflict surfaced on 6 September with a strike by doctors and medical workers at the state health service, the Instituto Colombiano de Seguros Sociales (ICSS). In two days it was labelled illegal by the government, which was hostile to the public sector organizations involved in the dispute. Although the interior minister threatened doctors with imprisonment if they rejected emergency cases, the strike was joined by most of the 35,000 workers affected. For three weeks the two combatants exchanged angry charges in what became a major political confrontation. By October López reimposed a state of siege once again, arguing that the fallout from the medical strike was provoking a new round of disorders at the Universidad Nacional, as well as an increase in kidnappings. Only after fifty-two days was the strike finally resolved, with the disputants compromising on a complicated set of agreements.

The capacity of the government to exercise effective and legitimate authority was next to be challenged in 1977 by a different set of problems—charges of corruption that reached to the presidential family itself. Months of rumors had originated with a newspaper column by Bertha Hernández de Ospina Pérez on 5 September 1975. Doña Bertha had claimed that friends and relatives of López had been engaged in improper commercial dealings. While noting amid the resultant outcry that she had named no names, she staunchly remarked that "*cuando el sapo salta y se estaca, la culpa no es de la estaca.*"[10] After a spate of reports and allegations the storm seemed to have passed, only to be resurrected with a vengeance on the pages of *El Espectador* on 15 February 1977. At center stage was the president's son, Juan Manuel López Caballero, member of a syndicate reportedly involved in the purchase of property through improper government financing. A corporation in which Juan Manuel was primary shareholder was also charged with gaining improper access to soft loans from the state. The purported icing on the cake was the claim that the government had built a new main road to service the country estate of the president's son.

As congressional investigation later revealed, this construction had actually taken place before López had been elected. In the meantime, however, another son, the president's private secretary—Felipe López Caballero—had also been charged with improprieties. He had received some 285,000 pesos as a consultant for the Federación Nacional de Cafeteros. The latter was state-supported, and the son's acceptance of money was deemed a conflict of interest. The attorney-general declared

that the money should be repaid and began an investigation. The resultant furor rocked the government, rumors of a military coup were widespread, and on 27 March at a meeting with Alberto Lleras Camargo and
Darío Echandía, López threatened to resign.

By the close of April the López family had managed to weather the
storm. A congressional commission found no impropriety in the land
deals and related business activities of Juan Manuel, while Felipe returned the payments in question. It was generally agreed that he was
guilty of bad judgment rather than a crime. López Michelsen was thus
able to redirect his attention to other matters. At the same time, these
events underlined growing public suspicion about the rectitude of the
administration. None of this was conducive to an effective handling of
social and political controls, and problems with labor were recurrent.

In August of 1977 a series of overlapping disputes broke out, first
centered on the demands of the Communist-dominated Confederación
Sindical de Trabajadores de Colombia (CSTC) and the smaller
Confederación General del Trabajo (CGT). Within three weeks they were
joined by the two traditional confederations, the Conservative-related
Unión de Trabajadores Colombianos (UTC) and the pro-Liberal
Confederación de Trabajadores Colombianos (CTC). There was una-
nimity over the need for immediate wage increases as compensation for
inflation, although specific proposals differed. In the end, leaders of the
four federations scheduled the first general strike in history for 14 September. A potential of 3 million workers could have been affected. President López banned reporting on radio and television while imposing an 8
PM curfew in Bogotá and army troops in battle dress with rifles and
submachine guns roamed the streets of the capital. Violence soon broke
out, and for two days there were flashes of rioting and even looting.

The official death toll for the first two days reached sixteen, while no
more than half the city's stores and shops opened their doors. By government count, 100,000 soldiers and policemen were on duty throughout the
nation. Only by the third day did the street fighting draw to a close.
While the government termed the strike a failure, it also conceded that
nearly 5000 had been detained in Bogotá and Barranquilla, where disturbances were greatest. The outburst was easily the worst in two decades,
and authorities for a time were holding detainees in open-air soccer fields
and bullrings. City authorities in Bogotá estimated the damages at some
$2 million.

While President López and his government (including new ministers following a speedy cabinet shuffle in the wake of the violence) insisted that the unrest was the product of internationally inspired troublemakers, labor leaders at the other extreme spoke of the nation as teetering on the brink of social revolution. On the one hand, UTC leader Tulio Cuevas, also a Conservative congressman, spoke of a powder keg. "Colombia is going through a grave institutional crisis that is reflected in political, moral and social decomposition." At the same time a prominent Liberal newspaper executive and supporter of Alfonso López referred to a sword of Damocles while reporting his worry "that the Government has failed to see the real emergency."[11]

Periodic outbursts marked the remainder of the López administration. Early in 1978 there were strikes of oil producers in Barrancabermeja and in Medellín; the teachers' union threatened a new work stoppage; meanwhile the UTC and CTC were deeply involved in political machinations with both the Liberals and Conservatives. In May of the same year, barely a month before presidential elections and three months before the inauguration of a new government, López's minister of labor had to be replaced, the victim of controversy with the workers as well as allegations of links to the drug industry. And the very growth of the drug trade during the 1970s was becoming recognized as a major national problem for the first time, suggesting yet another increasingly serious challenge to the authority of the state.

It was during López's first two years in power that headlines began to demonstrate the rising profile of drug activism: "$20 Million Pot Crop Found in Colombia"; "Colombia Moves on Drugs"; "Kidnappings to Drugs—Crime Grips Nation"; and "Drug Traffic Turns Colombian Coast into Zone of Terror." The Colombian-U.S. collaboration began to take shape, and the participation of the latter was etched on public awareness when the chief agent of the Drug Enforcement Administration in Bogotá was shot in December of 1976. At this early point the bilateral effort was somewhat constricted, owing in part to the prickly attitudes between Bogotá and Washington during the López years. More generally, Colombia saw an acceleration of social protest and antisystem violence from 1974 to 1978. Alfonso López Michelsen was no more successful than his predecessors in this regard, and the problems appeared increasingly resistant to the authority of the state.

Much of López's strong popular support in 1974 was progressively dissipated by his state of siege and the 1978 strike, underlying his problems in providing the level of leadership necessary to move the nation ahead significantly in either administrative or managerial terms.[12] Whether or not one regards the López government as an extension of the old National Front, it was evident that Colombia's system of governance was not dealing successfully with national problems. Social and political control was decreasingly dependent on public support or a genuine sense of legitimacy, but rather on armed force and counterviolence, too often including the use of repression as the final arbiter.

The Politics of the National Front

The Party Competition

Almost before the 1974 elections had faded, party leaders began to point toward 1978. The Conservatives, less fragmented than the victorious Liberals, nonetheless faced internal disagreements. More progressive elements, never happy with the Gómez candidacy, called in September 1974 for both organizational reforms and doctrinal modernization. Alfredo Vásquez Carrizosa, the former foreign minister under Pastrana, was joined by Augusto Ramírez Ocampo and Emilio Valderrama to form the so-called Comando Nacional Progresista in an effort to gain control of the party. Alvaro Gómez meanwhile was collaborating with President López to a degree, which further separated his followers from the *pastranistas*. Despite such partisan problems, however, the Conservatives maintained a modicum of internal unity until the April 1976 elections, while providing half of López's cabinet and thus moderating their criticisms of the Liberal president.

Ironically, the divisions within the majority party were intensifying. Alfonso López Michelsen had convened a party convention on 26 July 1974 to win official approval of his campaign document *El Mandato Claro*. However, its acceptance did not mask the presence of three distinct currents. The *lleristas* remained determined to achieve a genuine democratization of the Liberal party, although Carlos Lleras had stayed out of the public eye since losing the candidacy. Julio César Turbay Ayala, after helping López win both the nomination and election, imposed former foreign minister Germán Zea Hernández as party president over the protests of progressives. In April of 1975 he moved to Washington as Colombian ambassador, thereby distancing himself from everyday political controversies while remaining commander of the most traditionalistic forces in the party.

As President López encountered problems of governance and was perceived as reluctant or unable to pursue a reformist path, more progressive Liberals began to call for Carlos Lleras's return to party affairs. By late 1975 the former president was back in the fray, preaching as always for basic reforms, modernization of the party, and an end to political clientelism in Colombia. He constructed a Movimiento de Democratización that attracted support from nonparty leftists, such as the 1974 presidential candidate Hernán Echeverri Mejía and others from the small but vocal Unión Nacional de Oposición. He also succeeded in blocking selection of a new party directorate at the December 1975 convention, as well as a new set of party statutes. While unable to regain full party command, he did enjoy sufficient influence to exercise a virtual veto over major doctrinal and organizational proposals. In due course the *lleristas* put together their own slate of candidates for the April 1976 elections; also, a group of unreconstructed reformers clinging to the legacy of the MRL deepened internal cleavages. The party eventually entered the elections under a new official leadership that could only speak for a minority of the membership (its members were senate president Gustavo Balcázar Monzón, Chamber president Alberto Santofimio Botero, and Senator Víctor Mosquera Chaux).

The angry confusion over campaign issues was further compounded by López Michelsen's call for constitutional and electoral reforms. In his 1975 year-end address the president proposed that local and departmental elections be separated by three months from those for national offices. He demanded special elections for members of a constituent assembly that would formulate a basic reform of the judicial system, along with a restructuring of municipal and departmental government. This engendered controversy on all sides. Although López later asked that his project be delayed until after the elections, ongoing street demonstrations continued to plague the government, while the state of siege remained in effect. In March the cabinet publicly proclaimed its fear that democratic institutions were endangered, while a disinterested public—presumably reflecting both frustration and cynicism—threatened yet another exercise in electoral abstentionism. The process of registration moved slowly and, when the lists closed on 19 March, it was reported that only 130,000 voters in Bogotá had registered as compared with 198,000 four years earlier; in Barranquilla there were only 30,000 in contrast to 92,000 in 1972.[13]

Public disorder increased as elections neared. On 2 April the government banned political demonstrations in Bogotá, and on the twelfth, all electoral meetings and public gatherings were halted, while the Universidad Nacional remained closed indefinitely. An unexpected event came on 14 April with the sudden death of Maríano Ospina Pérez. A week after undergoing surgery for intestinal bleeding, he passed away from lung and heart complications at age eighty-four. The grand old man of the Conservatives had retained personal influence inside the party while providing a stabilizing influence nationally as the most senior surviving former chief executive. His final legacy to the party was the advice that should the Conservatives poll less than 40 percent of the vote, they should withdraw all six ministers and other senior party members from the government and go into outright opposition.

On the eve of elections President López broadcast an appeal to the voters, "I want it to be shown with a plebiscite, as voluminous as possible, that 90 percent of Colombians are for the institutions and against crime, against extortion."[14] Nonetheless, the turnout was very light. Based on estimates of the electorate for 1976, participation for both departmental assembly elections and for municipal councils was barely 30 percent.[15] While abstention data could only be estimated, the turnout was obviously low. Results showed a total of 3,265,974 votes for departmental offices; the Liberals with 1,698,081 votes to the Conservatives' 1,276,229 thereby enjoyed a margin of 52 to 39.1 percent. In races for municipal council the Liberals polled 1,740,256 for 52.4 percent, to the Conservatives' 1,274,178 and 38.4 percent. The remainder was divided almost equally between the diminished number of ANAPO and candidates for small leftist miniparties.

There was disappointment on all sides. For López, while he could claim his magical 90 percent in favor of National Front parties, the high level of abstention was clearly a damning public response. The Conservatives barely reached Ospina's modest figure of 40 percent. The Liberals remained divided while saddled with the government's unpopularity. Even Carlos Lleras, whose candidates won a substantial victory in the race for the Bogotá council, had been unimpressive in working-class neighborhoods to the city's south; his margin had come from the wealthy northern suburbs. His forces also had a mediocre performance in rural races. This led the Turbay regulars to claim that Lleras's fate was sealed, and they openly called for his withdrawal from politics. However, the Liberals remained divided into the followers of the three dominant *caudillos*. And for the Conservatives, the death of Ospina Pérez removed the brakes from an increasingly bitter rivalry between Alvaro Gómez and Misael Pastrana. In sum, the unofficial perpetuation of National Front practices continued to be accompanied by interparty feuds and clientelistic rivalries that nourished public disenchantment.

Candidate Selection

The struggle for the Conservative candidacy was strongly linked to the party's relationship with the government. This was compounded by controversy over López Michelsen's proposals to separate presidential, congressional, and local elections in 1978. Alvaro Gómez and his followers maintained their cooperative stance toward López, while the *ospino-pastranistas* announced their unqualified opposition. Pastrana himself argued that the issue of electoral reform was merely an instrument designed to resolve internal Liberal conflict; he also sought to gain personal control of the party, given the passing of Ospina Pérez. And at the same time Belisario Betancur, after a period of inactivity, mounted his own drive for the 1978 Conservative candidacy.

Alvaro Gómez endorsed Betancur in a television appearance on 13 March 1977. In June he agreed to drop demands for a shift in the sequence of elections, reasoning that this would pacify Pastrana and improve the chances of an uncontested nomination of Betancur. The perversity of internal factionalism was not so readily dissipated, however, and rival conventions were held in mid-October. Each of them eventually chose Betancur as candidate, although the two directorates were sharply at odds with one another. In the meantime Betancur held himself aloof from such internecine warfare, quietly reaching out to minor parties and to prominent independents with the hope of building a movement that would reach beyond Conservative loyalists, who by themselves remained a minority.

On the Liberal side of the aisle the competition between Lleras Restrepo and Turbay gradually intensified. The latter held the upper hand organizationally, and was aiming for official nomination at the Liberal convention set for December 1977. However, in that case the *lleristas* might walk out, thereby jeopardizing Turbay's chances in 1978. Extended talks among a number of ranking Liberals led to proclamation of "The Consensus of San Carlos" on 21 September 1976. With López Michelsen serving as guarantor, factional leaders met in the Salon Bolívar of the Palacio de San Carlos to set new rules of the game. It was agreed that the next convention would not select the candidate; that all Liberals would support the presidential plan to separate elections; and that any faction could campaign independently in the projected February 1978 congressional context. This would serve as a form of electoral primary to produce as candidate the leader of the winning faction.

The San Carlos accord was soon shredded by warring factions. Julio César Turbay Ayala moved about Colombia tightening his control on the Liberal machinery, most notably in Caldas, Santander, and Antioquia. On 25 February 1977 he accepted the endorsement extended by the Antioquia party director; others soon followed, and on 5 March he initiated his Bogotá campaign. The forces of *democratization* meanwhile fought for Carlos Lleras. Their congressional leader Augusto Espinosa Valderrama referred to Turbay bluntly as unfit to rule the nation; others worked more quietly, seeking the backing of business leaders. And amid this competition there were inevitably other aspirants, the most notable of whom were Carlos Holmes Trujillo, Virgilio Barco Vargas, and Hernando Agudelo Villa. In due course Holmes failed to attract support outside his native Cauca Valley, and Barco declared on 12 February 1977 that in the interests of party harmony he would not pursue the nomination. Agudelo remained an active pre-candidate until shortly before the February 1978 elections.

Amid the high-stakes Liberal struggle, President López's own role became an additional factor. By this time his government had been rocked by charges of corruption and nepotism; many of his original reform proposals had been diluted or rejected by the legislature. However, a special session of congress near the close of the year did adopt a separation of congressional and municipal from presidential elections. More limited changes dealt with the composition of the electoral tribunal, party access to the media, and modest state financing of campaigns. Separation of the date of elections—the single most crucial element in the process of candidate selection at this juncture was passed by congress on 19 December

1977. Carlos Lleras, who had found himself outgunned by Turbay in congress, promptly took the initiative through renewed attacks on traditional clientelism and the corruption of the political process generally. He also sought to link his rival to the unpopularity of the administration. Like Turbay, he was targeting the *mitaca* elections, which now constituted in effect a presidential primary for the Liberals.[16]

It was the Liberal candidacy that nourished uncertainties over the 1978 competition, for the Conservatives were clearly committed to Belisario Betancur. With the virtual disappearance of ANAPO, the only other contender was General Alvaro Valencia Tovar who, since his June 1975 dismissal as army commander, had maintained a public presence. A frequent columnist for *El Tiempo,* he was an iconoclast whose September 1977 proclamation of candidacy issued a cry for national moral regeneration. Claiming that corruption and decay had infected the body politic to the point of systemic disintegration, he promised an uncompromising drive for purification as representative of his Movimiento de Renovación Nacional. None of this was of basic electoral or popular significance, however. The Liberal conflict properly remained at center stage in the process of candidate selection.

The selection was more sharply etched with the withdrawal of Hernando Agudelo Villa on 9 December 1977. For many years one of the Liberals most uncompromisingly committed to genuine change, he had demanded an end to coalition government and a total renovation of the Liberal party in attacking clientelism. New national leadership was also critical, for "our political regime is affected by acute arthritis because of the lack of mobility and competition, since the same personages have occupied the political scene for over thirty years."[17] Although well-known within the party leadership, Agudelo Villa could not compete with either the visibility of Lleras or the organizational control of Turbay, and thus his resignation as a precandidate was inevitable. He did not endorse either of his rivals.

The contrasts between those two were vivid. Carlos Lleras Restrepo, although having disappointed some of the more avowedly reformist elements in the party, nonetheless remained the candidate of change. Vigorous, opinionated, sometimes abrasive, he was the bourgeois reformer par excellence, envisaging a modernized governmental apparatus supported by a more responsive, less somnolent and complacent Liberal party. Lleras had not turned his back on historic elite control, but thought it could better be maintained and legitimized if the masses were brought more fully into the system. He consistently denounced traditional clientelism, which he saw personified by the López-Turbay relationship. For Lleras, clientelism demonstrated the artificiality of democracy in Colombia while continuing to draw upon *gamonalismo* at the regional and local level. While the future was dependent upon the Liberal party, it was destined for burial unless meaningful changes were introduced:

> What I propose to the country in the present political circumstances—with grow-ing electoral abstentionism, with a greatly increasing number of people without a party, and with clientelistic politics carried out for the benefit of a few—is a great impulse to free itself from that decadence.... The country requires political regen-eration. If we want democracy not only to function, but also to be efficacious, we have to give as a base political parties which, because of their internal organiza-tion, may be capable of reflecting faithfully the opinions of the people.[18]

Lleras remained firm in his reliance on the state. The function of govern-ment in his eyes was to forge a modern society, one characterized "by quality of life, by education of the people, and by a redistribution of income that might avoid...the tremendous differences between those with nothing and those with an excess of riches."[19]

All of this stood in contrast with Julio César Turbay Ayala, a lifelong politician who had loyally toiled in the Liberal cause while laboriously building his strength within the organization. Customarily viewed as a source of industrious if uninspired work on behalf of the party, Turbay had nonetheless assumed a position of power through skillful manipula-tion of traditional clientelist interests. Having assured his organizational power base through negotiation of the virtual partnership with López in 1974 and thereafter, he could confront Lleras directly, even going so far as to claimed that his was "the candidacy of the merging Colombia, of the classes in ascent." Indeed, he claimed, "I am the flagbearer of a move-ment of nonconformity without the dynastic tendencies demonstrated by the titular leaders of aberrant privileges."[20] However, Turbay was un-questionably the status quo candidate, sustained by the support of re-gional clientelistic leaders inside his party. These were influential sources of power that could more than counterbalance the pro-Lleras posture of both *El Tiempo* and *El Espectador*. For Turbay, the road to the presi-dency was defined by special interests whose leaders he had cultivated for years; the impact of public opinion could presumably be controlled or directed by traditional local and regional *caciques*. It was scarcely surprising that, unlike Lleras, Turbay devoted minimal attention to spe-cifics as the campaign unfolded.

Campaign and Elections

On 26 February 1978, the *mitaca* round of elections took place. Clearly the highly publicized contest between Lleras and Turbay proved far more important to political elites than to the electorate, for abstention once again was high. Barely 34 percent of the eligible voters had gone to the polls, while two-thirds had stayed at home. Turnout was lower in urban than rural areas. Bogotá showed only 22 percent voting, while the figure barely reached 30 percent in such important departments as Antioquia and Valle. In elections for the Chamber the Liberals resoundingly defeated the Conservatives by 2,302,230 (55 percent) to 1,645,496 (39.4 percent). More notably, Turbay candidates outpolled those of Lleras by a resounding margin of more than two to one. The Liberals dropped a total of 6 seats while winning 173 of 311 (62 in the senate and 111 in the Chamber), of which 121 went to *turbayistas*—some 70 percent of the Liberal total. *Lleristas* captured 46 seats, or 27 percent of the total (the remaining 6 went to other Liberal lists). Although Lleras supporters swept two-thirds of the Bogotá vote, they could not carry a single department against Turbay.

Within three days of the elections, Carlos Lleras Restrepo announced that he would respect the San Carlos accord and withdrew his candidacy. At the same time he withheld any endorsement of Turbay, as did *El Espectador*. So it was that the oft-maligned Turbay, labelled by his political peers as a boss dependent upon clientelism and the prevailing corruption of the system, had triumphed through his very command of these skills. Years dedicated to the party machinery and to solidifying personal ties with local *gamonales* had made possible his official proclamation as Liberal candidate for president, which was formalized on 17 March 1978. This also prepared the way for the campaign against his Conservative opponent, who had been unencumbered by the rigors of a "primary" testing even as the party had once again been defeated nationally by the Liberals.

The Conservatives' delegation had increased from 103 to 132 (forty-nine in the senate and eighty-three in the Chamber), largely as defectors returned from ANAPO, which lost the twenty-two seats it had held since 1974. The *alvaristas* retained their majority with 52 percent of the Conservative seats (sixty-nine legislators) compared with 39 percent (fifty-one legislators) for the *ospino-pastranistas*. Overall the party showed its greatest strength in the customary Conservative strongholds of Boyacá and Norte de Santander. All of this further underlined Belisario Betancur's determination to build a national rather than partisan candidacy. His Movimiento Nacional therefore sought to broaden his appeal. While denouncing the failures of the Liberals, Betancur insisted that national problems required national rather than partisan solutions. For Colombia, then, the only possible path was

> the route I have proposed incessantly—to form a great national movement, drawn from my own party, the disenchanted, the skeptics, and the uncommitted, in order to put in motion formulae that will pull Colombia out of the economic, social, and moral morass in which it is sunk.[21]

While accompanied on his campaign trips by María Eugenia Rojas de Moreno and by leaders of several minor parties, he spoke of personifying a "new style" of Colombia politics.

Betancur presented a mildly populist approach by emphasizing his preoccupation with poverty. He affirmed traditional attitudes in citing the Christian foundation of the nation, thereby legitimizing his criticism of existing patterns of income distribution and the prevailing inequality of opportunity. In place of Gómez's 1974 *desarrollista* model he proposed a *contratación de desarrollo,* which he described somewhat vaguely as a means by which the state could contribute through collaborative agreements with the private sector. The Betancur message, delivered with a popular touch lacking in his opponent, differed only mildly in terms of substance. The Conservative was at one with Turbay in attacking government corruption, tax evasion, and a deterioration of public order. He also shared the view that the path to social and economic equity was dependent upon a stimulation of the business sector, and in fact his program had few specifics about the role of the state.

With Turbay, appearances on television were nearly as deadening as those on the campaign trail. He benefitted from frequent public appearances by Alberto Lleras Camargo at his side; beyond this, he was of course relying heavily on the Liberal network of regional and local *patrones*. He took a carefully noncommittal approach to major issues. There were few proposals on industrial, agricultural, or fiscal policy. Neither did he speak of major reforms or structural change. As one Colombian observer put it, the Liberal candidate sought to offer a positive vision for every voter, "in such a way that the hypothesis could be formulated that the Turbay government will not base itself on a special sector of the bourgeoisie, but will seek the support of the entire Colombian capitalist class."[22]

On 4 June 1978 Colombians went to the polls. With a total of 12,580,851 citizens eligible, 5,075,719 (40.3 percent) cast ballots. Julio César Turbay Ayala edged past Betancur by 2,503,681 to 2,356,620, or 49.3 percent to 46.4 percent. In contrast to the López landslide of 1974, the Liberals under the Turbay candidacy fell short of their February 1978 vote in all but three departments. Betancur won a plurality in traditionally Liberal Bogotá and added five departments to the Conservative ranks from 1974 (Antioquia, Boyaca, Cundimarca, Huila, and Risaralda). Four minor candidates divided the remaining votes. General Valencia Tovar polled 1.3 percent, over half of it in Bogotá. Three rival Marxist candidates received a combined total of less than 3 percent.[23]

There were no real surprises to the 1978 results, with the possible exception of the narrowness of Turbay's victory. Abstention remained omnipresent, aggravated by the impact of the 1976 extension of suffrage from a minimum of age twenty to eighteen, which therefore expanded the number of disillusioned and alienated Colombian youths. The severity of internal Liberal dissidence, the unpopularity of the López government, the uninspiring political persona of Turbay, and the freshness of the Betancur campaign, all combined to reduce the electoral gap between the two parties. The Liberals' 55-39 percent sweep in February had therefore shrunk by June to a bare 49-46 percent. In August of 1978, then, the latest of the Liberal leaders entered office with the need to establish its own identity while removing the tarnish that voters saw in the record of the López administration.[24]

Notes

1. The World Bank, *Economic Development and Policy under Changing Conditions* (Washington, D.C.: The World Bank, 1984).
2. A brief overview presenting a partisan perspective is Rafael Ballén, *Liberalismo hoy: Opción de cambio o agónica supervivencia* (Bogotá: n.p., 1985), 179–89.
3. The López government would publish a substantial number of collections of presidential speeches, conferences, and documents. For an expensively produced and illustrated example, which proved a useful if self-interested review of the administration, see Administración López Michelsen, *Una gestión con proyecciones hacia el año dos mil* (Bogotá: n.p., 1978).
4. This López statement was quoted in John Sheahan, *Aspects of Planning and Development in Colombia* (Austin: Institute of Latin American Studies, 1977),

23–24, as reported in turn by Harvey F. Kline, *Colombia: Portrait of Unity and Diversity* (Boulder: Westview Press, 1983), 110.

5. Malcolm Gillis and Charles E. McLure, Jr., "The 1974 Colombian Tax Reform and Income Distribution," in R. Albert Berry and Ronald Soligo, eds., *Economic Policy and Income Distribution in Colombia* (Boulder: Westview Press, 1980), 47–48. Also see the extended discussion in Rodrigo Losada Lora, *Realidades de la concentración/dispersión del poder político en Colombia 1966–1978* (Bogotá: Pontificia Universidad Javeriana, 1983).

   A more recent and far-reaching exploration, a rich treasure trove of data, is Charles E. McLure, Jr., John Mutti, Victor Thuronyi, and George R. Zodrow, *The Taxation of Income from Business and Capital in Colombia* (Durham: Duke University Press, 1990).

6. World Bank, *Economic Development*, 46.

7. Colombia receives substantial attention in a fine treatise on rural underdevelopment in Latin America by Merilee S. Grindle, *State and Countryside: Development Policy and Agrarian Politics in Latin America* (Baltimore: The Johns Hopkins University Press, 1986); see especially pp. 104–07 and 143–53.

   For a detailed study of Bogotá describing the López administration's modifications of Pastrana's housing policy, which had heavily concentrated on the capital, thereby increasing its primacy over Colombia's other large cities, see Francis Violich, in collaboration with Robert Daughters, *Urban Planning for Latin America: The Challenge of Metropolitan Growth* (Boston: Oelgeschlager, Gunn & Hain Publishers, Inc., 1987), chapter 6, "Bogotá: Metropolitan Dualism," 199–253.

8. For an exhaustive analysis see Harvey F. Kline, *The Coal of Cerrejon: Dependent Bargaining and Colombian Policy-Making* (University Park: Pennsylvania State University Press, 1987).

9. *Washington Post* (28 June 1975).

10. "Colombia," *Latin American Weekly Report* (19 September 1975).

11. *New York Times* (17 October 1977).

12. For a discussion of Colombian administrative reform and policy formulation beginning with the National Front and including an examination of the López record, see Linn A. Hammergren, *Development and the Politics of Administrative Reform: Lessons from Latin America* (Boulder: Westview, 1983), 133–71.

13. "Colombia," *Latin American Weekly Report* (2 April 1976).

14. *Miami Herald* (16 April 1976). A thorough study of the elections is Rodrigo Losada Lora, *Las elecciones de mitaca de 1976: participación electoral y perspectiva histórica* (Bogotá: Fedesarrollo, 1976).

15. There were no official figures between 1974 and 1978. Thus, we calculated the difference over the four-year period and halved it to arrive at an estimate of 10,772,661.

16. The long-running feuding inside the Liberal party, accompanied by an analysis of doctrinal disputes, is set forth in Ballén, *Liberalismo hoy.*

17. Statements illustrating his dedication to a new and modernized party are found in Hernando Agudelo Villa, *Hacia un liberalismo moderno* (Bogotá: Tercer Mundo, 1968); and Agudelo Villa, *Retorno al liberalismo,* 2d ed. (Bogotá: Tercer Mundo, 1975).

18. Oscar Delgado, ed., *La campaña por la presidencia, 1978–1982: los temas en controversia* (Bogotá: Tercer Mundo, 1978), 248–49.

19. Ibid., 83.
20. Ibid., 236.
21. Ibid., 194.
22. Ernesto Parra Escobar, *Elecciones 1978: Plataformas económicas* (Bogotá: CINEP, 1978).
23. J. Mark Ruhl provides an informed account in his "Party System in Crisis? An Analysis of Colombia's 1978 Elections," *Inter-American Economic Affairs* 32, no. 3 (Winter 1978): 29–47.
24. Another general assessment of the outgoing president and administration is Hernando Gómez Buendía, *Alfonso López Michelsen: Un examen crítico de su pensamiento y su obra de gobierno* (Bogotá: Tercer Mundo, 1978).

   An interesting retrospective view published recently by Alfonso López Michelsen is his *Grandes compatriotas* (Bogotá: Tercer Mundo, 1993). Here he is conciliatory and generally dispassionate in his remarks about such former adversaries as Alberto Lleras Camargo, Eduardo Santos, and Jorge Eliécer Gaitán.

9

Traditionalism and Repression: Turbay (1978–82)

The Policies of Governance

The National Environment

As Julio César Turbay Ayala took power in August he faced a citizenry that had become increasingly disenchanted over the course of the four previous years. The hopeful optimism that accompanied the inauguration Alfonso López Michelsen had been dissipated. The damaging inflation, declining real wages, memories of the general strike in September 1977, and the spreading influence of the drug industry all played a part, as did popular perceptions of excessive corruption in the government. By mid-1978 the population had reached 24,906,000, while the migration from countryside to city proceeded steadily. A total of 15,566,000 Colombians lived in urban environments, reaching an unprecedented 62.5 percent.

The 1978 elections had suggested a potential shift in patterns of party control. Although traditional clientelism had been underlined by Turbay's successful quest for the presidency, it also showed a deterioration that constituted the historical trend. The Liberal margin had been uncommonly small; the Conservatives had won Bogotá in a presidential election. At the same time there was little evidence of a new or modernizing form of clientelism that might supplant the traditional version as a mechanism for exercising social and political controls by the hegemonic elite. As Francisco Leal Buitrago observed, biparty depoliticization was on the rise, the old partisan mystique was in decline, and generational loyalties and allegiances were being progressively shredded by the process of urbanization.[1]

The economic panorama held little promise for either a sharp upswing or an attack upon distributive distortions. High inflation and a shrinking growth rate had been inherited, while coffee prices were dropping from the postwar high reached in 1977. While international reserves in the first half of 1978 had risen to $2,113,000,000, the outgoing government had not adopted protective safeguards. Despite the heavy emphasis on control of the money supply in the latter stages of his government, López had been concentrating on the inflow of dollars from exports. Julio César Turbay Ayala could therefore anticipate the possibility of economic recession unless adjustments were adopted and implemented promptly. Unlike his predecessor, who had entered office with resources sufficient to reshape national priorities, President Turbay could only hope that the impending decline might be averted. His followers contended that the pragmatism that had marked Turbay's career was ideal for the situation; in contrast, critics argued that structural problems basic to the society were at the heart of everyday difficulties, and were beyond Turbay's grasp or capacity to reshape.

Policies of the Administration

While a lifelong politician deeply enmeshed in public affairs, Julio César Turbay Ayala was not the characteristic product of a socially and politically eminent family—as, for instance, López Michelsen and Gómez Hurtado. A descendant of Lebanese immigrants, he was born of a middle-class Bogotá family on 8 June 1916. He entered politics without a university degree, became a councilman at age twenty-two, and in 1943 began a ten-year stint in the Chamber of Deputies. In 1957 he became labor minister for the provisional government, and from 1958 to 1961 served as foreign minister to Lleras Camargo. From that juncture he moved to the forefront of the Liberal party, gravitating between the senate, where he was presiding officer on several occasions, and diplomatic assignments. He was chief delegate to the United Nations from 1967 to 1969, ambassador to Great Britain from 1970 to 1972, and ambassador to the United States from 1975 to 1976. His evolving alliance with López Michelsen, of course, was the means whereby he further solidified his organizational position while gaining López's acceptance of his own subsequent presidential candidacy. Given high marks as a political boss and a shrewd judge of conditions and opportunities, Turbay as a backroom politician compensated for his unexciting public personality.

Having reached Colombia's highest office, Turbay faced the challenge of exercising a form of leadership that had never been his forte. From the start he spoke of the necessity for expansion. With the private sector slow to invest, he moved the state into further financing of development. A countercyclical economic approach was adopted. By early 1979 Turbay had announced in preliminary form the government's so-called Plan de Integración Nacional (PIN). Although criticized for vagueness and a lack of clarity, it did attempt to specify four broad objectives: (a) economic decentralization and regional development; (b) stimulus to transportation and communications; (c) development of mines and energy; and (d) formulation of a new social plan. The definitive version was presented in late May of 1980. Based on studies by the Departamento Nacional de Planeación, the PIN explicitly operated on the assumption that, in the words of its architect Eduardo Wiesner Durán, Colombian development was "more a problem of policies and diagnoses than insufficient resources."[2]

As a plan to inject large sums of public money into the economy, the PIN represented a change from economic policy since 1975, which had seen a decline in government investment. For the 1979–82 period some $22 billion were to be provided, with one-third to come from external credit. Large sums were required for transportation and communications, energy and mining, and expanded social services. At the same time, it was further noted that the state could not cope with the magnitude of activities, and that responsibilities should therefore be transferred to the regions. Investment priorities, moreover, were not to include Colombia's four largest cities. Such notions of decentralization and regional development paralleled Turbay's political style and perspective. In practice they also facilitated his practice of seeking clientelistic support through the direct provision of goods and services—patronage—to those on whom he relied politically. The president implicitly planned on utilizing his network of linkages to local and regional caciques as the mechanism of implementation.

The PIN's avowed intention of increasing the growth rate of public investment to 19 percent annually was unprecedented. Foreign credits were to provide the fiscal linchpin. An estimated $6.8 billion was projected, thereby doubling Colombia's external foreign debt. In due course the government also entered Colombia's financial markets in the quest for needed investment capital. This in turn provoked new increases in interest; the inflation rate rose, and recession deepened. The industrial and financial sectors angrily opposed the PIN from its very inception, but ultimately suffered from its effects and saw their own role in economic development reduced. By the close of Turbay's term, the manufacturing sector had grown by an annual average of merely 1 percent, while agricultural growth was running slightly above 2 percent. Both figures essentially halved those experienced by Colombia during the preceding decade.

An important if underpublicized government objective was a reduction of inflation. For two years there was a determined effort to raise wages sufficient to outdistance inflation. By introducing the largest increases in fifteen years in January of 1980, the government found itself under attack for aggravating rather than improving the situation. Notwithstanding minimum wage increases, which ranged as high as 56.7 percent in rural areas, the benefits were modest. The official 1979 inflation rate hit 29 percent, the highest of the 1970s. With the arrival of the 1980s, Colombia was undeniably approaching a general recession, one that mirrored a slowing of economic growth after the pronounced growth during the 1970s—an average of 6 percent annually. The reasons were multiple, as Kline aptly explained: wages had not kept up with inflation; Colombian consumers preferred foreign goods, whether imported legally or clandestinely; the peso was artificially high in value, thereby discouraging Colombian exports; investments were being diverted from productive industry; protectionism in the industrial world was stifling; and Colombia remained in a condition of economic dependency.[3]

By the conclusion of his term, President Turbay could claim that many of the objectives in the Plan de Integración Nacional had been realized. Public construction, for one, had increased by 5.4 percent in 1979, by 14.9 percent in 1980, by 12.3 percent in 1981, and by 5.8 percent in 1981. At the same time, the recession produced the most unfavorable macroeconomic performance in a decade. In 1980 the growth rate was down to 4.2 percent. A year later it fell to 2.5 percent, and in 1982 the gross national product grew by only 1.4 percent, the lowest figure since World War II. At the same time this was complemented by the income from drugs, which produced a spectacular growth in the Colombian financial sector. The newer financial organizations progressively challenged, then in many cases moved ahead of industrialists and other groups. This gradually evolved into a wave of transactions that triggered further concentration of economic power.

The López administration had facilitated the process of concentration by removing a panoply of state controls. When this continued under Julio César Turbay Ayala, the relative absence of regulations seemed further to insure that financial power rested in only a few hands. As former Liberal finance minister and sometime presidential aspirant Hernando Agudelo Villa put it, the trend showed "that the country is one step away from the point where four or five people handle the main controls of the economy, with the inevitable consequences of an outrageous concentration of wealth, income, and personal power, destroying the democratic bases of the nation."[4] An overzealous view, perhaps, but a telling statement about the readjustment of economic power in Colombia.

Turbay eventually would leave to his successor a host of unresolved problems: inflation raged unchecked; the industrial sector was resistant to all efforts at resuscitation; decentralization had complicated rather than simplified the tasks of governance; and national budget deficits ranging from 3 to 3.5 percent of the gross domestic product had accumulated. For the World Bank, characteristically seeking a balanced perspective, the problems were serious:

> In the 1978–82 period the administration attempted to lay the basis for sustained future growth by increasing investment in infrastructure, particularly energy and transport. However, the downturn in the world economy also gave its policies a countercyclical economic twist. Although economic growth decelerated, the downturn was not nearly as severe as in most other Latin American countries. Inflation, nevertheless, remained stubbornly high. In addition, the slowdown in devaluation that commenced in the previous administration was not reversed; this policy, while helping to restrain inflation, also contributed to a growing balance of trade deficits and discouraged firms which could have competed internationally under a more realistic exchange rate.[5]

Within the context of Colombian public policy, the Turbay administration was unexceptional. His attempts to respond to inherited problems were in every sense consistent with prevailing centrist policy. They stood out as illustrative of the president's attempt to reincorporate clientelism into the emergent modernizing system through the devolution of authority to local and regional levels. Ultimately, however, Turbay's administration would be remembered less for socioeconomic policy than for its concerted campaign to established unchallenged systemic controls, whatever the cost in repression and the potential weakening of democratic values.

Social and Political Controls

Political violence had risen perceptibly toward the close of the López administration, constituting a growing threat to National Front leadership. For Turbay, traditional measures were predictable, meaning harsher action by the military and the police. He had inherited the state of siege declared by López Michelsen, and soon after assuming office was faced with the first anniversary of the disruptive 1977 general strike. On 6 September 1978 Turbay promulgated executive decree number 1923, the Estatuto de Seguridad Nacional.[6] As authorized by the state of siege, the National Security Statute called for draconian measures in the pursuit of subversive elements. According to Interior Minister German Zea, the government found itself "in the presence of a challenge which leaves no room for vacillation, and it will not falter under threats or protests from those who feel affected by this action which is demanded clamorously by national opinion."[7] Violence and disturbances of public order would all be punishable—in some cases up to thirty years imprisonment. There was little differentiation between killings and kidnappings, on the one hand, and street demonstrations or strikes on the other. With scattered exceptions, all those charged with crimes under the statute would be tried by military courts-martial. Thousands of "subversives" were to be arrested.

The president's decree had been developed in close consultation with General Luis Carlos Camacho Leyva, the tough-minded new minister of defense. Under his direction the military moved promptly to implement the statute. Within a month, for example, five radio stations had been fined for broadcasting information about labor demonstrations—"threats to public order." The pattern of repressive action was speedily established, and would continue under the sanction of the national security statute throughout the administration. Turbay rescinded it only in July of 1982, on the eve of his departure from office. But by this time the guerrilla problem had actually worsened; the FARC, ELN, and EPL had all renewed their attacks from the moment of Turbay's inauguration. The M-19 further complicated the situation, and proved a particular irritant to security forces.

While its initial members were drawn largely from radical elements of ANAPO, the M-19 was subsequently joined by dissident members of the FARC, moving to develop the first truly urban guerrilla front in Colombia. By early 1979 some 1000 arrests had been carried out as a part of the anti-M-19 campaign, with detainees including the internationally renowned sociologist Orlando Fals Borda and actor/director Carlos Duplat. By April 1979 arrests were proceeding on a daily basis, and the government spoke of a mass court-martial for at least 1500 suspects. In the meantime, military operations had grown in rural areas, and there were increasing references to the "Bordaberrización" of Colombia.[8] J. Emilio Valderrama, a prominent Conservative, declared firmly that "President Turbay, a recognized democrat, is now giving generals the powers that President Bordaberry did when he turned himself into a marionette of the military and then got ousted." And from Turbay's own party, the distinguished elder statesman Darío Echandía spoke of "an official military government, and the dictator is Camacho Leyva."[9]

The general himself, a confidante of Turbay, stated in November 1979 that since the introduction of the National Security Statute a total of 1633 had been arrested while 140 soldiers and 88 police had been killed fighting subversives. He also rejected charges that the government, in the process of its campaign, was also moving against peasant and Indian organizations in the rural areas. ANUC took the lead in denouncing military interference with its organization and its members. Official claims to have improved security were mocked on 27 February 1980 when the Movimiento 19 de Abril captured the Dominican Republic's embassy and held hostage the ambassadors of fourteen nations. The captors demanded the release of 311 political prisoners in exchange for the diplomats. Among those held by the guerrillas were the representatives to Colombia of Austria, Belgium, Brazil, Costa Rica, Mexico, and the United States, along with the papal nuncio and of course the Dominican host. The ordeal lasted sixty-one days, after which sixteen M-19 members and twelve hostages flew from Bogotá's El Dorado airport to Havana, where the prisoners were released. Colombia released no prisoners, although undisclosed amounts of money, provided by private sources, were carried away by the guerrillas.

The government continued to increase its antiguerrilla activities in the countryside, basically employing "search and destroy" tactics. At the same time Turbay spoke of the need for amnesty. Congressional discussions led to proposals in 1980 that were tantamount to surrender by the guerrillas. Turbay sought a less unrealistic formula, and in January 1981 put forward his own proposed legislation while expressing the desire that "the armed rebels join the democratic structure, parliament, and the public square."[10] After extensive bargaining between Turbay and congressional leaders, he signed amnesty into law on 23 March 1981. It was conditioned by a number of caveats, including the provision that the government would released imprisoned guerrillas only if comparable numbers came in from the field and surrendered their weapons. The offer was limited to a four-month period. Both the FARC and the M-19 repudiated the measure as unduly exclusionary, and only a few hundred guerrillas surrendered.[11]

For the armed forces, tough counterinsurgency measures continued unabated. A characteristic campaign was centered in Caqueta at the close of 1980 and the beginning of 1981, with heavy bombing followed up by a sweep of some 5000 troops. Several thousand inhabitants were driven from their homes in the process. Despite such efforts, however, rural violence continued unabated throughout the remainder of Turbay's term. In July of 1981 the FARC ambushed government troops, while the ELN conducted periodic attacks on small towns near the Venezuelan border. The M-19 had already launched an offensive in southern Nariño; termed by the government an "invasion" sponsored by Cuba, it led to a break of diplomatic relations with Cuba (which had been restored by the López government in 1975).

The armed forces, despite the toughening of government policy, was disappointed by the proposed amnesty and by similar signs of an official willingness to negotiate with the guerrillas. General Camacho saw all critics as potential subversives; in a November 1981 speech he declared that Colombian democracy was endangered by guerrillas, teachers of sedition, and leftist labor organizations. The nation, he said, "cannot continue looking at subversion as if it were a simple phenomenon between the government and bandits."[12] Shortly thereafter the deputy commander of the army attacked the Comité Permanente por la Defensa de los Derechos Humanos, Colombia's human rights organization, for sympathizing with the guerrillas and exaggerating alleged military atrocities.

Turbay, disappointed by his inability to curb the violence, reluctantly chose to move outside traditional policy lines, naming a special Peace Commission to be headed by Carlos Lleras Restrepo. The Commission was empowered to negotiate with the guerrillas and to incorporate representatives of the Church and the military. Early in 1982 the Commission presented a set of specific policy recommendations, accompanied by a call for direct dialogue with the guerrilla organizations. All sentences issued for political crimes were to be suspended. According to Lleras, there were indications that the M-19 might compromise on its demands for an immediate end to the state of siege and the national security decree. However, General Camacho and his colleagues were unconvinced.

When Lleras Restrepo delivered the report to the acting defense minister and the joint chiefs of staff, he was sharply rebuffed. He then repaired to a meeting with President Turbay, who sided with the military and rejected the work of the Commission. Lleras Restrepo and the entire Commission promptly resigned, issuing a blistering denunciation of the administration and its refusal to negotiate. Turbay issued another amnesty through 1982 Decree Law 474, which was no less complex and impractical than the earlier one. His final presidential action in these matters came with his announcement on 5 June 1982 that the state of siege would be lifted in fifteen days. Flatly declaring that the guerrillas had been defeated, the president stated that Colombia was no longer threatened by subversion. In actuality, the iron-fisted approach that dominated during this administration had not seriously reduced guerrilla activity, although the influence of the military had grown. At the same time the armed forces found themselves engaged increasingly in efforts to curb the rapidly expanding drug industry.

By the end of Turbay's period Colombia was exporting at least 70 percent of all marijuana reaching the United States, along with no less than 60 percent of cocaine. Methaqualone had also become a large "offshore" industry with the powder arriving from abroad, being processed into Quaalude pills, and fed to the world market. Some 80 percent of Quaaludes consumed in the United States came from Colombia. All of this led to estimates that easily $3 billion annual earnings were being realized. Despite cooperation between Colombian police and the U.S. Drug Enforcement Agency, the magnitude of the drug industry continued to expand. Occasional operational successes were announced, as in February of 1982 when a joint operation seized some 6.4 million pounds of marijuana. The Colombian authorities confiscated an estimated 4.7 million pounds, while U.S. personnel took 1.7 million, and nearly 500 persons were arrested.

Even so, inroads into drug production were modest. In the Guajira Peninsula alone, for instance, an estimated 125,000–175,000 acres were planted in marijuana, the weed-like plant growing to maturity in three or four months.[13] It was difficult at best to restrict such activities. In the meantime, the sums of money involved continued to rise, the drug barons were growing more powerful, and the tainting of the political system by bribery and criminality was progressively worsening. Notwithstanding a drug-control agreement with the United States and an attitude of cooperation that stood in sharp contrast to that of the López government, conditions deteriorated with the passing of time.

The Turbay administration left a legacy of repressive actions that bespoke its failures in exercising legitimate authority on behalf of its citizens. Social and political controls of unparalleled severity were undertaken, only to produce a further deterioration of conditions. War zones, arbitrary and institutionalized torture, and a military obsession to annihilate the guerrillas—most especially the M-19—had become the order of the day.[14] Enlarged rural areas were militarized in the process. As Leal wrote, a sense of political autonomy grew within the armed forces, and the formulation of antisubversive military ideology also served to weaken civil authority and the traditional parties.[15] As Julio César Turbay Ayala left office, the political establishment found itself more than ever incapable of maintaining its authority by means of clientelism and traditional controls. Certainly the repressive tactics had not proven effective. Gabriel Silva Lujan put it well:

> In conclusion, the government of Turbay Ayala was a bankrupt effort to carry to the extreme the repressive alternative in controlling dissent and socio-political nonconformity. This response to the political conflict by the State, which had been gestating under the National Front, flowed primordially into a greater radicalization of conflicting forces, into the polarization of social sectors in dispute, eroding the precarious consensual ideology. At the same time, the guerrilla struggle and deinstitutionalizing political action were seen as fully legitimate in popular circles.... In short, a crisis of restricted democracy marked the Turbay government.[16]

The Politics of the National Front

The Party Competition

The lineup of Conservative and Liberal factions remained unstable in the wake of the 1978 Turbay victory. Leaders on both sides were jostling one another in the effort to establish a power base for the next four years. The president-elect chose to maintain an alliance with the opposition, and the National Front lived on. Colombia's political elite intended a continued defense of its hegemonic role, and this was dramatized when

Turbay awarded his Conservative opponents five cabinet seats to seven for the Liberals. Both the *alvaristas* and the *ospino-pastranistas* received two posts, while one self-described independent Conservative received a post. Defense minister General Abraham Varon Valencia gave way to the previous commander of the armed forces, General Luis Carlos Camacho Leyva. The Liberal ministers were in most cases known followers of the president, although some had been viewed as relatively independent.

Prior to inauguration Turbay had called a special Liberal convention on 2 August in order to name a tripartite directorate that would succeed him. This was viewed as a swift move to prevent departing president López Michelsen from becoming the effective *jefe único* of the party, although he had denied any such intentions. It was followed by Liberal preparations for a presumably less ritualistic convention set in March of 1979. By that time Turbay's grip on the party machinery had badly slipped, reinvigorating Liberal progressives. Hernando Agudelo Villa bluntly condemned administration policies at a meeting on 23 February 1979, denouncing the security statute, military influence, and what he termed shapeless economic policies. Carlos Lleras Restrepo, while declining to attend such party meetings, was active in encouraging party dissidents. In his weekly *Nueva Frontera* he called for a Liberal reorganization that would encourage local participation and popular input for the formulation of decisions. He also worked to encourage the incorporation of non-Liberal leftists into the party.

When the Liberals met in convention, *turbayistas* managed to exclude followers of Carlos Lleras from the National Directorate. The latter remained vocal, however, and were among those Liberals protesting the signing in May of an accord between the two party directorates, which pledged cooperative support to the Turbay government. This reflection of continuing *frentista* intentions was further demonstrated by congressional passage of an electoral reform that institutionalized "parity" in the national electoral court. Its membership would include four apiece from the traditional parties, with a ninth selected from a minor party. The electoral machinery would also include two *registradores del estado civil* (civil registrars) for Bogotá and for all cities above 100,000 in population; they would of course be one Liberal and one Conservative.

Disaffected Liberals, many but not all of whom were *lleristas,* formalized their anti-Turbay status in May 1979 by creating the so-called Unión Liberal Popular. Although promptly denounced by the Liberal

Directorate, it prepared to launch further attacks on the party organization. It also took all possible advantage of scandals revolving about the influential *turbayista* from Tolima, Alberto Santofimio Botero. Already a vigorous pre-candidate for the Liberals, Santofimio denied all public charges and unofficially offered himself for 1982, contrary to tacit Liberal agreements. Yet this provided further fodder for party insurgents. As the Liberals began to focus on the forthcoming elections, President Turbay's efforts to maintain control over the party clashed with the dissident progressives. In November of 1979 three Liberal ex-presidents— Lleras Camargo, Lleras Restrepo, and López Michelsen—backed Agudelo Villa's proposal that March 1982 elections would serve as a primary. A postelection meeting in Bogotá would name as candidate anyone whose followers gained above 50 percent, or choose from those who received at least 20 percent. This was designed in effect to parallel the February 1978 elections based on the San Carlos consensus.

On 9 March 1980, Colombians had some 37,000 candidates from whom to choose 8617 municipal councillors and 406 members of the 22 departmental legislatures. The contest for the Liberals was seen as a test for the Union Liberal Popular (ULP). For the Conservatives, *ospino-pastranistas* were championing the cause of Belisario Betancur while hoping to marginalize Alvaro Gómez. Once again, low turnout testified to public disinterest in the maneuvering of the party elites. Of 13,772,836 registered voters, 4,192,079 (30.4 percent) voted for municipal officials, and 4,130,802 (29.99 percent) for departmental assemblymen. Within this restricted electorate, the Liberals showed their customary superiority over the Conservatives. They won in municipal races with 2,287,764 (54.6 percent) to 1,585,053 (37.8 percent); their departmental margin was but a shade smaller, at 2,244,677 (54.3 percent) to 1,591,609 (38.5 percent). While Liberal party regulars easily won against the dissidents, the low turnout had defied President Turbay's public call for a vote of confidence in his leadership. For the Conservatives, little was changed by the 1980 elections; Belisario Betancur remained the party's leading option for 1982, although by no means a unanimous choice.

Candidate Selection

The maneuvering next centered on the party conventions. For the Liberals, three pre-candidates stumped the nation in search of support: Alberto

Santofimio and fellow congressman Augusto Espinosa Valderrama, along with former Bogotá mayor and current ambassador to the United States, Virgilio Barco Vargas. Preparations had included a December 1980 meeting at which the three Liberal former presidents were named party directors and empowered to stipulate the rules for candidate selection. The process began to move forward in early 1981 under the active guidance of Carlos Lleras. In January a special Comisión Política Central (CPC) was named, which in turn convoked a series of regional fora to discuss the party program. On 4 April the directorate issued a so-called Liberal Preamble, edited by Alfonso López, to be discussed at the regional gatherings.

Behind the existence of the triumvirate of directors was the notion of both Lleras Camargo and Lleras Restrepo that López Michelsen would help to oversee the entire process but not participate as a would-be candidate himself. Lleras Camargo himself had a personal preference for Virgilio Barco Vargas, and in the spring launched that pre-candidacy in the pages of *El Tiempo*. This action provoked some criticism, while such other possible candidates as Alberto Santofimio and Augusto Espinosa Valderrama, the latter a candidate favored by many in Lleras Restrepo's camp, sought to further their own positions. Lleras Restrepo himself was of course strongly opposed to López. While all this was going on, President Turbay was seeking to exert his own authority on the nomination, as suggested by the resignation of his loyal interior minister German Zea Hernández in mid-May. At age seventy-six Zea Hernandez did not seem a likely finalist in the competition, but he was a shrewd political tactician who could be expected to look after the president's interests.

Although López's name barely appeared in polls ranking potential precandidates, his ambitions for a second term were becoming evident. In protest, Lleras Restrepo withdrew from the directorate in May of 1981, followed in August by Alberto Lleras Camargo. While both men declared their sympathy for Virgilio Barco, López began working behind the scenes in anticipation of a party convention set to open on 19 September in Medellín. He directed particular attention to *turbayista* caciques at the 14 August round of regional conventions, winning declarations of support from several key departments. Both *El Tiempo* and *El Espectador* charged that López had improperly used his position in the directorate to control the selection of delegates—so-called *manzanillos,* or political hacks. Lleras Camargo and Lleras Restrepo refused to attend the September meeting, and Virgilio Barco let it be known that he would not go forward as an anti-

López pre-candidate. The other two would-be aspirants, Alberto Santofimio and Augusto Espinosa, withdrew from the contest after an August meeting with López in Sincelejo, where an exchange of commitments included agreement that López would be the candidate with the other two serving as campaign coordinators.

The former president himself denied any improprieties during the preconvention period. In a public letter on 9 September 1981, he claimed that there had been nothing novel or unethical about his behavior as director:

> It would really stretch the imagination to describe as a "concealed candidate" someone whose name comes up from the provinces. This is opposed to "the candidate of the 'big press' and of the ex-presidents, who has been displayed in a window for more than a year as if he were the official candidate.[17]

Certainly the Sincelejo accord had assured the nomination of the former president. And so it was that Alfonso López Michelsen, once the establishment-gestated rebel who had mounted a challenge to the National Front from the outside, demonstrated his own mastery of the intricacies of Gaitán's so-called *país político*.

When the Liberals trekked to Medellín, López acknowledged his critics by devoting more than half his acceptance speech to a defense of his nomination. Denying that it was an exercise in "abominable clientelism," López told some 400 delegates that, "if not united [on all significant matters], at least we are reunited in seeing the need to keep Liberalism in government for the good of Colombia."[18] Yet there was little question that he had effectively manipulated the political system within the context traditional clientelistic practices. This was best illustrated by his success in further negotiations with Alberto Santofimio, the powerful Liberal boss in Tolima. *Latin American Weekly Report* put it superbly:

> Santofimio and his like in the other main regions of Colombia are what make the current system operate; they are the *caciques* who deliver the votes and hand out the political favours that percolate down from the central government in Bogotá. As long as there is lots of largesse to distribute, the system can continue to function....
> The very indifference of the vast majority of the population to what the government does, and how it operates the political system, may eventually contribute to its undoing; nobody would lift a finger to save *la clase política* if the tanks began to roll.[19]

There were still Liberals unwilling to accept the return of the former president, and a number began to focus on Luis Carlos Galán Sarmiento.

A young collaborator of Lleras Restrepo, Galán had formed his so-called Nuevo Liberalismo in 1979. An especially sharp critic of the Turbay government, Galán also attacked the López candidacy as an opportunistic and clientelistic move that symbolized the corruption of Colombia's hegemonic caste. With the encouragement of Carlos Lleras and other progressive Liberals, he had gradually developed a program that constituted a challenge to the political establishment. In June 1981 Galán had presented a twelve-point program that included, among other things: the transformation of congress and reform of its traditional domination by political elites; state intervention in large urban centers; defense of human rights; reorganization of the state in order to combat the influence of multinationals; restoration of Colombian cultural identity and true national values; defense of indigenous populations; and an encouragement of progressive unionism.[20] In October his own convention in Rionegro formalized Galán's candidacy.

With the Liberals thus at odds as the 1982 elections loomed ahead, the Conservatives managed to negotiate their own candidacy without undue internal wrangling. Belisario Betancur, given his strong 1978 showing against Turbay, was not seriously challenged. The *ospino-pastranistas* saw his candidacy as the best means of preventing Alvaro Gómez and his followers from capturing the party. Gómez himself was widely viewed as too rightist and partisan to reach the independent and Liberal voters necessary to compensate for the minority status of the Conservative party. When the national party convention met on 27 November 1981, it demonstrated a degree of unity in stark contrast to 1977, when the two competing factions had convened separate gatherings. Alvaro Gómez formally withdrew his own candidacy and sought to draw nearer to Betancur in the event that he might upset the Liberals.

Campaign and Elections

In the Liberal campaign for March 1982 congressional elections, López reverted to his early reformist days by advocating Liberal membership in the Socialist International while painting himself as a leftist. In a February speech, for instance, he was quite insistent:

> It is very clear: either the party becomes conservative or it becomes socialist. If you want it to become conservative you only have to vote for us to remain being an appendage of the Conservative party under the National Front. If you want it to be

socialist you only have to vote for those of us who align ourselves to social democracy and who put into practice leftist programs. You have the decision and I am certain that you will decide to vote for the official lists of the Liberal party in the month of May.[21]

López sought to paint Galán as a puppet of Carlos Lleras and, although himself sixty-eight years old, contended that a vote for Galán meant a vote for the older generation of party leadership. Reiterating his commitment to change and reform while avoiding allusions to his first presidency, López also relied on the weight of official machinery. A month before the congressional elections Nuevo Liberalismo raised an outcry about the financial and organizational support of Bogotá's pro-López mayor. Central to one angry exchange was the convening of a López campaign rally in a Bogotá neighborhood recently named for President Turbay's daughter Diana. With the candidate accompanied by the mayor and other members of the city council, it was but one illustration of the typically clientelist and machine-oriented tactics that were still *de rigeur* in Colombian politics.

Luis Carlos Galán, some thirty years younger than his opponent, called for a reorganization of Liberalism as a means of preparing to confront the problems of a modernizing nation. In rhetoric reminiscent of Agudelo Villa in 1978 as well as Lleras Restrepo, he urged "the reorganization of Liberalism to give direction to popular forces." This was the only means of combatting interests opposed to socioeconomic change and to greater participation in the governance of Colombia. This would honor the fact that for 150 years "Liberalism has been the primary creative energy in our society and in each stage of national history...the Liberal spirit was decisive for Colombian progress."[22]

As the 14 March elections neared, Nuevo Liberalismo set its goal at a vote total at 500,000; presumably support at or above three-quarters of a million might pressure López to withdraw. Galán insisted that there was no way he would withdraw from the subsequent presidential race. His votes were nontransferable; "they belong to independent citizens who have a free conscience and cannot be herded around like a flock of sheep."[23] In turn, the former president warned that Liberal divisions could lose the race to the Conservatives. He promised to meet after the first round of elections to discuss party structures and the possibility of reform. He also indicated a target of 2 million votes as his objective.

The week before elections was marked by greater violence than usual, and the military was out in force. Even so, buses were burned in Bogotá,

Medellín, Cali, and Barranquilla in the days before the vote, and on 10 March a car bomb exploded on the street outside the presidential palace. Election day itself was relatively calm, and turnout was up somewhat from the low percentage in 1978 congressional elections. The Liberal margin over the Conservatives was, as usual, a healthy one; with 3,140,868 votes to 2,248,602, the Liberals polled 56.3 percent to 40.3 percent for the Conservatives. Luis Carlos Galán exceeded his minimal target by winning 600,000 votes as his lists polled 12 percent. This compared with 44 percent for López's lists. After application of proportional representation, this ultimately produced *lopista* control of 47 percent of the seats in the chamber, Nuevo Liberalismo 9 percent, and the Conservatives 42 percent.[24] By themselves, *lopistas* were less than 200,000 above the Conservative totals, demonstrating the electoral uncertainty as Colombia moved toward the presidential contest.

This left Galán's position for the runoff as a major question mark. He had achieved significant victories only in Cundinamarca and in his native Santander. The charge by traditional Liberals that he represented an urban elite of the middle and upper-middle class was not entirely empty. Yet there was certainly a constituency that Galán was reaching.

His earlier statements rendered it virtually impossible to withdraw unless there was a bargain whereby López Michelsen would also step aside. While the latter had agreed to meet for discussion of the Liberal program, he was clearly not about to relinquish his candidacy at any price. The divisiveness that had so poisoned the atmospherics of the Liberal primary campaign rendered an accord virtually impossible. The result was Luis Carlos Galán's decision to remain in the race, risking the possibility that like Jorge Gaitán in 1946, he might become the spoiler to have cost the Liberals national power. Alfonso López sought to fortify his own claims to reformism, redistributive policies, and an intellectual commitment to social democracy. Although contradicting much of his first-term record, this might yet have proven effective against a traditional Conservative, such as Alvaro Gómez. Against a Betancur candidacy, however, it was quite another matter.

As in 1978, Betancur developed his Movimiento Nacional as extending beyond the Conservative party alone, "attaching my political survival to the national flag, as a representative of the National Movement, with the conviction that the problems of my people are neither Conservative nor Liberal."[25] Endorsed by the daughters of Gustavo Rojas Pinilla and Jorge Eliécer Gaitán, as well as Christian Democrats and other small centrist groupings, Betancur also enjoyed a more effectively united Conservative party organization than in 1978. His financial resources were also more ample this time around. Betancur's campaign strategy accurately took into account changing demographics. In the rural areas he played to traditional Conservative allegiances where appropriate; in the urban areas, where party identification was steadily weakening, he minimized partisan rhetoric and stressed his personal style of populism. Selected policy issues that received emphasis were low-cost housing without down payments, university education by correspondence, and a promise to curb both inflation and unemployment. He spoke of easing credit, providing tax incentives for new companies, and direct credits for business. He was also a sharp critic of "the clientelistic system of governing." Betancur offered "to maintain myself irreparably at the head of a campaign of purification…. I understand that to obtain that moral tone it is necessary to destroy the existing political chieftainships. I can do it because I have no connections to them, because I owe them nothing."[26]

Alfonso López Michelsen attempted to trump Betancur's populism with competing claims of his own. He reiterated his social democratic orientation and, in a calculated disagreement with President Turbay, called for reincorporation of the guerrillas into everyday life and society. Where Betancur said relatively little on the issue, López underlined his determination to resolve the issue by means other than force and coercion. López spoke of the need to alter provisions of national government for, he conceded, the two post-1974 administrations had in effect prolonged the National Front. He believed that Article 120 needed to be changed, that there be a legislated normalization of relations between the government and opposition parties. López also called for a "federalization" of Colombia, with greater authority extended to regional and municipal governments.

In the final analysis, the former president chose to rest his bid for reelection on the tradition of the Liberal electoral majority. Efforts to paint Betancur as a rightist—sometimes bracketed with Ronald Reagan and Margaret Thatcher—had created few sparks. Thus, with the slogan of "La Paz es Liberal"—Peace is Liberal—López rested his hopes on historic Liberal allegiances, and on the anticipated intervention of the government in his behalf. A final campaign peroration reiterated his electoral call for support: "I invite all Colombians, but especially my fellow Liberal party members, that together we may participate in an act of faith in Colombia."[27] His appeal to Liberals, however, was muted by the firm opposition of Luis Galán, whose own campaign reiterated earlier pronouncements. His television appearances reached largely the same electoral clientele with which he was already in contact. While tours of the interior spread his image more broadly, it still left Galán without an extensive penetration of the electorate. Meantime the leftist candidate, Gerardo Molina, conducted a competent campaign within the severe limitations on his organizational and financial resources.[28]

On 30 March 1982 the presidential elections took place. Turnout was 49.2 percent as 6,759,351 of an electorate of 13,734,093 cast ballots.[29] This was an increase of almost 10 percent over congressional elections, repeating the 1978 pattern. Participation also exceeded that of the 1978 presidential election by nearly 10 percent, although more than 8 percent lower than the 1974 presidential totals. On the Liberal side, Alfonso López received 2,778,214 votes, for 41.1 percent of the total; Luis Carlos Galán won 730,162, or 10.9 percent. Belisario Betancur emerged as the victor with 3,168,592 votes at 46.8 percent. For the Conservatives, it was their first presidential victory in a competitive contest since 1946—and, like 1946, had been achieved when the Liberals were so split as to divide their votes between two candidates. Alfonso López Michelsen was swift to blame his loss on Luis Galán, although the backers of the latter claimed that their voters would have preferred Betancur to López. Either way, there was little shortage of explanatory theories in the wake of the vote.

Certainly the reduced turnout along the Caribbean coast, where Turbay had traditionally been strong, was damaging to López. His margin of roughly 100,000 was insufficient to balance Betancur votes elsewhere. In Bogotá, where Galán had outpolled López, Betancur consequently won by a healthy margin. Some analysts read the results as suggesting a party realignment, while others argued that the Betancur victory signified the decline of electoral clientelism in the face of a populist candidate who reached across partisan boundaries. It was also possible to argue that the perception of a failed López presidency from 1974 to 1978, combined with criticism of the Turbay performance, virtually assured the decline of the Liberals. Extending interpretations further, there were striking indications of electoral shifts between the March and May voting.

Hartlyn singled out three in particular. For one, the vote for López along the Atlantic coast, where the purchase of votes and regional clientelism were historically deeply entrenched, fell by some 230,000 votes; Betancur rose by almost 60,000. Second, although López's Bogotá vote increased by 100,000, that of Betancur grew by more than 200,000. And finally, in Betancur's own state of Antioquia, he won 170,000 more than the March total for the Conservatives.[30] There were also some indications of broader trends developing over time. Mario Latorre elaborated on several of these, including marked shifts in the character of solid, hard-core Liberal loyalties.[31] In general, there was no escaping the obvious if basic fact that the Galán candidacy had been a decisive element.

Beyond this, however, Alfonso López had been forced to fight two terms of increasing popular dissatisfaction over Liberal rule, four years of which had been his responsibility. The economic recession and state of civil violence and societal agitation, the weakening of party loyalties, and important demographic changes were all relevant factors. Gary Hoskin reported that public opinion data showed that in Bogotá, only 64 percent of respondents identified with the two traditional parties in 1978, compared with 73 percent in 1974 and 80 percent in 1970.[32] Beyond all such analyses, many of which focused on reasons for the presumed failure of López, was the fact of Belisario Betancur's success. His perceptions had nearly carried him to the presidency in 1978 and, four years later, these solidified his electoral appeal as a populist in style who sought a national rather than partisan electoral victory. As he moved into office, Colombia seemed increasingly susceptible to a legitimacy crisis that would endanger the bureaucratic centralist state of the enduring National Front pattern. If the president-elect was an uncommon figure who contradicted usual patterns of national leadership, this scarcely diminished the magnitude of problems he confronted upon his August 1982 inauguration.

Notes

1. This theme is expressed at length in a number of his writings, notably including Francisco Leal Buitrago, *Estado y política en Colombia* (Bogotá: Siglo Veintiuno Editores, 1984).
2. For the text see República de Colombia, Dirección Nacional de Planificación, *Plan de integración nacional, 1979–1982* (Bogotá: DNP, 1980). The views of its architect, Eduardo Wiesner Duran, appear in his *Devaluación y mecanismo de ajuste en Colombia* (Mexico City: Centros de Estudios Monetarios Latinoamericanos, 1980). A succinct overview of Turbay's economic policies appears in Edgar Reveiz and María José Pérez, "Colombia: Moderate Economic Growth, Political Stability, and Social Welfare," in Jonathan Hartlyn and Samuel A. Morley, eds., *Latin American Political Economy: Financial Crisis and Political Change* (Boulder: Westview Press, 1986), 279–81.
3. Harvey F. Kline, *Colombia: Portrait of Unity and Diversity* (Boulder: Westview Press, 1983), 117–18.

4. *The Financial Times* (19 February 1982).
5. The World Bank, *Economic Development and Policy under Changing Conditions* (Washington: The World Bank, 1984), 50.
6. For the text of the so-called Estatuto de Seguridad, see Ministerio de Defensa Nacional, *Compilación de disposiciónes legales vigentes,* Tomo XVII (Bogotá: Imprenta de las Fuerzas Militares, 1978), 31 ff.
7. *Miami Herald* (16 September 1978).
8. This referred to the process in Uruguay wherein the military received ever-increasing controls from President Bordaberry, ultimately resulting in outright military rule.
9. *New York Times* (14 November 1979).
10. "Colombia," *Latin American Andean Report* (23 January 1981).
11. Hopes for the amnesty were dimmed by the news that M-19 guerrillas had killed Chester Allen Bitterman of the Summer Institute of Linguistics (SIL) several weeks after the kidnapping of this member of the controversial Wycliffe Bible Translators program.
12. *Miami Herald* (3 November 1981). Increasing attacks and violence during the later Turbay years were the handiwork of local death squads such as Muerte al Secuestadores (Death to Kidnappers, MAS), which was formed by Medellín drug dealers and encouraged by the military. The deterioration of human rights, notwithstanding the wave of indiscriminate detentions and military trials, was accepted by much of the business community, especially in light of the dangers of kidnapping that had become manifest in the late 1970s.
13. *Miami Herald* (14 October 1981).
14. "Colombia," *Latin American Weekly Report* (15 January 1982).
15. Leal, *Estado y política,* 262–75.
16. Ricardo Santamaría S. and Gabriel Silva Lujan, *Proceso político en Colombia: Del Frente Nacional a la apertura democrática* (Bogotá: Fondo Editorial CEREC, 1984), 56.
17. *Miami Herald* (24 September 1981).
18. Ibid.
19. "Colombia," *Latin American Weekly Report* (30 October 1981).
20. Luis Carlos Galán, *Nueva Colombia* (Bogotá: Coeditores Ltda., 1982), 32.
21. *El Espectador* (14 February 1982).
22. Galán, *Nueva Colombia,* 32–33.
23. *Miami Herald* (18 March 1982).
24. Gabriel Silva Lujan, "Factores de incertidumbre en la elección presidencial de 1982," *Estrategía* (March 1982). Also see Silva's subsequent "Las elecciónes parlamentarias por dentro," *Estrategía* (April 1982).
25. Belisario Betancur, *Si, se puede!* (Bogotá: Tercer Mundo, 1982), 61.
26. Ibid., 61–62.
27. *El Tiempo* (16 April 1982).
28. Gerardo Molina, an eminent intellectual and educator, had participated in politics from López Pumarejo's Revolución en March forward, including his 1982 presidential candidacy. Among his many works are the three-volume *Las ideas liberales en Colombia,* 10th ed. (Bogotá: Tercer Mundo Editores, 1990).
29. Extended analyses by a leading public opinion expert are found in works by Carlos Lemoine, such as his *Como conseguir el voto de los colombianos* (Bogotá: Oveja Negra, 1986).
30. Jonathan Hartlyn, "Colombia: Old Problems, New Opposition," *Current History* (February 1983): 62–65, 83.

31. See Mario Latorre, *Hechos y crítica política* (Bogotá: Universidad Nacional de Colombia, 1986).
32. Gary Hoskin, "Belief Systems of Colombian Political Party Activists," *Journal of Interamerican Studies and World Affairs* 21, no. 4 (November 1979): 481–504.

III

Modernization and Restructuring

10

"Apertura" and the Reformist Impulse: Betancur (1982–86)

The Policies of Governance

The National Environment

Belisario Betancur was the first Conservative to win power by competitive means in more than three decades. His government was also faced with a congressional majority in opposition hands. The optimistic view anticipated a new party emerging from the Movimiento Nacional, one that might move away from traditional clientelism. However, while the new president was not cut from the customary cloth, his electoral campaign had offered few indications that a truly different approach might be undertaken. What was scarcely open to debate, by 1982, was the deterioration of political civility and the decline of the economy.

With the rate of population growth remaining at the 2 percent level, there were an estimated 26,965,000 Colombians when Betancur took the oath of office. The level of urbanization had also continued to rise, having reached 65.4 percent of the population. Unemployment had increased during the four previous years. The World Bank, studying seven Colombian cities, found that the total had climbed from 8.2 percent in September 1982 to 9.3 percent in September 1982. Colombia's highest urban jobless rate continued to be found in Medellín, which was 15 percent; for Bogotá the figure was 6.8 percent. The national total in 1981 was some 7 percent, but a year later it stood at 12.5 percent. Inflation under Turbay had jumped to 25 percent annually in 1979, and had stubbornly resisted efforts to reduce it. By 1982 the real GDP growth rate was barely 1.4 percent, while the fiscal deficit had widened to 3.4 percent of GDP.

The intention of the Turbay government to prepare for lasting growth through investment in infrastructure—especially in transportation and communications—had been frustrated, and the downturn in the world economy produced a countercyclical economic turn. Redistributive measures and social programs had been pushed aside, even before the end of the coffee bonanza and the decline in growth from the 1978 high of 8.9 percent to a mere 1.4 percent. The eventual recourse to external borrowing had resulted in a debt of $8 billion which, if modest by continental standards, was high for Colombia. Agricultural productivity had not improved, while the stagnation of industrial expansion begun under López Michelsen had turned to a virtual recession. By 1982 overall industrial production was in decline, hampered by the monetary policies, which meant tight credit and high interest rates.

As detailed in chapter 9, the Turbay government had been penalized by the unpreparedness and incapacity of the López administration to respond constructively to the unparalleled world market prices for coffee during that period. The impact of the drug-fueled underground economy had also been unanticipated. By 1982 it was estimated at anywhere from $2 to $4 billion annually. Nevertheless, the four years under Turbay had marked the further weakening of the economy, leaving for Belisario Betancur both a recession and a critical fiscal deficit. Thus, he entered office challenged by perhaps Colombia's most severe economic problems since World War II. At the same time, with guerrilla violence still rising and the repressive efforts of the military having proven counterproductive, there was also a legitimacy crisis of major proportions. As Luis Alberto Restrepo wrote, "The logic of the National Front exhausted itself with Turbay Ayala," and Betancur, as well as his own successor, was "obliged to deal with the grave deterioration of the regime in a serious manner."[1]

Policies of the Administration

Belisario Betancur Cuartas went to his inauguration in a business suit rather than the customary cutaway, and after the ceremonies opened the doors of the palace to greet the people. This break with tradition demonstrated the informality and the persona that characterized the new chief executive. Charming and unpretentious, he was unapologetic for his humble origins. Of his twenty-one sisters and brothers, only five reached adulthood, the others dying of what he often called "a disease named underdevelopment." From his birthplace of Amaga, a coal mining town in Antioquia, he had studied law and economics at Medellín's Universidad Pontificia Bolivariana, and in 1946 at the age of twenty-three he had been elected deputy as a follower of Maríano Ospina Pérez. He progressed steadily through Conservative ranks, although always something of a maverick.

Jailed several times for opposition to the Rojas dictatorship, he supported the National Front from the beginning and served subsequently as deputy, senator, minister, and ambassador to Spain. Betancur had bid for the presidency in 1962, 1970, and 1978, during which his populist style had been developed and polished. Having failed to gain officialist Conservative backing in 1970, he ran eight years later with the backing of the hierarchy and of Pastrana Borrero, winning many cities in his hard fought challenge to Turbay and the majority party. His 1982 defeat of López Michelsen had brought him to power on a wave of popular approval. Moreover, while his campaign had included promises of reforms— most particularly an ambitious housing program—they were sufficiently vague to leave Betancur considerable flexibility as he was sworn in.[2]

Although he was soon to enunciate his quest for a reformist "opening" or *apertura*, Betancur had given little indication of his plans to negotiate with Colombia's guerrillas. Indeed, it had been Alfonso López Michelsen who proclaimed his dedication to "peace" during the campaign, and his appeal seemed not to have been an electoral plus. At the inauguration on 7 August 1982, the new president promised internal peace, a nonaligned foreign policy, and major reforms in housing, including a campaign promise of housing without down payment. The intended sense of his presidency was a renewal of direct communications with the people:

> There is a consensus to return to the genuine meaning of democracy.... That was the criterion that oriented my electoral promises and permitted me to formulate a concrete policy proposal: to ennoble habits, correct justice, attenuate the inequalities that threaten to dissolve the nation, and to stand up to the terrible conflict between those with everything and those with nothing.[3]

Having once assumed office, Betancur also sought to remedy economic problems, and immediate priority was directed toward control and regulation of the financial sector. Nearly a decade of freely moving interest rates and generalized instability had led to major scandals in the financial world. The so-called *financieras* had grown exponentially during the preceding decade, flourishing in conjunction with Colombia's "parallel economy" and benefitting from the protective sympathy of banking authorities under both the López and Turbay governments.

The *financieras* constituted an effective linkage with the subterranean economy for the Colombian business establishment. Easily the largest was Grancolombiana de Promocíones (PRONTA), which had been racked by irregularities of its investment fund. This was followed shortly after installation of the new government by a major scandal in a smaller financial conglomerate, the Grupo Colombia. The Financiera Furatena, one of its virtual subsidiaries, was intervened by the bank superintendent early in July. The crisis soon spread to Furatena's bank, the Banco Nacional. Withdrawals by panicking small investors forced its liquidation in September. Meanwhile, similar actions forced the government to intervene the Grupo Santa Fe. The Banco del Estado, Colombia's fourth largest, was nationalized while the rapidly expanding but shaky Banco Comercial Antioqueno was forced to change management.

Dealing with these matters required crisis management on the part of President Betancur and his advisors, rather than long-range economic planning. Efforts to attack more basic problems were described in a September 1982 television address by the president, in which he described anticipated steps designed to turn around the economy: spending cuts, financial reforms, austerity for imports and export incentives. Orthodoxy suggested the desirability of tight policy constraints, notwithstanding popular pressures for expansionist initiatives. Almost from the outset, it was evident that the government would be squeezed between efforts to brake the wage-price spiral and at the same time to spur economic recovery. Speaking after his first 100 days in office, Betancur lamented the difficulty in realizing his intended social reforms.

Closest to his heart was the promised program of low-cost housing, which he had reiterated in general terms during the campaign. María Eugenia Rojas de Moreno, an electoral supporter, was appointed to head an intended bureau in charge of the initiative, although Betancur noted that adequate funds were not immediately at hand. The same was true of other proposed reforms, leaving the president with the classic problem of resources inadequate for the realization of electoral promises. The official development plan, labelled "Cambio con Equidad," was forced to blend new ideas with existing programs, spiced by a few novelties such as a guaranteed university education by correspondence courses. Housing construction retained its high priority, and there was a tacit repetition of the old Pastrana strategy of stimulating the economy through reliance on building as a leading sector.

The balance of payments crisis grew rapidly during the early months of the government. The trade deficit in the first two months of 1983 reached some $200 million, while the previous twelve months had totalled $572 million. Foreign reserves, which were $5.6 billion in January of 1982, were down to $3.6 billion by July 1983.[4] Government officials recognized the necessity of adjusting the balance of payments in order to achieve domestic expansion of the economy. At the close of 1982 Betancur had announced a fifty-day economic emergency, accompanied by measures to curb the excesses of the financial system and control the growth of the money supply. While these measures were retained, the psychological value was minimized in February 1983 when the Supreme Court declared the bulk of the decrees unconstitutional.[5]

By this time Belisario Betancur was already deeply enmeshed in his quest for a negotiated end to domestic violence (see *Social and Political Controls* below), and his attention to economic issues was largely a matter of responding to immediate problems. Concerted measures to make possible broad, overarching long-range objectives were more the exception than the rule. It was not until 1984, midway in his term, that Betancur and his economic policymakers attempted to mount a coordinated attack on the most nagging issues. The balance of payments problem had continued to deteriorate; a 1983 deficit of $1.9 billion brought the reserves to a mere $1.6 million by October 1984—barely enough for three months of imports. The public sector deficit, 0.5 percent of the 1979 GDP, had risen above 8 percent. In 1984 the foreign debt stood at $10.6 billion, and the debt service had more than doubled in two years, to $2.005 billion—42.7 percent of exports. As Kline wrote, Colombia was in a deep recession and, although previous governments and international conditions both shared the blame, it was also true that the Betancur government was at least a year late in responding.[6]

Early in 1984 Colombia adopted an accelerated rate of minidevaluations, set at some 28 percent—a rate higher than inflation—which favored exports rather than imports. As Reveiz and Pérez put it, "Management of the crawling peg exchange rate, essential to the country's economic and political stability since 1967,...again became the key tool of economic policy."[7] Income tax reform was adopted, while a government job freeze and budget cuts in official agencies sought to encourage savings and austerity. At the same time, Colombia sought foreign loans to help fund the *Cambio con Equidad.* By the end of the year the government's IMF-style austerity was being applied more rigidly, and in early 1985 the World Bank gave approval for added international funding. A subsequent "enhanced surveillance" accord with the IMF further reassured foreign commercial bank creditors. Betancur also signed an agreement with the US Overseas Private Investment Corporation (OPIC) to enhance investment security.

As the administration drew toward its close, Belisario Betancur remained more engaged personally with political reforms, the quest for *apertura,* and negotiations with the guerrillas. The economic outlook had improved modestly, largely the result of the succession of austerity and stabilization measures. The somewhat belated implementation of an orthodox economic adjustment program in the latter months of 1984 had gradually strengthened Colombia's creditworthiness internationally. When this was followed by renewed financial assistance through the IMF, the subsequent increase in foreign investment—especially the huge Cerrejón coal project—further stimulated the economy. By the time of the May 1986 elections, inflation was down somewhat. In contrast, however, the government deficit was growing at a record rate, while the official unemployment rate had risen to 14 percent. All of this represented an overall stabilization of the economy, but one in which redistributive inequities and social programs changed little.

While much of Betancur's domestic agenda concerned issues of security and peace, there was unanticipated attention devoted to foreign affairs. This contrasted with his predecessor's inclinations, and had not been suggested by Betancur's campaign. It was therefore surprising when he announced in his inaugural address that Colombia would join the organization of nonaligned states. Despite public criticisms from both his own party and from such eminences as Carlos Lleras Restrepo, Betancur and his foreign minister, Rodrigo Lloreda Caicedo, did indeed bring about Colombia's membership in 1983.

The president also called for greater independence in regional affairs, at the same time reversing the strong support for Reaganite policy so firmly embraced by Julio César Turbay Ayala. The crisis of the Malvinas/Falklands led Betancur to urge an immediate regional summit as a means of preserving the inter-American system. This reflected his belief that Colombian and regional independence of Washington's influence was crucial—the more so given his disapproval of the hard-line positions emanating from the White House. This led to his unprecedentedly tough talk during Ronald Reagan's state visit to Bogotá in December 1982. He complained publicly that Colombia was treated by the United States with "olympic disdain," and was determined not to be a satellite of any super-power, including the United States.[8]

A month later Lloreda Caicedo attended the conference on the Pana-manian island of Contadora, which would initiate the so-called Contadora Group. Constituted by Colombia, Venezuela, Panama, and Mexico, it contemplated regional cooperation in seeking a peaceful solution to Cen-tral American strife. The basic rationale was expressed on countless oc-casions, including Betancur's October 1983 address before the United Nations. Again attacking the superpowers' pursuit of their own special interests, he contended that in Central America, "violence,...under-development, and injustice are all symptoms of a crisis in which coexist-ence and self-determination have been forgotten and which sees the superpowers shamelessly interfering in lands where peasants leave their sowing to take up alien arms and to dig their own graves."[9]

For the remainder of his term Belisario Betancur was the single most active leader in the group. He succeeded in establishing a personal pres-ence acceptable to Central American leaders of the warring camps, as in the case of Salvadoran revolutionary leaders and President José Napoleón Duarte. As the peace efforts continued through the remainder of his term and beyond, Betancur was taxed increasingly by domestic critics who argued that domestic affairs were more important, along with the good-will of the United States. In his determined independence, however, the president proceeded with the Contadora process while also altering ear-lier Colombian policy toward both Cuba and Nicaragua.

With Fidel Castro serving as president of the Non-Aligned Movement when Betancur took office, a possible improvement of relations seemed timely. While formal normalization did not take place, the sharp hostility of the Turbay administration was ended. Betancur was also mindful that both alleged and real ties between Cuban and Colombian guerrilla forces comprised a linkage that could affect his drive for pacification. By a quiet if implicit courting of Cuba, the concrete support of the latter for domestic rebels and insurgents might at the least be minimized. Despite periodic claims that there were significant ties with Cuba—a belief held by many Colombian military officers—the improvement of relations continued throughout the life of the administration. The case of Nicaragua was similar although not identical.

A decisive factor was the shifting character of exchanges between Managua and Bogotá over claims to San Andrés and Providencia, islands off Nicaragua's Caribbean coast that had long been regarded and treated as Colombian territory. Except for one flurry of charges in 1985 that the Sandinistas were tied to Colombian drug traffickers, public exchanges were largely conciliatory in character. Betancur recognized the need for healthy ties with Nicaragua if Contadora initiatives were not to be doomed from the start. It was consistent with such factors that Colombia also supported Nicaragua's candidacy for a seat on the Security Council of the United Nations. Even when Betancur later felt the need to close somewhat the gap with the United States, treatment of Nicaragua was largely untouched. At the August 1986 transfer of power from Betancur to Virgilio Barco, one of the foreign guests to be received cordially—and with great curiosity from the Colombian media—was Daniel Ortega.

President Betancur also undertook an active role more generally in hemispheric affairs, including discussions of the debt question. He hosted a meeting of Latin American leaders in May 1983; a year later he cosigned a letter to the heads of industrial nations in conjunction with the Brazilian, Argentine, and Mexican chiefs of state. Colombia was also vocal in the long succession of debt-related economic conferences that convened. When Colombia's own debt situation began to deteriorate, Betancur became even more energetic in discussions of the question, although showing more sensitivity to domestic economic constraints. The unavoidable adoption of austerity programs, plus discussions with the IMF, suggested the limits on those earlier initiatives. As in some other areas, the Betancur style and presence was sometimes greater than the actual substantive accomplishments. By the close of his term, ambitious foreign policy undertakings seemed to have combined nationalistic rhetoric with either unrealistic or failed objectives.

In the meantime, there were also constant debates over his domestic campaign of pacification. This was unquestionably the central question of his entire administration, and one with potentially historic proportions for Colombia and for the system of the National Front. It also involved initiatives and a personal commitment that were not readily evident before August 1982. In the exercise of power and the effort to resuscitate declining systemic legitimacy, he would be fighting simultaneously on several fronts: pacification and the guerrillas, drug trafficking, and generalized crime. All were encompassed by the broad rubric of a political opening—his vaunted *apertura*.[10]

Social and Political Controls

The rise in systemic repression and official violence under President Turbay had epitomized the orthodoxy of Colombian political traditionalists. It was a logical extension of the reasoning that had evolved during the years of the National Front. Only when rising violence failed abjectly to break the back of guerrilla activism did that government, as already described, turned toward a half-hearted amnesty with little chance of acceptability to the insurgents. The amnesty legislation signed on 23 March 1981 had elicited from Betancur only a promise to continue the pursuit of negotiation. When he took office, however, Betancur faced a new configuration of conditions: violence was on the rise, the legitimacy crisis was increasingly clear to the national elites, and he came to office on a wave of goodwill.

As he began to formulate specific plans, Betancur gradually evolved a four-pronged strategy, as Chernik noted: unconditional amnesty for guerrillas; a plan of national rehabilitation; formal cease-fire agreements; and constitutional reforms to open the system.[11] The first major official action—something of a stopgap measure to clarify general intentions while buying time—was the naming of a new forty-member Peace Commission in late October 1982. This was linked with Law 35, signed by Betancur on 20 November, which softened somewhat the previous amnesty. It specified that guerrillas already in jail for pardoned crimes would be released; all those who had fought the government qualified for pardons unless undue cruelty or noncombat-related killings had been involved. Adoption of the measures was a significant victory for the government, especially given the necessity of winning approval from the military. General Fernando Landazábal, as minister of defense, had agreed to the measure while emphasizing that the armed forces had demonstrated their ability to combat subversion.

At the same time, he shared the fear of other officers that greater legitimacy for the guerrillas might in the long run be damaging. In accepting the legislation, he contended,

The amnesty offer must not, and cannot be confused with the belief that the Armed Forces lack the capacity to conquer subversion.... The Armed Forces obey and support with enthusiasm the amnesty,...feeling pride for having complied and promise to continue watching over the peace dispassionately and quietly.[12]

If the military was somewhat grudging in its response, that of the guerrillas was also mixed. Inured to government promises, there was suspicion over the lack of clear signals from the incoming administration. At the same time, the new amnesty law helped to promote the notion that Betancur's peace strategy might indeed be legitimate. Among the results were a series of meetings between guerrilla and government representatives, something virtually unheard of in earlier years.

Indeed, by November 1983 there had been more than a dozen meetings, while the administration was moving forward in guerrilla-affected areas with projects described as economic rehabilitation. Among the most dramatic was the conference between Belisario Betancur and the two senior M-19 leaders, Ivan Marino Ospina and Alvaro Fayad. Conducted in Madrid, the exchange facilitated an exchange of proposals between the contending groups. Back home, the FARC was engaged in similar communications with the government. However, such efforts were soon overshadowed by new outbursts of violence. There was particular notoriety over the so-called Magdalena Medio, a populated region in which fighting continued to erupt with uncommon ferocity. Investigations merely exacerbated tempers, with military leaders defending their activities and denying any use of excessive force.

In defending military actions, General Landazábal bluntly insisted that the basic problem was subversion supported by an anonymous "international conspiracy," while further stating his objections to a cease-fire. It was the duty and responsibility of the armed forces, he contended, to defend Colombian institutions by means of counterviolence. The theme of foreign intervention was repeated by General Gustavo Matamoros, second in military seniority, when he declared unequivocally that Cuba was collaborating with the guerrillas in Colombia and elsewhere. Advocates of amnesty and negotiation reacted angrily, although Betancur remained quiet. On 22 November, tensions mounted with the kidnapping of the president's brother Jaime by the pro-Castro ELN.

All political parties, including the Communists, denounced the action, while Fidel Castro publicly called for Betancur's release. ELN demands included both economic and political objectives, but were slowly if undramatically turned aside by the government. In December Jaime Betancur was released without any of the demands having been met, while the president pushed ahead with his own efforts at pacification. He also moved to reassert his control over the armed forces, which resented the Peace Commission. Early in January of 1984 the minister of defense had told Betancur of military displeasure with the handling of public order, discussions with the guerrillas, and foreign policy toward Nicaragua. Betancur indicated his intention of seeking talks with guerrilla organizations while insisting that the military was a nondeliberative body.

On 18 January the dispute came to a head when the president retired Landazábal as defense minister, along with both the army and air force commanders and the head of the joint chiefs of staff. While praising General Landazábal profusely, Betancur sent him abroad as ambassador to the Low Countries two months later, while General Matamoros succeeded to the defense ministry. Betancur declared in a speech at Cartagena that there could be no question of executive authority, for the president of the republic was "the commander of the armed forces, which obeys his decisions. These are not submitted for discussion or approval to any other organization."[13] Having presumably curbed military dissidence, at least for the time, Betancur then proceeded in his pursuit of dialogue. In repeating his conviction that political violence was largely a response to socioeconomic difficulties, Betancur agreed with the guerrilla groups that a negotiated peace process was but the first step toward a comprehensive accord. In seeking to do so, the president followed a strategy of pursuing signed truces without the guerrillas handing in their arms.

The basis for a possible breakthrough in negotiations came in early March of 1984 with a joint communique from the M-19 and the FARC. It spoke favorably of a truce with the armed forces, praised Betancur's preoccupation with peace, and approved of a dialogue and cease-fire. This led to a pair of agreements, the first signed on 28 March 1984 between the FARC and the Peace Commission. A one-year cease-fire would go into effect on 28 May, a special "High Level Commission" would verify the honoring of the agreement, and rehabilitative measures would be developed. Members of the FARC were not officially pardoned, but were invited to return to political legality without qualification.

A second agreement was negotiated in May with the EPL and the M-19, and was signed on 24–25 August 1984. Its general thrust resembled that with the FARC, although speaking in more vague terms about government commitments and systemic reforms. However, the heralded national dialogue reverberated with dissident opinion. There were three major questions before Colombia at this point, as Kline wrote. First was the meaning of dialogue, which the FARC in particular saw as leading to a Constituent Assembly or similar body in which it would be represented. Carlos Lleras Restrepo was prepared to consider some form of democratization or electoral modification, although the government itself spoke only of "ample consultation." Second was the tricky question of guerrilla arms, for many argued that an accord should be conditioned on the surrender of weapons, as was the case in 1953 under Rojas Pinilla. The third dealt with cost and feasibility of rehabilitative programs, about which there were widely differing views.[14]

The much-heralded dialogue began in Bogotá late in October. Ten subcommissions were created with representatives of both the guerrillas and congress: they were to consider such themes as constitutional, agrarian, labor, health, and economic reforms. As these proceeded sporadically in the months to come, periodic outbursts of violence repeatedly endangered the cease-fire agreement while sapping the vigor of the Betancur initiatives. Internal guerrilla divisions were dramatized by the August killing of former M-19 leader Carlos Toledo Plaza by a faction opposed to the cease-fire. In December fighting broke forth in the mountains of Cauca between the M-19 and the army. The Peace Commission eventually negotiated a settlement, but not without the army insisting once again that the basic problem remained that of public order rather than reforms. The military generally felt responsibility for implementation of the peace process.

Betancur was periodically forced to back away from the peace process rather than directly challenging armed forces. In February 1985 his government minister, Jaime Castro Castro, denied the M-19 permission to convene a meeting in Los Robles, Cause. The following month Alvaro Fayad, newly appointed head of the M-19, complained that the truce was being violated. The M-19 was not persuaded that the peace process might endure. In March Fayad expressed M-19 reservations:

> The real problem of peace is not the arms, but unemployment, illiteracy, the economic crisis, the moral crisis, the crisis of the parties, the lack of political will to carry out reforms; the bankruptcy of the oligarchy, that has no answers for the new country in which it lives. Arms are but a result of all of this.[15]

Further skirmishes marked the next few months until, on 20 June, the M-19 called a twenty-four-hour strike and proclaimed the truce broken. From this juncture it proceeded with further attacks, especially in Cauca and Valle, before mounting the attack on the Palace of Justice described shortly. In the meantime the FARC, while issuing its own denunciations of cease-fire violations, firmly moved toward a political opening. In March a new political party was created, the Unión Patriótica (UP).

A twenty-point platform stressed electoral reforms and *apertura,* and the emphasis was on negotiation rather than violence, although there was no mention made of arms. With representatives from several leftist groups in addition to the Partido Comunista, the UP insisted that it was not the civilian organization of the FARC, a claim that was met with skepticism. Spokesmen also stressed that the UP would seek to develop during the truce period of the FARC, and that its appearance marked not the disappearance of the FARC but rather a shift toward civil structures and processes. The creation of the UP, which was soon examining the possibility of electoral participation in 1986, came at a time when the pessimism of the M-19 seemed more justified by events.

For it was precisely during the second half of 1985 that the peace process visibly stumbled. The military became more assertive, violence increased, an EPL representative was murdered, and in October Betancur was forced to reconstitute the Peace Commission. Moreover, the opposition of the political elite was becoming more forthright. Liberal and Conservative leaders were far from agreement, complicating the president's need to wrest reforms from the congress. He had sought changes concerning parties, elections, and a decentralization of power, but as early as 1983 government bills were being rejected in congress. With Betancur lacking a firm legislative majority, party leadership disunited, and negotiations taking place without congressional input or participation, this was unsurprising. Once the 1984 truces had been signed and the ten subcommissions convened, moreover, there were few meaningful institutional links with the legislature.

During the 1984 sessions President Betancur placed particular emphasis on those political reforms he identified with an *apertura democrática.*[16] Of particular importance was the proposed constitutional reform establishing direct popular election of mayors. For Betancur, this would encourage a democratization of the overcentralized system, also helping to free the parties from caudillistic domination. Colombian reformists ardently championed the measure, while traditionalist forces were opposed. Betancur's own Conservative Party Directorate failed to support the measure, while former presidents Lleras Restrepo and Turbay Ayala entertained strong reservations. For the Bishop's Conference, Monseñor Héctor Rueda Hernández declared that electoral tensions would merely divide the citizenry unnecessarily.

Only after herculean efforts did the administration secure passage of this constitutional reform on 21 November 1984. Winning the mandatory two-thirds margin with one vote to spare, it provided that mayoral elections by direct vote of the citizenry would become effective in 1988. Under the determined leadership of Government Minister Jaime Castro Castro, the administration convened an extraordinary session of congress in March 1985, at which a number of other proposals were laid out: further political democratization, administrative and fiscal decentralization, and special economic measures. Most of these were stalled, however, and then delayed until the July 1986 postelection congressional session. Given the intervention of presidential and legislative elections during the interim, this effectively killed adoption of further reforms.[17]

Much of the lingering momentum—and the unflagging conviction of Belisario Betancur—was crudely and rudely disrupted by the events at the Palace of Justice, which shook both the nation and the government in November 1985. On the sixth of the month members of the M-19 attacked and seized control of the palace, situated on the Plaza Bolívar in the heart of the city. Hundreds were held captive, including Supreme Court justices. The apparent intention—or at least a major one—was that of conducting negotiations and venting grievances both real and imagined before the eyes of the world. To a degree, this had been a central fact in the 1980 scenario of the Dominican Embassy. If such was indeed the principal objective, it was a miscalculation of classic proportions. The military swiftly decided to respond by force of arms in lieu of negotiations.

Tanks, artillery, and special attack troops were mobilized. After twenty-eight hours of fighting, much of it recorded with grim fascination on the live television screens of millions of Colombians, the palace fell. The president and eleven associate justices of the Supreme Court were slain, as were some forty members of the M-19. The imposing palace itself had been fired, and the insides were virtually gutted. At the August 1986 inauguration of the next president, it stood as mute testimony to the harsh realities of Colombian politics, the shell-pocked exterior only partially hidden by an inadequate cosmetic draping of large banners. Among the other results of the attack was the virtual destruction of Colombian legal records, including extensive documentation of past and pending cases notably involving drug producers and traffickers.

On the evening of 7 November Belisario Betancur went on television, accepted full responsibility for the decision to attack, and emphasized that the democratic institutions of the republic were not negotiable. He also declared that his actions had been taken in consultation with, and with the approval of, the full cabinet. The array of multiple investigations to follow, many of which continued well after Betancur's departure from office, raised more questions than provided answers. As to the crucial issue of decision-making authority, it was evident that in a sense Colombia had undergone what some termed a twenty-eight-hour coup. Confidential accounts from knowledgeable Venezuelan as well as Colombian authorities have persuaded this observer beyond reasonable doubt that the armed forces swiftly took the decision and were not to be deterred. One account has it that Betancur was informed telephonically in vividly obscene language that if he had any objections, he would be removed from the presidency within the hour.

Whatever the truth of such anecdotal details and reports, under prevailing circumstances Betancur was essentially powerless. For the armed forces, smarting over restrictions imposed by the government and persuaded that the president was either a fool or a knave, authority had to be exerted. The institutional honor of the military as a corporate body was at stake, if not the very reputation and dignity of the nation itself. Therefore, negotiation was unthinkable and no quarter was to be given. M-19 calls for negotiations were never heeded by anyone exercising governmental authority. The armed forces responded to a perceived need that brooked neither questions nor qualifications. The resulting toll was a heavy one.[18]

Among the many conspiratorial theories that inevitably swirled about events of this magnitude has been the allegation that links between the M-19 and Colombia's huge drug industry were important. It was at least plausible to argue that major drug producers urged on the M-19. Records would be destroyed, proceedings eliminated, and justices who sat on drug cases and considered the extradition of Colombians from the United States for trial might be punished. In fact, the entire system of justice might thereby be further intimidated. The political survival of Betancur himself could have been in question had it not been for another tragedy barely a week later, when the eruption on 13 November of the Nevada del Ruiz volcano killed over 20,000. In its humanitarian response to this act of nature, Colombians were distracted from the Palace of Justice horrors wrought at the hands of man.

The November trauma, coming as it did within six months of presidential elections, effectively closed the door on most of Betancur's initiatives. The nearest approach to *apertura* came with the eventual participation of Unión Patriótica at the urns. This will be noted in the later section on the campaign and elections. Otherwise, the Betancur initiatives had ground to a halt, and would necessarily await the wishes and inclinations of the next government. Whatever the final verdict of history regarding Betancur's pacification efforts, it will also have to judge administration policy with regard to crime, justice, and the drug industry. In Colombia as in no other nation on the continent, the challenge to systemic social and political controls was profound. And although problems had been experienced by previous National Front governments, it was with Belisario Betancur that the difficulties assumed previously unimagined proportions.

Crime rates had been rising for some years, and the system of justice was increasingly incapable of meeting the needs of public security. Rodrigo Lara Bonilla, Betancur's minister of justice noted in late 1983, for example, that there was an accumulation of 1.3 million cases to be handled; 24,000 of the 30,000 prisoners in the country were awaiting trial; trained judges were lacking; and so forth. Despite a high crime rate, nearly 90 percent of all crimes went unreported. An estimated 53 percent of crimes concerning economic matters, while 35 percent threatened life and personal integrity.[19] Medellín was increasingly compared with Chicago of the 1930s, while the southern Colombian garden spot of Cali was tainted by violence and crime. An imposing array of data testified to the growing inability of the system to meet civic needs and exercise effective controls. And beyond this lay the problem of the drug industry.

The economic benefits had been on the rise, dollars were produced by the trade, and a special window at the Banco de la República facilitated open exchanges of currency. But as conditions grew more extreme, President Betancur gave a free hand to his dedicated justice minister. The latter directed an attack on both dealers and their production facilities while vehemently issuing denunciations, some of which suggested the involvement of Colombian politicians in the burgeoning source of wealth and influence. In March of 1984, by which time U.S. officials from the Justice and Treasury Departments were working actively with the Colombians, a series of raids on cocaine-processing plants produced a rich harvest—one alone, near the Yari River, seized 12,500 kilograms of cocaine valued at $1.2 billion. The plant had been operating under the protection of FARC guerrillas, leading to new charges about collaboration between the two groups.

If Betancur still entertained any reservations about the magnitude of the problem, these disappeared when Rodrigo Lara was gunned down on the streets of Bogotá on 30 August 1984. The president declared a state of siege, proclaimed a war to the death on *narcotraficantes,* and unleashed a massive wave of raids and arrests. An extradition agreement with the United States was dusted off, and in January 1985 the government extradited the first four Colombians under indictment in the United States. The action produced the counterthreat that one U.S. diplomat would be killed for each extradition. Members of the embassy staff were placed under exceptional security safeguards, and the ambassador himself soon left the country for vacation and subsequent reassignment.

Betancur's next New Year's address to the nation underlined his personal determination to curb the industry:

> This is an unconditional struggle; there is no place for false compassion for those who directly or indirectly engage in this filthy and degrading business; whoever might be surprised in this activity should pay all consequences absolutely because...he is a bad son of Colombia and should be punished. We will do so. Threats are useless. We will not retreat a single millimeter.[20]

As the year unfolded, there were further extraditions of those held in Colombia but accused of drug offenses in the United States. Attitudes seemed to be changing on the part of Colombian officials, especially as the growing use of "bazuco"—a coca paste or cocaine base mixed with marijuana or tobacco—was recognized as a domestic problem. Furthermore, the drive against ranking leaders of the industry also picked up momentum. This seemed only to spur the drug *capos* to greater activity.

The near-capture of Carlos Lehder in May 1985—perhaps a harbinger of his eventual apprehension in March 1987—spurred officials to continued efforts. The obstacles were nonetheless pronounced, and by the close of the year it was true that most of the 3600 Colombians jailed on narcotics charges were local drug dealers, student distributors, and retailers. It was increasingly apparent that the drug trade was easily the best—and one of the very few—routes for aspiring Colombians to rise within the stratified class system and better themselves financially. Yet the macroeconomic impact was mixed. As two economists wrote in the powerful *Los Condenados de la Coca,* the lack of a coherent government policy toward narcotics earnings contributed to inflation, phony investments, the laundering of drug money, and an overextension of the banking industry.[21] All of this, of course, said nothing about the social impact of the drugs themselves on Colombians, let alone nationals of other countries. This is not the place for a technical or detailed evaluation of the drug industry. The significance here rests with the level and capacity of social and political controls under the incumbent administration. With the magnitude of the subject greater than ever, Betancur attempted at great political and physical cost to respond in kind.

From its origins in the early 1970s, the industry had gradually developed and refined the production and processing of cocaine, while Colombian and U.S. authorities had concentrated on marijuana from Santa Marta and the Caribbean coastal area. As the so-called Medellín Cartel took shape, that city became the major center for business operations; coca paste from Bolivia and Peru was refined and processed in Colombia, then shipped to U.S. markets through Miami and other cities. Millions of dollars were laundered in South Florida banks as the business flourished.

By the decade of the 1980s many of the founders had been voluntarily or forcibly retired. A new generation of drug barons bore such names as Ochoa and Escobar, while Carlos Lehder and José Rodríguez Gacha were especially notorious. A drive to assure collective self-defense produced the December 1981 manifesto, signed by 223 traffickers, which created Muerte a Secuestradores (MAS)—Death to Kidnappers—as a right-wing terrorist organization. This was the first such collaborative effort, and was followed for three years by the Cartel's so-called golden age. As U.S. market demand soared, the industry grew to meet it. Judges and government officials were threatened or assassinated if bribery failed; shipments of cocaine grew enormously, and the profits were staggering. Such known *capos* as Pablo Escobar, the brothers Fabio and Jorge Luis Ochoa Vásquez, and Lehder lived amid unparalleled opulence; many of their estates were widely known, as well as heavily defended by private guards.

Signing of the U.S.-Colombian reciprocal extradition treaty in 1979 and its ratification in 1981 stimulated cartel efforts toward a reversal. In addition to threats of death and reprisal, the *narcos* even offered to pay $3 billion on the international debt if extradition were reversed or barred. Arguments based on Colombian nationalism and independence were also employed, as were attacks on the presumed U.S. interference. As seen, the reluctance of Belisario Betancur disappeared with the murder of Rodrigo Lara Bonilla on 30 April 1984. Symbolic of the president's change of heart was his signing on 8 May of Carlos Lehder's extradition order. Escobar, Jorge Luis Ochoa, and others slipped across the border to Panama, while Lehder went into hiding in the jungle. Cartel leaders sought an understanding with authorities while playing upon the prevailing sentiment that U.S. demand was solely responsible for the thriving industry.

Shortly after the shooting of Lara Bonilla, top drug bosses quietly met with Alfonso López Michelsen in Panama, attempting to distance themselves from the killing. On 26 May 1984, industry leaders proposed in writing a truce and reconciliation with the administration. Claiming control of at least 70 percent of the cocaine produced domestically, they pledged to bring their money home, retire from the business, and proceed to be reincorporated into society. Discussions in political circles in Bogotá and elsewhere were animated, although the government itself was not swayed by the purported olive branch. In time, the conflict reheated, with the industry returning to any and all conceivable methods of influence and intimidation.

One anecdotal example of reality came when Jorge Luis Ochoa was arrested in August of 1986, just as Betancur was leaving office. A young local jurist sentenced Ochoa for smuggling bulls, then released him on $11,500 bail. Ochoa was soon seen walking the streets of Medellín with Escobar, and then dropped from the scene. The dismissal of the judge and his immediate superiors was of no avail. As the Betancur period drew to a close, killings of particular prominence included that of DEA informant Barry Seal in Baton Rouge, Louisiana by a Colombian hit squad on 19 February; Avianca Airlines executive Luis Francisco Briceño Murillo by motorcycle killers on 3 July in Bogotá; and Supreme Court Justice Hernando Baquero Borda in similar fashion as he drove away from his Bogotá home on 30 July 1986.

The conflict between the drug industry and the Colombian authorities continued with the next government. The capture of Carlos Lehder and his extradition to the United States in early 1987 was a significant event; it was counterbalanced by further killings, including additional judges and, on 17 December 1986, that of Guillermo Cano, crusading editor of Bogotá's noted daily *El Espectador*. New links between drug dealers and the guerrillas, including both the FARC and the EPL, began to surface. But with the long struggle far from resolved, the pernicious influence of the traffickers on the lives of ordinary Colombians, as well as national elites, constituted a continuing problem requiring relentless attention from the regime. Moreover, this continued to occur within a general context of violence and criminality. By 1986 there was a growing public awareness of the problem, one that neither Belisario Betancur nor his predecessors had been able to curb.

Data and statistics were imprecise and subject to diverse interpretations, both disinterested and partisan. Basic patterns were not readily deniable, however. The U.S. Department of State's 1985 human rights report, for one, recorded that political killings and disappearances for 1980–85 ran in the thousands. Drawing upon numerous sources, including the Colombian attorney-general, official military data, and reports of the human rights organization, it detailed disappearances and kidnappings, political killings, and torture. The department, by no means a hostile source, could but conclude that despite a "tradition of electoral democracy, Colombia continues to experience high levels of political and criminal violence."[22] Far sharper and harsher opinions came periodically from Amnesty International.

Reporting on the first half of 1986 in July of the year, it denounced an intensified campaign of disappearances and killings conducted by the military and security forces. It alleged that over 600 Colombians had been victimized since January, including some 300 in violence-racked Cali alone. Such charges were rejected by the armed forces, which claimed that the level of killing was predominantly the work of the MAS and other civilian vigilantes, which it did not control. Characteristically, the ranking military commander, General Augusto Moreno Guerrero, attacked Amnesty International for a campaign to discredit the armed forces. Similar ripostes came from other security officials, and even from some civilians who denounced foreign meddling. President Betancur himself chose not to speak out.

Yet even allowing for the difficulties in tracking such events, and acknowledging the zeal of Amnesty International, there was little doubt that conditions had been worsening with the gradual deterioration of the truce and the M-19 attack on the Palace of Justice. On 10 May Carlos Jiménez-Gómez, the attorney-general, had warned that an Argentine-style "dirty war" might be in the offing. In an accompanying report delivered to Betancur, the defense minister, and the director of the National Police, Jiménez-Gómez cited specific names and cases while speaking of "intolerable illegal waves of violence...carried out with the excuse of controlling guerrilla actions." He also criticized the "nocturnal homicides" being carried out in Cali and other centers.[23]

By the close of the Betancur period, basic crime rates and occurrences of nonpolitical violence were higher than four years earlier. Guerrilla activism and tough military action, while having been reduced for a time, seemed again on the rise as the architect of *apertura* left office. The drug industry had extended its tentacles ever further throughout society. Social and political controls had been designed and implemented with diversity and imagination; the excesses of blunt *turbayista* methods had been reduced. At the same time, the level of civil unrest and violence suggested a generalized worsening of social conditions. Given the stubbornness of such elements in the face of a perspective sharply different from that of the preceding government, the capacity of the National Front system to satisfy or ameliorate societal ills and needs remained in question, even as the political setting was slowly but unmistakably beginning to open up.

The Politics of the Biparty Government

The Party Competition

Facing the opportunities and difficulties in leading a minority government with congress firmly in opposition hands, Belisario Betancur invariably invoked national unity and nonpartisanship. At least in the wake of elections, he could draw some comfort from the disarray of the Liberals, who were sharply divided. Alfonso López Michelsen remained an unpopular figure, further tainted by his defeat despite a lengthy array of advantages—money, party machinery, media approval, and government backing. His control of the apparatus had been weakened, while the positions of Galán and especially of Lleras Restrepo were enhanced. When Betancur had earlier referred wryly to López Michelsen as "Lleras

Restrepo's intimate enemy," it said much about the past and present of the Liberal party.

Betancur's initial appointments were broadly representative. The cabinet included six members from each party, and reflected a number of different factions. General Fernando Landazábal Reyes was named to defense, while the crucial post of government minister went to the Liberal Rodrigo Escobar Navia. Eight vice-ministries were assigned to women, and a blue-ribbon economic advisory commission included Lleras Restrepo and Lauchlin Currie. In the congress, the final breakdown after last-minute shuffling left the Liberals with sixty-two Senators (nine with Nuevo Liberalismo), fifty-one Conservatives, and one from the leftist UNO. In the Chamber, 115 Liberals included sixteen from Nuevo Liberalismo, along with eighty-three Conservatives and one from the UNO. On 25 November there was sufficient bipartisan agreement to select Alvaro Gómez Hurtado as designado.

Betancur's problems with the Liberals responded to the sharp division between the orthodox followers of López and Turbay, and Luis Carlos Galán with Nuevo Liberalismo. Internal party maneuvering was continuous; in March of 1983 the Comisión Política divided its seats equally between López and Turbay followers, leaving Galán supporters in the cold. This necessarily influenced Betancur when he restructured his cabinet in August after completing his first year in office. With the six original Liberal members having served without the official approval of the party orthodoxy, the president reluctantly conceded the necessity of securing the so-called *legitimista* approval of López and Turbay. Escobar Navia resigned, along with the twenty-three governors and four mayors appointed by the government minister. In the new cabinet, Escobar was shifted to education, while Alfonso López Gómez succeeded him on behalf of Liberal *legitimistas*. Nuevo Liberalismo was represented by Lara Bonilla at justice, while *turbayistas,* whose leader remained absent abroad, had no one in the cabinet.

With López Michelsen still on the scene but discredited in many Liberal eyes, there was some talk of Turbay as the party standard-bearer in 1986. On 23 August he returned home and issued a statement in *El Tiempo,* which served as a reminder that he had not withdrawn from party politics. Within a month he was proposing that López Michelsen and Lleras Restrepo join him to plan greater party unity. By November Turbay indicated his veto of a Galán candidacy for 1986. The latter promptly re-

torted: "I am the undertaker for *clientelismo* and I am terminating the
negative influence of Turbay in the Liberal Party, who since leaving the
presidential office has sought to be the keeper of the palace door in order
to determine who enters the presidency."[24] The level of internal dissension became a matter of almost daily press reports, none of which aided
the Liberals in moderating their combativeness. As the March 1984 *mitaca*
elections neared, the situation did not improve.

The lineup in Bogotá was especially telling, given the capacity of even
the poorly organized factions to present their own slates in the capital.
The deepest rift was that between Nuevo Liberalismo and the party orthodoxy; this latter, however, was itself fragmented with López followers headed by Ernesto Samper Pizano, *turbayistas* under former Bogotá
mayor Hernando Durán Dussán, and the aspiring Alberto Santofimio
with his own list. The Conservatives, almost lost in the wake of Liberal
dissension, saw their Bogotá lists headed by former president Pastrana's
son Andrés. In the *mitaca* elections for departmental assemblies and city
councils on 11 March 1984, roughly 100,000 candidates contested 9326
offices. Public apathy to internecine feuds was predictably high, with an
abstention rate of 62.1 percent. There was little significant difference
between the patterns of the 1982 presidential contest. Thus, the total
Liberal margin over the Conservatives was 52.5 to 41.2 of the 5,446,721
votes cast. For the majority party, the officialists polled 41.3 percent to
11.3 for Nuevo Liberalismo. The latter again demonstrated both their
strength in Bogotá and their inability to reach voters elsewhere in the
country. Under the image of Galán they took the capital's electoral district with 34.6 percent to 22.1 for the officialists and 30.5 for the Conservatives. The overall vote produced for the departmental assemblies a
total of 132 Liberal officialists, 41 from Nuevo Liberalismo, 176 Conservatives, and 11 from other party lists.

None of this clarified or simplified the political scenery. Emerging presidential possibilities for 1986 included Liberal *oficialistas* Virgilio Barco
Vargas, Augusto Espinosa Valderrama, Otto Morales Benítez, and
Hernando Durán Dussán, while Galán was the countercandidate for the
self-proclaimed reformers. On the Conservative side, Alvaro Gómez
Hurtado appeared well on his way to an easy nomination, with only J.
Emilio Valderrama prepared to contest the party selection. However, during the Betancur period the midterm elections, even granting the exclusion
of national legislative elections, bore less weight than was customarily the

case. The Betancur policies concerning reforms and *apertura,* along with the Contadora efforts and purported domestic amnesty and pacification, attracted much greater attention than the partisan struggles of 1984.

Candidate Selection

Once the elections were past, Betancur renewed efforts to introduce delayed reforms. Theoretically capable of mounting a congressional majority if the Galán faction could be added to the Conservatives, the president found that his own party support was by no means monolithic. On 28 June he reshuffled his cabinet. Senator Jaime Castro Castro, president of the central committee of Liberal *oficialistas,* was named the new minister of government. A onetime justice minister under Pastrana Borrero who enjoyed links with both parties, his congressional ties were seen as useful. Foreign relations passed to the Conservative Augusto Ramírez Ocampo, former coordinator of Betancur's campaign and subsequently mayor of Bogotá. Roberto Junguito Bonnet, with ties to Alvaro Gómez, became the new finance minister, while Conservative Senator Alvaro Leyva Durán, a *pastranista,* was assigned mines and energy. In balance, the new lineup recognized continuing Liberal factionalism while favoring close associates of Misael Pastrana over Alvaro Gómez, who had recently gone to Washington, D.C., as Colombian ambassador.

Greater success with congress was not to come Betancur's way, however, and the Liberals' internal struggles continued. A national convention was convened in December of 1984, at which the government was strongly attacked for its alleged pursuit of rightist positions. The Liberals decreed that collaboration by party members would be "personal and technical" without bearing any official sanction. While it was impossible to arrive at fully acceptable rules of the game for the candidate selection, the majority adopted the notion of a nominating convention sometime between 15 May and 15 August 1985. Carlos Lleras Restrepo, still backing Luis Carlos Galán, was among those calling instead for a nomination based on the March 1986 congressional elections. Galán himself continued to push Nuevo Liberalismo while tilting with the *oficialistas.* He refused to negotiate with "the clientelistic political class":

What is at issue is the search for political and social modifications. I am going to win the parliamentary elections, but if I lose them, I will not sit down at a table for conversations with those we have been fighting in recent years.... Win or lose in parliamentary elections, our objective is the presidency.[25]

While Galán fought ahead, the officialists were increasingly inclined toward Virgilio Barco Vargas or Augusto Espinosa Valderrama; the latter publicly withdrew on 14 March 1985.

The Conservatives were meantime moving much more quietly toward the selection of a candidate. There seemed no obvious *betancurista* heir-apparent, although in January of 1985 J. Emilio Valderrama announced his candidacy under the rubric of *Conservatismo Progresista,* pledging a movement that would draw the backing of ANAPO, Christian Democrats, and other small groupings. However, there was little doubt that Alvaro Gómez Hurtado would carry the Conservative banner for the second time. Misael Pastrana Borrero, whose influence had reached its highest point inside the party, maintained an official silence while indicating privately his willingness to back Gómez. At their November 1985 national convention, the Conservatives officially proclaimed Gómez their candidate. Such critics as Valderrama and Berta Ospina joined in the display of unity, and Gómez's acceptance speech promised a strong hand in government, especially concerning public order.

The Liberals continued their dispute throughout 1985 and into the election year. Galán maintained the drumbeat of criticism that had been alienating party fathers since the beginning of the decade. Critical of clientelism and insisting upon meaningful reforms, Galán was especially acerbic in his longstanding attacks on Julio César Turbay Ayala and the tradition he represented. He also suggested the necessity of reaching out to the political left, and in August 1985 held discussions with Unión Patriótica. The talks proved fruitless, and in September the UP opened its own campaign. For Galán, the key was apparently the extent to which voter abstention and public alienation might be attracted to his camp. Without major organizational efforts and a truly nationwide effort, he was likely to find his success circumscribed, as in earlier elections, by the metropolitan Bogotá voters.

Public opinion polls, which were evolving rapidly after a rather belated introduction to Colombia, consistently recorded public dissatisfaction with the prevailing system. In December 1984 a major survey firm reported a trend toward increased pessimism, a decline in Betancur's popularity, a conviction that economic problems would worsen in the year ahead, and identification of unemployment as even more serious than inflation.[26] By mid-1985 the electoral impact was viewed with grave misgivings; the noted financial magazine *Estrategia* reported that private polls showed that 75 percent of the electorate would vote for neither Barco nor Gómez. In the five most populous cities, the abstention rate was projected at 80 percent, with the highest rates located in urban slum neighborhoods. This suggested the advisability for the traditional elite of responding to the failures of orthodox clientelism in the urbanizing electorate, but even Galán seemed more inclined to employ the longstanding practices and techniques of campaign politics.

With the arrival of 1986, attention concentrated first on the March congressional races. For Barco, who had been formally proclaimed both candidate and Liberal Party *jefe* in August of 1985, the challenge was not only to crush Nuevo Liberalismo, but to dissipate widespread doubts about his public persona. Although long a public servant with extensive experience in the party, Barco nonetheless bore the image of a bloodless technocrat whose forte was the abstract solution of problems. As a colorless candidate, he was an easy target for Liberals willing to move to another candidate unless his appearances improved. The former mayor and onetime cabinet minister stepped up his public appearances, and succeeded only in underlining prevailing opinion. Barco speeches were dull, rambling, and diffidently delivered; he was ineffective at pressing the flesh, and local leaders came away from his visits shaking their heads in dismay.

Luis Carlos Galán, a far more effective speaker who projected an image of strength and decisiveness, was less adept in organizing his supporters or managing regional and local efforts. There was notable weakness in overall campaign strategy and tactics. The necessity of relying on local political supporters, on stressing the campaign outside Bogotá, and even the mounting of an effective electoral campaign went unrecognized. Programs, slogans, media images—all were disappointingly traditional and unimaginative. For those seeking new ideas and approaches, Nuevo Liberalismo in the 1986 campaign seemed to offer little. Galán too easily and too often gave the impression that his concern was wresting power from the party hierarchy for the sake of his own personal success, rather than modernizing a decrepit system in danger of total collapse.

For the Conservatives, Alvaro Gómez Hurtado wavered between the hard-line orthodoxy that he had long represented, and the necessity of reaching out to thousands of voters who preferred broader-based policies and a less partisan orientation. Relying on modern, media-oriented advice from North American consultants, Gómez sought to project a candidate image at odds with prevailing popular attitudes about the place of his father Laureano in recent Colombian history. He willingly appeared in the company of Luis Carlos Galán on television on 11 February, where both men responded to questions from the press. Virgilio Barco refused to participate, calling it a mere publicity stunt; given his shaky public appearances to date, this was the course of prudence.[27]

A second-round presidential debate changed things little, although some felt that Galán had been less imprecise than Gómez. The broader electoral question was still whether Nuevo Liberalismo might draw enough from Barco to permit a minority win for Gómez. In the meantime, there was a disproportionate interest in the activities of minor groups, most particularly the UP and others on the Left. By February there were initial discussions that eventually produced a number of alliances between the FARC and the Liberals at the local level. In such departments as Caqueta, Nariño, Huila, and Tolima, collaboration was seen as useful for the congressional races. This became more meaningful when the government and the FARC signed a new cease-fire on 2 March, thereby providing greater credibility to the UP in its alliances with the Liberals.

Such matters, however, were of greater interest to political insiders than to the Colombian electorate. The latter saw the contest as reminiscent of many others. Barco, notwithstanding a favorable record as Bogotá mayor, was but the newest product of the Liberal party apparatus. Gómez was a capable and articulate figure who could not be seen without stirring memories of the 1950s violence and of his extraordinarily controversial father. Galán seemed to a degree a younger version of Barco, trying vainly to resuscitate his image as *enfant terrible* when first a cabinet minister at age twenty-six in 1970. Even the Unión Patriótica was playing the game by systemic rules; *clientelismo* emerged in its pacts with departmental and local Liberal *caciques*. For Colombians fond of describing politics as "*aquí no pasa nada*," it was difficult to place great importance in either the March or May elections. At the same time, there were some 5000 citizens contesting 124 congressional seats, while nearly 40,000 were seeking local office.

Campaign and Elections

On Sunday, 9 March 1986, Colombians went to the polls, awarded the Liberals a substantial victory, and rejected Nuevo Liberalismo. While abstention was some 52 percent, nearly 7 million cast their ballots. Projections gave the Liberal lists 3,402,800 votes for 49 percent, easily out-distancing the Conservatives' 2,590,200 for 37 percent. Nuevo Liberalismo fell short of 500,000 for a shade under 7 percent, while the Unión Patriótica polled some 280,000 for 4 percent. The magnitude of the Galán loss was demonstrated by the Bogotá vote; after having run first in both 1981 and 1984, his followers now ran a distant third. Nuevo Liberalismo dropped over 12 percent from 1984, the regular Liberals picking up 20 points while the Conservatives dropped slightly. At the same time, it appeared that appeals to the disenchanted electorate had gone unheeded.

To be sure, there were those who argued that the Liberals were modernizing in message and technique; the slogan of *"continuidad o cambio"* presumably had reached some of Colombia's growing number of independents. The more frequent interpretation, however, was typified by María Jimena Duzán and Antonio Caballero in *El Espectador,* where it was argued that the elections signified a return to the past—a consolidation of traditional clientelism, with the parties unable or unwilling to change, and the Galán challenge a meaningless distraction. The failure of the latter was probably the most widely discussed aspect of the elections. It was unquestionable that Nuevo Liberalismo dropped in no fewer than fifteen of the twenty-three departments, many patently dissimilar in culture and demographics.

Perhaps most fundamental was the fact, already alluded to, that Galán and company had demanded a renewal of party leadership without concomitant attention to the formulation of specific new policies. There was far too little by way of direct responses to major urban preoccupations, notably unemployment, inflation, and deteriorating public services. Added to this was an internal structure that was shaky at best, disconnected from local and regional leadership, and unresponsive to the interests of the latter. In light of these NL campaign characteristics, it was not difficult for the orthodox Liberals to reverse the apparent deterioration of more recent years. There had at last been a programmatic reorientation since 1982, a series of widely publicized "ideological fora," and a technologizing of the machinery. Policies responding to the needs of the cities had been reshaped, and urban decline for orthodox Liberals since 1974 had seemingly been checked.[28]

For the Conservatives the elections were frankly discouraging. After improving their position in previous parliamentary elections, it now became evident that the presence and impact of Belisario Betancur had been decisive in reaching beyond traditional Conservative boundaries. The widely used slogan of "National Participation" had been insipid and ineffective. Given the margin by which they trailed the Liberals, the presidential race seemed a certain loss. This became even more definite when Luis Carlos Galán announced his withdrawal from the May contest. While refusing to pledge NL electoral support to the Liberals, Galán's action was positive for Virgilio Barco. In relative terms, one other tangible victor was Unión Patriótica, which, while attracting only limited support, had improved upon the left showing of the past. Aided in some cases by alliances with the Liberals, they at least argued that there might be some shifting from bullets to ballots, justifying renewed political negotiation rather than military suppression.

In the new congress, which was after all the focus for voter choices, the Liberals won fifty-nine senate seats to forty-four for the Conservatives and seven for the NL. In the Chamber, the Liberals led the Conservatives by 102 to 82 with Nuevo Liberalismo capturing 7. The Liberal party was left with an outright majority in each house, regardless of NL votes. Its solid victory also helped to silence any remaining complaints about the candidacy of Virgilio Barco. Whatever his problems on the stump, and notwithstanding charges that he was not adept as a political leader, Barco had headed the party success. As eyes turned to the May contest, Barco also perceptibly improved his public style.

With experience and repetition, Barco's set speeches became more natural and less stilted. Local and regional leaders stepped up their organizational efforts, and crowds swollen in size and enthusiasm lent an aura of triumphalism to the Barco campaign. The Liberal candidate was also able to proclaim vague if high-minded generalities rather than specific proposals. To be sure, Barco speeches and statements were compiled and published in a 200-page book, but these were more often analyses of longstanding difficulties than about remedial policies.[29] All of this meant that Barco could enter office without a heavy burden of explicit campaign promises. It also left his political outlook something of a puzzlement; his image makers concentrated on projecting and praising his long experience as an administrator and problem solver.

For Alvaro Gómez Hurtado, there were few tactical cards to be played. His party remained a distinct minority, and necessarily had to attract wavering Liberals, independents, and nonvoters. Belisario Betancur had won with this approach, aided mightily by a divided Liberal party as well as his own distinctive style and personality. Yet the president's own popularity had declined substantially, and was of limited value to the Conservative candidate. Gómez was further handicapped by a lifelong reputation for toughness and orthodox Conservatism; the task of reproducing the Betancur movement was a practical impossibility.

The Conservatives' *"Participación Nacional"* issued populist statements and promises that many found disingenuous and others simply disbelieved. Among the campaign commitments were: creating 500,000 new jobs annually; providing 500,000 new homes, with the cost held at 30 percent of the minimum salary or less; delivering a country without guerrillas by the end of the term; and a moral renaissance of the political system. Gómez campaigned energetically across the nation, but party support was often uneven, local leaders were preoccupied with maintaining or solidifying their personal situations, and public receptivity was unexceptional. Skillful use of the media, shaped in part by U.S. advisors, was nonetheless ineffective in presenting to the electorate a new or different Alvaro Gómez. At age sixty-six, he was scarcely a new face nationally—far less so than Barco, although the Liberal had himself been born in 1921.

On Sunday, 25 May, 41,140 voting tables were installed at 7247 locations throughout the nation. Government Minister Jaime Castro guaranteed the security of elections, although the administration had earlier decided not to lift the state of siege. In addition to the major presidential candidates, three others were officially inscribed. Jaime Pardo Leal had continued through the campaign for the Unión Patriótica. Whimsical or off-beat candidacies were those of the self-proclaimed witch Regina Betancourt de Liska for the Movimiento Metapolítico and Juan David Pérez García for the Partido Humanista. Television crews and reporters prepared for the vote count at the Gómez and Barco headquarters in the Hotels Tequendama and Hilton respectively; even before nightfall, all the activity was centered at the latter.

Virgilio Barco Vargas won with a record landslide, polling 4,214,510 for 58.4 percent of the vote. Gómez received 2,588,055 for 35.8 percent. Jaime Pardo Leal won 328,752 votes, or 4.5 percent. Barco's win was truly national, as he prevailed in twenty-one of twenty-three departments; even the Conservative stronghold Antioquia fell to the Liberal candidate. The great Liberal advances in Bogotá, Medellín, Cali, and Barranquilla represented a major recovery from recent elections, demonstrating renewed Liberal strength in urban areas. The Liberals swept the capital with a margin of well above 300,000. The Liberals had improved significantly over their showing in March, while the Conservatives dropped comparably. The Liberals increased their percentage in thirteen departments, while the Conservatives dropped off in fifteen. The latter also lost accustomed centers of strength, including the ten departments where Betancur had won in 1982. The UP was cheered by its pronounced increase—more than double its March vote. Along with the 50,000 for Regina, there were still, however, no more than 6 percent who voted against the biparty system.

President-elect Barco, with his historic victory a matter of record, could move toward inauguration secure in the knowledge that he was his own man. He was correctly perceived as being the puppet or protege of none of the several Liberal ex-presidents. While Turbay had joined in some of the campaigning, Barco was clearly independent. The congressional majority was his, and the prospect of a party-based government emerged. During the campaign Barco had emphasized the Liberal character of his candidacy. This raised the possibility that he might move further from Article 120, perhaps rejecting a continuation of de facto National Front governments. There were early postelection echoes from Misael Pastrana Borrero, the dominant Conservative leader. With the party having sunk well beneath the "magical" 40 percent cutoff, he suggested that the party might best go into full opposition while attempting to rebuild its strength and popular appeal in the next few years.[30]

In the maneuvering between elections and the August inauguration, speculation on these issues was rife. For the first time in a decade, there was serious question about the character of the regime, the relationship between the two parties, and the future course of the prevailing National Front arrangements. The Conservatives were badly in disarray, casting about for scapegoats and angry over the course of events. The Liberals celebrated the Barco triumph and awaited his guidance over the future of the system, as well as the character of his administration and its policies. It was possible that a new era was about to open. For skeptics, in contrast, the expectation was more of the same; "aquí no pasa nada" remained the motto of many observers. Given the admittedly unrealistic expectations that had accompanied the election of Belisario Betancur, such questioning of forthcoming changes or reforms was the course of prudence as the nation awaited Virgilio Barco Vargas's assumption of power.[31]

Notes

1. Luis Alberto Restrepo, "The Crisis of the Current Political Regime and Its Possible Outcomes," in Charles Bergquist, Ricardo Peñaranda, and Gonzalo Sánchez, eds., *Violence in Colombia: The Contemporary Crisis in Historical Perspective* (Wilmington: Scholarly Resources Books, 1992), 279.
2. Belisario Betancur, *Colombia cara a cara* (Bogotá: Ediciónes Tercer Mundo, 1983), 28
3. *El Espectador* (8 August 1982).
4. "Colombia," *Latin American Andean Report* (7 October 1983).
5. The critical economic situation was sharply etched in Mario Latorre, "La emergencia económica: presentación para profanos," *Estrategia* 65 (April 1983): 19–22.
6. Harvey Kline, "New Directions in Colombia?" *Current History* 84, no. 499 (February 1985): 68. A most useful analysis by Betancur's minister of finance for the second half of his administration is Roberto Junguito, "The Colombian Debt Problem," in Rudiger Dornbusch and Steve Marcus, eds., *International Money and Debt: Challenges for the World Economy* (San Francisco: International Center for Economic Growth, 1991), 61–87.
7. Edgar Reveiz and María José Pérez, "Colombia: Moderate Economic Growth, Political Stability, and Social Welfare," in Jonathan Hartlyn and Samuel A. Morley, eds., *Latin American Political Economy: Financial Crisis and Political Change* (Boulder: Westview Press, 1986), 282.
8. *New York Times* (4 December 1982).
9. *New York Times* (6 October 1983).
10. For a succinct overview from one of the more ambitious and sweeping works in the recent literature, see Daniel Pecaut, *Crónica de dos décadas de política colombiana 1968–1988* (Bogotá: Siglo Veintiuno Editores, 2d ed., 1989), 358–65. A detailed and authoritative treatment of the administration and its fundamental doctrinal outlook is Alfredo Vázquez Carrizosa, *Betancur y la crisis nacional* (Bogotá: Ediciónes Aurora, 1986).

    Yet another useful source, a work that provides an excellent perspective on the nation's international relations and includes analyses of both Betancur's and Barco's efforts in this realm, is Rodrigo Pardo and Juan G. Tokatlian, *Política exterior colombiana: De la subordinación a la autonomía?* (Bogotá: Tercer Mundo Editores, 1988).
11. See Mark W. Chernick, "Insurgency and Negotiations: Defining the Boundaries of the Political Regime," unpublished Ph. D. dissertation, Columbia University, 1990; among others, also see Chernik, "Negotiated Settlement to Avoid Conflict: Lessons from the Colombian Peace Process," *Journal of Inter-American Studies and World Affairs* 30, no. 4 (Winter 1988–89): 53–89, and Chernik and Michael F. Jimenez, "Popular Liberalism, Radical Democracy, and Marxism: Leftist Politics in Contemporary Colombia, 1974–1991," in Barry Carr and Steve Ellner, eds., *The Latin American Left: From the Fall of Allende to Perestroika* (Boulder: Westview Press, 1993), 61–81.
12. *El Espectador* (31 October 1982).

13. "Colombia," *Latin American Weekly Report* (27 January 1984).
14. Kline, "New Directions," 66–67.
15. *Semana* (15 March 1985).
16. For a statement representative of administration views see Jaime Castro, *Elección popular de alcaldes* (Bogotá: Editorial La Oveja Negra, 1986).
17. An extensive multiauthored collection of reformist statements, prepared by Cristina de la Torre, is *Reformas políticas: apertura democrática* (Bogotá: Editorial La Oveja Negra, 1985).
18. A detailed journalistic account of events, including extended discussion of the M-19 background and past government efforts at negotiation, is Germán Hernández C., *La justicia en llamas,* prólogo de Carlos Lemos Simmonds (Bogotá: Carlos Valencia Editores, 1986).
19. *El Espectador* (5 June 1983).
20. *El Espectador* (31 December 1984).
21. Mario Arango Jaramillo and Jorge Child, *Los Condenados de la coca* (Bogotá: 1984).
22. U.S. Department of State, *Country Reports on Human Rights Practices for 1985* (Washington, D.C.: U.S. Government Printing Office, 1986).
23. "Colombia," *Latin American Weekly Report* (23 May 1986).
24. *El Tiempo* (2 November 1983).
25. *El Tiempo* (20 March 1985). For a closer account of Liberal divisions and maneuverings at the convention and after, see Rafael Ballén, *Liberalismo hoy: opción de cambio o agónica supervivencia* (Bogotá: n.p., 1985), 234–39.
26. "Colombia," *Latin American Andean Report* (14 December 1984).
27. Both Gómez and Galán broadly praised development, attacked the inadequacies of agricultural policy, urged an end to violence, and condemned rural injustice. There were few differences on such issues as foreign investment and the exploitation of Colombian petroleum. They also agreed on the importance of improving the state of human rights.
28. A more detailed discussion appears in Jorge Ramírez Aljure, *Liberalismo: ideología y clientelismo 1957–1986* (Bogotá: Fotolito Inter 2000, 1986), including pp. 28–31 ff.
    A useful source on Nuevo Liberalismo, notably its specific policy proposals and related materials, is found in Ballén, *Liberalismo hoy,* 240–303.
29. Virgilio Barco, *Hacia una Colombia nueva: Liberalismo, democracia social y cambio* (Bogotá: Editorial La Oveja Negra, 1986).
30. For a solid journalistic overview in the wake of the election, see the Informe Especial, "Camino despejado para Barco Vargas," *Visión* (14 July 1986).
31. A penetrating analysis of the Betancur government, which includes consideration of a possible system-breaking third party under the aegis of the president, by an eminent public servant as well as social scientist, is the previously cited Vázquez Carrizosa work, *Betancur y la crisis nacional.*
    Since leaving office, Betancur has defied Colombian presidential tradition by holding himself largely aloof from the politics of the day. He remains reluctant to discuss his own administration and its policies at length. However, for an interview that captures something of his essence, see Paul H. Boeker, *Lost Illusions: Latin America's Struggle for Democracy, as Recounted by Its Leaders* (New York: Markus Wiener Publishing, for the Institute of the Americas, 1990), 219–27.

11

The Shift from Biparty Government: Barco (1986–90)

The Policies of Governance

The National Environment

When candidate Virgilio Barco followed the advice of Colombian and North American campaign advisors to eschew calls for a national movement in favor of avowedly partisan appeals, he was promising voters a Liberal government committed to his official program and unfettered by Conservative participation. Notwithstanding Barco's sweeping victory, however, conversion to a uniparty administration was not a foregone conclusion. The president-elect subsequently promised in general terms to heed Article 120, while Misael Pastrana announced a Conservative commitment to a so-called *oposición reflexiva*. The latter set forth the details on 26 May and soon after forced grudging agreement from the Directorio Nacional Conservador despite opposition by Bertha Hernandez de Ospina and other party elders. In July Barco told the Liberals' Comisión Política Nacional that he stood by his commitment to a Liberal government; later, however, he honored Article 120 by offering three ministries on an individual basis to members of the Conservative party. Misael Pastrana instructed them not to accept appointment, thus clearing the way for the first single-party government in more than thirty years. In his inaugural day address to congress, Barco consequently declared that changing generations were altering the very structure of society: "Nothing has stayed the same. Today's country is not the same. Why maintain, then,...a constitutional precept that constrains the full exercise of democracy and was only justified by a stage of our history?"[1]

Colombia faced a new model of governance, then, as the *desmonte* from the Frente Nacional progressed.[2] While the political context therefore held the potential for change, prevailing demographic trends endured. An annual population growth rate of 2.2 percent from 1980 through 1985 had brought the national total close to around 30 million, and 70.8 percent were classified as urban (an increase of over 5 percent from 1986). The continuing rural migration led to an increase in urban unemployment beyond the 1985 figure of 14.2 percent, which itself was the highest figure in three years. It was estimated that over one-half million unemployed lived in Colombia's four largest cities; another 2 million, or 55 percent of the economically active population, were jobless in the ten largest cities. In Bogotá, two-thirds of its 4.5 million inhabitants lived in slum areas.[3] Underemployment, moreover, was believed to be approaching 30 percent.[4]

The continuing devaluation of the peso in 1986, which at 27.2 percent was the third highest annual figure in history, inevitably impacted upon the majority of Colombians. At the same time, these and related microeconomic hardships did not alter the relative macroeconomic successes of the day. The economy, rebounding from recession, was growing at 5.4 percent. The position of international reserves had improved in response to booming coffee revenues, and stood at approximately $2.75 billion. While the foreign debt by the close of 1986 had reached $12,185 million (as compared with $5,990 million at the end of 1982), Colombian creditworthiness was superior to that of most South American nations. Still subjected to the system called "monitoring," which the IMF and World Bank had set up two years earlier, it was sufficient for the two international institutions to praise Colombian efforts and then to set aside the practice effective October 1986.

The growth in GNP during the 1960s and 1970s had been favorable, as detailed in earlier chapters. By 1980, the GNP was some 75 percent higher in real terms than twenty years earlier, while social development indicators had been positive in such areas as literacy, infant mortality, and life expectancy. However, the overall rate of economic growth, by no means immune to international or regional difficulties, had slowed during the Betancur years. This had led to his government's eventual adoption of IMF-style measures. For the incoming Barco administration, then, its major challenges included that of reviving and stimulating overall economic growth. Added to this was the growing impact of the underground economy, estimated at some $3 billion annually. As Bagley put it tellingly, its "massive corrupting effects on every aspect of Colombia's economic and institutional life…[served to] undermine central government control over monetary policy [and] distort the rational allocation of economic resources and entrepreneurial energies in the economy."[5]

The president-elect, in short, had inherited from Belisario Betancur an economy that did not require emergency measures. However, selective continuation of Betancur's austerity policies seemed advisable if the growth rate were to be solidified and increased. Furthermore, having flatly promised to end all "absolute poverty," Barco was committed to action. He and his advisors believed that the major tasks, then, were to create jobs, along with meaningful agrarian reform (especially as a means of combatting rural violence) and a promotion of export trade. The first of these was to receive the highest priority. In his inaugural address Barco lamented that "immense sectors of the population are excluded from…nutrition, potable water, health, housing, work, and recreation."[6] The goal for Barco and his advisors was to be a program that would first generate employment within the growing economy, subsequently stimulating the growth of the internal market while projecting an international image expected to attract a healthier flow of foreign savings.

Policies of the Administration

Despite a long public career and his huge electoral victory, Virgilio Barco entered office as something of an enigma. *Semana* called him the most unknown president to have entered office in decades. Recalling López Michelsen's earlier statement about the Liberal candidacy, "If it isn't Barco, then who?" the newsweekly added its own query: "If it is Barco, who is he?"[7] Yet he had spent much of his life in public service and, while regarded as an administrator and technician, had literally never worked in the private sector, unlike most Colombian politicians. Neither had Barco ever owned or managed a *hacienda* or any other form of agricultural holding.[8]

Born in 1921 in Cúcuta, Norte de Santander, Barco studied at the Universidad Nacional and subsequently at Massachusetts Institute of Technology, where he earned a degree in civil engineering as well as a Ph.D. in economics. His first elected position came as concejal of Duranía from 1945 to 1947. Reaching the national level for the first time in 1947 through election to the Chamber of Representatives, Barco later served in the senate, as well as occupying a host of ministerial and ambassadorial positions. From 1966 to 1969 he was mayor of Bogotá, an experience often cited as indicative of his administrative talents. Service with the World Bank and participation in numerous international commissions further underlined the perception of his technical orientation, as well as strengthened his credentials outside Colombia.[9]

Gradually ascending inside the Liberal party, he had been regarded as a likely future president until his 1982 performance, when waffling over a possible competition with López Michelsen and the eventual retreat from his pre-candidacy weakened Barco's image. He had also been overshadowed by Luis Carlos Galán; had the latter returned to the Liberal fold earlier, Barco's aspirations might have been stymied. As it was, he ultimately was accepted as the next in the *"fila india"*—the unspoken file of presidential candidates awaiting their turn. He also benefitted greatly in elections from the reunited Liberal efforts in opposition to Alvaro Gómez, as well as the enduring public negativism toward the Conservative candidate, which memories of Gómez's youth and especially of his father's partisanship had long spawned.

Coming to office with a uniparty cabinet, Barco proceeded with an elaboration of plans already being fleshed out by his key advisors. Its contours, while scarcely secret, were not revealed in detail until Barco's speech to congress at the close of its session in December 1986. A "National Plan of Struggle against Poverty and for Employment" called for such measures as improved urban housing, universal health care, and education for all. The preoccupation with job creation remained a particular concern for the administration and, as with other new or expanded programs, was to be financed from greater coffee- and petroleum-based income. Agrarian reform was also proposed, while an early and immediate emphasis was placed on tax reform. Finance minister César Gaviria Trujillo, one of Barco's major advisors, presented a tax bill to congress in November, where hostility was manifest.

Designed to modernize and rationalize the system, rather than alter the level of tax revenue, it included rate unification for both individuals and tax businesses, eliminated many exemptions, and improved the process of record keeping and collection. A new tax on special benefits was promptly cited by opponents as penalizing the upper-middle class, along with a mistaken protest that common wage earners would also suffer.

Opposition was voiced primarily by Conservatives on partisan more than economic grounds. They were largely content to attack it as a "Reaganite" program, even while some Liberals were troubled by what they saw as an unduly conservative measure. Not until April 1987 was the legislation passed, and only then after it had been diluted.[10] The political lesson for Barco was the difficulty of dealing with congress, including members of his own party. The problem with fellow Liberals, however, would prove one to which he never adequately responded. By the close of 1987 the president had sent some twenty projects to congress, only one of which—a watered-down version of agrarian reform—was adopted. The absence of economic crisis, the regionalized character of the political parties, and Barco's evident unwillingness or inability to exercise his authority as party leader, effectively defenestrated many of his carefully wrought, technically sound plans.

By midterm the political situation for the government had worsened; the honeymoon had waned. The official growth rate had dropped to 4.1 percent, the inflation rate for 1988 was 28.1 percent, and both business and industry were sagging. Wages fell behind inflation for the first time in several years, and the labor force was restive. There was also growing criticism of an alleged insensitivity to social needs. Although the administration continued to insist that social investment was a major priority, its planning agency preferred to stress the need to control public spending. There was also official concern over Colombia's total external debt of $16.5 million. On 30 December 1988 the government reached agreement with creditor banks, thus postponing impending payments. At the same time, a loan of $1.7 billion was included. While useful, it fell short of the $2.6 billion projected as necessary to maintain the existing level of international reserves.

By mid-1989, as the administration entered its final year, the economic outlook had been clouded by declining coffee and petroleum revenues. The government decreed a freeze on spending. Related measures included a freeze as well on government salaries in conjunction with a reduction in military spending. A tilt toward trade liberalization and export-induced growth began to emerge. Privatization plans had already been drawn up, and these proceeded when the government announced in August 1989 that a number of state-managed banks and lending agencies could sell up to 65 percent of their assets to the private sector. Plans were also drafted to restructure key industries, drawing upon foreign as well as domestic expertise. In February of 1990 the administration put into effect a variety of additional measures within the context of economic liberalization, which had been accepted as the basic approach to economic policy.

While pursuing a mild reorientation of economic policy, Barco had consistently sought political and constitutional reforms as well. This enterprise included efforts on behalf of Betancur initiatives in undertaking a renewed drive for institutional decentralization. In January 1987 the president issued twelve executive decrees designed to transfer a host of activities—transportation and communications, education, health, urban development, among others—from the national to local government. The process, to be completed by 1992, significantly included the transfer of funds from the central government to the *municipios*. While constituting a revision with great potential, this was soon overshadowed by widespread debate over constitutional reform.

Barco had indicated at the outset of his term that stimulation of the government-opposition model plus the popular election of mayors were basic to a resolution of fundamental political tensions and discontinuities. Added to this, somewhat to his surprise, was a growing call for constitutional reform, which generated increasing public support. By early 1988 the topic was the single hottest political issue in the media, and the administration moved up its plans for extensive conversations with the political elite. The president himself preferred a plebiscite, to be followed by a Constituent Assembly and then another vote, this time on proposed reforms. For critics, such an open-ended plebiscite was viewed as constituting no less than a quasi-legitimized coup d'etat—a virtual blank check lacking any curbs on executive authority.[11]

It was opposed by a Conservative plan (also backed by Carlos Lleras Restrepo), which would effectively be more dependent upon elite negotiation than extensive plebiscitary review by the electorate. The eventual result was a document signed by Virgilio Barco and Misael Pastrana on 20 February 1988, labelled the Agreement of the House of Nariño. It called for proposed constitutional reforms by congress, thereafter subjected to a nationwide referendum on 9 October. The accord was soon jettisoned, however, when the Council of State declared it unconstitutional in early April. A new round of negotiations led to the May unveiling of a plan endorsed by Barco and Liberal leaders Luis Carlos Galán and Hernando Durán Dussán. Among other features was the elimination of Article 120; a "statute of opposition" would be produced by congress which would assign such posts as attorney-general to the opposition party. Misael Pastrana indicated his sympathies toward the plan, but pro-Gómez Conservatives, among others, were largely unpersuaded. It was subjected to lengthy congressional debate in the session beginning in August 1988. While the legislation was ultimately set aside, the entire issue became one of major national concern. Moreover, it became intricately interrelated to the series of elections scheduled for 1990. Further treatment is therefore deferred for later analysis.

Social and Political Controls

Virgilio Barco inherited a somewhat tattered peace policy from his predecessor. While the FARC had proceeded with a political party— Unidad Patriótica—which was participating in congress, this scarcely altered the fact that new initiatives were in order. What emerged over time was consistent with Barco's search for a middle ground between the draconian iron fist of Turbay and the conciliatory approach of Betancur. Even during the campaign, moreover, he had indicated that the extragovernmental commission would be dismissed, with the process of dialogue and communication entrusted directly to his ministers. Once in office, the new president therefore stressed the importance of institutional channels while effectively centralizing the effort.

In his inaugural address Barco promised a plan of "Rehabilitation, Reconciliation and Normalization," which would promote economic and social development, especially in those regions most in conflict. This also enabled Barco to differentiate his peace policies from those of his predecessor. Faithful to his technocratic orientation, he resumed programs of rehabilitation that were so designed by the PNR as to resemble an extended and permanent civil version of traditional civic-military action.[12] Given his belief that poverty was the root of violence, the incoming president was initially committed to structural reforms. As Hoskin wrote at the time,

> The major programmatic thrust of the Barco government is oriented toward a frontal attack on the structural inequalities of the society, which are viewed as the underlying causes of the violence. The magnitude of the problem is stressed in a recent government study that reveals that 43.2 percent of the population— 13,250,000 people—do not have the income necessary to meet basic human needs.[13]

Barco undertook a reinvigoration of Betancur's Plan Nacional de Rehabilitación (PNR; National Plan for Rehabilitation), with which the state would reach out to the most neglected areas of the nation. The Plan contra Pobreza Absoluta (PPA; Plan against Absolute Poverty) also sought to deal directly with problems of poverty.[14] Within a matter of months, however, killings by paramilitary death squads increased, guerrilla activism rose to new highs, and there was a generalized recrudescence of violence. Carlos Lleras Restrepo declared that Colombia was "currently experiencing one of the worst crises of its history. The lack of security and the proven inefficacy of the judicial system are reaching terrifying new heights."[15] The notion of dialogue progressively receded as the political environment worsened. Barco's efforts to produce structural reforms were slow to come. When Attorney General Carlos Mauro Hoyos Jiménez was murdered on 25 January 1988, Barco responded by introducing tougher antiterrorist measures, including a broadening of arresting powers for security forces and creation of nearly 5000 new judicial posts.

The kidnapping that same month of Andrés Pastrana, son of the former president who was running for mayor of Bogotá, dramatized for the public the gravity of the situation. This contributed further to the continuation of military and counterguerrilla measures that gained priority over those of reform and societal restructuring. Assassinations and massacres became ever more frequent in 1988, and the Conservatives' most recent presidential candidate, Alvaro Gómez, was himself kidnapped on 29 May and held hostage for a time. The government proclaimed its antiterrorist Statute in Defense of Democracy, while the perceptions of military inefficiency encouraged an expansion of the armed forces' budget.[16] The tilting of government policy toward the use of force continued, especially when the president's own peace plan, announced with fanfare on 1 September 1988, was widely criticized on all sides and was promptly cast aside.

The climate of death and terror during the Barco years was also powerfully affected by the growth of drug-related violence. Despite occasional victories such as the capture on 4 February 1987 of Carlos Lehder Rivas, the *narcotraficantes* largely operated with impunity. Colombia and the United States engaged in lengthy debate over the issue of extraditability; Bogotá and Washington found themselves increasingly at odds, even as the industry flourished.[17] Concerted military action against the drug traffickers came only in the wake of the August 1989 murder of

Luis Carlos Galán at an outdoor campaign rally. The death of the probable next president of the republic spurred an intensification of conflict. Yet this did not prevent the 1990 assassinations of two more presidential candidates: Bernardo Jaramillo Ossa of Unión Patriótica at Bogotá's El Dorado Airport on 22 March, and the M-19's Carlos Pizarro Leóngomez on 27 April during an Avianca flight to Cartagena. Threats against Colombian judges also undergirded the air of intimidation, along with such periodic episodes as a mid-April car bomb explosion in Medellín which killed twenty and wounded another one hundred.

Over the life of the Barco administration, the norms for national security and measures to curb violence were not altered fundamentally in practice. Among the most significant was the 1989 creation of an elite force, the Cuerpo Especial Armado de la Policia, dedicated to fighting death squads and drug-related terrorists.[18] In 1990 Barco also formed a series of special mobile brigades in the army, especially trained and equipped to conduct sophisticated counterguerrilla actions. As Colombia stepped into the 1990s under a young new president, it was evident that the Barco administration had failed to alter conditions significantly. Granting its shortcomings, however, it remained true that problems were systemic. As Zamosc wrote, Colombia's ongoing violence was "a direct reflection of the breakdown of state authority"; the weakness of the state required a rebuilding of the foundations of state through a deepening of democracy.[19] This message would be writ large with the coming of the Gaviria administration in August 1990.[20]

The Politics of Uniparty Government

The Party Competition

For the first time in nearly four decades, a new government had taken office with the intention of ruling without an alliance or biparty coalition.[21] In light of campaign pledges as well as the failed dialogue with the Social Conservatives, Virgilio Barco undertook a so-called *gobierno de partido* in which the Liberal party bore sole responsibility. There seemed grounds to believe that this might prove a beneficial step in systemic reform, with a government-opposition model producing a more competitive and representative form of governance.[22] The Liberals had won a resounding victory, and Virgilio Barco was relatively free from constraining ties to earlier presidents. The Betancur-inspired impetus toward *apertura,* whatever its manifest policy failures, also offered a basis on which Barco might build.

The president's advisors had labored to formulate the government-opposition structure; the single major proponent was the incoming minister of government Fernando Cepeda Ulloa, a prominent political scientist who had built the notable program at the Universidad de Los Andes. He argued that interparty competition would permit an institutional restructuring of the anachronistic Frente Nacional system.[23] Among the most important by-products would presumably be a reorganization and reunification of both the Liberal and Conservative parties; in the meantime, the M-19 and other groups would also be empowered to contest elections.[24] However, circumstances proved less propitious than had been anticipated, and before the conclusion of its first year in office the Barco administration was awash with partisan turmoil and internal confusion.

The causes were multiple. On the Liberal side, the new president was soon demonstrating that his leadership and personality were less than forceful. The party itself remained a confederation of regional *caciques,* and it was difficult to translate the rhetoric of the campaign into a meaningful government program. With patronage and positions now essentially restricted to the Liberals, party demands were greater than ever, and the balancing act was a delicate one. All of this was reflected in congress, where the solid Liberal majority was far from responsive to presidential leadership. Entrenched local and regional interests manifested themselves in the business of the legislature, often ignoring or even defying Barco and his ministers. As *El Tiempo* put it while assessing the first year of the Barco government, there was sadly a "difficult and chaotic situation within the government party."[25] In short order, then, the Liberals and President Barco found that the theoretical benefits of a strong party-based electoral victory were inoperative.

In addition to these problems, the unusual experience of a government-opposition model was complicated by the internal problems of the Social Conservatives themselves. While Misael Pastrana had formalized the party's acceptance of its role as a "thoughtful opposition" through the Directorio Nacional Conservador, Bertha Hernandez de Ospina and other party notables disagreed. This dissension worsened relations with Barco and the Liberals in congress. As an example, Government Minister Fernando Cepeda Ulloa opened a speech to the lower house in November 1986 by declaring that he would permit statements only from fellow Liberals; the Conservatives immediately walked out. The result was similar action in the senate and a period during which the lack of a quorum paralyzed all congressional action, as well as government legislation then on the table.

All of this led to what one observer characterized as agitated politics rather than an institutional reinvigoration of the political system.[26] The situation did not improve significantly. By June of 1988 *El Espectador* bluntly expressed the view "that the president does not understand what is going on."[27] Yet Barco was doggedly plodding forward, including his support for the election of municipal officials on 13 March 1988, the first such in national history.[28] As a realization of Belisario Betancur's *apertura*, it attracted some 55 percent of the 11 million eligible voters; 1009 mayors and some 10,000 municipal representatives were to be selected. The period leading up to the election was marked by violence and intimidation; twenty-nine of the eighty-seven Unidad Popular candidates were killed during the six months preceding elections, and over 100 other municipal office seekers were slain. Death threats and murder also discouraged voters in small towns and outlying rural areas. Thus, the level of participation was widely viewed as surprisingly solid.[29]

The Liberals won their customary victory, electing 498 mayors in contrast to the Conservatives' 442; Nuevo Liberalismo captured 53 and the Unidad Patriótica 17. This reflected 51.8 percent for the Liberals, 36.5 for the Conservatives, along with the New Liberals' 4.8 and a mere 0.9 for the UP.[30] The Liberal success included victory in seventeen of the twenty-three departmental capitals and in twenty-four of the thirty-one principal cities. However, they lost Medellín by a narrow margin to the editor of *El Colombiano,* Juan Gómez Martínez, who ran on a strong antidrug campaign. Even more serious for the Liberals was their unnecessary loss of the mayoral race in Bogotá. After months of complicated negotiations the Liberals had failed to reach agreement, leading to the candidacies of Carlos Ossa Escobar and Juan Manuel Caicedo Ferrer. The former was chosen by a transitory alliance between Ernesto Samper Pizano and Luis Carlos Galán, while a separate Bogotá convention had opted for the latter.

This Liberal disunity allowed the ultimate victory of the thirty-four-year-old Andrés Pastrana Arango, son of the former Conservative president. Polling 324,275 votes, he outdistanced Caicedo with 236,567. Ossa received 215,704; thus, the two Liberal candidates amassed 452,291 votes, a substantial margin above their rival. Liberal disunity had cost them the nation's second most important elected position while catapulting Pastrana into a strong position as future presidential timber. None of the would-be Liberal hopefuls benefitted. Aside from their reluctance to cooperate, which in fact had extended to many mayoral races elsewhere in the nation, none could claim success in Bogotá races for councilmen. The number of Samper supporters dropped to two, and Galán enthusiasts to three. Senator Hernando Durán Dussán had championed the stronger Liberal candidate in Caicedo, but otherwise had not greatly advanced his presidential prospects.

Virgilio Barco was the subject of recriminations for having allegedly stood aside while the Liberals divided over the Bogotá mayorship. Yet he customarily held himself apart from such matters, including the coming period of competition over the Liberal presidential nomination. At the least, the Liberals' future had been brightened by the return of Nuevo Liberalismo. A month after mayoral elections, Luis Carlos Galán reiterated the goals of his movement while committing himself to agreement with the government on legislative plans for 1988–89.[31] This movement toward a reunification of disparate Liberal forces was realized at the party convention in August 1988, where Galán made his peace with a party whose formal leader at the time was, ironically, none other than Julio César Turbay Ayala. It was also tacitly understood that, while competition would not be suppressed, Galán would be acceptable to the party *jefes* as presidential candidate in 1990. This did not assure his nomination, but opened the door for his legitimized participation in the process of candidate selection.

Candidate Selection

While some viewed Galán as the next Liberal candidate, many party stalwarts still treated him as an upstart, and he had serious rivals.[32] Hernando Durán Dussán was regarded by many Liberals as next in the "fila india," and former president Turbay, serving once again as party director, clearly leaned in his direction. Many of the regional party caciques also saw Durán as a candidate who would pursue traditional paths and leave their own power and patronage untouched. They had not been converted to *galanismo* with the latter's return to the party, and were also suspicious of the young Ernesto Samper Pizano, a senator and former minister who reflected left-of-center elements among the Liberals. As the pre-campaign gradually unfolded, the prevailing folk wisdom held that Galán would secure the nomination and subsequently win the May 1990 general elections. All of this came to an abrupt halt with Galán's assassination at a political rally on 18 August 1989.

This had a stunning impact on the nation and prodded Virgilio Barco into an intensification of the crackdown against the *narcotraficantes*. It also left the Liberal candidacy up in the air. The Galán forces announced their support for César Gaviria Trujillo, who had earlier resigned from the Barco cabinet to serve as Galán's campaign manager. In the wake of Galán's murder, the campaigning for nomination moved increasingly from street rallies to television appearances. Ernesto Samper remained the nominee of the quasi-social democratic Liberals while Durán Dussán, at age seventy, offered both a generational and a programmatic contrast. He took a hard line on security issues, while the other two stressed a solution to social problems and further political decentralization. All three were unsympathetic to the Barco policy toward the drug barons. In addition, another trio of well-known Liberals had entered the race, although without any real chance for nomination: Alberto Santofimio, Jaime Castro Castro, and William Jaramillo.

The Liberals' previous decision to choose their candidate for the first time by *consulta popular*—in effect, a nominating primary—had been designed both to democratize the process and, even more importantly for many party leaders, to assure a unity candidate. In early 1990 there was a spate of rumors that if support among the contenders was relatively evenly distributed, Julio César Turbay Ayala might seize the nomination. Both Gaviria and Samper appealed to Lleras Restrepo and López Michelsen, and the two ex-presidents issued a statement endorsing the *consulta popular* in February. This effectively assured the candidacy of the victor although, once again, a major decision had been affirmed only by the direct intervention of two ranking figures rather than action of the organization as a whole.[33]

While Gaviria increasingly appeared the preference of the party rank-and-file, observers doubted his ability to win a majority, in which case an agreement with Samper over major policy initiatives might have emerged. In the balloting on 11 March, however, Gaviria won decisively with 59.9 percent of the vote; Samper followed with 18.5 percent and Durán Dussán with 14.4.[34] The regional caciques had suffered a blow to their old-style clientelistic practices, while the cloak of *galanismo* plus the reformist public mood and solid connections with the Barco government had all contributed to Gaviria's margin of victory. The forty-three-year-old victor had also conducted a shrewd campaign whereby he had successfully seized the political center, pushing Samper to the Left and Durán to the Right. The Liberals were meanwhile whipping the Social Conservatives in mayoral races, capturing seventeen departmental capitals. They won Bogotá with Juan Martín Caicedo Ferrer and Medellín with Omar Flores Vélez as well, although losing in Cali.

Public interest had been divided between the Liberals' *consulta popular* and the legislative and municipal races. Encouraged by Virgilio Barco's continuing urging of more competitive politics, there was a proliferation of contenders. For example, no fewer than seventy-nine separate slates participated in the race for Bogotá's twenty council seats. While the Liberals were sorting out their affairs, then, the level of activity was substantial for both the Social Conservatives and for small opposition groups. With the former, the failure to define and to fulfill the role of opposition to the Barco government aggravated the party's internal divisions. The current manifestations of the historic *laureanista-ospinista* rivalry had grown so severe that in November a cover story in *Semana* asked "Is the Conservative Party Finished?"[35]

Despite decades of defeats at the hands of the Liberals, the party had not only shared power and patronage during the Frente Nacional, but in subsequent governments until that of Barco. The experiment as opposition party had proved discouraging. Alvaro Gómez spoke of possibly supporting a Liberal candidate, and such stalwarts as Juan Diego Jaramillo wrote that for all practical purposes the Conservatives were dead.[36] Misael Pastrana remained the *jefe único,* and there were few other names with national recognition. A poll in late 1989 showed that among presidential pre-candidates, the Liberals captured some 80 percent while the three Conservatives listed—Gómez, Pastrana, and Rodrigo Lloreda Caicedo— totalled a mere 12 percent.[37] Belisario Betancur had largely withdrawn from party affairs and Alvaro Gómez was about to chart his own personal political course when the official convention of the Social Conservative party convened on 9 November 1989.

Three presidential pre-candidates were on parade: Lloreda, Alvaro Leyva, and Carlos Holguin. Each spoke harshly of the Liberals and the

Barco government. Pastrana was more moderate toward the administration, but shared in harsh attacks on Alvaro Gómez, who was not in attendance. There was a move to delay the naming of the candidate until new approaches might be made toward the Gómez forces but, after extended debate, it was decided to proceed. Of the 715 official delegates, only 508 were on hand for the vote, which Lloreda won with 346 votes to 72 and 71 for Leyva and Holguin respectively. This meant in effect that Lloreda would be the official party candidate, but without the support of Alvaro Gómez or his colleagues and supporters. As Rodrigo Marín declared for the latter, it remained uncertain whether Gómez would run himself, support another candidate, or simply sit out the 1990 elections.

In Lloreda, the Social Conservatives had selected a respected figure who at age forty-seven had served in numerous elected posts and a variety of diplomatic and international positions, including foreign minister under the Betancur administration.[38] His political and diplomatic acumen was notable and there were hopes that, notwithstanding an inevitable electoral defeat in 1990, he might contribute to a reunification of the Social Conservatives and a redefinition of the party in the last decade of the century. However, the prospects—at least in the short run—were dimmed when Alvaro Gómez Hurtado rejected all overtures and shaped his own Movimiento de Salvación Nacional (MSN) in support of his own 1990 presidential candidacy. The March electoral results were also discouraging, for, although the losses were not dramatic, they extended the party's electoral decline that had set in most notably in the years since 1978.

The Social Conservatives' global vote was one-third, continuing the decline from virtually 40 percent in 1978. Three seats were lost in the senate, leaving 41 to oppose 72 Liberals. Eleven seats were dropped in the lower house, leaving 72 representatives as against 117 Liberals. The panorama was also darkened by a drop in mayorships, from 40 to 36 percent; the Liberals increased from 45 to 55 percent.[39] It remained for Lloreda to carry the official, Pastrana-endorsed banners in the May elections against Alvaro Gómez, constituting in effect the kind of *consulta popular* that the Social Conservatives had rejected. The importance for the future of the party, then, was greater by far than for the outcome of the national elections. And in addition to the anticipated Liberal victory, there were questions about other participants, most notably the M-19 and Unión Patriótica.

For the M-19, electoral participation was hinged upon continuing negotiation with the government. In March of 1989 the M-19's leader Carlos Pizarro Leóngomez signed a cease-fire agreement with Interior Minister Raul Orejuela setting forth stages of transition, demobilization, and reincorporation of M-19 guerrillas. In mid-July this led to a further accord signed by Pizarro and Rafael Pardo, Barco's peace representative. As discussions moved forward, Pizarro announced in October his intention of running for the presidency. A final pact was signed a mere two days before elections, with the M-19 agreeing to surrender its arms in exchange for legal participation in the congressional and local elections. Running in alliance with three small parties under the label of Acción Nacionalista por la Paz (ANP), they outpolled the Unión Patriótica.[40] This included Carlos Pizarro's 8 percent in the Bogotá mayoral contest versus 1 percent for the UP's Carlos Romero, while winning a few mayoral races. The overall decline of the UP, including the loss of two congressional seats and mayoral control of Remedios and Segovia, among others, reflected in no small part the depredations suffered during its five years of legal existence. The toll exceeded 1000 and, for 1990 alone, had already reached 75.

Campaign and Elections

The interim between the March and May elections were marked more by death and violence than by orthodox political campaigning.[41] Bernardo Jaramillo Ossa, thirty-five-year-old presidential candidate for the Unión Patriótica, was fatally shot by a contract killer at Bogotá's El Dorado airport on 22 March. A critic of violence who had fought for the independence of the UP from the FARC movement, Jaramillo had been a voice of moderation on the Left. His murder, coming as it did amid a renewal of hostilities between armed guerrillas and right-wing paramilitary groups, stimulated calls for a delay of the presidential elections. The government rejected the proposal, and at the same time Carlos Pizarro Leóngomez was formally named as presidential candidate for the M-19. A movement on behalf of a Nueva Izquierda coalition began to take shape, but on 26 April, a day before its general congress was to convene, Pizarro was assassinated aboard an Avianca jetliner. He was the seventh M-19 commander to die since Jaime Bateman Cayon in 1983; into his shoes stepped his second-in-command, Antonio Navarro Wolff.[42]

As with Jaramillo, responsibility for the killing of Pizarro was generally laid at the feet of the drug industry, whose leaders were determined to force a reversal of the existing policy to extradite drug traffickers to the United States. There was also widespread criticism of government security forces—not to mention airport officials—for laxity, incompetence, or even complicity. The campaign itself, already limited in the interests of security, became even less open or participatory than before. César Gaviria temporarily suspended his campaign, and later appearances were largely televised rather than presented from public fora. Other candidates were similarly cautious, while the public was more alienated as well as personally fearful of the campaign process. Thus, Alvaro Gómez Hurtado limited his otherwise vigorous campaign largely to press conferences, closed meetings, and television appearances.

Granted the constraints, Gómez campaigned generally with uncommon zest. Recognizing that victory in the presidential race was not within his reach, he sought his vengeance against Misael Pastrana in reprisal for many years of insults and intraparty harassment. Gómez soon built a solid lead over Rodrigo Lloreda in the polls, although in effect this represented an impending triumph over Pastrana himself. Some fifteen years of near-Napoleonic *pastranista* control of the party had led to a basic decline from 40 to 30 percent in the electorate, and the weakness of party structures could not withstand the onslaught of Gómez's own candidacy. At the same time, impartial observers asked whether the two *jefes* were in effect willing to sink their party rather than permit a triumph for the other. In any event, the Gómez campaign was a forceful one, with the MSN candidate displaying his experience on television as well as in personal appearances. All of this left Rodrigo Lloreda little realistic chance of carrying the official Social Conservative party and *pastranista* interests to victory.

His campaign was fuller and more open than any of the others. Appearing regularly in public plazas, Lloreda stomped the country as if he were on the brink of victory. His official program of government, the first to be announced, was filled with concrete proposals. His familiar campaign slogan "Misión: Colombia!" spread across Colombia and was supplemented by generally skillful media presentations. Lloreda was also viewed favorably by the electorate in the polls, although his reputation did not carry over to a concomitant share of the actual vote. None of this was sufficient to combat Alvaro Gómez, a far more recognizable public figure, let alone the youthful Gaviria whose campaign placards were often superimposed upon an image of Luis Carlos Galán.

On 27 May Colombians went to the polls. Citizens were faced with the ongoing wave of bombings and violence, as well as a degree of disinterest owing to the universal expectation of an easy Gaviria win. A total of 6,047,576 votes were cast; the abstention rate of 48 percent was higher than the average for presidential races. César Gaviria secured a comfortable victory with 2,891,808 votes—47.8 percent of the total. This doubled Alvaro Gómez's 1,433,913 for 23.7 percent. Third, surprisingly, was the M-19's Navarro with 754,740 for 12.4, followed by Lloreda in fourth place with 735,374 and 12.1 percent. Given the fragmentation of his opposition, Gaviria ran first in every department and major city. If he saw the results as less than ideal, it was due to the fact that his totals were well short of a majority of eligible voters.

Nonetheless, the voters' verdict gave him a reasonable mandate with which to enter office. The other "winner" was Navarro; although an unknown to the public who had entered the race barely thirty days before elections, his underfunded campaign had more than doubled the highest total ever before achieved by the left in Colombia. A somewhat professorial and far from charismatic figure without the resources for television campaigning, he benefitted from public revulsion over the recent deaths of Pizarro and Jaramillo, along with a general sympathy for the reincorporation of guerrillas into civil life.

Alvaro Gómez was also a winner in gaining his revenge against Misael Pastrana; it was the latter, rather than Rodrigo Lloreda, who was humiliated by the elections. Yet Gómez and his MSN controlled no more than 30 percent of the basically Conservative seats in congress, where Pastrana still held the upper hand. Whatever the broad repudiation of the former president, it still left the remnants of the party organization in his hands. Indeed, the Social Christian crisis showed no signs of abating, with neither caudillo capable of unifying the party and without a possibility of meaningful reconciliation between the two.

Toward Constitutional Reform

A rather different element in the May elections related to the movement toward constitutional reform, which in intermittent fashion had been underway for some time. When President Barco's reformist proposals had been shot down by both the legislature and the courts in 1988, the initiative passed elsewhere. As the notion of congressional action ceded to that of a Constituent Assembly, other groups came to the fore, including a number of dedicated student activists. On 15 August 1989, five days after the burial of Galán, over 20,000 held a silent march to protest the murder. A document that denounced violence and called for support of all democratic institutions in the struggle also demanded the convocation of a national Constituent Assembly. This proved a relatively easy idea to sell, and public support mounted. *El Espectador* campaigned relentlessly for the idea and, along with others, demanded that the electorate be asked its opinion.

Congress had not yet definitively yielded its own role, and late in 1989 sought to frame a variety of constitutional changes, which would then be presented to popular vote in January of 1990. However, the ineffectiveness of traditional party leadership—notably including Barco, Turbay, and Pastrana—left the legislature rudderless, and it was finally decided not to proceed further.[43] The popular campaign in favor of a plebiscite gained momentum and, with the students again in the vanguard of the fight, it was agreed that the 11 March elections would included the so-called *séptima papeleta*. This was consequently added to the six other electoral options, and asked if the voters favored a plebiscitary test of the proposed constitutional assembly. The result was a favorable vote from over 2 million Colombians.[44]

The presidential response was Virgilio Barco's issuing of Decree 927 of 1990, which called for inclusion of the plebiscitary question on the May ballot.[45] The presidential edict ordered that the populace be given the opportunity to vote up or down on the following proposition:

To strengthen participatory democracy, do you vote for the convocation of a Constitutional Assembly, with representations of the social, political and regional forces of the Nation, constituted democratically and popularly to reform the Political Constitution of Colombia?[46]

On 27 May, 86.6 percent of those voting (5,236,863) supported the convening of an Asamblea Constituyente. Within two weeks the Barco government had named a commission to study the matter and on 2 August, shortly before the inauguration of César Gaviria, an accord was signed by representatives of the Social Conservatives, M-19, and the Liberals (Gaviria as party director) concerning the procedures for the selection, composition, and thematic responsibility of an Asamblea Nacional Constituyente.

The agreement was ratified on 23 August 1990, but soon began to unravel. By this point the mantle of leadership had passed from Virgilio Barco to César Gaviria. It remained for the latter to grapple with the issue as a part of the ongoing drive for *apertura,* which had seized public opinion and which had been cited as a major element in the president-elect's commitment to structural modernization of the state. This would constitute a major challenge to the movement away from the Frente Nacional and the necessity of redefining or adapting patrimonial clientelism to the realities of Colombian life, society, and politics as the nation approached a new century.

Notes

1. For the full text see Virgilio Barco, *Discursos 1986–89,* vol. 1 (Bogotá: Presidencia de la República, 1990), 19–33.
2. A theoretical discussion of the government-opposition model, along with other político-institutional reforms, is Jesús Pérez González Rubio, *Gobierno y oposición: elementos para una reforma del estado* (Bogotá: Pontificia Universidad Javeriana, Facultad de Estudios Interdisciplinarios, 1987).
3. "Colombia," *Latin American Andean Report* (16 May 1986).
4. "Colombia," *Latin America Weekly Report* (21 August 1986).
5. Bruce Michael Bagley, "Colombian Politics: Crisis or Continuity?" *Current History* 86, no. 516 (January 1987): 23. This article provides an informed overview of conditions and problems as power passed from Betancur to Barco.
6. Barco, *Discursos.*
7. *Semana* (2 June 1986).
8. A characteristic statement reflecting his professional outlook and interests is Virgilio Barco, *Economía, planeación y política social* (Bogotá: Carlos Valencia Editores, 1981).
9. A complete CV appears in Virgilio Barco, *Hacia una Colombia nueva: Liberalismo, democracia social y cambio* (Bogotá: Editorial La Oveja Negra Ltda., 1986), 223–27. This collection contains Barco policy statements and campaign promises from 1985 and 1986, as well as the official Liberal party program adopted on 4 December 1985 when he was officially designated the party candidate.
10. Indications of both achievements and frustrated proposals were evident in the president's message to the nation on 20 July 1987, subsequently published as Virgilio Barco, *Diálogo democrático: ni hegemonía, ni sectarismo* (Bogotá: Editorial Oveja Negra Ltda., 1987).
11. Luis Alberto Restrepo, "The Crisis of the Current Political Regime and Its Possible Outcomes," in Charles Bergquist, Ricardo Peñaranda, and Gonzalo Sánchez, eds., *Violence in Colombia: The Contemporary Crisis in Historical Perspective* (Wilmington, DE: SR Books, 1991), 283.

12. For Barco's view at the time see his *El restablecimiento del orden público* (Bogotá: Presidencia de la República, 1988).

13. Gary Hoskin, "Colombia's Political Crisis," *Current History*, 87:525 (January 1988), 12.

14. See Ayala O. Ulpiano, "Aproximación al Plan de Lucha Contra la Pobreza y para la Generación de Empleo," in *Debates de coyuntura económica* (Bogotá: Fedesarrollo y Fescol, 1987).

15. Quoted in Clara Ponce de León, "Colombia: Another Dirty War?" *NACLA Report on the Americas* 21, no. 4 (July/August 1987): 4.

16. Barco, *El restablecimiento*, 437 ff.

17. For discussions that briefly review the highlights of the recent conflict and debate between Colombia and the United States, see John D. Martz, "Colombia's Search for Peace," *Current History* 88, no. 536 (March 1989): 128, and Martz, "Colombia at the Crossroads," *Current History* 90, no. 553 (February 1991): 72.

18. Barco, *El restableciemiento*, 843 ff.

19. León Zamosc, "The Political Crisis and the Prospects for Rural Democracy in Colombia," *The Journal of Development Studies* 26, no. 4 (July 1990): 70.

20. An insightful analysis presented shortly after the conclusion of the Barco administration is Francisco Leal Buitrago, "Political Crisis and Drug Trafficking in Colombia," *Papers on Latin America* (New York: Columbia University, The Institute of Latin American and Iberian Studies, 1990).

21. For a complete listing of ministers throughout the Barco period, see Pontificia Universidad Javeriana, *Los gabinetes ministeriales como élites políticas—Colombia (1930–1990)*, Tomo II (Bogotá: Pontificia Universidad Javeriana, Facultad de Estudios Interdisciplinarios, 1991), 735–45. This two-volume collection is a definitive source of information, accompanied by succinct summaries, for each Colombian administration.

22. A valuable compendium of essays and relevant documents, dating back to President López Pumarejo's 1934 letter to the Conservatives offering collaboration in government, is Patricia Pinzón de Lewin, *La oposición en Colombia* (Bogotá: CEI, UNIDANDES y FESCOL, 1986).

23. Official declarations elaborating the virtues of the government-opposition model are found in Fernando Cepeda Ulloa, *El esquema gobierno-oposición* (Bogotá: Ministerio de Gobierno, 1987).

24. An extensive collection of supportive statements, television interviews, and op-ed pieces in the Bogotá press is found in Virgilio Barco, *El fortalecimiento de la democracia: el esquema gobierno-partidos de oposición, la democracia participativa y la paz* (Bogotá: Imprenta Nacional de Colombia, 1990).

25. *El Tiempo* (7 August 1987).

26. Hoskin, "Colombia's Political Crisis," 12.

27. *El Espectador* (15 June 1988).

28. For an authoritative review of the process that includes both analytic essays and detailed factual information, see Pontificia Universidad Javeriana, *Mercadeo electoral: elección de alcaldes* (Bogotá: PUJ, Facultad de Estudios Interdisciplinarios, 1988).

    A government-based publication that provides excellent historical background, along with a variety of congressional documents, including Law 78 of 1986, which regulates mayoral elections, is Fernando Cepeda Ulloa, ed., *La reglamentación de la elección popular de alcaldes* (Bogotá: Ministerio de Gobierno, 1987.

29. A helpful overview is Angelica Ocampo and Germán Ruiz, "Las elecciónes," in Rubén Sánchez David, ed., *Los nuevos retos electorales—Colombia 1990: antesala del cambio* (Bogotá: CEREC, 1991).

30. Somewhat different totals emerge if Liberal votes are combined and if coalitions as well as small local parties are included. Cf. Ocampo and Ruiz, "Las elecciónes," 175.

31. The text appears in *El Espectador* (24 April 1988).

32. For detailed political profiles of four leading aspirants compiled prior to Galán's death, see Asociación de Politólogos Javerianos, *Los Presidenciables 1990* (Bogotá: Pontificia Universidad Javeriana, 1989).

33. A detailed report is "Hablan los Muebles Viejos," *Semana* (13 February 1990): 22–23.

34. An analysis of Gaviria's cooly skillful trajectory from *galanista* campaign manager to official Liberal candidate appears in "El Elegido," *Semana* (13 March 1990) 24–27.

35. "Is Conservative Party Finished?" *Semana* (6 November 1989).

36. Juan Diego Jaramillo declared the Conservative party dead in his *De la política la vida pública* (Bogotá: Tercer Mundo, 1991).

37. "Is Conservative Party Finished?" *Semana* (6 November 1989).

38. Lloreda's complete CV plus a selection of policy statements are found in *Los Presidenciables*, 123–48.

39. Pastrana's rationalizing of defeat appears in a letter to *Semana* published 29 March 1990, p. 28.

40. Frente Democrático, Colombia Unida, and Democracia Cristiana.

41. Several essays dealing with the elections of 1990 are contained in Rubén Sánchez David, ed., *Los nuevos retos.*

42. An informative biographical summary was published in *Semana* (1 May 1990): 26–27.

43. "Eutanasia," *Semana* (19 December 1990): 32–33.

44. An informative analysis that traces the evolution of the idea and the politics of the Constituyente is John Dugas, Rubén Sánchez D., and Elizabeth Ungar B., "La Asamblea Nacional Constituyente, expresión de una voluntad general," in Sánchez, ed., *Los nuevos retos,* 187–215.

45. For the text of the decree, Barco's accompanying televised statement, plus the complete decision of the Court, see *Una constituyente para la Colombia del futuro,* 2d ed. (Bogotá: FESCOL and Departamento de Ciencia Politica, Universidad de los Andes, 1990). The volume incorporates papers delivered at a Forum sponsored by the UNIANDES Department of Political Science.

46. Jaime Buenahora Febres-Cordero, *El proceso constituyente: De la propuesta estudiantil a la quiebra del bipartidismo* (Bogotá: Tercer Mundo Editores, 1991), 169.

12

Modernization and Restructuring: Gaviria (1990–94)

The Politics of Governance

The National Environment

Under a chilly Bogotá sky on 7 August 1990, the youngest chief executive in Colombian history was inaugurated. Following in the wake of the laconic and uncommunicative Virgilio Barco, César Gaviria was expected to provide a positive contrast in leadership style. Enjoying an 89 percent approval rate, Gaviria represented not only a younger generation but, in many ways, political elements that were not totally beholden to longstanding traditional elites. He had come to the candidacy prematurely in the wake of the Galán assassination, won the nomination despite opposition by the Liberal old guard, and proceeded to a decisive victory over a divided opposition. Despite the high level of abstention and the diluted quality of his electoral mandate, Gaviria was in a position to call for a wide array of reforms. *Apertura* was the buzzword of the hour and, ill-defined as it was, gave the new president further leeway in setting forth his own program. This took shape in his inaugural address, which focused on three basic issues: peace, institutional modernization, and an internationalization of the economy. These emphases were perhaps pedestrian at the outset. However, the incoming government expressed a realization that Colombia was fast approaching a historical conjuncture at which forces were susceptible to meaningful change.

Prevailing demographic trends had continued during the Barco years. By 1990 the population had passed 32 million while the growth rate was running at some 2.3 percent annually. The increase was almost exclusively in the urban sector, which constituted three-quarters of the population; the rural population remained steady at 10 million, not having shown any change for more than twenty years.[1] It was officially estimated that Greater Bogotá would reach 5.2 million by 1992, with Medellín at 2.3 million, Cali 1.7 million, and Barranquilla passing the 1 million mark.[2]

While the general pace of growth was showing a decline, the rural-urban migration plus natural increase in the cities contributed to the continuation of urban growth. Unlike most other Latin American countries, this was of course shared by the capital with the three other cities of more than 1 million, while cities of 200,000 or more were also being affected by migration from the countryside. At the same time unemployment remained a problem, notwithstanding an annual growth of the economically active population in the four major cities estimated at 170,00 persons. It was calculated that some 120,000 entered the work force naturally upon coming of age, with the rest resulting from broadening participation. Many of those officially labelled as employed were working in the informal sector, where productivity was low.[3]

The incoming administration therefore inherited a host of problems from its predecessor. The overall economic rate of growth, which earlier dropped from over 5 percent in 1987 to 3.7 percent in 1988, had fallen to 3.1 percent by 1990. The annual inflation rate of 28 percent, although low for Latin America, was high for Colombians. Moreover, consumer prices had risen in 1989 by 25.8 percent and, over the period from October 1989 to May 1990, consumer price inflation had reached 32.9 percent annually.[4] The foreign debt stood at $16 billion, the rate of export growth was slowing, and declining coffee prices were costing the nation dearly in export earnings—no less than $200 million in the twelve months preceding Gaviria's inauguration.[5] Economic resources were also continuing to be stretched by the demands of the struggle to assert control over both the guerrillas—whose attacks on oil pipelines had become especially costly—and the drug industry. Indeed, the cost of the drug war between 1988 and 1989 alone had grown by nearly 300 percent, making the defense sector Colombia's largest importer.

The new administration was basically persuaded of the need to seek a modernization of Colombian institutions, much of which was related to the forthcoming Constituent Assembly. It was also committed to renewing the quest for internal peace, and Gaviria himself believed in political dialogue, demobilization of armed organizations—including private informal self-defense units—and justice for all combatants willing to accept the authority of the state. Detailed policies were to be formulated and implemented by the new set of counselors and advisors put together by the incoming president. They numbered representatives of diverse groups in the cabinet, importantly fleshed out by a small inner circle of confidantes. The mean age of the former was forty-eight and the latter less than forty, leading in time to what many Colombians termed Gaviria's *kinder*. The prominence of this relatively unknown new generation of policymakers further underlined widespread expectations of nontraditional approaches to fundamental difficulties.[6]

Policies of the Administration

The rise of César Gaviria to the presidency was one of the most meteoric in Colombian history. It brought to office a politician whose command of economics had not been seen in the presidency since Carlos Lleras Restrepo. His personal style was also reminiscent of Lleras in his openness to extensive debate and an airing of differing views—a sharp contrast from the virtual monasticism of Virgilio Barco—after which he would privately reach his decision and then pursue it decisively. And while Gaviria in some ways had built his career by challenging the traditional political class, he also appreciated its power and influence sufficiently to deal with its barons. Thus, his ties to Galán and the political inheritance of Nuevo Liberalismo had in no sense isolated Gaviria from the prevailing establishment. Neither had his past career and performance produced a figure as inscrutable as his predecessor. Gavaria's trajectory reflected both fortuitous circumstances and hard, determined toil in a series of important posts—almost always with positive ties to major national leaders.

Born in Pereira in 1947, Gaviria's early years and education were in the provinces. One year was spent as an exchange student in a California high school, after which he returned home and continued to excel academically. Moving to Bogotá for his university studies, he shifted from industrial engineering to economics at the University of the Andes, where he recorded the most distinguished record in twenty-five years. Turning to politics on the Pereira council, he was named the city's mayor by López Michelsen at age twenty-six. He was soon elected to congress, served as vice minister of development in the Turbay government, directed the Barco election campaign, and later held two critical ministries in the Barco administration—finance, and then government. His subsequent commitment to Luis Carlos Galán led the son of the latter to name Gaviria as heir apparent two days after Galán's murder. And as described in chapter 11, he outmaneuvered several opponents to gain the nomination and move to an electoral victory.

During his campaign Gaviria had appeared ideologically as balanced between a center-left foreign policy and a center-right domestic policy. The latter generally included a tough stance in the war against the drug industry. While indicating an openness to negotiation and flexibility, accompanied by a willingness to distinguish between drug trafficking and drug terrorism, Gaviria saw a restoration of civic peace as fundamental. Indeed, in his inaugural address he spoke of "the historic responsibility of pacifying Colombian life, modernizing its institutions,...and strengthening the economy."[8] There were only veiled references to the neoliberal economic policies that would soon emerge. There was a denial of the need for shock programs such as those proliferating elsewhere in Latin America. Key commitments in the realm of economics emerged more clearly in the months immediately following the inauguration.[8]

The basic Gaviria program was comprised of three fundamental elements: (1) an economic streamlining designed to improve attractiveness for foreign investment; (2) a shrinking of the state, primarily through decentralization and privatization; and (3) adoption of a developmental plan designed to improve conditions for the poor via improvements in health, water, education, and transport. This meant in general an avowed "internationalization" of the economy to meet social objectives of improved living standards, while deriving benefits from austerity and from stripping away existing state responsibilities in ports, railways, and telecommunications, among others. An early indication of governmental priorities came barely a month after Gaviria's inauguration, when officials from the ministry of agriculture—the single largest contributor to GDP—announced measures relaxing existing controls, emphasizing the role of the private sector, and liberalizing agricultural imports.

The new administration speedily undertook economic reform after taking office.[9] Measures to control inflation were emphasized, while efforts to reduce state sector employment and the initiation of privatizations also occurred. The growth rate for 1990 was a solid 3.5 percent, especially as stimulated by rising agricultural output and steady progress in mining. Early in May of 1991 Finance Minister Rudolf Hommes completed a $1.575 million loan agreement with foreign banks. This covered the bulk of Colombia's debt service payments through 1994, and demonstrated the positive reaction to the government's economic reforms. Privatization of Colombia's state-owned banks was also moving ahead steadily. Early in 1992 a tax reform bill was introduced that was to generate additional revenues of nearly one-half billion dollars.

Despite these accomplishments, the government encountered vigorous opposition by major economic groups in Colombia, as well as manufacturing and industrial conglomerates. Moreover, the economic picture was clouded by drug money, the presence of which became more important as liberalization proceeded and trade barriers continued to be dismantled. By mid-1992, halfway through his term, Gaviria's popularity had dropped dramatically, owing in no small part to the electricity shortages that for more than a year mandated blackouts of six hours or more in virtually all Colombia's cities. A mishandled telephone strike, related to privatization efforts and accompanying labor protests, further cut into Gaviria's approval rating with the public. Yet the administration retained its commitment to modernizing the economy—to restructure the public sector and achieve *apertura* on behalf of greater international competition. Even as the fight against inflation continued, further reforms were applied in such programmatic areas as taxation, foreign exchange regulations, and foreign investment.

Gaviria insisted, as had Barco before him, that social progress constituted a fundamental obligation of the state. In effect, the modernization of the economy was seen as necessary to permit adequate investment human capital. On 16 October 1991 Gaviria presented his "Peaceful Revolution" as a national development plan giving special emphasis to transport and infrastructure. Projected at $6 billion, the plan was to lift up 4 million or more Colombians from the estimated 13 million poor in the nation. Infrastructural needs in education, water, and health sanitation were given slightly higher priority than transportation. Roughly half of the plan was to be financed from external borrowing. Other socially oriented policies included a liberalized labor code. Yet the government remained firm in its neoliberal policies even if—at least in the short run—their impact often seemed remote from the needs of the impoverished in Colombia.

As the Gaviria government gradually moved toward its final months, long-range economic prospects were dramatically affected by the massive Cusiana oil find.[10] By mid-1993 it was estimated that crude exports from this field would reach at least 600,000 b.p.d. (barrels per day) in the next four years, leaving Colombia second only to Venezuela among Latin American producers. The government began directing its attention to the potential problem of "Dutch Disease," wherein an abnormal inflow of foreign exchange leads to currency revaluation and a host of serious economic distortions (Ecuador, Mexico, and Venezuela present noteworthy variations on the dangers of the Dutch Disease). Notwithstanding these and other difficulties, the magnitude of Cusiana was obviously of great importance. It also emboldened the government to push its program further even in its final months in office.

Late in 1993 foreign exchange rules were further simplified, with the intention of greater *apertura* in the interests of avoiding Cusiana-related inflationary overheating. The G3 trade agreement with Mexico and Venezuela was signed in October and became effective in 1994. All trade barriers are to be eliminated by the year 2014. Trade with Venezuela continued to expand dramatically, notwithstanding political disputes between the two nations. A series of border clashes, basically minor in nature but explosive within the context of nationalistic paranoia in both nations, temporarily slowed binational exchanges in 1994. Indeed, they became the focus for sharp dispute, aggravated by Gaviria's belated candidacy for the position of OAS secretary-general in competition with two serious contenders, one the new foreign minister of Venezuelan President Rafael Caldera.[11] Even so, economic perspectives were generally positive as the Gaviria administration drew to a close. By the close of 1993 the inflation rate was 21.2 percent as compared with 25.1 for 1992. The GDP had risen from 1993's 3.3 percent to nearly 4 percent, while the foreign debt—just above $16 billion—remained at an acceptable level. Foreign investment, responding to a decade of economic stability and Colombia's record of competent management, had increased by 55 percent compared with the comparable nine months in 1992.[12] Non-oil investment had risen by more than 50 percent over 1992, while petroleum and the entire energy sector promised continuing growth. The government's Consejo Nacional de Política Económica y Social (CONPES) predicted a 5 percent growth of GDP for 1994, along with an inflation rate under 20 percent.[13] This was predicated on strongly positive prevailing indicators reflecting further expansion in construction and financial services. Industry also continued to thrive, notwithstanding stiff competition from imports as well as problems with textiles.

The administration's policies continued along established lines until its departure in August 1994. Privatizations were extended, the most dramatic example of which focused on the nation's second largest bank, the Banco de Colombia. Sales of other banks were destined to follow. At the same time, fiscal stability was underlined by abolition of the official exchange rate in late January, and continuing efforts were directed at controlling and protecting the potentially enormous economic bonanza produced by Cusiana's output. Gaviria's accompanying preoccupation with social problems was underlined through continuing measures working toward a massive restructuring of Colombia's social security system, which had not been altered or updated for a full half-century. In such ways the major policy perspectives that Gaviria brought to power in 1990 endured until he left office, and Colombia maintained an economic position generally more favorable than most Latin American nations. Notwithstanding all of this it remained true, as with previous administrations, that the realities of economic progress had to be judged alongside the ever-powerful impact of both guerrilla activities and the drug industry.

Social and Political Controls

Doubtless the most dramatic and highly publicized event in the Gaviria administration's efforts to strengthen systemic controls came with the killing of the notorious Medellín drug boss Pablo Escobar on 2 December 1993.[14] This not only extended the gradual breakup of the Medellín cartel but also compensated somewhat for the government's deep embarrassment the previous summer when Escobar had virtually walked out of the luxurious facility in which he had presumably been imprisoned. Yet the drug industry continued to thrive, even as the publicity-shy Cali cartel became more widely recognized known as the most powerful such organization in the nation. Furthermore, it represented an important proportion of Colombian national income as well as its exports.[15]

Gaviria had spoken at length on the drug problem when he first came to power. His inaugural address had included the statement that "no nation has paid as high a price as Colombia for fighting a crime of an international nature, and for confronting the most powerful organizations in memory."[16] While renewing a call for greater reciprocity from the United States as well as more concerted efforts by the industrialized countries to target the problem of drug consumption internationally, he also drew an explicit distinction between drug terrorism and drug trafficking. He saw his basic commitment as reducing *narcoterrorismo* and sought a more flexible and diverse approach than that of Barco. Indeed, as early as 5 September 1990 the newly inaugurated president issued a decree that softened greatly the virtually automatic extradition that had prevailed under the Barco administration. He suggested that drug traffickers surrendering to authorities would receive "a fair trial" from the Colombian courts, thereby removing any need to practice extradition. He sought thereby to assuage the preoccupation of major drug dealers by assuring relatively light sentences in Colombia. This spared the latter their fear of extradition to the United States and exposure to its judicial system.

In December of 1990 another presidential decree offered reduced prison sentences and no extradition to drug dealers who would surrender and confess. This was taken up by the Ochoa brothers, Fabio and Jorge Luis, who were major figures in the Medellín cartel. Gaviria's less confrontational stance subsequently brought about further surrenders, although generally of low-level traffickers. The exception was Pablo Escobar, who in June 1991 had agreed to accept a shortened sentence in lieu of the constant pressures as a fugitive targeted by both Colombian and U.S. personnel. However, he demanded and received untoward conditions, with the government building his own personalized lodgings near Medellín. There, at El Envigado, he enjoyed a luxurious life-style while maintaining direct control over his organization. When he and several colleagues walked out in July 1992, the entire fabric of the Gaviria policy fell under critical scrutiny. Expiatory goats were sacrificed and, in the end, the president was able to maintain his policy, if on a more cautious and guarded level. His basic approach was not altered and, in the aftermath of Escobar's eventual killing, his government attempted to deal in similar fashion with the kingpins of the Cali cartel. At the same time, there was praise for the so-called Bloque de Busqueda—a special force set up to hunt and run down Escobar.

In the final months of his administration, Gaviria energetically pursued agreement with representatives of the Cali *narcotraficantes,* including the Rodríguez Orejuela brothers, along with Francisco Herrera and José Santacruz Londoño. This proceeded even as it appeared that a new generation of drug barons was emerging in Cali and the vicinity, as well as in Medellín itself. There seemed a growing if undramatic increase in a pro-legalization movement, spurred especially by public prosecutor Gustavo de Grieff, an embattled and widely admired official who concluded that the existing struggle could never be brought to closure. Collaboration with the United States suffered, as officials from the U.S. Drug Enforcement Administration (not to mention Attorney General Janet Reno of the Clinton administration) were both apprehensive about and opposed to a feared Colombian retreat from tough measures. While the Gaviria approach brought both successes and defeats, it did not eradicate the drug industry, nor the violence surrounding it. This was starkly demonstrated by the kidnapping and eventual killing in early 1991 of Diana Turbay de Uribe, a prominent journalist and daughter of the former president.

If the Gaviria drug policy was something of a departure from prevailing patterns, its efforts to strengthen social and political controls vis-à-vis the guerrillas were also designed to introduce greater flexibility.[17] This evolved into four years of stop-and-start negotiations during which, more often than not, the government seemed to be responding to initiatives from the guerrillas. At the outset of his term Gaviria proclaimed his commitment to political dialogue, demobilization of all armed organizations, and just treatment for those accepting the authority of the state. He opportunely offered a handful of designated seats in the Constituent Assembly to those who heeded his call to lay down arms. Talks with the Maoist EPL progressed, and its leader Bernardo Gutiérrez eventually agreed, with the EPL shifting tactics toward the goal of broad leftist alliance working for change from within the system. The final peace accord between the government and the EPL was signed in early 1991. Negotiations with the FARC and ELN, in contrast, traversed a rocky road through the next four years.[18]

The former, shaken by the assassination of the UP candidate Bernardo Jaramillo on 22 March, was further inclined toward a rethinking of tactics and objectives following the death by natural causes of the FARC's longtime, near-legendary leader, Jacobo Arenas. Its orientation tilted back toward violence, while the ELN continued its damaging attacks on the oil pipelines and facilities in northeastern Colombia. Sabotage to the 490-mile pipeline cost some $500 million during the last half of the 1980s,

and the ELN was more unyielding than the FARC in resisting government peace overtures. A small dissident EPL faction joined them to form
the umbrella Coordinadora Nacional Guerrillera Simón Bolívar
(CNGSB). The Gaviria administration pushed hard for its first two years
in office; however, the eventual result was an outbreak of renewed violence, endless haggling and intransigence on the part of the CNGSB, and
an ultimate breakdown of talks. The government, in its carrot-and-stick
approach, had been strengthening counterinsurgency forces; all of this
led to a gradual worsening of conditions from 1992 on.[19]

Gaviria was indefatigable in continuing efforts to blunt the guerrillas'
activities. He and his advisors were eager to capitalize on such developments as successive divisions of the ELN, the most important of which
occurred in the final months of 1993. The CNGSB had promised a major
terrorist campaign under the rubric of "Black September." While it did
produce an outburst of bombings and sabotage in Bogotá and other major cities, its heralded impact proved grossly exaggerated. This in turn
encouraged further internal debate inside both the FARC and the ELN.
For the latter, it meant the breakaway of the so-called moderate wing, the
Corriente de Renovación Socialista (CRS). The longtime ELN leader
Manuel Pérez, a Spanish-born former priest, attempted to maintain his
centrist position, rejecting the diehard rightists of the Domingo Laín front.
The government thereby sought to emphasize ELN divisions while seeking further influence with the CRS splinter. Its antiguerrilla forces also
maintained pressure on the diverse guerrilla groups, which themselves
had recourse to selective violence, sabotage, and killing.

An apparent lessening of violence in the months following Black September was later disrupted as the electoral campaign was picking up
momentum in 1994. On 23 January nearly three dozen were shot to death
at a political meeting in Apartado, along the Caribbean coast in the Uraba
region; the FARC was blamed. Meanwhile the ELN was engaged in the
killing of local officials in eastern oil-producing cities, while the attempted
assassination of finance minister Rudolf Hommes on 17 January further
rattled political elites. All of this was complicated by deadly internal
conflict among the several guerrilla groups, especially the ELN and FARC.
The surface unity of the CNGSB, which had begun to crack with the
breakdown of direct talks with government representatives, shattered
further with the varied mixture of attitudes toward March and May elections. The lack of violence on the election days suggested that guerrilla

activities would remain moderately calm until the next government took office and revealed its own policy.

However, an unanticipated challenge to governmental authority had arisen with the dispatching of troops from the United States to Colombian soil. Late in 1993 it had been quietly announced that some 150 North Americans from the U.S. Southern Command were engaged in civic action programs. These were labelled "humanitarian missions," and focused on the building of a school at Juanchaco, near Cali. Following the year-end holiday hiatus, sharp doubts were enunciated from a variety of different political camps. President Gaviria was criticized for obfuscation and for ceding national sovereignty to foreigners. It was argued that, in the wake of Pablo Escobar's killing, U.S. pressure to tighten the screws on the Cali cartel had increased. The troops, critics alleged, would be collaborating in the effort while stationed near that city. This presumption was enhanced on 8 January when Crescencio Arcos, undersecretary of state for international narcotics, stated that "if we are really going to negotiate with these kinds of people there must be punishment at the end of it."[20] Then another 250 U.S. troops were revealed to be pursuing antidrug and counterinsurgency operations elsewhere in Colombia.

The flames of controversy were further fanned by rumors that César Gaviria had his eyes on the position of OAS secretary-general and was bidding for Washington's support. On the seventeenth of the month he publicly denied any trading of bases in Colombia for United States backing. Government officials subsequently announced that U.S. engineers and support units were indeed building a school, road, and health center at Juanchaco, while another fifty-six were constructing a river port at Puerto López. The political row did not subside, however, and even Liberal presidential pre-candidates felt free to question the official version. Front-runner Ernesto Samper said that Gaviria was looking foolish, while Enrique Parejo denounced the government for making fraudulent statements. Certainly the U.S. military presence eroded Gaviria's position while underlining existing policy differences between the two nations over the antidrug campaign.

The domestic furor threatened to overflow its banks on 9 February when the Council of State rejected Gaviria's explanation of the U.S. presence, denouncing him for "trampling" on national sovereignty and recommending that the lower house of congress put him on trial. While Gaviria was not at risk, the repercussions of the decision dramatized internal disagreement over antidrug policy in 1994. The potential constitutional confrontation was finessed when the Juanchaco troops were withdrawn, the last departing on 1 March with the construction works unfinished. A congressional committee launched a formal inquiry into Gaviria's authorization for the U.S. troops, but its work was soon buried by the crescendo of campaigning and electoral competition. At the same time, bilateral ill will was further nourished by ever-sharper differences over drug policy.

On 4 April the Drug Enforcement Administration charged in its annual report on the drug war that Colombia's ongoing policy of negotiating surrender terms with *narcotraficantes* had encouraged corruption of the political system, most notably the judiciary. The DEA soon admitted to having cut back drastically its cooperation with Colombian officials. Senator John Kerry, chairman of the drugs subcommittee, followed this by attacking Colombia as a "narco-democracy." There was an angry response from ranking Colombian officials, including the two major presidential campaigners. Before the close of the month Public Prosecutor Gustavo de Greiff was responding in kind, using a Washington press conference to charge Kerry and the deputy U.S. attorney general with lying about his contacts with Cali cartel leaders. As *fiscal general,* de Greiff was in considerable part an independent official; he was not a member of the executive branch, a fact that complicated matters for Gaviria and led to criticism from Justice Minister Andrés Gonzalez. De Greiff was undaunted; he pursued advocacy of drug legalization and, on the verge of automatic retirement at age sixty-five, blamed Washington for a campaign to discredit him.[21]

As the electoral campaign progressed, highly publicized charges of *narcotraficante* efforts to influence the outcome further fouled the atmosphere. Perspectives were darkened further with the July murder in Medellín of Andrés Escobar, a star of Colombia's national soccer team that had just returned home after its unexpected elimination in the first round of the World Cup. Thus, whatever the successes of Gaviria policies, both domestic conflict and international controversy were a part of his legacy to the new government.

The Politics of Power-Sharing

The Party Competition

The results of the presidential elections on 27 May had left the customary Liberal-Conservative hegemony seriously damaged, and new political actors were emerging on the scene.[22] César Gaviria was pledged to a degree of power-sharing, which would alter the one-party arrangement practiced by Virgilio Barco. He therefore planned to include representatives of opposition parties in his government. Furthermore, he made clear his commitment to widespread consultation. This also suggested a break from the Barco pattern, in which almost exclusive presidential reliance was placed upon a small, closely knit coterie of advisors (El Sanedrin, or the Sanhedrin). When the president-elect had put together his ministerial cabinet, it was composed of seven Liberals (including representatives of Durán Dussán and Samper in addition to four *galanistas*), four conservatives (two each from the Gómez and Pastrana factions), and one from the M-19, plus the customary military officer for defense.

Key ministers included Liberals Julio César Sanchez, interior; Rudolf Hommes, finance; Ernesto Samper Pizano, development; and Luis Fernando Jaramillo, foreign affairs. The Conservative Jaime Giraldo was named to justice, while the M-19's Antonio Navarro Wolff went to health. General Oscar Botero Restrepo was the sole carryover from the Barco administration, which he had served for two years in defense. In addition, Gaviria planned to draw upon an inner cabinet of close advisors. Among the most important were Rafael Pardo, advisor for national security; Jesús Bejarano, advisor for peace; Fabio Villegas, secretary-general to the presidency; Miguel Silva, private secretary; and María Emma Mejía, advisor for peace and rehabilitation in Medellín and Antioquia. The latter group collectively constituted an influential source of assistance and advice throughout the Gaviria presidency.

The notion of power-sharing had been embraced by Gaviria even before organizing the incoming administration, and an immediate challenge was raised by the national movement toward a Constituent Assembly. Certainly it was the major focus of party competition and interaction during Gaviria's first year in office. It had been February of 1990 when students from several universities launched the drive to include the so-called *séptima papeleta* or seventh ballot in the 11 March elections. Supported by important media outlets, the movement received the electoral approval of over 2 million Colombians. On 3 May the Barco government had issued Decree 927, empowering the Registraduría Nacional to count votes for or against convocation of an Asamblea Constitucional during the presidential elections of 27 May. This produced a positive vote by 5,236,863 Colombians—86.6 percent of those participating.

This led César Gaviria in his role as *director único* of the Liberal party to write Alvaro Gómez Hurtado, Alvaro Villegas Moreno, and Antonio Navarro Wolff, respective spokesmen of the MSN, Social Conservatives, and M-19. His message of 22 July set forth twelve principal points. On the twenty-eighth this was followed by a complementary statement proposing the major themes that should be placed before the Asamblea.[23] Contacts between Gaviria and other political leaders were intense. Meetings began officially on 2 August, leading to the formal signing of an agreement on the twenty-third. One day later Gaviria, having been officially sworn in earlier in the month, issued Decree 1926, which largely reflected the multiparty accord.[24] This in turn was very much the work of the new president, who wished to avoid the virtual blank check to the Asamblea approved by the previous popular vote. Those themes that were permissible included revisions concerning congress, the judicial system, human rights, political parties, mechanisms of participation, state-of-siege provisions, and the like.

Critics were swift to point out that the government was seeking to control the business of the Asamblea, very much in keeping with elitist traditions. It was noted, for example, that the Asamblea was denied authority over a long list of important potential reforms.[25] As one observer put it,

> The Constituyente is the creature being controlled. The president of the Republic is the true constituyente.... It is notable that discussion of presidentialism as a political regime is absent from the agenda.[26]

Certainly Gaviria, notwithstanding his reformist preferences, sought firm presidential control of the legislative body soon to be selected. However, the Procurador General questioned the constitutionality of the political agreement and sought a ruling from the Corte Suprema de Justicia. On 9 October following a lengthy session, Decree 1926 was declared constitutional, but with the caveat that as a sovereign body its powers could not be limited to the agenda that had been set forth.

Confounding the many experts on constitutional law who anticipated that Decree 1926 would be overruled, the Court proceeded to reject the constraints of the existing agreement on the agenda by a fourteen to twelve margin. Consequently, the Asamblea would be free to consider any and all issues. This judicial ruling assured that, as I wrote elsewhere, the powers of a Constituent Assembly were opened to the free rein of its members. Suddenly, President Gaviria and the nation's traditional elites were confronted with conditions which would not guarantee an automatic responsiveness to suggestions for change. The boundaries were effectively removed, and the framework for *apertura* was far more open than anyone had expected.[27]

This inevitably provoked a heated renewal of party competition. The seventy-member Constituent Assembly was scheduled to convene on 5 February 1991 and complete work on a new draft constitution by 4 July. Elections were slated for 9 December 1990.

The campaign was *sui generis* in Colombia's electoral history, combining characteristics of both presidential and legislative contests.[28] The Liberals, whose customary organizational disarray had led them to recall the septuagenarian ex-president López Michelsen to serve as *director único,* accepted his insistence on presenting forty separate lists, most of which were headed by local or regional leaders. The latter agreed upon this strategy as the most likely to provide an electoral victory. Known as "Operación Avispa" (Operation Wasp), this permitted maximal independence for heads of the competing lists, presumably appealing to local constituencies. It also underlined the disorganized and diffuse condition of the Liberal party, even as it insisted upon longstanding majority status. Given the inclination of the electorate to blame the Liberals for all the nation's problems, this clouded the party's immediate prospects.

The campaign was scarcely less difficult for the Social Conservatives. They also drew public criticism as a major element of the nation's political elite and its systemic shortcomings. In addition, the reverberations from the recent presidential elections had not subsided. The party eventually decided upon a single list headed by Misael Pastrana, who campaigned nationally. In addition, however, there were other Conservative lists inscribed as independent but headed in actuality by politically sympathetic local stalwarts. This contrasted with the Movimiento de Salvación Nacional, which concentrated on the effort to project a broad movement committed to fundamental changes. Alvaro Gómez presented himself as the standard bearer for revisionism within the political establishment. He reiterated themes from his recent presidential campaign—attacks on clientelism, corruption, and the inefficiency of the state while defending basic constitutional principles. The MSN emphasized its purported national character by offering a number of lists, many headed by Liberals sympathetic to Gómez's positions.

The most avowedly reformist campaign was put forth by the M-19 (officially the Alianza Democratica M-19) under the guidance of Antonio Navarro Wolff, who resigned from Gaviria's cabinet to promote the party's antisystemic position within a constitutional and democratic framework. Navarro himself was looking forward to the 1994 presidential race, and his personality loomed large in the campaign for the assembly. He necessarily sought to balance his calls for basic change with the necessity of lessening the fears and suspicions of the establishment. A single electoral list was put forward, numbering among others a heterogeneous group of candidates representing a variety of social and economic interests. A similarly broad and diverse set of candidates also headed a number of microparties and organizations. Only a few stood out, generally owing to the prominence of an individual leader and program—for example, the Unión Patriótica with Alfredo Vásquez Carrizosa, which fought on behalf of human rights.

The government itself and César Gaviria in particular labored on behalf of participation while seeking the smoothest possible handling of electoral machinery. Election day itself passed without serious disruptions. Indeed, Bogotá and other cities were relatively deserted for much of the day, and nonparticipation was high. Only 3.7 million of over 14.2 million eligible voters went to the polls; this 75 percent abstention was the highest in years. The largest total for a single list was 27 percent for the M-19, an increase from its previous 700,000 to nearly 1 million. The Liberals, thanks to Operación Avispa, polled 31 percent of the vote from forty-one lists, compared with 48 percent in the presidential elections and 61 percent in the March congressional race. It was the party's worst showing since the 1930 election of Enrique Olaya Herrera. The MSN dropped off from its 24 percent in presidential elections, drawing some 16 percent. The Social Conservatives drew but 6 percent, while Pastrana's own list was even lower. Once the dust had settled, the Liberal forces held twenty-five assembly seats, followed by the M-19's nineteen, eleven for the MSN, and nine for the Social Conservatives and their allies.[29]

This helped to set the stage for the work on the assembly in 1991, and the drafting of the new constitution, which is detailed in the final chapter. Once its work was done and the new charter was officially adopted, yet another round of elections was required to choose a new legislature. On 27 October 1991, voters chose 102 senators and 161 representatives; twenty-seven departmental governorships were also included. Two additional senate seats were reserved for representatives of indigenous communities. The government's security program, "Plan Democracia," deployed over 40,000 troops and police to protect nearly 16 million voters. Abstention nonetheless held at 70 percent. The results were a Liberal victory that reflected the reformist-oriented popularity of César Gaviria, whose approval rating in the polls had remained at or above 60 percent for months. Polling nearly 45 percent of the legislative vote, the government party won 56 of 102 senate seats and 87 of 161 seats in the lower chamber. The Liberals also captured 18 of the 27 governorships.

The Conservatives suffered by their continuing divisions. The Social Conservatives won nine senate and twenty-five chamber seats; Andrés Pastrana's NFD won eight and nine respectively; and Alvaro Gómez's MSN five and ten. Together, they and the Liberals controlled nearly three-quarters of the senate and 85 percent in the chamber, thus confirming the enduring if internally fragmented authority of the two parties. This was underlined by the disappointing performance of the M-19, which had expressed a center-left populism during the campaign. Barely surpassing 10 percent of the vote after having won more than a quarter of the votes in previous elections to the Asamblea Constituyente, the AD-M19 dropped to nine senate seats and thirteen in the chamber. Navarro Wolff remained a seemingly viable presidential candidate for 1994, and his party was clearly third in the nation. However, the heady expectations generated in the Constituyente elections had been dampened by the reassertion of two-party domination.[30] Despite the inevitable public exhaustion over the long succession of elections, yet another test stimulated renewed partisan activities with municipal elections on 8 March 1992. At stake were the seats of 12,639 mayors, city councillors, and state legislators. Barely one-third voted, notwithstanding a televised plea by President Gaviria. Of an estimated 15 million eligible voters, fewer than 6 million voted—nearly 2 million less than the March 1990 local elections, although higher than those who cast a ballot in the December 1990 competition. The rate of abstention ran from two-thirds to three-fourths in the most populous cities. While the Liberals won in eighteen of Colombia's twenty-third largest cities, they lost to Conservative mayoral candidates in both Cali and Medellín, while the Salesian priest Bernardo Hoyos triumphed in Barranquilla as the M-19 candidate. The Liberals did win Bogotá with its mayoral selection Jaime Castro Castro, but the city council's two major lists were headed by former ministers Carlos

Lemos Simmonds and Enrique Parejo, both avowed critics of Gaviria policies. The president was meantime continuing his power-sharing approach, shuffling ministerial and other high positions in response to electoral considerations. All of this became more pronounced as the next presidential elections began to preoccupy Colombian politicians.

Candidate Selection

The disorganized condition of the Colombian parties was manifest throughout the Gaviria years. While the 1992 elections had reasserted Liberal domination over the Conservatives, with the M-19 struggling to maintain its electoral credibility, severe internal problems complicated the process of choosing presidential candidates. For the Liberals, it had been necessary to recall López Michelsen to direct that campaign. The former president then attempted to restructure the party leadership and withdrew from daily politics. In less than a year Liberal factionalism tore apart the leadership, and once more the party turned to a *jefe único*—again, a septuagenarian former president. Julio César Turbay Ayala eventually returned from his ambassadorship in Rome to take the reins. He found a number of active pre-candidates, while there was no automatic aspirant from the Gaviria camp. The claimant closest to heading a *fila india*, however, was Ernesto Samper Pizano.

Following his 1990 participation in the Liberals' *consulta popular,* he had entered Gaviria's cabinet as minister of development. Differing with the president over the speed and extent of neoliberal economic policies, he resigned and was sent to Madrid as ambassador. Thereby removed from Bogotá's daily political vicissitudes, Samper did not return home until late 1993.[31] He soon found himself in a crowded field. Among the best-known were Carlos Lemos Simmonds and Humberto de la Calle Lombana. The first had held many high-level positions for years, and was a sharp critic of the government. De la Calle, in contrast, had been Gaviria's minister of government and represented a continuity of policy.[32] Two younger competitors, mirroring the tradition of political families, were David Turbay Turbay and Carlos Lleras de la Fuente. Longtime Comptroller General (1982–90) Rodolfo González García was also in the race, as was Enrique Parejo Gonzalez. The latter, another sharp critic of Gaviria policies, was the only candidate rejecting Julio César Turbay Ayala's otherwise successful tactic of persuading all the Liberals in the *consulta popular.*

Samper, constantly subjected to the political spotlight, floundered at the outset. Although his Liberal rivals seemed unlikely to defeat him, critical attention focused far more on his competition with the presumed Conservative candidate, Andrés Pastrana Arango. The latter consistently led Samper in the polls, which heightened criticism of the Liberal. This was dissipated only on 16 February 1994 when, for the first time, Samper led Pastrana in a nationwide poll by 38 to 33 percent in the first round of presidential elections, and by 50 to 43 in a runoff.[33] From that point forward, Samper rode the crest of growing popularity to a decisive victory in the Liberal primary on March 13th. Defeating De la Calle by over four to one—with the other Liberals trailing even farther behind— he was officially proclaimed at the party convention on 18 March. This was followed a week later by a meeting in Rionegro at which a reorganization of the party was announced.

His opponent, Andrés Pastrana Arango, had played a shrewdly effective waiting game for months. As head of his own personalized Nueva Fuerza Democrática (NFD), Pastrana had sought to broaden his political base. The NFD held a cabinet position throughout the Gaviria administration, and often stood somewhat aloof from controversial debates in congress. The former mayor of Bogotá, more recently a senator, who had been a visible journalist and wore the badge of former kidnap victim, Pastrana played up his image of independence, of somehow being above party. While Pastrana's attractive public image was shrewdly managed by his handlers, his combative father held his peace on his son's relationship with the party. Other Conservative aspirants found themselves consistently frustrated by Andrés Pastrana's looming shadow. Periodic efforts to mount a unity convention of Conservatives, including the NFD and Alvaro Gómez's MSN, foundered and were rejected. Pastrana scored well in the polls, and kept his political silence until 10 February 1994, when he officially announced his candidacy.[34] In due course he was endorsed by all the Conservative factions—most importantly of all, the bitter opponent of Pastrana's father, Alvaro Gómez.

The Liberal-Conservative rivalry was again being challenged by the ADM-19 and its prevailing leader, Antonio Navarro Wolff. Following his influential role and the active participation of the party in the deliberations of the Asamblea Constituyente, some had envisaged an eventual collapse of Colombia's traditional two-party hegemony. César Gaviria included an M-19 representative in his cabinet, and by the early months of 1993 Navarro was polling more than 30 percent as a potential presidential nominee. At the very least, party strategists hoped to win sufficient congressional representation to hold the balance of power between Liberals and Conservatives in the next government. However, despite Navarro's extensive campaigning in the runup to the March 1994 elections, he and his party progressively declined in the polls. In the meantime, the climate for campaigning had intensified with an extended wave of violence.

The murder on 7 November 1993 of the Liberal vice president of the senate, Darío Londoño, shocked the political establishment; the head of the security police was moved to announced formation of a special protection unit for candidates. The anti-election campaign of the ELN hardline, led by Manuel Pérez, later took responsibility for Londoño's death, as well as a bomb attack on 17 January directed at Finance Minister Rudolf Hommes. While charging Hommes with perpetrating "policies of poverty," the ELN promised further terrorism. In conjunction with other guerrilla factions, the CNGSB promised to disrupt the elections. February was marked by the kidnappings of several congressmen and mayors, while bombs were placed in several local party headquarters. The government resisted proposals that the elections be suspended or rescheduled and, shortly before the thirteenth, the CNGSB suspended its campaign. Even so, more than 50,000 were mobilized by the defense ministry to assure security for the voters.

If fears of violence were minimized to a degree, confusion over the new system of ballots was little short of intimidating. In accordance with the 1991 constitution, separate lists of nearly 1000 congressional candidates appeared—each one of which included accompanying candidates whose names did not appear. On the senate ballot, for example, a large wall-sized poster included no less than 251 names and photographs. With names having been drawn from a hat to determine the order, the result was "a bewildering array of parties and organisations, all jumbled up."[35] Ultimately, no fewer than 5333 legislative candidates were entered; 3355 competed for 154 seats in the lower house, plus another 1978 for 102 senate seats.[36] All of this compounded customary abstentionism, which reached 70 percent in much of the country. Even so, the results were unequivocal. Ernesto Samper was the unquestioned Liberal victor in the *consulta popular*; Humberto de la Calle secured a favorable position for a possible 1998 candidacy; and Andrés Pastrana could hope that votes for Liberal right-wingers Lemos and Lleras de la Fuente might be drawn to his own candidacy in May presidential elections. Navarro Wolff saw his own ambitions virtually obliterated by the crushing defeat of the M-19, as the Liberal-Conservative hegemony reasserted itself.

For the ADM-19, it won but two of the 163 seats in the lower chamber, while losing eight of its nine existing senate seats. Although Navarro Wolff insisted that an alternative to the hegemonic parties was viable, the results were devastating for his forces. Furthermore, Alvaro Gómez's MSN could capture but two seats in the house of representatives while falling from five senators to only one. Pastrana's own NFD dropped from eight to five senators. As usual, the Liberal victory over the Conservatives was substantial. Indeed, the Liberals had recorded their most decisive congressional victory in many years. Their margin in the 102-seat senate was sixty-six to twenty-seven; fifty-nine of these were identified with Samper, which would obviously be beneficial should he reach the presidency. Their victory was equally decisive in the lower house. For the Conservatives, their accustomed total of 35 to 40 percent had dropped to little more than a quarter of the vote.

The two traditional parties drew over 90 percent of the vote, confounding those who had believed that the 1991 constitution would promote new and reformist elements. In sum, the March elections confirmed in capital letters the majoritarian status of the Liberals; reversed the earlier inroads of the ADM-19 and MSN; and certified Pastrana's approach to the presidential race. As had been widely assumed for some months, his necessary course was clearly an effective replication of Belisario Betancur's 1982 campaign, in which 30 percent of the vote was independent, and crossover votes from Liberals. Pastrana's appeal to these voters, and Samper's efforts to hold onto party loyalists, became central to the campaign for the presidency.

Campaign and Elections

As contenders began preparations for the first-round presidential election on 29 May (which the constitutional court had moved back from 8 May), the choice of vice presidential running mate—a novelty introduced by the 1991 constitution—was an immediate necessity. Samper maximized his opportunities by persuading a reluctant De la Calle to join his ticket. This helped to assuage the feelings of anti-Samper Liberals while shoring up his right wing, which had threatened a defection to Pastrana when De la Calle lost the *consulta*. Pastrana was less successful, failing in his effort to recruit a prominent Liberal or, at the least, a non-Conservative. He settled on Gaviria's Conservative labor minister, Luis Fernando Ramírez Acuña. As campaign activity gradually mounted, speculation centered on the significance of Antonio Navarro's declining fortunes. For the first time, it appeared that a second round runoff might be unnecessary, although public opinion surveys consistently showed Samper with a small margin over Pastrana but falling short of the necessary 50 percent. In a televised debate on 12 May Samper surprised many analysts by holding his own against the telegenic Pastrana, a former TV personality. Indeed, the exchange was interrupted by Navarro, who, having been excluded, took it upon himself to force his way on camera.

During the time leading up to the elections there were periodic outbursts of violence, intermingled with anti-election threats from a variety of dissident guerrilla spokesmen. However, those voters who went to the polls on the twenty-ninth enjoyed an unusual degree of peace and freedom. Fewer than 6 million of a potential 17 million voters took part; the unofficial totals gave Samper a victory over Pastrana by a bare 20,000 votes (2,586,103 to 2,566,464). This represented a cliff-hanging margin for Samper. Navarro Wolff for ADM-19 received less than 4 percent of the vote; of the other eighteen candidates listed on the ballot, the only one to exceed 1 percent was the self-declared witch Regina Betancourt of her Movimiento Uniterio Metapolítico (1.1 percent).

The decisive runoff was then set for 19 June. Given the first-round results and the similarity between the programs for the two contenders, it was not surprising that further rounds of public opinion polls suggested a virtual toss-up.

Inevitably, complicated partisan maneuvering and outright dirty tricks began to emerge in the final weeks of the campaign. There were ill-conceived charges of drug money having entered the campaign; the Bishop of Bucaramanga urged Liberal Catholics to cast blank ballots; Samper was alleged to have made deals with the leaders of Protestant sects; and the like. Meantime, both candidates lamented that the scheduling for Colombia's soccer team in the 1994 World Cup would encourage even greater abstention on the nineteenth. As it developed, Colombia was defeated by Romania 3–1 on the eve of elections, and voter turnout was greater than expected, nearly 45 percent. The result was a strikingly close contest, clearly a rarity for Colombia. Ernesto Samper squeezed past Andrés Pastrana by a bare margin of some 2.2 percent—some 133,000 votes—and the latter promptly expressed his recognition of defeat. Nonpartisan cordiality was then dissipated in a matter of hours.

Pastrana claimed to have tapes that allegedly suggested that Cali drug money had gone into the Samper campaign, and claimed that President Gaviria had ignored the materials on the case that he had been sent. The Samper camp retorted that it had named an "ethical monitor" precisely to protect itself against such problems, and the exchange of charges and countercharges was inflammatory. All of this was damaging to the electoral process, while further clouding Colombian relations with the United States.[37] Samper, who still carried bullets from a drug-related attack in 1989 at the Bogotá airport, welcomed an investigation, and it appeared that the intrusion of drug money into the campaign generally was an obvious fact, which, indeed, had occurred recently in the December 1993 Venezuelan elections as well. Further investigation was scheduled, while Ernesto Samper began to put together an extra-partisan administration to be inaugurated in August.

More than any of his predecessors, he confronted a nation that had undergone important changes under the outgoing administration. Political *apertura*, while introducing a number of institutional reforms and weakening the organizational control of the political parties, had also seen a reassertion of traditional biparty hegemony. Market liberalization had encouraged economic growth and attracted greater foreign investment, while the prospect of petroleum riches was opening up new and challenging developmental vistas. As one observer wrote, Colombia had set aside a forty-year model of development in 1990, and the testing of new policies and guidelines, such as introduced under César Gaviria, was far from complete as the new government assumed the reins of power in August 1994.[38] And in addition, endemic violence continued to plague the nation. As Samper took office it was reported that for 1993, Colombia had exceeded even the United States in murders (28,000 to 15,800), or 10 percent of the 280,000 homicides recorded worldwide.[39] Civic peace and security had yet to be achieved.

Notes

1. Inter-American Development Bank, *Latin America in Graphs: Demographic and Economic Trends* (Washington, D.C.: IADB, 1992), 16 and 80.

2. DANE (Martínez and Escobar), *Proyecciónes nacionales de población: Colombia 1950–2025* (Bogotá: DANE, 1989).
3. *Revista del Banco de la República* (Bogotá) (December 1991): 256.
4. A convenient summary of these and more detailed data are presented in *The Latin American Times* 10, no. 4 (July–October 1990): 20–26.
5. Trade remained an important element in developmental policy. For a detailed treatment see Carlos E. Juarez, "Trade and Development Policies in Colombia: Export Promotion and Outward Orientation, 1967–1992," *Studies in Comparative International Development* 28, no. 3 (Fall 1993): 67–97.
6. A statement representative of international opinion is found in *Business Latin America* (26 March 1990): 94.
7. The text appeared in the Bogotá press on 8 August 1990.
8. A broad overview is John D. Martz, "Colombia at the Crossroads," *Current History* 90, no. 553 (February 1991): 69–73 and 80.
9. For a timely survey that includes statements by Rudolf Hommes as well as a number of Colombian economists, see Alvin Cohen and Frank R. Gunter, eds., *The Colombian Economy: Issues of Trade and Development* (Boulder: Westview, 1992).
10. The macroeconomic context is described in John D. Martz, "Colombia: Democracy, Development, and Drugs," *Current History* 93, no. 581 (March 1994): 134–38.
11. Inaugurated in February 1994, Rafael Caldera appointed Miguel Angel Burelli Rivas as foreign minister, thereby emphasizing his government's backing of the Venezuelan candidate.
12. Banco de la República, *Reportaje* (October 1993).
13. "Colombia," *Latin American Andean Report* (16 December 1993): 7.
14. For a bleakly detailed journalistic portrayal of security problems as Gaviria took office, see "Colombia," *The Latin American Times* 19, no. 4 (July–October 1990): 20–26.
15. For an elaboration of this and related themes, see Salomon Kalmanovitz, "Violencia y Narcotráfico en Colombia," *Conference Paper No. 44,* presented to the conference on "Violence and Democracy in Colombia and Peru," Columbia University, New York City, 1990.
16. *El Espectador* (Bogotá) (8 August 1990).
17. A thoughtful and well-informed review is Eduardo Pizarro, "Insurgencia Crónica, Movimiento Guerrillero y Proceso de Paz en Colombia," *Conference Paper No. 45,* presented to the conference on "Violence and Democracy in Colombia and Peru," Columbia University, New York City, 1990.
18. The contribution of paramilitary forces to endemic violence should not be minimized. See Alejandro Reyes Posada, "Paramilitares en Colombia: Contexto, Aliados y Consecuencias," *Conference Paper No. 46,* presented to the conference on "Violence and Democracia in Colombia y Peru," Columbia University, New York City, 1990.
19. Harvey F. Kline has been conducting a major study that includes extended analysis of peace policies and government-guerrilla negotiations. An excellent preliminary statement is his "Negociaciónes del Gobierno de César Gaviria Trujillo con los Grupos Guerrilleros Colombianos, 1991–92," paper presented to the Annual SECOLAS Conference in Antigua, Guatemala, February 1993.
20. "Colombia," *Latin American Andean Report* (3 February 1994): 8.

21. For an expression of his views, see De Greiff's interview in *The New York Times* (8 July 1994).

22. These elections and their political implications are treated in Andrés López R., "Elecciónes del 27 de Mayo: Piezas Surtidas para Armar un Escenario," *Análisis Político*, no. 10 (mayo-agosto 1990): 55–60.

23. For the specifics of both messages see Jaime Buenahora Febres-Cordero, *El proceso constituyente: De la propuesta estudiantil a la quiebra del bipartidismo* (Bogotá: Tercer Mundo Editores, 1991), 181–218.

24. The texts of this and other relevant documents are reproduced in the lengthy annex of Buenahora Febres-Cordero, *Una constituyente para la Colombia del futuro* (Bogotá: FESCOL, 1990), 107–404.

25. Edmundo López Gómez, *La verdadera Constituyente* (Bogotá: Editorial Librería del Profesional, 1990), 105.

26. Ricardo Sánchez, "El presidencialismo y la Reforma Constitucional," *Foro* (Bogotá) (October 1990).

27. John D. Martz, "Contemporary Colombian Politics: The Struggle Over Democratization," in Cohen and Gunter, eds., *The Colombian Economy*, 21–47.

28. John Dugas, Rubén Sánchez David, and Elizabeth Ungar B., "La Asamblea Nacional Constituyente, expresión de una voluntad general," in Rubén Sánchez David, comp., *Los nuevos retos electorales; Colombia 1990: antesala del cambio* (Bogotá: CEREC, 1991), 192–93.

29. See Dugas in ibid. for electoral data, pp. 209–15. A breakdown of the 161 competing lists plus individual totals appear in Buenahora Febres-Cordero, *Una constituyente*, 347–57.

30. A useful review of recent Colombian elections, running through the October 1991 contest, is Rubén Sánchez David and Patricia Pinzón de Lewin, "Elecciónes y Democracia en Colombia," in Rudolfo Cerdas-Cruz, Juan Rial, and Daniel Zovatto, eds., *Una tarea inconclusa: Elecciónes y democracia en América Latina 1988–1991* (San José, Costa Rica: IIDH, 1992), 287–311.
The data are, as usual, reported by the Registraduría Nacional del Estado Civil.

31. For an anecdotal collection of observations and commentary by his family and friends, as well as by Samper himself, see Juan Mosca, comp., *Querido Ernesto* (Bogotá: 1993).

32. Announcement of his pre-candidacy was accompanied by publication of Rosa Jaramillo and Beatriz Gómez, comps., *De la Calle; Anatomía del cambio; de los 60 al siglo XXI* (Bogotá: Planeta, 1994).

33. A detailed journalistic examination is "La Resurrección de Ernesto Samper," *Semana* (22 February to 1 March 1994): 22–28.

34. For his first interview following proclamation of his candidacy, see "Pastrana se destapa," *Semana* (8–15 February 1994): 26–31.

35. "Colombia," *Latin American Weekly Report* (17 March 1994): 119.

36. *The Miami Herald* (12 March 1994).

37. For a characteristic North American report, which was predictably negative in tone, see "Colombia: The Narco-Candidate?" *Time* (4 July 1994).

38. Andrés López Restrepo, "El cambio de modelo de desarrollo de la economia colombiana," *Análisis Político*, no. 21 (enero-abril 1994): 14–35.

39. Eight percent of Colombia's deaths were reported as related to guerrilla actions, 10 percent to sociopolitical conflicts, and the remainder to "normal daily violence." See *North-South* (July-August 1994): 58–59.

Conclusions: Corporate Clientelism and the Political Future

Toward a Reshaping of Politics?

The New Constitutional Framework

The last major constitutional reforms had been those of 1968, when Carlos Lleras Restrepo had sought to modernize Colombia by institutionalizing economic development and systemic planning. After extended battle with the traditional political elites, Lleras eventually emerged with enhanced executive powers.[1] Congress was largely stripped of its budget powers, in exchange for which it received the benefits of *auxilios*. Thus, each legislator received funds targeted for civic improvement in his district; in practice, the congressman typically used the money to finance reelection campaigns. Ballots were printed and distributed, which encouraged the wholesale buying of votes and strengthening clientelism at the regional and local level, most especially in electoral terms. In addition, the path to a higher level of guerrilla activism had been set in place, while cocaine traffic flourished and violence spread. As Eduardo Pizarro put it years later, "The political class put Colombia in a straitjacket. Citizen protest was criminalized. Despite its extraordinary stability, the civil regime became embedded in violence."[2]

In the years to follow, disenchantment with many of the 1968 reforms nourished renewed efforts to revise or amend the system. The government of Alfonso López Michelsen proposed a constitutional assembly to explore reforms appropriate for the shifting administrative and political realities of the Colombian state. However, the Supreme Court in 1978 rejected the convocation of the Assembly on constitutional grounds. Later, President Turbay sought reforms through regular congressional action. Once again the court intervened, denying congress the necessary legal authority to alter the constitution. Belisario Betancur, an avowed advocate of a series of reform measures, was also frustrated by congress. Then in January 1988 Virgilio Barco proposed in a letter to *El Espectador* that a constitutional amendment might permit the government to convoke a referendum wherein citizens could ratify institutional reforms. This gave way to an agreement between Barco and Misael Pastrana that would look for other procedures. It was termed unconstitutional in April by the Council of State, thus blocking Barco in his desire for significant reforms. However, both the Colombian public and political elites were becoming insistent that traditional political procedures needed to be updated and redefined, then reified as the constitutional law of the land.

The process leading to the 1991 Constituent Assembly—touched upon only briefly in the preceding chapter—therefore unfolded within a context of growing public disillusionment. The prevailing system was evidently incapable of providing effective social and political controls; the drug industry was thriving, guerrilla activism continued, ordinary crime was serious, and murder had become the major cause for deaths in the country. Given Colombia's long experience with Constituent Assemblies, dating all the way back to 1827, there was a rising clamor for constitutional reform. Although the constitution of 1886 required congressional approval at two consecutive sessions, many were willing to ignore or somehow circumvent these provisions. As early as 5 July 1987 former president Carlos Lleras Restrepo had called for an assembly devoted to a "rehabilitation" of the rule of law. Although López Michelsen insisted that a Constituent Assembly was unconstitutional, the Liberal party's National Directorate soon called for government initiative in exploring the possibilities.

While the Barco government had dropped all serious efforts by the close of 1989, the student movement had already picked up the issue, and on 9 February 1990 they sent a letter to President Barco with some 30,000 signatures, demanding a plebiscite on the proposed reform of Colombia's constitutional structures. Their demand for a seventh ballot was supported by *El Tiempo*, López Michelsen, and four Liberal precandidates for the presidency, including César Gaviria. The latter suggested a two-party agreement to seek and identify an extra-constitutional method to reform the constitution. The question was eventually included on the ballot in conjunction with the presidential vote on 27 May 1990. As noted previously, some 86 percent answered in the affirmative to the question: "In order to fortify participatory democracy, do you vote for the convocation of a Constituent Assembly with representation of social, political, and regional forces, integrated democratically and popularly, to reform the Constitution of Colombia?"[3]

President-elect Gaviria, after extended consultation, issued Decree 1926 to identify those topics he viewed as legitimate for discussion. Thus, a characteristically elitist approach sought to assure that Gaviria and his collaborators might control and restrict the work of the Assembly.[4] However, to the surprise of many, the Supreme Court by a fourteen to twelve vote ruled that the assembly was free to consider any and all themes.[5] On 6 December 1990 voters proceeded to elect 70 members, using proportional representation with a national constituency.[6] The session was projected for 150 days beginning on 5 February 1991, with the new constitution to become operative on 4 July 1991. Meanwhile, the congress elected in 1990 was dissolved. As the assembly began its activities, three co-presidents were chosen: Horacio Serpa Uribe for the Liberals, Alvaro Gómez from the MSN, and Antonio Navarro Wolff from the M19. The assembly itself was divided into five commissions, with each member choosing the one that was preferred.[7]

Politically, the Constituent Assembly reflected something of a partisan realignment, given the rough parity gained by the M-19 vis-à-vis the traditional parties. Members included Indian tribal elders and disarmed guerrilla leaders, along with two protestant evangelicals (much to the dismay of the Catholic church). This was personified by the three co-presidents. Some three years earlier Gómez had been kidnapped and held for fifty-three days by the M-19, after which Serpa Uribe as government negotiator arranged his release. The three men collaborated effectively as floor debate and the work of the commissions unfolded. A fundamental democratization of the constitutional system was envisaged and, as proceedings went further, there was a broad national consensus expressing hopeful optimism over the outcome. The journalist Enrique Santos Calderón penned a characteristic statement that captured Colombian opinion:

The democratic spectacle of the Constituent Assembly has no precedent.... Never before has such a heterogeneous group of Colombians gathered...to discuss and write a new Constitution. It was in this sense an emotional scene of national reconciliation, the spirit of which will no doubt be radiated over the entire community.[8]

The eventual institutional changes were pronounced.[9] With the executive branch, the assembly first ruled that the president would be chosen by absolute majority, thereby introducing the notion of a second round of voting if necessary. In addition, there was an absolute prohibition of more than one term in office. Another reform was the adoption of a vice president to be selected in general elections, although not necessarily coming from the party of the presidential candidate. This did away with the previous practice in which congress chose a so-called *designado* every two years. Such provisions were in effect when Ernesto Samper won office in the second round of elections. Fellow Liberal Humberto de la Calle became the vice president by winning his own electoral competition. While such changes were scarcely negligible, they paled beside the series of reforms intended to restructure the unpopular and much maligned congress. Many of the powers and practices most associated with clientelism and elitist rule thus came under attack. Congressmen could no longer hold other public positions simultaneously, nor would alternates be elected who could serve temporarily as substitutes. Any member missing six votes in plenary sessions would be replaced. Clientelism in the form of nepotism, pork barrel legislation, and especially of the *auxilios,* was banned; unauthorized foreign travel was also prohibited. All of these actions were designed, as a plenary session of the assembly was told, as means of restoring lost congressional prestige, which had been "seriously affected by the inefficiency in recent times, immorality,... clientelistic practices that became common in elections, and the unmeasured urge to accept honors and power and to use their positions to gain personal benefit."[10] The only change that strengthened rather than weakened the legislature came from granting it the power of censure against ministers. This parliamentary procedure was justified as assuring greater presidential consultation with congress.

Even greater reforms were introduced into the judiciary, which had been rendered virtually powerless by the violence and drug trafficking of recent years. A new Constitutional Court was assigned responsibility to preserve and safeguard the constitution itself. At the same time, the Supreme Court of Justice remained the regular court of law appeals, while the Council of State was retained to oversee executive decrees. The new constitution also created a Superior Council of the Judiciary, which bore responsibility for the management and administration of the judicial system. Additional reforms were introduced at lower levels, including the election of justices of the peace at the municipal level. Perhaps the most important change of all was a new Office of the General Prosecutor, which replaced the National Directorate of Criminal Instruction and its 600 judges. The prosecutor, now to be elected by the Supreme Court, was assigned responsibility over the judicial police. At least in theory, the entire criminal investigation system would be overturned and restructured, with the Office of the General Prosecutor becoming the key to the functioning of the entire system. It was granted access to state security services for the investigation of crimes. This freed judges from this task, which had been handicapped in the past by reliance on the aid of poorly paid judicial police.

Such institutional reforms to the three branches of national government were accompanied by measures designed to encourage electoral participation and democratize national politics. State governors were to be popularly elected rather than appointed by the president. The recall was also authorized, whereby elected officials could be removed by the voters. New electoral regulations called for use of the *tarjeton*— a multiple-choice card administered by a newly created independent electoral branch. This was intended as a way of sanitizing voting, which in the past had relied on one-party ballots prepared and distributed by individual parties and candidates prior to election day. Additional government funds would be allocated to the campaigns of smaller parties, enhancing electoral prospects for new parties in both local and national elections. Another set of changes designed to foster genuine democratization centered on human rights. A major target was the "state of siege" power authorized by the 1886 constitution in the event of foreign wars or internal upheaval; it could be maintained indefinitely. In practice this had led to a nearly permanent state of siege and its incumbent restrictions on individual rights for more than a half-century. The new constitution substituted a "state of exception," which was much more constrained in character. Congress and the courts could no longer be suspended during the period of emergency; furthermore, human rights and individual liberties could not be denied.[11] Beyond these specifics, the new charter also reified individual rights, which went beyond political provisions to such matters as health, housing, environment, and social security. Workers' rights were also spelled out in considerable detail.

The constitution of 1991 was a voluminous volume—at 397 articles one of the world's longest, and criticized by some for both its unwieldiness and for a lack of internal coherence and consistency. It included important provisions that were largely responsive to problems of the moment as, for example, the prohibition of extradition. There were others specifying such civil rights to Indians, children, and even more generally to consumers. Indians were guaranteed two seats in the senate. A broad commitment to decentralization called for the transfer of over 40 percent of the national budget to departments and municipalities for health and education. A separate reform legalized civil divorce for Catholic marriages, a measure predictably criticized by the Church. There were additional provisions that in some cases compounded apparent constitutional inconsistencies and organizational disarray.[12]

Criticisms have been numerous ever since the adoption of the charter in 1991; for one, opponents hit the presumed timidity of the assembly in dealing with the military. For others, there were flaws in a failure to provide means of implementing a number of reforms, including many of the broad pledges of civic rights. Notwithstanding these and other targets for opponents, there was no questioning the importance of the new constitution.[13] As Eduardo Pizarro noted, "You can have a thousand objections to the text of the new constitution, but you cannot object to its greater political significance"—the elimination of the two-party system that had long restricted political participation. For Gustavo Gallón, many Colombians "felt that the state belonged not to us but to the elite few. Domination by two parties was ensured by legal and constitutional mechanisms that we couldn't do anything about."[14]

The 1991 constitution has already been tested on a number of particulars since its adoption. Implementation of many provisions is in its early stages, and legislation is necessary in many areas to flesh out general statements of principle. There is insufficient experience on which to formulate a definitive assessment. At this early juncture, the judgment is effectively encapsulated by a terse and direct statement by Harvey Kline. In his words,

> The Constituent Assembly of 1991 was called at a desperate time in Colombian history, one in which the entire country seemed to be coming apart. Clearly the new Constitution will take years to put into effect and will have to overcome both tradition and the lack of funds that come with underdevelopment. It is based on the assumption that the lack of democracy was more important than the lack of authority.
>
> Hopefully in the next century we will conclude that it was a new constitution that helped bring the country out of its difficulties, and not that it was simply another one written for angels, worth only the paper that it was written on.[15]

Samper's Government: The First Year

Samper's arrival at the Casa Nariño in a sense had been anticipated for the better part of a decade. Yet it had only been realized after a difficult personal and political passage of rites. By the time Samper narrowly defeated Andrés Pastrana for the presidency, his credentials as a survivor had been firmly established. On 5 March 1989 he had been gravely wounded during a shooting at the El Dorado international airport; doctors informed the family that his chance of survival was only 5 percent. His determined medical recovery was paralleled by a roughly comparable political return from the brink.

Having become the leader of the Asociación Nacional de Institucións Financieras (ANIF) at the age of twenty-five (succeeding Belisario Betancur, who was an important early mentor), he soon came to the attention of Alfonso López Michelsen, and became the political coordinator of his second presidential campaign in 1982. With López's loss, Samper's star temporarily faded; he founded the Poder Popular movement, which in time carried him to the senate. By 1988 Samper had become one of five members of the Liberal Directorate and, as a foremost figure in the party's rising generation, came to be viewed as second in the *fila india,* after Luis Carlos Galán. When Galán was murdered, Samper's name swiftly came to the fore, to be confronted by Hernando Durán of the Liberal old guard and by César Gaviria, most recently the coordinator of Galán's campaign. This led to Samper's 1990 defeat—a bitter and painful political setback. Nonetheless, Samper remained the candidate to beat for the Liberal candidacy in 1994. Such visible rivals as Lemos, De la Calle, and Carlos Lleras de la Fuente, among others, were largely seeking to position themselves for 1998.

After having served the inevitable term as cabinet minister for Gaviria—during which time he often clashed with Rudolf Hommes over economic policy—Samper also followed the customary Colombian practice accepting an ambassadorship, in his case Madrid. Upon his subsequent return home Samper then effectively assumed leadership of the Liberal electoral machinery. The narrowness of his victory over Andrés Pastrana in the first round compounded the pressures preceding the second, which he was to win. All of this, then, resulted in a new president—youthful and vigorous, full of ideas backed by experience, a veteran of party politics who nonetheless stood somewhat apart from Liberal traditions, especially regarding social and economic policies. Having survived both personal and professional setbacks of the most serious kind, Samper took office with predictions about his policy orientation mixed. Certainly there was much to suggest that the new president had his feet to the left of Liberal traditionalism. Yet Samper had more recently been associated with Gaviria's trade liberalization. During the campaign he had promised to emphasize greater state interventionism as well as extending social programs.

Such critical policy questions, however, were initially sidetracked by the furor over alleged drug penetration of the 1994 campaign. Following the official announcement of the Samper electoral victory, Andrés Pastrana charged that a secret tape strongly hinted at a contribution of some $3.6 million from the Cali cartel to the president-elect's campaign. Samper vigorously denied all accusations while Pastrana, who had gained the tapes before the runoff, insisted that if the charges were proved, Samper should resign. A wide variety of theories subsequently took shape, with involvement linked by some to conspiracies from the Colombian and U.S. intelligence communities, to rivalries between the foreign ministries and drug enforcement agencies, and the like. No meaningful documentation emerged and, at least in the short run, Pastrana had damaged his own reputation for what was perceived as petulant partisan mishandling of the affair.[16] The matter was seemingly closed in August when the public prosecutor's office cleared both candidates, ruling that the tapes of telephone conversations had been tampered with and were unreliable. Yet doubts persisted, and by mid-1995 Samper's status was badly damaged in the eyes of North American officials, adding to the deterioration of Colombian-U.S. relations that had begun in the final months of the Gaviria administration.[17]

Despite the ongoing distraction, the president-elect sought to define more fully his policy objectives. Both before and after his inauguration he emphasized the importance of social spending. While praising the neoliberal economic policies of Gaviria, Samper sought to cushion their impact. With coffee prices booming and oil exports increasing, he saw encouragement of trade and investment as a major means of financing an improved social net. All of this, he argued, would permit social investments to rise from 8.2 to 15 percent of the GDP; some $15 billion would be directed into roads, railways, health, housing, and education.[18] On 10 August 1994 he promised a great social leap forward while establishing directly under his own office a "social solidarity network" program that would provide subsidies for the poorest third of the population. Some 12 million were to be covered, while an emergency plan was assigned the task of filling 110,000 new jobs in urban investments projects plus a similar number in rural areas.[19]

While extending the government's commitment to these and other social policies, Samper also pledged his determination to tackle anew the endemic problems of public security. In his inaugural address the new president proclaimed a dream that his government would progress in the quest for peace. A multipronged attack was to be directed against guerrillas, the manifest inadequacies of the judiciary, and of course the drug industry. Problems with the first of these were underlined when a guerrilla offensive in late July killed a number of civilians as well as military personnel, including the commander of the army's Fourth Division. The Departamento Administrativo de Seguridad reported that the Coordinadora Nacional Guerrillera had been building up its forces for several months, while incoming Defense Minister Fernando Botero announced that in the first six months of 1994, 787 guerrillas and 366 government troops had been killed in combat. The CNG's offensive was designed to increase the pressure on Samper for a renewal of peace talks. The president had responded favorably to a letter from the FARC responding his inaugural call for meaningful talks, even as the commander of the armed forces criticized such efforts. Samper stuck to his guns despite continuing rumbles of complaint from the military, strongly supporting his newly appointed high commissioner for peace, Carlos Holmes Trujillo. A continuing military drive against both the guerrillas and drug dealers was to go hand in hand with a comparably strong commitment to peace an observance of human rights. Key figures included Holmes, an experienced politician, along with the new Interior Minister Horacio Serpa—himself a former peace commissioner—and Defense Minister Fernando Botero. The last of these, with the unqualified approval of Samper, named a new human rights office with representatives to be assigned to all military bases and garrisons. It was Botero in particular who sought to punish military violators of human rights, both by regular and by irregular and unofficial personnel. Private antiguerrilla paramilitary units continued to be organized, however, with names such as Muerte a Comunistas y Guerrilleros (Mucogue), which was believed responsible for the murder of Colombia's only Communist senator, Manuel Cepeda Vargas, only two days after the inauguration.

As Samper moved into office and began to set his agenda for 1994–98, the quest for peace and internal security inevitably remained inextricably linked to reforms of the judiciary as well as a reshaping of Colombia's approach to the longstanding antinarcotic campaign. The state of the judiciary was especially notorious, and had largely resisted the restorative efforts of the Gaviria administration. Similarly, the constitutional reorganization introduced by the 1991 document had not yet taken hold—nor had its internal contradictions been resolved. It was unsurprising when human rights ombudsman Hernando Valencia announced that in the previous year, the judiciary had found guilty only 2717 defendants despite a total of nearly 28,000 murders. Threats by both *narcotraficantes* and guerrillas, combined with healthy bribes to underpaid (and underprotected) judges, had led to a virtual collapse of the judiciary. Its revival would not be susceptible to swift change, but efforts at reform were especially critical regarding the government's drug policy.

Even before his inauguration, Samper had been in Washington and New York assuring government and business leaders that his government was dedicated to eradication of the drug industry, especially the Cali-based bosses. He promised to step up both military and judicial activity while seeking penalties tougher than the leniency of Gaviria's *sometimiento* policy. Samper reiterated his earlier statements pledging a tightening of terms under which *narcotraficantes* could negotiate their voluntary surrender. Harsher penalties and more rigorous conditions were to be employed. At the same time Samper voiced the oft-repeated Colombian complaint that consumer as well as producing nations bore responsibility for the basic problems, calling for coordinated international action in addition to a broader understanding and a concomitant commitment from the United States.

With the replacement of Gustavo de Greiff by Alfonso Valdivieso as public prosecutor, cooperation did show some progress during the transition period, although Colombians were outraged by periodic denunciations from the floor of the U.S. Congress. An outspoken statement by the new Ambassador Myles Frechette a few months after Samper took office also exacerbated relations, and they remained troubled in 1995. At the same time, on 8 March a special commission recommended a strengthening of sentencing policy while expanding Valdivieso's authority.[20] The carrot-and-stick policy was already in effect, as Valdivieso sought and secured greater penalties against drug dealers, while police operations unfolded at a higher level. In early March of 1995 they arrested 135 suspects and seized a number of specially equipped vehicles. For the new government, policy sought to introduce harsher measures without reigniting a major drug war.[21]

The struggle to enhance public safety and national security found Samper plagued, as were his predecessors, by the difficulty in balancing sharply conflicting views and constituencies. The effort to curb violence and reduce murders—whether political or otherwise—led to continuing denunciations both at home and abroad.[22] Ernesto Samper, defense minister Botero, and other government spokesmen conceded that the state apparatus bore the responsibility for many deaths.[23] At the same time, their efforts at pacification registered some progress during the early months of the new administration, while Vice President Humberto de la Calle travelled the globe to defend Colombia and explain that the government was doing its utmost. He also explained *ad nauseum* that many deaths came from the abuses of guerrillas, whose tactics often failed to discriminate between innocent civilians and uniformed military personnel. The Samper administration, in short, publicly conceded that a dirty war had been waged for some years, at the same time offering no apologies for the basic effort to reestablish civilian rule and extend more effectively the protection of the innocent through policies designed first to control, and then destroy the violence of physical terrorism and psychological intimidation.

Partisan politics and competition largely took a back seat during the rather rocky transition period from Gaviria to Samper and the formative months of the incoming administration.[24] The selection of the cabinet was not in itself unduly contentious. Its sixteen members included twelve Liberals, three Social Christians, and one representative of the Alianza; a few had served with or been generally linked to César Gaviria, and many of the new ministers were well-known on the political scene.[25] There was general approval of Samper's choices, and party-based disputes only surfaced with the approach of elections for departmental and local offices on 30 October. All thirty-two state governorships were contested, along with 1,043 mayors, 502 provincial deputies and 11,066 city councillors. The results led some to argue—*Semana,* for instance—that a new era of "antipolitics" was at hand, although such a judgment may well have been premature.

On the one hand, abstention of nearly 70 percent was not unusual. Furthermore, the customary pattern of Liberal domination was reflected by the party's capture of twenty-two of Colombia's thirty-two governships; the Conservatives won only seven seats, while the remaining three went to coalitions of parties and civic groups supporting independent candidates. Moreover, "anti-politics" mayoral candidates generally fared well, winning seats in such departmental capitals as Armenia, Barranquilla, Cali, Cartagena, Cúcuta, Ibaque, Montería, Neiva, Pasto, and Riohacha.[26] Most striking of all was the sweeping victory of Antanas Mockus as mayor of Bogotá. A mathematician and philosopher who had recently served as rector of the Universidad Nacional, the highly eccentric and unorthodox son of Lithuanian immigrants dramatized his antipolitics stance by cancelling all campaign appearances the week before elections. Mockus explained his unexpected victory by a two to one margin as characterizing that political change and broadening democracy, which he saw as the fundamental contribution of the 1991 constitution. Mockus seemed a personification of antipolitics. The noted academic Fernando Cepeda Ulloa saw him as demonstrating popular alienation from career politicians in Bogotá; the virtual absence of policy proposals was overridden by his popular status as a recognized critic of the existing system. Vice President Humberto de la Calle saw the electoral victories of Mockus and other newcomers, along with the defeat of many traditional politicians, as "a new phase of political pluralism." Samper himself recognized the success of nontraditional forces the day after elections when he called for all new governors and mayors "to begin a process of *concertación*."[27]

Despite the narrowness of his electoral margin, Ernesto Samper had come to power with a wealth of knowledge and experience. His administration was ready for a swift transition and a running start on a wide range of policy issues. Having achieved primacy inside his own party while the opposition was querulously fragmented, he was relatively free from the more extreme partisanship that had so swiftly dissipated the honeymoon periods of several earlier presidents. At the same time, however, the transition was plagued by a series of unanticipated challenges. First came the controversy over drug-related funding of campaigns, which distracted Samper as well as tainted his administration at the outset. This in turn aggravated Colombia's relationship with the United States, which was already suffering during the final period of the Gaviria government. The external implications of Colombia's policies vis-à-vis both the narcotics industry and the guerrilla war thus intruded further upon the Samper administration. And on top of this came an unexpected border crisis with Venezuela, which exploded in late February of 1995 and continued to simmer in the months that followed.

The dispute arose on 26 February when Colombian guerrillas crossed the border, attacked a Venezuelan outpost, and killed eight in the process. Venezuelan President Rafael Caldera warned in his annual address to congress on 10 March that Venezuela might exercise its right to defense of the border if there were recurrences. General Moisés Orozco, his minister of defense, discussed the right to hot pursuit, and Venezuelan public opinion was soon inflamed. Despite a series of meetings between officials from both countries, the climate worsened during the following month. Statements by Venezuela's Frontiers Minister Pompeyo Márquez further aroused sentiment in Caracas, and by late March Humberto de la Calle was lamenting that the situation was "serious in the extreme."[28] Colombian opinion, initially less confrontational in character, gradually toughened toward Venezuela, especially after the latter had deported some 1700 illegal Colombian immigrants before refugee camps and facilities had been prepared. When Venezuelan human rights spokesmen charged abuses against Colombian civilians by Venezuelan military personnel, reports of further reprisals along the border area received greater credence.

At the conclusion of his first year in office, Ernesto Samper found himself the center of a major controversy that threatened to force him from office. This evolved from the earlier charges that his presidential campaign had received contributions from members of the Cali cartel. Renewed investigation led to the arrest of Santiago Medina, his campaign treasurer; Medina unwaveringly point a finger at President Samper, his campaign director Fernando Botero Zea, and others. Botero, the widely acclaimed defense minister, resigned to fight the charges, while Samper firmly repeated earlier denials and urged the appropriate congressional committee to conduct a full-blown investigation. Polls showed that a cynical electorate, already immunized by assumptions that drug money had for years penetrated to the highest levels of Colombia's political and social elite, tended to disbelieve the president's denials. At the same time, they expected him to survive his four-year term. As the administration circled its wagons against attack, it was ironic that in the last few months virtually all of the major leaders of the Cali drug cartel had been captured and arrested. Thus, it counterposed these impressive successes to charges that the same *narcotraficantes* had funnelled millions into the Samper electoral campaign. The president also sought to regain the initiative by organizing a broad-based national movement committed to the eradication of violence. This incorporated a hardened policy against guerrilla organizations, which had responded to the government's original offers of negotiation and compromise with a renewed wave of violence initiated in the early months of 1995.

All of these matters, then, rendered the 1994 government transition far more difficult than it would otherwise have been. It also delayed and complicated the uncertain process whereby the Colombian political system was grappling with the new constitutional framework. It is premature to judge at this early point the eventual significance of the struggle over a potential reshaping by the new constitutional framework. As this gradually unfolds, the impact of a modernizing, corporate clientelism remains critical. Whatever the outcome of the "Cali-gate" investigations, which exploded during the author's mid-1995 research in Colombia, it is unlikely in the broader sweep of politics to nullify or reverse the powerful modernizing pressures and the further elaboration of bureaucratized rule and corporate clientelism as exercised by national elites.

Clientelism and Democracy

Redefining Clientelism

The literature on clientelism has experienced continuing scholarly scrutiny over the better part of a half century. Subjected to a variety of diverse definitions, based on field research in a host of different societies across the face of the globe, and often placed on the defensive against more fully developed as well as modish trends in the social sciences, clientelism has been hard pressed to maintain itself as a heuristically valid perspective for the study of politics. The very question of its survival into modern times has provoked a plethora of disagreement through the years. At first there was a chorus of voices insistently holding that urbanization, industrialization, mass mobilization, and rising participation rendered clientelism an increasingly atavistic concept. Traditional forms of clientelism, as discussed and differentiated in chapter 1, were not generally expected to survive.

Given its anthropological roots, the original concept of clientelism focused on dyadic interpersonal relationships involving a direct exchange between the actors. Unequal reciprocity and personalism were writ large, with resources increasingly controlled by the patrons. The eventual rise of brokers brought about a transformation into what I have identified as patrimonial clientelism. In time, first local and then national leaders developed political channels to incorporate the emergent urbanized masses. The activism of political parties and the expansion of the state helped to assure the breakdown of old loyalties and the sapping of strength from traditional networks. The unilinear developmentalist caste of mind entertained by many social scientists, then, led naturally to the expectation that P-C relationships would fade away, to be replaced by one or another presumably modern form of politics and broadening participation. Yet there were those unprepared to relegate the concept to the social science dustbin. Luis Roniger remarked recently that the "study of patronage and clientelism—which has burgeoned in the social sciences since the late 1960s—can be considered part of a broad reaction against evolutionary assumptions regarding the allegedly generalized move toward Western liberal forms of political development and bureaucratic universalism."[29]

The role of mass participation and, in a very real sense, democratization led students to seek clarification about the impact of presumably nonmodern clientelism and its mechanisms. One view held that clientelism was capable of moving ahead within a more refined notion of political development. Thus, it would draw together national and regional elites while serving better to redistribute resources through a powerful centralized state. Clientelism thus was viewed as functional for political development.[30] A contrasting school of thought criticized this approach as being unduly deterministic. Furthermore, they preferred to move away from the unilinearism of prevailing developmental literature. In so doing, they contended that clientelism did not necessarily assure political modernization, let alone a more participatory system. Thus, neither democratic nor authoritarian patterns could be assured. In most cases, however, this perspective pessimistically concluded that contemporary clientelism would mitigate against greater participation and civic involvement. The popular will would be fragmented while leaning toward preservation of the status quo.[31]

While this debate was very slow to move toward theoretical resolution, at least an emergent if qualified consensus accepted the vitality of clientelism amid a modernizing society. Even before the 1990s there was a grudging repudiation of the earlier denial that modernization axiomatically guaranteed the irrelevance of clientelism. A collective voice was enunciated in July 1990 by participants in sessions on clientelism convened by the Committee on Community Research at the XII World Congress of Sociology. Later published in expanded form, it declared in the preface that the contributors dissented from earlier approaches "in their shared conviction that...clientelism should not be expected to disappear as a necessary corollary of political change and development." Rather, the authors claimed that "in many modern and contemporary politics clientelism is a major focus for research into the interplay of structural and cultural factors that affect the prospects of consolidation of the new democracies."[32] Thus, clientelism could not be dismissed as a remnant of the past.

As the senior editor remarked in his own contribution to this volume, by the 1970s and 1980s "a myriad of empirical analyses and a number of theoretical works made social scientists increasingly aware of the near ubiquity of patronage and clientelism in modern societies."[33] He argued persuasively that the increasing flow of theoretically sophisticated studies had led to reconceptualization along several lines. As already discussed, there was a broad sensitivity to the survival of clientelism even as político-economic modernization was progressing, thereby requiring renewed study. The question was not whether clientelism still existed but, rather, centered on a redefinition of P-C relationships.

Another basic theme reflected a realization that there was a variability across societies in the institutional and conceptual character of P-C relationships. Out of this came the contention by some scholars that there was a societal and cultural regionalization that allowed for cross-national generalizations at a less than global level. This formed the basis, for instance, for those claiming to identify meaningful clientelistic parallels between and among the nations of the Mediterranean and Latin America.

The effort to redefine clientelism also recognized the importance of greater attention to historical conditions, and especially to matters of timing and circumstance. This bore particular relevance for Third World nations where, as Rene Lemarchand pointed out, the demands and frustrations of the rural sectors found an outlet in electoral channels before the crystallization of social identities along class lines. The result, therefore, "has been a process of fragmented restructuration which offered ample scope for the re-emergence of patron-client ties in the guise of nominally modern institutions.... *It is primarily where social change has lagged substantially behind political modernization that clientelistic forms of dependency have been more resilient.*"[34] A variant, also stressed by some of the works based on Third World research, has considered in detail the contextual importance of political culture. Authors of these works generally regard political culture as composed of values, norms, and expectations that are held as political givens by groups of citizens. Thus, conditions of the macro-setting may well be critical to P-C relationships.

All of the preceding suggests that there is little remaining dissension over the persistence and transformation of clientelism in the modernizing world. Still, explanations are necessary for the coexistence of clientelism with modern forms. Günes-Ayata argues that "with the increasing participation of the masses and changing patterns of political activity and recruitment in developing societies, clientelism is likely to evolve and persist along with other forms of participation that once were considered to be on the wane."[35] Granted the survival of clientelism into the modern era, then, other issues and debates that dot the literature have not been resolved. Neither is this likely in the foreseeable future. Scholarship requires the detailed empirical investigation that is sensitive to the richness of prevailing theories while seeking to refine insights that result in fresh new conceptual constructs.

Moreover, it must address perhaps the single most important difficulty of all, namely, a reconciliation of relationships between clientelism and the modern (or modernizing) state. For there is little doubt that democracy, especially when attempting to move toward more inclusionary participation, runs contrary to many of the classic elements of clientelism. Meaningful democracy in modernizing societies suggests a degree of fragmentation, the weakening of systemic state controls, and an empowerment of civil society that further encourages the rise of the individual as an active player in politics. Some of this is encouraged by, or evolves through the growth of political parties—an important element within the Colombian context (see next section). As political democracy is reshaped by the newly emerging civil society, there must be new channels of communication as the impact of urbanization and industrialization compete with older clientelistic principles of deference and social status. The representative basis for a more broadly inclusionary politics of democracy is therefore confronted by the challenge of clientelism that is ultimately derived from patronage and exchanges between patrons and clients.

P-C relationships in modernizing systems are destined to reflect contradictions that were not present in older, more traditional societies. Major demographic shifts, urbanization, industrialization, economic diversity and diversification, the expansion of regulatory and distributive activities on the part of the state, and the complexities of providing public security to the citizenry—all of these have called for the development of new clientelistic channels. In the case of Latin America, clientelism has been powerfully influenced by the deep-seated history of hierarchical controls and fundamentally unequal relationships of patron and client, accompanied by the conceptions of personalism and the importance of the individual being (as elaborated in chapter 1). This brings us to a reprise of the Colombian experience, set within the broader theoretical framework of clientelism and the contradictions of the democratic state. To cite Roniger once more, "As modern capitalistic and democratic settings endorse the openness of the system in universalistic or quasi-universalistic terms, clientelism is opposed by countervailing forces: political organizations within civil society, social forces willing to support autonomous channels of communication with the center, and constituencies for bureaucratic autonomy."[36]

Colombian Clientelism in the 1990s

The traditional definition of clientelism elaborated in chapter 1 and derived from such writers as Powell and Mainwaring, among others, was applicable to Colombia during its first century of independence. As Leal and Davila wrote, "clientelism forms part of Colombian history. The weak presence of the State and the consequent inefficiency of institutions...have influenced this type of relations in politics."[37] Mass political participation was largely unknown, with the P-C relationship resting on economic power and prestige, especially at the local level. Clientelistic values, attitudes, and practices became deeply rooted in Colombia's traditional social structure. Rewards came largely from the resources available to local leaders. Reliance upon national leaders through developing brokerage networks was not appreciable until the 1930s, at which time the major political parties began to elaborate their organizational structures. The *revolución en marcha* of López Pumarejo and the activities of such other political figures as Eduardo Santos and Laureano Gómez began to build the foundations for more effective and truly national political parties. López in particular led the way toward broader and more extensive responsibilities on the part of a gradually expanding state.

Still, in the absence of significant mass incorporation into politics, the brokerage-based functioning of traditional clientelism held firm; cliques of party-affiliated notables remained the dominant force. New, enlarging government jobs and services represented a growing resource for the leadership, thereby cementing the loyalties of local patrons. Yet none of this altered the fact that the rapid emergence of a modernizing and industrializing state—propelled by major changes in demographic and economic conditions—dated essentially from the 1950s. Thus, it largely coincided with the restoration of constitutional government under the limiting elitist provisions of the National Front. Both the parties and the state found themselves necessarily engaged in seeking new clientelistic relationships, in moving away from patrimonial patterns as a means of preserving their traditional political hegemony.

With the advent of the National Front, first the Lleras Camargo and then the Valencia administrations effectively isolated economic policies and their implementation from partisan decisions. Lleras Restrepo further centralized the state administration while reducing congress to legalistic approval of executive decisions as a legitimizing function for the state. The 1968 constitutional reforms, with the so-called *desmonte* of the National Front, secured an extension of the existing biparty monopoly over the state. Yet this did little to enhance or revitalize the role of the parties, whose tightly knit groups of notables continued to coordinate the definition and realization of state policies under highly exclusionary circumstances. Rather, the result was an invigorating of the parties at the regional and local levels. While this was transpiring, the context within which clientelism operated was progressively altered.

The rise of corporate clientelism, as we call it, emanated in no small part from the state as a means of substituting for the accustomed role of the political parties. Certainly the parties and the state have both been central of P-C relationships for generations. For the parties, the provisions of the National Front altered substantially the rule of the game under which they had long been operating. Clientelism and the involvement of the local *cacique* had been tied historically to a backward, precapitalist society in which the institutions of the state were weak. The local party chiefs, many of them longstanding leaders linked to rural landowning patterns, had come to work more through evolving broker-age networks with regional and national party leaders. Under the post-1958 cooperative arrangement, however, party competition was stifled. The biparty monopoly of power and its resulting emphasis on establish-ing a consensus over major national issues effectively weakened the links from national to regional and local levels. The *jefaturas naturales* were in a sense eclipsed; party discipline weakened; and organizational activ-ity was greater at the subnational level.

All of this ran parallel to the growth of state institutions.[38] This repre-sented a necessary response to the complexities of the emerging moderniz-ing state, but also was politically motivated by the bureaucratic parity mandated by the National Front. The state to a degree was absorbing the earlier activities and resources of the parties, weakening national party discipline in the process. The coming and implantation of the National Front not only allowed for an hegemonic two-party system, which effectively limited competition and thereby discouraged participation, but also pro-vided Liberals and Conservatives the opportunity to reshape their clientelistic networks in conjunction with the growth of the modernizing state.[39]

In practice, what resulted was an inflammation of internal party rival-ries. Even while the state was becoming increasingly important as a pur-veyor of resources, Conservatives extended and exacerbated the bitter animosities of the Gómez and Ospina clans. For the Liberals, conflict be-tween reformers and supporters of the status quo raged for years, with *jefes naturales* fighting for domination. Local and regional *caciques*, al-though seeking to maximize their benefits through opportunistic links to the dominating national *jefe* of the moment, also relied increasingly on the largesse of the state. Many forms of the patronage that had customarily flowed from party leaders gradually fell under the aegis of the state. Public jobs, for one, were controlled increasingly by the state, although party loyalists in the government were not without influence. Openings in public schools, the securing of retirement benefits, the providing of scholarship, public access to housing and medical services, a favorable treatment in the awarding of public concessions and licensing—these and a myriad of other benefits and rewards were determined through the patronage of the state.

Over time the local leaders and their own clients became dependent upon the state and its representatives more than upon party authorities, especially as the distinction between Conservatives and Liberals was blurred by the realities of the National Front. Partisanship was also weakened in the process. As the modernizing bureaucracy was slowly professionalized, personal rather than partisan allegiances were emphasized. One's loyalty to the Liberals, for example, was less relevant by the 1970s than, say, a commitment to Lleras Restrepo rather than López Michelsen. This shift became more pronounced after presidential elections reverted to competitive contests in 1974, when remaining provisions of the National Front expired in 1978, and then with the 1982 election of Betancur marking more fully the conclusion of the Front experiment.[40] The parties found it difficult to respond to the impact of modernizing changes, not the least of which were the more competitive and participatory measures—*apertura*—which the public was demanding.

Electoral partisanship was also redirected toward a greater emphasis at the local and regional levels. Congressional races were especially notable, where legislators relied heavily upon their own electoral machinery. Clientelistic networks proliferated, with office seekers soliciting the fullest possible degree of state patronage. Ties with aspiring presidential contenders remained, but diminished in significance as campaigns became more dependent upon modern techniques, means of mass communication, and sophisticated public relations approaches to the winning of votes. Gary Hoskin also pointed to the shift of electoral behavior produced by modernization, thereby weakening party clientelism:

> Clientelistic practices have always been more effective in rural zones, and with growing urbanization...the clientelistic networks no longer constitute such a significant resource for the mobilization of the vote. Another manifestation of the weakening of [party] clientelism is the growing size of the middle class, which in part has upset clientelist practices of the traditional parties."[41]

Local studies bear out Hoskin's views. Junco Veloso's examination of Boyacá clientelism from 1930 to 1990, for one, first presented a lengthy study of traditional patterns. He then analyzed the Front and its biparty depoliticization as responsible for "a new clientelism," which changed from the old to the new patron, the state. He saw a shift toward the machinery lodged in government agencies. Personal loyalties toward *jefaturas naturales* gave way to more material interests that could best be served by the state and its agents. The sense of party affiliation weakened while the state was strengthened through its control of new and expanding activities and services. Old-style politicians were replaced by professionals with the knowledge and capacity to manage the political machinery of the state.[42]

A somewhat contrasting perspective emerges from Cristina Escobar's study of peasant politics in the northern province of Sucre, where traditional clientelism endured into contemporary times despite a strong peasant movement and two decades of related attempts at popular mobilization. She concurs with the view that even in rural villages, traditional P-C relationships have been altered under the force of the developing market and bureaucracy. She follows the earlier work of Powell in recognizing that peasant organizations help to integrate peasants into the national political system, but leave them still in a condition of subordination. The Sucre study richly documents the role of local leadership, the incorporating impact of modernization, and the reshaping of clientelism. The role of the parties had diminished. Escobar concludes that in peasant communities—now with a small proportion of the population—PC-relations had not evolved into corporative forms. Elsewhere, however, she saw that "corporatism has become a major mechanism for the control of social conflict by combining party or state political cooptation of peasant organizations."[43] Even the rural, peasant-based communities of the interior, then, were increasingly susceptible to corporate clientelism.

Perhaps the most searching, empirically based study was that of Leal Buitrago and Davila on the municipio of Rionegro in Santander, with local clientelism personified by Don Tiberio Villareal. Here again is a case where the setting for clientelism has shifted in recent years. First the National Front diluted the unadulterated Liberal-Conservative rivalry of the past century. The government of the state moved to establish its own monopoly of resources. As always, the Achilles heel for clientelism and patronage lay in budgetary constraints. More broadly, the flourishing of ever-expanding demands, which can only be met by official moneys, necessarily extends to businessmen and impresarios who can buy functionaries. This situation has proven beneficial to the narcotraficantes, whose massive wealth invites intrusion into the system. Another important resource was that of the congressional auxilios, which until their elimination by the Constitution of 1991 enabled congressmen to participate effectively in the buying of votes at election time, notably along the Atlantic. For the parties, then, a significant by-product of the transition to corporate clientelism was the renewal of regional caciquismo, at the same time detracting from the authority of national political leadership and damaging what little real party discipline had survived.[44]

The contemporary literature has provided further justification for the contention that patrimonialism went out of style as modernization emerged with a vengeance, accompanied by the political dynamics of the National Front. While there are differences of opinion over details, conditions unquestionably changed. Whether or not one accepts the argument that the Front effectively drew to a close with the Betancur administration, it is clear that his promotion of *apertura* through such reforms as the direct election of mayors required the introduction of new clientelistic practices and networks. The modernizing state and the growing availability of its resources sapped the vitality of traditional clientelism, and patterns of brokerage networks were inevitably altered. Impoverished municipalities require clientelistic goods and services far beyond the capacity of local and regional bodies, necessitating eventual recourse to the national state (and to its burgeoning presence through representative officials). In electoral terms the predominantly rural heritage of the political parties has weakened. Presidential candidates have found their own personal campaigning critical in pursuing the urban electorate. They benefit relatively little from the electoral efforts of congressional candidates, who in most cases can still survive by reliance on time-tested clientelist tactics in rural areas as well as mixed constituencies, which include at least one urban center. This general failing of the party system nationally, confronted with the powerful changes produced by the process of modernization, has consequently helped to reorient clientelistic attitudes and expectations toward the state and away from the parties.

The resources, organization, and scope of the modernizing state in Colombia have reshaped clientelism into a bureaucratized, corporate model.[45] The statist momentum accelerated during the Betancur administration and thereafter as party allegiances further diminished. Virgilio Barco, notwithstanding his ultimate failure to realize a fundamental political redemocratization, nevertheless presided over an administration in which both the efficiency and scope of state agencies quickened. The pace was ratcheted even higher with the arrival of César Gaviria and his youthful advisors (the much-maligned *kinder*). Policy initiatives were not startling, and in a general sense Gaviria pursued a path regarded by many as slightly to the right of center. Although concerted rethinking of approaches to the treats of drug dealers and the guerrillas preoccupied the administration, its actions left many Colombians disappointed, especially after the fiasco of Pablo Escobar's escape from imprisonment. Ernest Samper has become only the most recent in a long line of presidents pledging to find solutions which would contradict longstanding state failures in the realm of public security. It is also worth noting that Samper's narrow margin of victory over Andres Pastrana, despite the Liberal wins in congressional races, was consistent with the declining relevance of the parties and party organization.

It has been the symbiotic relationship between the state and the political parties that underlies a redefinition of clientelism in corporate terms; the newer form constitutes the contemporary phenomenon seeking to provide those services so long taken for granted by the citizenry via the older patrimonial mechanisms. If the prevailing clientelistic system is not to decay in the face of modernization, benefits must still be available and deliverable. Otherwise the legitimacy of the clientelistic system is destined to decline; in Colombia, the depth of historic clientelism strongly propelled the system toward a redefinition for survival rather than a retreat into obscurity. This again encouraged the drive—no matter how accidental or unplanned—toward that bureaucratization that would meet societal needs. Contemporary forms of clientelism thus have questioningly reconsidered the nature of state power.

Important elements in the structure of the state are sympathetic to the clientelistic impulse. For one, the state possesses a hierarchical organization, accompanied by the growing state monopoly over resource control and allocation. While the state organization contains an unequal linkage between and among officials at different bureaucratic levels, it also allocates benefits to those below and outside the state structure. The system allows for the vote as a mechanism of representation, but in the Colombian case the realities of the National Front and the prevailing levels of abstention and nonparticipation have worked against those committed to a democratization of the system. Where electoral manifestations of clientelism are marginal to national politics, the role of the state necessarily expands. The hierarchical nature of the state structure becomes a guiding feature of bureaucratic clientelism, with the patron's interests shaped in accordance with his hierarchical status. This is consistent with the notion that the clientelism of control is linked to organizational politics.[46]

A final retrospective look reminds us that forms of clientelism change over time in response to the nature of society, the state, and the political order. Within the traditionalist order, the most elemental form of clientelism—the feudal—was succeeded by the stage of patrimonialism, set first within a rural context. What Schmidt termed agrarian patrimonialism was inevitably altered as Colombia moved forward toward modernization of society and the state. The demographic and socioeconomic data presented for the succession of administrations since 1958 amply document Colombia's modernization. The emergent bureaucratic system has meant centralization and statism; urbanization and the breakdown of regional and rural practices and attitudes; internal immigration; industrialization; the infrastructural elaboration of transportation and communications; and economic diversification. The exercise of social and political control, especially in terms of public security and the safety of the ordinary citizen, further multiplies the need for new clientelistic mechanisms.

With the state consequently assuming increasing responsibility for tasks once performed primarily by the parties and interrelated brokerage networks, the rise of corporate clientelism was unavoidable. While adjectival descriptions in the literature have included such labels as modern, post-modern, industrial, and the like, the reality is clear: clientelism lives on, but wearing new and different garb. Furthermore, a redefined clientelism may function under either civilian or military government. While the Colombian case has stimulated attention to the former, it is also true that while the role of the parties recedes even further under authoritarian rule, this does not obviate the need for corporate clientelist mechanisms. Rather, it assures that democratic participation is either barred or else rigorously controlled. Under authoritarian rule, therefore, the model is preeminently exclusionary.

Whether or not the rulers are civilian and constitutionally legitimized—as in Colombia since the fall of Gustavo Rojas Pinilla more than three decades ago—corporate clientelism requires the activism of technocrats and bureaucrats. If participation and mass mobilization is present, then the inclusionary element is dominant. Although most students of clientelism have agreed that inherently antidemocratic qualities endure, they have also argued that these need not prevent pluralist activism and the growth over time of representational mechanisms. The momentum toward greater participation in Colombia, toward a meaningful process of democratization as encompassed by the popular rubric of *apertura,* has been manifest for some two decades.

Beyond question, the debate in Colombia over clientelism will no more die than will the shifting qualities manifested by its modernizing corporate form. As Gilhodes remarked, there has been a tendency for Colombians to view clientelism from a moral perspective as fundamentally evil. Yet he has predicted that the democratizing influence of mayoral elections and greater local participation will produce a redefinition rather than disappearance of clientelism.[47] And while Colombian scholars have eclectically dealt with clientelism as a reality of national life—sometimes in relatively positive terms—the political leadership has largely maintained a sharply critical view. It was powerfully projected into the public mentality by the series of excoriating editorials by Carlos Lleras Restrepo published in 1975 by his magazine *Nueva Frontera*. The former president saw clientelism as having developed a range of levers that enslaved the electorate and subordinated public needs to the satisfaction of selfish personal interests.

The former president's view was later taken up by others, perhaps most notably Nuevo Liberalismo and Luis Carlos Galán. As this perspective gradually spread within the nation's political elites, it was first adopted at the presidential level by Belisario Betancur. His advocacy of such measures as the election of mayors, among others, moved Colombia toward a less atavistic form of clientelism. Virgilio Barco fought for greater public participation via the path of constitutional reform, although with little success.[48] Then the student-initiated campaign for democratization took form in the movement that led to the ultimate adoption of a new and significantly different constitution in 1991. The newly inaugurated César Gaviria hailed the charter as a powerful tool supporting his campaign pledge to dismantle clientelism.[49] Ernesto Samper later voiced similar rhetoric. For skeptics, however, the reality was an emergent new generation inheriting the legacy of their elders. By the mid-1990s, such fraternal or maternal surnames as Lleras, Turbay, López, Rojas, Trujillo, and others were personified by younger political leaders.[50] Both 1994 presidential rivals, of course, enjoyed a lineage including former presidents and party notables. The elitist drive for power and control, now framed by new inclusionary mechanisms, caused the turn toward bureaucratization and state corporatism.

In recent years first César Trujillo and then Ernesto Samper have been confronted with the necessity of making functional the newly defined inclusionary constitutional principles. These have elaborated more fully the presumed decentralization that is part and parcel of the Colombian version of *apertura*. It suggests potential problems and an uncertainty over democracy and civic participation in the corporate clientelist model. This very model fits Colombian politics in theory and practice where the older patrimonial experience does not. The state has acquired and exercised far more extensive duties in the distribution of resources and the servicing of citizens' needs. In so doing it has operated with increasingly complex and intricate interrelationships with business. Labor has also been brought into the process. It is not coincidental that Samper in late 1994 elaborated a set of policies labelled the Pacto Social or social pact, the success of which will depend upon the effectiveness of formal agreement as negotiated and then signed by representatives of the state, business, and labor.

This endeavor provides institutional testimony to the corporate clientelism that is now operative. At the same time, a meaningful extension of state decentralization and heightened responsibilities for regional and local officials suggests the possible for a more truly inclusionary system. Broadened participation may be encouraged as state authority is dispersed. The future role of the political parties has also been raised once again. Logic would suggest that *apertura* and state decentralization may provide an impulse for the resuscitation of the parties and a higher level of civic participation. Yet there have been few signs that the parties are being truly revitalized. Even such a basic participatory act as that of voting is still ignored by a majority of Colombians. Electoral data show that abstention rates remain high, especially for races at the subnational level. Liberals consistently defeat Conservatives, with local and regional *caciques* delivering the party vote for the small number of loyalists who participate, at least beneath the presidential competition. This was manifest from both the first and second 1994 presidential rounds, with the Conservative Pastrana only narrowly losing his challenge to the Liberal Samper. The relative weakness of the two traditional parties was evident, yet the decline of the M-19 and its allies also repeated the classic pattern of dissident Colombian parties or factions being co-opted into the world of biparty hegemony.

Two lines of reasoning can be constructed and elaborated to anticipate the possible future course of Colombian politics as shaped by the powerful clientelistic impulse. The first would expect corporate clientelism to endure. The state would remain a prime dispenser of favors, services, and patronage; it would maintain the responsibility for assigning and distributing resources to the citizenry. Colombians would not indulge themselves greatly in participatory activities, and democratizing reforms would not be effectively adopted. Socioeconomic and political elites would still control national affairs. At the same time, centralized security forces would be unable to improve substantially the condition of public safety; instead, they would continue as lightning rods for many domestic and international charges of human rights violations.[51] Both official and unofficial armed bands would still be engaged, as would be the guerrilla bands and armed enforcers of the drug industry.[52] Drug money would remain a vital element to the economy while thriving on a capacity to penetrate Colombian life, society, and politics. Corporate clientelism would be exclusionary, and the practice of democracy would be limited to narrowly formalistic, electorally oriented political dynamics.

An alternative scenario—comparatively more promising and forward-looking—is that of true and fuller democratization in which there is a revival of the political parties as nationally organized, internally developed entities with identifiable doctrinal or programmatic messages. No longer will they require the temporary electoral leadership of septuagenarian former presidents to run a campaign.[53] Local membership and grass-roots activism will contribute to the process of systemic democratization. The parties will in effect be taking away some of the clientelistic duties of the state, while the relationship of the two will be couched within the context of the modernizing society. The role of labor will be enlarged while business will remain a partner in matters of policy formulation. A reformed judicial system will help with the marginalization of the guerrillas, while the drug industry will have gradually shifted much of its activity from Colombia to other nations. Decentralization will encourage local participation, thereby reinforcing the opportunities for the revival of the parties in more open rather than closed elitist politics.

Whether a version of either scenario may ultimately prevail or, more likely, some amalgamation of key features of the two ideal types occurs—Colombia is unlikely to shed basically clientelistic impulses. As the modernizing corporate form proceeds, the fate of inclusionary reforms will determine whether or not the state can construct a system in which the citizenry influences the course of national politics. The policies of governance ceded to this point by traditional socioeconomic and political elites—often in begrudging fashion—have demonstrated the fundamentally conservative impetus that still motivates the defense of their own interests through the exercise of power. The outcome of the present historic clash between reformist, participatory *apertura* and the customary exclusionary elites will speak eloquently about democracy and the state as the nation moves toward the twenty-first century. Whatever the assessment, it will have drawn upon both old and modern manifestations of Colombian clientelism.

Notes

1. While it is true that executive authority was increased in many areas, there were also provisions that augmented the president's accountability to the legislature. "Introduction of a State of Economic Emergency," contrary to the earlier "State of Siege," was of limited duration and subject to modification by congress. Other restrictions on the executive included greater congressional power in questioning ministers and their policy proposals.
2. Pizarro, a political scientist at the Universidad Nacional, was quoted in *The Los Angeles Times* (30 April 1991).
3. An excellent electoral analysis, accompanied by useful data, is John Dugas, Rubén Sánchez David, and Elizabeth Ungar B., "La Asamblea Nacional Constituyente, expresion de una voluntad general," in Rubén Sánchez David, compilador, *Los nuevos retos electorales; Colombia 1990: antesala del cambio* (Bogotá: CEREC, Universidad de los Andes, 1991), 187–215.
4. An informative overview published in August of 1990, based on a Forum at the University of the Andes, is FESCOL, *Una constituyente para la Colombia del futuro* (Bogotá: Fundación Friedrich Ebert de Colombia, 1990).
   An earlier study of reforms of the state that expressed concerns over the quality of popular participation is Jesús Pérez González Rubio, *Gobierno y oposición: elementos para una reforma del estado* (Bogotá: Pontificia Universidad Javeriana, Facultad de Estudios Interdisciplinarios, 1987).
5. A helpful discussion and analysis of the court proceedings and sentence appears in Jaime Buenahora Febres-Cordero, *El proceso constituyente: De la propuesta estudiantil a la quiebra del bipartidismo* (Bogotá: Pontificia Universidad Javeriana, 1991), chap. 6, pp. 219–73.
6. Two additional members were designated for selection by indigenous organizations. As noted in chapter 12, twenty-five seats (from a number of lists) went to the Liberals, followed by nineteen for the M-19, eleven for Alvaro Gómez's MSN, nine for Conservatives (five from the Social Christians and four from Independent Conservatives), and eight independents. For a breakdown of lists and accompanying information, see Buenahora, *El proceso constituyente,* especially chap. 8, pp. 317–65. Short biographical sketches of Constituyente members appear in the Annex, pp. 365–89.
7. The five commissions were: (1) fundamental principles, rights, liberties, participation, electoral system, political parties, opposition rights, and so forth; (2) territorial organization plus local and regional authority; (3) reforms of the executive, congress, the military, state of siege; (4) judicial reforms; and (5) socioeconomic and ecological affairs, finances.
8. From *El Tiempo* (4 July 1991), as quoted by Harvey F. Kline.
9. A juridical study that focuses on the organization of the state and especially reforms to public administration under the new document is Alvaro Tatur Galvis, *La constitución de 1991 y la modernización del estado colombiano: la par-*

ticipación, la colaboración convenciónal, las empresas publicas, la privatización (Bogotá: Universidad Externado de Colombia, 1993).

A broader analysis that probes the document in detail while also considering the broader issue of participatory democracy is Diego Uribe Vargas, *La constitución de 1991 y el ideario liberal* (Bogotá: Universidad Nacional de Colombia, 1992).

10. *Gaceta constitucional* (22 May 1991): 79.
11. The president could declare a state of exception for no more than ninety days in a calendar year, which could be extended by senate vote for another ninety days. Thus, the condition was limited to a maximum of six months per calendar year.
12. In addition to works already cited in this section, an stimulating evaluation is contained in John Dugas, ed., *La constitución política de 1991: un pacto político viable?* (Bogotá: CEREC, 1993).
13. The general significance of the 1991 constitutional reforms for governance in Colombia is also discussed by Gabriel Murillo Castaño and Rubén Sánchez David, "Procesos y Factores Determinantes de la Recurrencia de la Crisis Gubernativa en Colombia," in Gabriel Murillo Castaño, ed., *Hacia la consolidación democratica andina; transición o desestabilización* (Bogotá: Tercer Mundo Editores, UNIANDES), 1993), 85–151.

For an excellent examination of the partisan and electoral situation as based on the several 1994 elections, see Matthew Soberg Shugart, *Economic Adjustment and Political Institutions; Foreign vs. Domestic Constituents in Colombia,* Graduate School of International Relations and Pacific Studies, University of California, San Diego, February 1992.

14. Both quotations were reported by Stan Yarbro in his "Colombia's New Constitution Tackles Old Corruption," *Los Angeles Times* (8 July 1991).
15. The quotation comes from Harvey F. Kline, "Conflict Resolution through Constitution Writing: The Colombian Constituent Assembly of 1991," paper presented at the Annual Meeting of the Southern Political Science Association, Atlanta, Georgia, 5–7 November 1991, p. 24. This is one of several conference papers by Kline based on a larger research project concerned with conflict resolution efforts in Colombia. My thanks are extended to Professor Kline for sharing his findings and interpretations as reported in these essays.
16. A poll by Gallup Colombia in Colombia's four major cities, carried out between 9 August and 11 August, gave a favorable rating of 57 percent to Ernesto Samper, with 18 unfavorable; Humberto de la Calle had almost identical evaluations. The opinion for Pastrana, in contrast, was 39 percent favorable and 47 percent unfavorable. See further details in *Semana* (23 August 1994): 21. 17. Issues of *Semana* in July and August effectively summarized assorted Colombian opinions. For a convenient and accessible English-language overview as the dispute first flared up, see *Latin American Regional Reports—Andean Group* (4 August 1994): 8.
17. Later events further threatened Samper's political survival.
18. "Colombia," *Latin American Weekly Report* (28 July 1994): 327.
19. Samper's social programs were to be financed by $163 million from internal resources, $698 million from the 1995 budget, plus an anticipated $500 credit with the International Development Bank. For details see "Columbia," *Latin American Weekly Report* (25 August 1994): 382.
20. The commission included Justice Minister Néstor Humberto Martínez, Supreme Court President Carlos Jaramillo, Attorney General Orlando Vásquez, and Valdivieso.

21. A cleanup of the police also continued. The national director of police, General Rosso Serrano, announced on 8 March 1995 that 50 officers and over 7000 additional personnel had been dismissed as part of the anticorruption drive.

22. A characteristic denunciation, which centers especially on the August 1994 murder of Senator Manuel Cepeda of Unidad Patriótica while giving a telling if partisan and impassioned account, is Ana Carrigan, "A Chronicle of Death Foretold: State-Sponsored Violence in Colombia," *NACLA Report on the Americas* 28, no. 5 (March/April 1995): 6–11.

23. An official admission of guilt for the killing of civilians at the town of Trujillo from 1988 to 1990, a sharp departure from customary government denials, is detailed in "Columbia," *Latin American Regional Report, Andean Group* (13 April 1995): 2.

24. The political and electoral context is clearly outlined in Eduardo Pizarro Leóngomez, "Elecciónes, partidos y nuevo marco instituciónal: en que estamos?" *Análisis Político*, no. 22 (mayo-agosto 1994): 81–99.

25. Among the more noteworthy were Horacio Serpa Uribe (interior), Rodrigo Pardo García-Peña (foreign relations), Fernando Botero Zea (defense), Guillermo Perry Rubio (finance), Néstor Humberto Martínez (justice), Juan Gómez Martinez (transportation), and Rodrigo Marín Bernal (development). Brief sketches of the cabinet plus ministerial priorities and selected interviews and comments appear in *Semana* (9 August 1994): 34–48.

26. The victor in Pasto was the ADM-19 leader Antonio Navarro Wolff.

27. Both quotes come from "Colombia," *Latin American Regional Reports*, Andean Group (17 November 1994): 2–3.

28. *El Espectador* (24 March 1995): 1.

29. Luis Roniger, "The Comparative Study of Clientelism and the Changing Nature of Civil Society in the Contemporary World," in Roniger and Ayse Günes-Ayata, eds., *Democracy, Clientelism, and Civil Society* (Boulder: Lynne Rienner Publishers, 1994), 3.

30. Among the more prominent advocates of this position were Jerry Boissevain in his work on patronage in Malta, including such works as "Patronage in Sicily," *Man* 1 (1966): 18–33, and *Friends of Friends; Networks, Manipulators and Coalitions* (New York: St. Martin's Press, 1974; John Duncan Powell with his research on Venezuela and Italy in such contributions as "Peasant Society and Clientelistic Politics," *American Political Science Review* 64, no. 2 (April 1970): 411–25; and Alexander Weingrod in his "Patrons, Patronage and Political Parties," *Comparative Studies in Society and History* 10, no. 4 (July 1968): 377–400, also "Patronage and Power" in E. Gellner and John Waterbury, eds., *Patrons and Clients in Mediterranean Societies* (London: Duckworth, 1977), 41–52.

31. Those who prominently shared this perspective while criticizing those who called contemporary clientelism a force for progress and modernization numbered, among others, Lemarchand, Legg, Eisenstadt, and Schneider. Representative expressions are found in such works as Rene Lemarchand and Keith Legg, "Political Clientelism and Development: A Preliminary Analysis," *Comparative Politics* 4, no. 2 (1971): 149–79; S. N. Eisenstadt and Rene Lemarchand, eds., *Political Clientelism, Patronage, and Development* (Beverly Hills: Sage Publications, 1981); and P. Schneider et al., "Modernization and Development," *Comparative Studies in Social History* 14 (1972): 328–49.

32. The quotes come from pp. vii and viii of the collection of papers published in Luis Roniger and Ayse Günes-Ayata, eds., *Democracy, Clientelism and Civil Society*.

33. Roniger, "The Comparative Study of Clientelism." He provides extensive citations in support of his views, nearly all of which appear in either the introduction to this work or in the present chapter.

34. Lemarchand, "Comparative Political Clientelism," in Eisenstadt and Lemarchand, *Political Clientelism*, 19. The emphasis is mine.

35. Ayse Günes-Ayata, "Clientelism: Premodern, Modern, Postmodern," in Roniger and Günes-Ayata, eds., *Democracy, Clientelism, and Civil Society*, 20.

36. Roniger, "Conclusions: The Transformation of Clientelism and Civil Society," in ibid., 213.

37. An important source for consideration of both national and local clientelism, as well as the historical evolution of P-C relationships, is Francisco Leal Buitrago and Andrés Dávila Ladrón de Guevara, *Clientelismo: El sistema político y su expresión regional* (Bogotá: Tercer Mundo Editores, 1990). This work includes a detailed empirical study of regional clientelism in Rionegro from 1970 to 1988, as cited later in the text. The quote is found on p. 353.

38. The growth of the central state in contemporary Colombia, along with the rise of major economic conglomerates, is probed in A. H. J. Helmsing, *Firms, Farms, and the State in Colombia: A Study of Rural, Urban, and Regional Dimensions of Change* (Boston: Allen & Unwin, Inc., 1986), esp. chap. 5, pp. 105–201.

39. Among the more recent studies of Colombian parties is the collaborative volume by Oscar Delgado, Pierre Gilhodes, Alirio Gómez, Fernan González, Carlos A. Sánchez, and Rubén Sánchez, *Modernidad democracia y partidos políticos* (Bogotá: FIDEC and FESCOL, 1993). The focus in most of its chapters is more upon party systems than upon the internal dynamics of individual parties. Considerable attention is given to past history and to electoral trends over time. The most recent years are not stressed, other than references to the "crisis of the 1990s" and the new constitution.

40. A superb collection by prominent Colombian scholars is Francisco Leal Buitrago and León Zamosc, eds., *Al filo del caos: crisis política en la Colombia de los anos 80* (Bogotá: Tercer Mundo Editores, 1991). Of particular relevance for the present discussion are the chapters by Ana María Bejarano, Leal Buitrago, and Francisco E. Thoumi.

41. Gary Hoskin, "Los partidos tradiciónales: hasta donde son responsables de la crisis política?" in ibid., 153.

42. Junco Veloso, *Clientelismo de Boyaca, 1930–90* (Bogotá: n.p., 1991), 24–29 and 211–18.

43. Cristina Escobar, "Clientelism and Social Protest: Peasant Politics in Northern Colombia," in Roniger and Günes-Ayata, *Democracy, Clientelism and Civil Society*, 81.

44. For an informative discussion that describes contrasting forms of Colombian clientelism and the role of parties, see the treatment of three diverse cases (occurring in 1904, 1930, and the late 1960s) by Steffen Schmidt, "Patrons, Brokers, and Clients: Party Linkages in the Colombian System," in Kay Lawson, ed., *Political Parties and Linkage: A Comparative Perspective* (New Haven: Yale University Press, 1980), 266–89.

45. A collection of brief, highly critical commentaries by a businessman with long experience in Colombian public and private administration is Rogelio Villamizar J., *Como nos gobiernan en Colombia* (Cali: Impresora FERIVA S.A., 1993).

46. A useful airing of these and related issues is that of Christopher Clapham, "Clientelism and the State," in Clapham, ed., *Private Patronage and Public*

Power; Political Clientelism in the Modern State (New York: St. Martin's Press, 1982), 22 ff.

47. See Pierre Gilhodes, "Elección de alcaldes, descentralización y clientelismo," in *Mercadeo electoral: elección de alcaldes* (Bogotá: Pontificia Universidad Javeriana, Facultad de Estudios Interdisciplinarios, Programa de Estudios Políticos, 1988), 9–21.

48. For an excellent collection on the Barco years that has recently appeared, see Malcolm Deas and Carlos Ossa, eds., *El gobierno Barco: política, economía y desarrollo social en Colombia, 1986–1990* (Bogotá: FEDESARROLLO, Fondo Cultural Cafetero, 1994).

49. *El Espectador* (11 September 1990): 5-A.

50. "Curules por herencia," *Semana* (29 March 1994): 34–37.

51. The long succession of reports over human rights violations more than amply document the many violations committed by military and security forces as well as by guerrillas ad drug-employed armies of "persuaders" functioning as goons. See the discussion of Samper's policies on this topic elsewhere.

52. A work that investigates in detail the November 1985 attack on the Palace of Justice, while also voicing concern about the entire phenomenon of violence and counterviolence, is Ana Carrigan, *The Palace of Justice: A Colombian Tragedy* (New York: Four Walls Eight Windows, 1993).

53. An extreme case arrived for the Liberals in the early 1990s when first López Michelsen and later Turbay temporarily assumed the position of party director for the organizing and conducting of the national party campaign at the turn of the 1990s.

Bibliography

Books and Monographs

Agudelo Villa, Hernando. *Hacia un liberalismo moderno.* Bogotá: Tercer Mundo, 1968.

———. *Retorno al liberalismo,* 2d ed. Bogotá: Tercer Mundo, 1975.

Aguirre Lozano, Maria Isabel. *Análisis del sistema electoral colombiano.* Bogotá: Editorial Kelly, 1980.

Alape, Arturo. *El bogotazo.* Bogotá: Editorial Pluma, 1984.

———. *La paz, la violencia: testigos de excepción.* Bogotá: Editorial Planeta, 1985.

Alcántara Sáez, Manuel. *Sistemas políticos de America Latina,* vol. 1. Madrid: Editorial Técnos, S.A., 1989.

Allies, Paul, et al. *Elección popular de alcaldes; Colombia y la experiencia internacional.* Bogotá: FIDEC, FESCOL, PROCOMUN, 1988.

Alonso Pinzon, Martín. *Historia del conservatismo.* Bogotá: Tercer Mundo, 1979.

Alvarez, Luis Alberto et al. *Colombia hoy: perspectivas hacia el siglo XXI.* Bogotá: Siglo XXI, 1991.

Angulo Bossa, Jaime. *Mi encuentro con la constitución.* Bogotá: Plaza y Janes, 1986.

Angulo Novos, Alejandro, y Pedro Santana B. *La miseria de los partidos; análisis de las elecciónes 1980.* Bogotá: CINEP, 1980.

Apuleyo Mendoza, Plinio. *Los retos del poder: carta abierta a los ex presidentes colombianos.* Bogotá: Intermedio Editores, 1991.

Arango, Carlos. *FARC 20 años: de Marquetalia a La Uribe.* Bogotá: Editorial Aurora, 1984.

Arango Jaramillo, Mario. *El proceso del capitalismo en Colombia,* 4 vols. Medellín: Aurora, 1976.

Araoz, Santiago. *Historia del Frente Nacional y otros ensayos.* Bogotá: Presencia, 1977.

Arenas, Jacobo. *Cese el fuego.* Bogotá: Editorial Oveja Negra, 1985.

———. *Diario de la resistencia de Marquetalia.* Bogotá: Ed. CIES, 1972.

Arias Carrizosa, José Manuel. *Amnistia e indulto para la democracia.* Bogotá: Talleres de Editorial Presencia Ltda., 1986.

Arocha, Jaime et al. *Colombia: violencia y democracia.* Bogotá: Universidad Nacional de Colombia, 1988.

Arrubla, Mario, et al. *Colombia hoy,* 2d ed. Bogotá: Siglo XXI Editores, 1978.

Asociación de Politólogos Javerianos. *Presidenciables 1990.* Bogotá: Facultad de Estudios Interdisciplinarios, Pontificia Universidad Javereiana, 1990.

Atehortua Cruz, Adolfo León y Humberto Vélez Ramírez, *Estado y Fuerzas Armadas en Colombia (1886–1953).* Bogotá: TM Editores, 1994.

Ayala, Ulpiano, et al. *La problemática urbana hoy en Colombia.* Bogotá: Centro de Investigaciónes y Educación Popular, 1982.

Bagley, Bruce M., and William O. Walker III, eds. *Drug Trafficking in the Americas.* New Brunswick: Transaction Publishers, for the North-South Center, University of Miami, 1994.

Ballén, Rafael. *Liberalismo hoy: opción de cambio o agónica supervivencia.* Bogotá: Editorial Carrera 7a, Ltda., 1985.

Barco Vivas, Virgilio. *Economía, planeación y política social.* Bogotá: Carlos Valencia Editores, 1981.

———. *Hacia una Colombia nueva: Liberalismo, democracia social y cambio.* Bogotá: Editorial La Oveja Negra Ltda., 1986.

———. *Diálogo democrática.* Bogotá: Editorial Oveja Negra, 1987.

———. *Reformas para el cambio.* Bogotá: Banco de la Republica, 1988.

———. *Discursos 1986–1990.* Bogotá: Presidencia de la Republica, 1990.

———. *El fortalecimiento de la democracia: el esquema gobierno-partidos de oposición; la democracia participativa y la paz.* Bogotá: Imprenta Nacional de Colombia, 1990.

Bateman Cayon, Jaime. *Oiga hermano.* Bogotá: Ediciónes Macondo, 1984.

Behar, Olga. *Las guerras de la paz.* Bogotá: Planeta Colombiana Editorial, 1985.

———. *Noches de humo.* Bogotá: Planeta Colombiana Editorial, 1988.

Bejerano, Jesus Antonio. *La economía colombiana en la década del 70.* Bogotá: Fondo Editorial CEREC, 1984.

———, ed. *Construir la paz: memorias del seminario paz, democracia y desarrollo.* Bogotá: Presidencia de la República, 1990.

Bergquist, Charles. *Labor in Latin America: Comparative Essays on Chile, Argentina, Venezuela, and Colombia.* Stanford: Stanford University Press, 1986.

Bergquist, Charles, Ricardo Peñaranda, and Gónzalo Sánchez, eds. *Violence in Colombia: The Contemporary Crisis in Historical Perspective.* Wilmington: SR Books, 1992.

Berry, R. Albert, ed. *Essays on Industrialization in Colombia.* Tempe: Arizona State University, 1983.

Berry, R. Albert, and Ronald Soligo, eds. *Economic Policy and Income Distribution in Colombia.* Boulder: Westview, 1980.

Betancur, Belisario. *A pesar de la pobreza.* Bogotá: Tercer Mundo, 1967.

———. *Si, se puede!* Bogotá: Tercer Mundo, 1982.

———. *Reformas políticas; apertura democrática.* Bogotá: Editorial La Oveja Negra, 1985.

———. *Tránsito hacia la paz.* Bogotá: Banco de la República, 1985.

Boeker, Paul H. *Lost Illusions: Latin America's Struggle for Democracy as Recounted by Its Leaders.* New York: Markus Wiener Publishing, 1990.

Boissevain, Jeremy. *Friends of Friends; Networks, Manipulators and Coalitions.* New York: St. Martin's Press, 1974.

Botero, Camila, ed. *Propuestas de descentralización en Colombia.* Bogotá: CIDER, Cámara de Comercio de Bogotá, 1982.

Botero Jimenez, Nodier. *Crisis del bipartidismo y mitos del sistema en Colombia.* Bogotá: Lerner, 1985.

Botero Montoya, Mauricio. *La caída del partido liberal (1982).* Bogotá: Tercer Mundo, 1983.

———. *El MRL.* Bogotá: Publicaciónes Universidad Central, 1990.

Braun, Herbert. *The Assassination of Gaitán: Public Life and Urban Violence in Colombia.* Madison: University of Wisconsin Press, 1986.

Buenahora Febres-Cordero, Jaime. *El proceso constituyente: de la propuesta estudiantil a la quiebra del bipartidismo.* Bogotá: Pontificia Universidad Javeriana, 1991.

Buenaventura, Nicolás. *Unión Patriótica y poder político.* Bogotá: Ediciónes CEIS, 1987.

Buenaventura, Nicolás et al. *Tregua y Unión Patriótica.* Bogotá: Ediciónes CEIS, 1985.

Burbano Burbano, Ary Alfredo. *El nuevo liberalismo y Galan: concepto sobre la renovación de la democracia.* Bogotá: M.A., Javeriana, 1984.

Bushnell, David. *The Making of Modern Colombia: A Nation in Spite of Itself.* Berkeley: University of California Press, 1993.

Calderon Rivera, Mario. *Un nuevo municipio, un nuevo pais.* Bogotá: BCH, 1987.

Campaña '82: Belisario Betancour, Alfonso López, Luis Carlos Galán; tres campañas, tres estilos. Bogotá: Universidad Javeriana, Fundación Simon Bolivar, 1982.

Campos, Judith de, and Jose Martin. *El comportamiento electoral en Cali 1978.* Cali: CIDSE and Fundación Friedrich Naumann, 1980.

Campos, Judith de, and John McCamant. *Cleavage Shift in Colombia: Analysis of the 1970 Election.* Beverly Hills: Sage, 1972.

Carbonell, Abel. *La quincena política.* (Bogotá: Ministerio de Educación Nacional, 1952.

Carrigan, Ana. *The Palace of Justice: A Colombian Tragedy.* New York: Four Walls Eight Windows, 1993.

Castro, Jaime. *Elección popular de alcaldes*. Bogotá: Editorial Oveja Negra, 1986.

——. *Proceso a la violencia y proceso de paz*. Bogotá: Editorial Oveja Negra, 1986.

Castro, Jaime y otros. *Paz? Paz!; Testimonios y reflexiones sobre un proceso*. Bogotá: Editorial Oveja Negra, 1987.

Cataño, Gonzalo. *La sociología en Colombia: balance crítico*. Bogotá: Plaza & Janes, 1986.

Cavelier Lozano, Carlos Enrique. *Preludio a la nueva Colombia: dos años de reflexión sobre nuestro devenir*. Bogotá: PRODEMOCRACIA, 1992.

Centro de Investigación y Educación Popular (CINEP). *Elecciónes 1978: legislación, abánico político, resultados de febrero 1978*. Bogotá: CINEP, 1978.

——. *Elecciónes 1978; plataformas económicas*. Bogotá: CINEP, 1978.

——. *La izquierda colombiana y las elecciónes de 1978*. Bogotá: CINEP, 1978.

Cepeda, Manuel José. *Como son las elecciónes en Colombia: guía del votante*. Bogotá: CEREC, FESCOL, and CIDER, 1986.

Cepeda Espinosa, Manuel José, ed. *Estado de sitio y emergencia económica*. Bogotá: Contraloría General de la República, 1985.

Cepeda Ulloa, Fernando. *El esquema gobierno-oposición; El ministro de gobierno ante el congreso*. Bogotá: Ministerio de Gobierno, 1987.

——. *La reglamentación de la elección popular de alcaldes*. Bogotá: Ministerio de Gobierno, 1987.

——, coordinador. *La corrupción administrativa en Colombia*. Bogotá: n.p., 1994.

Cepeda Ulloa, Fernando, and Claudia González de Lecaros. *Comportamiento del voto urbano en Colombia: una aproximación*. Bogotá: Universidad de los Andes, 1976.

Cepeda Ulloa, Fernando, and Rodrigo Pardo García-Peña, et al. *Contadora: desafío a la diplomacia tradiciónal*. Bogotá: Editorial Oveja Negra, 1985.

Chernik, Marc, and Michael F. Jimenez. *Popular Liberalism and Radical Democracy: The Development of the Colombian Left, 1974–1990*. New York: Conference Paper #43, Columbia University NYU Consortium, 1990.

Chubb, Judith. *Patronage, Power, and Poverty in Southern Italy*. Cambridge: Cambridge University Press, 1982.

Clapham, Christopher, ed. *Private Patronage and Public Power: Political Clientelism in the Modern States*. London: Frances Pinter, 1982.

Colmenares, German. *Partidos políticos y clases sociales*. Bogotá: Universidad de los Andes, 1984.

Colombia en las urnas; que paso en 1986? Bogotá: Carlos Valencia Editores, 1987.

Comisión de Estudios sobre la violencia. *Colombia: violencia y democracia.* Bogotá: Universidad Nacional de Colombia, 1987.

Constituciónalistas ante la Constituyente. Bogotá: Editorial Temis, 1990.

Corr, Edwin G. *The Political Process in Colombia.* Denver: The Social Science Foundation and Graduate School of the University of Denver, Monograph Series in World Affairs, nos. 1–2, 1972.

Cortes Arevalo, Fernando. *El asesinato de Galán.* Bogotá: La Planeta, 1994.

Cuellar M., Maria del Rosario. *El marketing político en las elecciónes 1982; el caso del Nuevo Liberalismo: Galán.* Bogotá: M.A., Javeriana, 1985.

Currie, Lauchlin. *The Role of Economic Advisers in Developing Countries.* Westport: Greenwood Press, 1981.

———. *Evaluación de la asesoría económica a los paises en desarrollo: el caso colombiano.* Bogotá: CEREC, 1984.

Dávila L. de Guevara, Carlos. *El empresariado colombiano: una perspectiva histórica.* Bogotá: Pontificia Universidad Javeriana, Facultad de Estudios Interdisciplinarios, 1986.

Davis, Robert H. *Historical Dictionary of Colombia.* Metuchen: The Scarecrow Press, Inc., 1977.

Deas, Malcolm. *Del poder y la gramática; y otros ensayos sobre historia, política y literatura colombianas.* Bogotá: Tercer Mundo Editrores, 1993.

Deas, Malcolm, and Carlos Ossa, eds. *El gobierno Barco: política, economía y desarrollo en Colombia, 1986–1990.* Bogotá: FEDESARROLLO, Fondo Cultural Cafetero, 1994.

De la Pedraja, Rene. *Energy Politics in Colombia.* Boulder: Westview, 1989.

Delgado, Oscar, ed. *La campaña por la presidencia, 1978–1982: los temas en controversia.* Bogotá: Tercer Mundo, 1978.

———. *Colombia elige; Mitaca 84, perspectivas 86.* Bogotá: Universidad Javeriana, 1986.

Delgado, Oscar et al. *Modernidad democracia y partidos políticos.* Bogotá: FIDEC y Fescol, 1993.

De Roux, Francisco. *Candidatos, programas y compromisos.* Bogotá: CINEP. 1978.

De Zubiria Samper, Andrés. *Por que la Constituyente? un pacto social para un nuevo país.* Bogotá: Rodríguez Quito Editores, 1990.

Díaz-Alejandro, Carlos F. *Foreign Trade Regimes and Economic Development: Colombia.* New York: Columbia University Press, for National Bureau of Economic Research, 1976.

Díaz Uribe, Eduardo. *El clientelismo en Colombia: un estudio exploratorio.* Bogotá: El Ancora Editores, 1986.

Dix, Robert Heller. *Colombia: The Political Dimensions of Change.* New Haven: Yale University Press, 1967.

———. *The Politics of Colombia.* New York: Praeger, 1987.

Drekonja Kornat, Gerhard. *Colombia: política exterior.* Bogotá: La Editora, 1982.

―――. *Retos a la política externa colombiana.* Bogotá: CEREC, 1983.

Dugas, John, ed. *La constitución política de 1991: un pacto político viable?* Bogotá: CEREC, 1993.

Dugas, John, Angélica Ocampo, Luis Javier Orjuela, y Germán Ruiz. *Los caminos de ls descentralización: diversidad y retos de la transformación municipal.* Bogotá: Universidad de Los Andes, 1992.

Duque Gómez, Diana. *Una guerra irregular entre dos ideologías: Colombia (1982–1990).* Bogotá: Intermedio Editores, 1991.

Duque Gómez, Maria Cecilia. *Mitaca 84: por que los eligieron.* Bogotá: Pontificia Universidad Católica, 1985.

Eastman, Jorge Mario. *Perfiles políticos.* Bogotá: Plaza & Janes, 1982.

Eastman, Jorge Mario, and Marco Gerardo Monroy Cabra. *El diferendo colombo-venezolano.* Bogotá: Editorial Oveja Negra, 1987.

Echeverri Uriburu, Alvaro. *Elites y proceso político en Colombia (1950–1978); una democracia principesca y endogámica.* Bogotá: Fundación Universitaria Autónoma de Colombia, 1986.

Edie, Carlene J. *Democracy by Default: Dependency and Clientelism in Jamaica.* Boulder, Lynne Rienner Publishers, 1991.

Eisenstadt, S.N. *Traditional Patrimonialism and Modern Neopatrimonialism.* Beverly Hills: Sage, 1973.

Eisenstadt, S.N., and Rene Lemarchand, eds. *Political Clientelism, Patronage, and Development.* Beverly Hills, Sage, 1981.

Elías del Hierro, Jose. *Los programas conservadores.* Pasto: Editorial Sur Colombiana, 1973.

Escobar Sierra, Hugo. *La constituyente: reforma nacional.* Bogotá: Editorial Temis, 1991.

Fals Borda, Orlando. *Campesinos de los Andes.* Bogotá: Iqueima, 1961.

―――. *Subversion and Social Change in Colombia.* New York: Columbia University Press, 1969.

―――. *Historia doble de la costa,* 4 vols. Bogotá: Carlos Valencia Editores, 1980–86.

FESCOL. *Una constituyente para la Colombia del futuro.* Bogotá: FESCOL and UNIANDES, 1990.

Flores, María Isabel. *Cuatro liberales responden.* Bogotá: Instituto de Estudios Liberales, 1988.

Florez E., Luis Bernardo, comp. *Economía pública y control fiscal; contraloría general de la República,* 2 vols. Bogotá: Contraloría General de la Republica, 1987.

Foros Nacionales del Liberalismo. *La democracia está en peligro.* Bogotá: n.p., 1988.

Fundación Naumann. *Clientelismo*. Bogotá: Enfoques Latinoamericanos, 1980.

Galán, Luis Carlos. *Nueva Colombia*. Bogotá: Coeditores Ltda., 1982.

———. *Ni un paso atrás, siempre adelante!* Bogotá: Fundación Luis Carlos Galan, 1991

Galbraith, W.O. *Colombia; A General Survey*, 2d ed. London: Oxford University Press, 1966.

Gallón Giraldo, Gustavo. *Quince años de estado de sitio en Colombia*. Bogotá: Editorial América Latina, 1979.

———, comp. *Entre movimientos y caudillos: 50 anos de bipartidismo, izquierda y alternativas populares en Colombia*. Bogotá: CINEP-CEREC, 1984.

Galvís, Silvia and Alberto Donadio. *El jefe supremo; Rojas Pinilla en La Violencia y el poder*. Bogotá: Planeta, 1988.

Gellner, E. and J. Waterbury. *Patrons and Clients in Mediterranean Societies*. London: Duckworth, 1977.

Gerlein Echevarría, Roberto. *La estructura del poder en Colombia*. Bogotá: Tercer Mundo, 1978.

Giraldo M., Javier, comp. *El camino de la niebla: La desaparición forzada en Colombia y la impunidad*. Bogotá: Liga Colombiana por los Derechos y la Liberación de los Pueblos, 1988.

Gómez, Elsa, et al. *La elección presidencial de 1982 en Bogotá: dinámica de la opinión pública*. Bogotá: ANIF-Fondo Editorial, 1982.

Gómez Buendia, Hernando. *Alfonso López Michelsen: un examen crítico de su pensamiento y de su obra de gobierno*. Bogotá: Javeriana, Ediciónes Tercer Mundo, 1978.

———, ed. *El liberalismo al banquillo*. Bogotá: Instituto de Estudios Liberales, 1989.

Gómez Buendía, Hernando, y otros. *Desarrollo social en la década del 70*. Bogotá: FEDESARROLLO, D.N.P. y UNICEF, 1984.

Gómez Hurtado, Alvaro. *Hoy en le pensamiento de Alvaro Gómez*. Bogotá: Populibro 21, 1967.

———. *Soy libre*. Bogotá: Ediciónes Gamma, 1989.

Gómez Hurtado, Alvaro, et al. *Una política conservadora para Colombia: bases para la nueva plataforma social del partido*. Bogotá: Centro de Estudios Colombianos, 1969.

Gómez Mejia, Alberto. *Derecho electoral colombiano*. Bogotá: Pontificia Universidad Javeriana, 1977.

González, Libardo. *El estado y los partidos políticos en Colombia*. Bogotá: Latino, 1975.

González G., Fernan E. *Partidos políticos y poder eclesiástico; reseña histórica 1810–1930*. Bogotá: CINEP, 1977.

Grindle, Merilee S. *State and Countryside: Development Policy and Agrarian Politics in Latin America*. Baltimore: The Johns Hopkins University Press, 1986.

Guillén Martínez, Fernando. *El poder político en Colombia*. Bogotá: Punta de Lanza, 1979.

Hammergren, Linn A. *Development and the Politics of Administrative Reform: Lessons from Latin America*. Boulder: Westview, 1983.

Hartlyn, Jonathan. *The Politics of Coalition Rule in Colombia*. Cambridge: Cambridge University Press, 1988.

Hartlyn, Jonathan, and Samuel A. Morley, eds. *Latin American Political Economy: Financial Crisis and Political Change*. Boulder: Westview, 1986.

Hartwig, Richard. *Roads to Reason: Transportation, Administration, and Rationality in Colombia*. Pittsburgh: University of Pittsburgh Press, 1983.

Helmsing, A.H.J. *Firms, Farms, and the State in Colombia*. Boston: Allen & Unwin, Inc., 1986.

Henderson, James. *Cuando Colombia se desangró*. Bogotá: El Ancora Ed., 1984.

Herman, Donald L., ed. *Democracy in Latin America: Colombia and Venezuela*. New York: Praeger, 1987.

Hernández Becerra, Augusto. *Las elecciónes en Colombia (análisis jurídico-político)*. San José, Costa Rica: Centro Interamericano de Asesoría y Promoción Electoral (CAPEL), 1986.

Hernández Benavides, Manuel. *Una agenda con futuro: testimonios del cuatrienio Gaviria*. Bogotá: Presidencia de la República, 1994.

Hernández C., German. *La justicia en llamas*. Bogotá: Carlos Valencia Editores, 1986.

Hernández Rodríguez, Guillermo. *La alternación ante el pueblo*. Bogotá: Ediciónes America Libre, 1962.

Herrera Soto, Roberto. *Antología del pensamiento conservador en Colombia*. Bogotá: Biblioteca Básica Colombiana, Instituto Colombiano de Cultura, 1982.

Holmes Trujillo, Carlos. *Colombia, drama y esperanza*. Bogotá: Plaza & Janes, 1987.

Holt, Pat M. *Colombia Today—And Tomorrow*. New York: Praeger, 1964.

Hunter, John M. *Emerging Colombia*. Washington, D.C.: Public Affairs Press, 1962.

Instituto de Estudios Socio-Políticos del Partido Conservador Colombiano. *Documentos Socio-políticos; nueva generación conservadora*. Bogotá: Impresa Limitada, 1976.

Jaramillo, J. *Estado, sociedad y campesinos*. Bogotá: Tercer Mundo, 1988.

Jaramillo, Juan Diego. *De la política y la vida pública*. Bogotá: Tercer Mundo, 1991.

Jaramillo, Rosa, and Beatriz Gómez, comps. *De la Calle; Anatomía del cambio; de los 60 al siglo XXI.* Bogotá: Planeta, 1994.

Jaramillo O., Hernán. *Momentos estelares de la política colombiana.* Bogotá: Tercer Mundo, 1988.

Jaramillo Uribe, Jaime, ed. *Antología del pensamiento político colombiano, 2 tomos.* Bogotá: Talleres Gráficos del Banco de la República, 1970.

Junco Velosa, Edmundo. *Del fraude y la violencia al clientelismo: Boyacá 1930–1990.* Tunja: Universidad Pedagógica y Tecnológica de Colombia, 1992.

Kern, Robert, ed., with the assistance of Ronald Dolkart. *The Caciques: Oligarchical Politics and the System of Caciquismo in the Luso-Hispanic World.* Albuquerque: University of New Mexico Press, 1973.

Klaren, Peter F., and Thomas J. Bossert, eds. *Promise of Development: The Politics of Change in Latin America.* Boulder: Westview, 1986.

Kline, Harvey F. *The Coal of El Cerrejon: Dependent Bargaining and Colombian Policy-Making.* University Park: The Pennsylvania State University Press, 1987.

———. *Colombia: Portrait of Unity and Diversity,* 2d ed. Boulder: Westview, 1996.

Asociación Nacional de Instituciones Financieras. *La abstención: libro del simposio 1980.* Bogotá: Simposio realizado por la Asociación Nacional de Institucionés Financieras, 1980.

La campaña por la presidencia, 1978–1982: los temas en controversia. Bogotá: Tercer Mundo, 1978.

Landazábal Reyes, Fernando. *El precio de la paz.* Bogotá: Editorial Planeta, 1985.

Lanzetta, Mario et al. *Colombia en las urnas: Que paso en 1986?* Bogotá: Carlos Valencia, 1987.

Fundación Friedrich Naumann. *La otra cara del liberalismo: el pensamiento de la juventud liberal 1972 al 78.* Bogotá: Fundación Friedrich Naumann, 1980.

Lara Bonilla, Rodrigo, Rodrigo Losada Lora, and Humberto Uribe Toro. *Los partidos políticos colombianos; presente y futuro.* Bogotá: Pontificia Universidad Javeriana, Fundación Simon Bolivar, 1985.

Las cinco maravillas millonarias de Colombia. Bogotá: Oveja Negra, 1982.

Latorre Rueda, Mario. *Elecciónes y partidos políticos en Colombia.* Bogotá: Uniandes, 1974.

———. *Política y elecciónes.* Bogotá: Universidad de los Andes, 1980.

———. *Hechos y crítica política.* Bogotá: Universidad Nacional de Colombia, 1986.

Latorre Vargas, Francisco. *Desarrollo histórico-político de la frontera colombo venezolana.* Bogotá: Editorial Kelly, 1988.

Leal Buitrago, Francisco. *Estudio del comportamiento legislativo en Colombia. Tomo I, Análisis Histórico del Desarrollo Political Nacional, 1930–1970.* Bogotá: n.p., 1973.

———. *Estado y política en Colombia.* Bogotá: Siglo XXI Editores, S.A., 1984.

———. *El oficio de la guerra: la seguridad nacional en Colombia.* Bogotá: Tercer Mundo Editores, IEPRI, 1994.

Leal Buitrago, Francisco, and Andrés Dávila Ladrón de Guevara. *Clientelismo: el sistema político y su expresión regional.* Bogotá: Tercer Mundo Editores, 1990.

Leal Buitrago, Francisco, and Juan Gabriel Tokatlian, comps. *Orden mundial y seguridad: nuevos desafíos para Colombia y América Latina.* Bogotá: Tercer Mundo Editores, IEPRI, 1994.

Leal Buitrago, Francisco, and Leon Zamosc, eds. *Al filo del caos: crisis política en la Colombia de los años 80.* Bogotá: Tercer Mundo Editores, 1991.

Le Grand, Catherine. *Frontier Expansion and Peasant Protest in Colombia, 1830–1936.* Albuquerque: University of New Mexico Press, 1986.

Lemieux, Vincent. *Le patronage politique.* Quebec: Presses de l'Universite de Laval, 1977.

Lemoine, Carlos. *Como conseguir el voto de los colombianos.* Bogotá: Oveja Negra, 1986.

Liévano Aguirre, Indalecio. *Los grandes conflictos sociales y económicos de nuestra historia,* 22d ed., 2 vols. Bogotá: Ediciónes Tercer Mundo, 1987.

Lijphart, Arend. *Democracies: Patterns of Majoritarian and Consensus Government in Twenty-One Countries.* New Haven: Yale University Press, 1984.

Lleras Restrepo, Carlos. *El liberalismo colombiano, 1972.* Bogotá: Tercer Mundo, 1973.

———. *Historia y política.* Bogotá: Osprey Impresores, 1980.

Lloreda Caicedo, Rodrigo. *La nueva política internacional de Colombia.* Bogotá: Editorial Prensa Moderna, 1985.

Lombard, Francois J. *The Foreign Investment Screening Process in LDCs: The Case of Colombia, 1967–1975.* Boulder: Westview, 1979.

López Gómez, Edmundo. *La verdadera Constituyente.* Bogotá: Ed. Librería del Profesional, 1990.

———. *Palabra que no: el misterio de la tractomula.* Bogotá: La Imprenta, Limitada, 1991.

López Michelsen, Alfonso. *El gobierno del mandato claro.* Bogotá: Secretaría de Información de la Presidencia de la República, 1975–78.

———. *Esbozos y atisbos.* Bogotá: Canal Ramírez-Antares, 1980.

———. *Grandes compatriotas.* Bogotá: Tercer Mundo, 1993.

Losada Lora, Rodrigo. *Las elecciónes de mitaca de 1976: participación electoral y perspectiva histórica.* Bogotá: FEDESARROLLO, 1976.

————. *Realidades de la concentración/dispersión del poder político en Colombia 1966–1978*, 2 vols. Bogotá: Pontificia Universidad Javeriana, 1983.
————. *Clientelismo & elecciónes*. Bogotá: Pontificia Universidad Javeriana, Programa de Estudios Políticos, 1984.
Losada Lora, Rodrigo, and Marco A. Muñoz Delgado. *Niños y jovenes frente al voto*. Bogotá: Pontificia Universidad Javeriana, 1988.
Losada Lora, Rodrigo, and Gabriel Murillo. *Análisis de las elecciónes de 1972 en Bogotá*. Bogotá: Universidad de los Andes, 1973.
Losada Lora, Rodrigo, and Eduardo Vélez. *Identificación y participación política en Colombia*. Bogotá: FEDESARROLLO, 1982.
Partido Conservador, *Los programas del Conservatismo*. Manizales: Editorial Renacimiento, 1967.
Malano, Alfredo. *Amnistía y violencias*. Bogotá: CINEP, 1980.
Malloy, James M., and Mitchell A. Seligson, eds. *Authoritarians and Democrats: Regime Transition in Latin America*. Pittsburgh: University of Pittsburgh Press, 1987.
Manrique, A. *Elección popular de alcaldes: retos y posibilidades*. Bogotá: FESCOL, 1986.
Manrique Reyes, Alfredo. *Consulta popular y ciarcumscripción nacional: dos intentos y renovación democratica*. Bogotá: FESCOL-CEREC, 1986.
Manuel de historia de Colombia. Bogotá: Instituto Colombiano de Cultura, 1982.
Martín L., José Francisco. *Campo y ciudad. Participación y abstención electoral en Colombia*. Cali: IDSE y Fundación Friedrich Naumann, 1981.
Martz, John D. *Colombia: Un estudio de política contemporánea*. Bogotá: Universidad Nacional de Colombia, 1969.
Maullin, Richard. *Soldiers, Guerrillas and Politics in Colombia*. Lexington: D.C. Heath & Co., 1973.
McGreevey, William Paul. *An Economic History of Colombia, 1845–1930*. Cambridge: Cambridge University Press, 1971.
Medellín, Pedro, comp. *La reforma del estado en America Latina*. Bogotá: FESCOL, 1989.
Medellín González, German. *La publicidad política en la campaña presidencial colombiana 1982*. Bogotá: Pontificia Universidad Javeriana, M.A., 1984.
Medina Gallego, Carlos. *Autodefensas, paramilitares y narcotráfico en Colombia*. Bogotá: Editorial Documentos Periodisticos, 1990.
Mendez Buendía, Rafael. *Misael Pastrana Borrero*. Bogotá: Bolivar, 1969.
Mendoza Díaz, Raúl. *Rojas Pinilla: un gobierno populista?* Bogotá: Pontificia Universidad Javeriana, M.A., 1984.
Miranda Ontañeda, Néstor. *Clientelismo y dominio de clase: el modo de obrar política en Colombia*. Bogotá: CINEP, 1977.

Molano, Alfredo. *Selva adentro: una historia oral de la colonización del Guaviare.* Bogotá: El Ancora Editores, 1987.

Molina, Gerardo. *Las ideas liberales en Colombia: Tomo 3, de 1935 al Frente Nacional.* Bogotá: Tercer Mundo Editores, 1990.

Moore, Jr., Barrington. *Social Origins of Dictatorship and Democracy: Land and Peasant in the Making of the Modern World.* Boston: Beacon Press, 1966.

Morales Benítez, Otto. *Papeles para la luz.* Bogotá: Arbol que Piensa, Editorial, 1991.

———. *El escritor Alberto Lleras Camargo.* Bogotá: n.p., 1991.

———. *Iconografía y fragmentos de prosas de Otto Morales Benítez.* Bogotá: Fundación Universidad Central, 1995.

Morawetz, David. *Why the Emperor's New Clothes Are Not Made in Colombia: A Case Study in Latin American and East Asian Manufactured Exports.* New York: Oxford University Press, for the World Bank, 1981.

Morner, Magnus. *The Andean Past: Land, Societies, and Conflicts.* New York: Columbia University Press, 1985.

Mosca, Juan, comp. *Querido Ernesto.* Bogotá: n.p., 1993.

———. *Jaime Castro: tres años de soledad.* Bogotá: OP Graficas, 1994.

Mosquera, Tomas Cipriano de. *Los partidos políticos en Colombia.* Bogotá: Editorial Incunables, 1984 (from 1874 original).

Murillo, Gabriel, ed. *Hacia la consolidación democrática andina: transición o deestabilización.* Bogotá: Tercer Mundo Editores, UNIANDES, 1993.

Murillo, Gabriel, Ismael Rivera Ortiz, y Patricia Pinzón. *Actividades y estructura de poder en los partidos colombianos.* Bogotá: UNIANDES, 1973.

Murillo, Gabriel, and Juan Carlos Ruiz. *Elecciónes, partidos políticos y democracia en los paises andinos.* Bogotá: UNIANDES, 1991.

Murillo, Gabriel, and Miles Williams. *Análisis de las elecciónes presidenciales de 1974 en Bogotá.* Bogotá: UNIANDES, 1975.

Nelson, Richard R., T. Paul Schultz, and Robert L. Slighton. *Structural Change in a Developing Economy: Colombia's Problems and Prospects.* Princeton: Princeton University Press, 1971.

Noriega, Carlos Augusto. *Lo que pasó aquella noche: 19 de 1970.* Bogotá: Tercer Mundo, 1977.

———. *Nuestra democracia: una farsa?* Bogotá: Editorial LEC, 1980.

Nuevo Liberalismo. *1984–86 Programa del Nuevo Liberalismo para Bogotá.* Bogotá: Editorial Carrera 7a. Limitada, 1986.

Ocampo, José Antonio. *Colombia y la economía mundial, 1830–1910.* Bogotá: Siglo XXI Editores de Colombia, 1984.

Ocampo, José Antonio, and Santiago Montenegro. *Crisis mundial, protección e industrialización: ensayos de historia económica colombiana.* Bogotá: CEREC, 1984.

Ocampo López, Javier. *Que es el liberalismo colombiano?* Bogotá: Plaza & Janes, 1990.

———. *Que es el conservatismo colombiano?* Bogotá: Plaza & Janes, 1990.

———. *Otto Morales Benítez: sus ideas y la crisis nacional.* Bogotá: Editorial Grijalbo S.A., 1993.

OMIDELAC. *Organización de militares por la democracia, la integración y la liberación de América Latina y el Caribe.* Bogotá: OMIDELAC, 1986.

Oquist, Paul W. *Violencia, conflicto, y política en Colombia.* Bogotá: IEO, 1978.

Orlando Melo, Jorge, comp. *Origines de los partidos políticos en Colombia.* Bogotá: Colcultura, 1978.

———. *Colombia hoy: perspectivas hacia el siglo XX,* 14 ed. Bogotá: Siglo Veintiuno Editores, 1991.

Ortiz Sarmiento, Carlos Miguel. *Estado y subversión en Colombia: La Violencia en el Quindío anos 5.* Bogotá: CIDER, 1986.

Ospina Sardi, Jorge. *Hacia un nuevo conservatismo.* Bogotá: Tercer Mundo Editores, 1989.

Palacio Ruedas, Alfonso. *El congreso en la constitución de 1991.* Bogotá: Tercer Mundo, Editores, 1992.

Palacios, Marco. *Coffee in Colombia, 1850–1970.* Cambridge: Cambridge University Press, 1980.

———. *Colombia no alineada: Memoria de un foro y declaración de Nueva Delhi, 1983.* Bogotá: Biblioteca Banco Popular, 1983.

———. *Estado y clases sociales en Colombia.* Bogotá: Serie Breve, Nueva Biblioteca Colombiana de Cultura, 1986.

———. *Entre la legitimidad y la violencia: Colombia 1875–1994.* Bogotá: Grupo Editorial Norma 1995.

Pardo, Rodrigo, and Juan J. Tokatlian. *Política exterior colombiana: De la subordinación a la autonomía?* Bogotá: Tercer Mundo Editores, Ediciónes UNIANDES, 1988.

Parra Escobar, Ernesto. *Elecciónes 1978: Plataformas económicas.* Bogotá: CINEP, 1978.

Pastrana Borrero, Misael. *Gran impulso: ideas y acción política para la nueva Colombia.* Bogotá: n.p., 1970.

———. *El partido social conservador.* Bogotá: Editorial Oveja Negra, 1988.

Payne, James J. *Patterns of Conflict in Colombia.* New Haven: Yale University Press, 1968.

Pearce, Jenny. *Colombia Inside the Labyrinth.* London: Latin American Bureau, 1990.

Pecaut, Daniel. *Orden y violencia: Colombia, 1930–1953.* Bogotá: Siglo Veintiuno, 1987.

———. *Crónica de dos décadas de política colombiana, 1968–1988.* Bogotá: Siglo Veintiuno, 1988.

Peeler, John. *Latin American Democracies: Colombia, Costa Rica, Venezuela.* Chapel Hill: University of North Carolina Press, 1985.

Peñarete Villamil, Fabio. *Por que somos liberales; antología.* Bogotá: Hispana, 1975.

Pérez, Hesper Eduardo. *Proceso del bipartidismo colombiano y Frente Nacional.* Bogotá: Universidad Nacional de Colombia, 1989.

Pérez González Rubio, Jesús. *Gobierno y oposición: elementos para una reforma del estado.* Bogotá: Pontificia Universidad Javeriana, Programa de Estudios Políticos, 1987.

Pinedo Vidal, Miguel, comp. *Presentación y compilación: legislación electoral 1986.* Bogotá: Colección "Pensadores Políticos Colombianos," Cámara de Representantes, 1986.

Pinilla Pinilla, Luis. *Como se ejerce el poder en Colombia? Análisis sobre procesos decisorios de importancia en la vida nacional.* Bogotá: Pontificia Universidad Javeriana, M.A., 1980.

Pinzón, Martin Alonso. *Historia del conservatismo.* Bogotá: Tercer Mundo, 1979.

Pinzón de Lewin, Patricia, comp. *La oposición en Colombia: algunas bases para su discusion.* Bogotá: FESCOL, 1986.

———. *Los partidos políticos colombianos (estatutos, reglamentos, programas).* Prólogo Fernando Cepeda Ulloa. Bogotá: FESCOL, 1987.

———. *Pueblos, regiones y partido.* Bogotá: Universidad de los Andes, CIDER-CEREC, 1989.

———. *El ejército y las elecciónes: ensayo histórico.* Bogotá: CEREC, 1994.

Premo, Daniel. *Alianza Nacional Popular: Populism and the Politics of Social Class in Colombia, 1961–1970.* Austin: University of Texas, Ph.D. dissertation, 1972.

Programa Democracia, Universidad de los Andes. *Una constituyente para la Colombia del futuro.* Bogotá: FESCOL, 1990.

Ramírez, Socorro y Luis Alberto Restrepo. *Actores en conflicto por la paz: el proceso de paz durante el gobierno de Belisario Betancur 1982–1986.* Bogotá: Siglo Veintiuno Editores, 1989.

Ramírez Aljure, Jorge. *Liberalismo: ideología y clientelismo, 1957–1986.* Bogotá: Fotolito Inter 2000, 1986.

Ramírez H., Luis Fernando. *La financiación estatal de las campañas y la democracia del sistema político colombiano.* Bogotá: Pontificia Universidad Javeriana, M.A., 1985.

Ramírez Tobon, William. *Estado, violencia y democracias: ensayos.* Bogotá: Tercer Mundo Editores, Universidad Nacional de Colombia, 1990.

Randall, Stephen. *Colombia and the United States: Hegemony and Inter-Dependence.* Athens: University of Georgia Press, 1992.

Restrepo, Antonio José. *El moderno imperialismo: protecciónismo y libre cambio.* Bogotá: Editorial Incunables, 1984.

Restrepo, Laura. *Historia de una traición.* Bogotá: Plaza & Janes, 1986.

Restrepo, Luis Alberto. *Actores en conflicto por la paz: El proceso de paz durante el gobierno de Belisario Betancur.* Bogotá: n.p., 1988.

Restrepo Jaramillo, Gonzalo. *El pensamiento conservador: ensayos políticos.* Bogotá: Futuro Colombiano, 1987.

Reyes Posada, Alejandro. *Latifundio y poder político.* Bogotá: CINEP, 1978.

Rezazadeh, Reza, and Joseph McKenzie. *Political Parties in Colombia; Continuity in Political Style.* Platteville: University of Wisconsin-Platteville, 1978.

Roa Suárez, Hernando. *La teoría política sistemática: una aproximación.* Bogotá: Escuela Superior de Administración (ESAP), 1984.

Robinson, J. Cordell. *El movimiento gaitanista en Colombia.* Bogotá: Ediciónes Tercer Mundo, 1967.

Rodríguez, Edmundo R. *Partidos políticos y autonomía universitaria.* Bogotá: Pontificia Universidad Javeriana, Facultad de Estudios Interdisciplinarios, 1979.

Rojas Ruiz, Humberto, and Alvaro Camacho Guizado. *El Frente Nacional: Ideología y realidad.* Bogotá: Punta de Lanza, 1973.

Romero, Joaquín. *The Colombian System of Territorial Administration: An Analysis.* The Hague: Institute of Social Studies, 1982.

Roninger, Luis, and S.N. Eisenstadt. *Patrons, Clients and Friends.* Cambridge: Cambridge University Press, 1984.

Roninger, Luis, and Ayse Günes-Ayata, eds. *Democracy, Clientelism, and Civil Society.* Boulder: Lynne Rienner, 1994.

Rosas Londono, Luis Fernando. *Nuevo Liberalismo, suprapartidismo con ideas liberales.* Bogotá: Pontificia Universidad Javeriana, 1992.

Safford, Frank. *The Ideal of the Practical: Colombia's Struggle to Form a Political Elite.* Austin: University of Texas Press, 1976.

Samper, Ernesto. *Colombia Sale Adelante!* Bogotá: E.C.M. Impresores, 1989.

Samper, José María. *Los partidos en Colombia.* Bogotá: Editorial Incunables, 1985 (from 1873 original).

Sánchez, Gonzalo. *Ensayos de historia social y política del siglo XX.* Bogotá: Ancora, 1984.

Sánchez, Gonzalo, and Donny Meertens. *Bandoleros, gamonales y campesinos.* Bogotá: El Ancora Editores, 1983.

Sánchez, Gonzalo, and Ricardo Peñaranda. *Pasado y presente de la violencia en Colombia.* Bogotá: 1986.

Sánchez, Gonzalo et al. *Colombia: violencia y democracia.* Bogotá: Universidad Nacional de Colombia, Centro Editorial, 1987.

Sánchez David, Rubén. *El comportamiento electoral de los bogotanos en las elecciónes de 1978.* Bogotá: Universidad de los Andes, 1981.

————, ed. *Los nuevos retos electorales—Colombia 1990: antesala del cambio*. Bogotá: CEREC, 1991.

————, ed. *El estudio de la ciencia política en Colombia*. Bogotá: Tercer Mundo Editores, UNIANDES, 1994.

Sanín, Javier, ed. *Mercadeo electoral: elección de alcaldes*. Bogotá: Pontificia Universidad Javeriana, Facultad de Estudios Interdisciplinarios, 1988.

Santa, Eduardo. *Sociología política de Colombia*. Bogotá: Ediciónes Tercer Mundo, 1964.

Santamaría S., Ricardo, and Gabriel Silva Lujan. *Proceso político en Colombia: Del Frente Nacional a la apertura democrática*. Bogotá: Fondo Editorial CEREC, 1984.

Santos Calderón, Enrique. *La guerra por la paz*. Bogotá: Fondo Editorial CEREC, 1985.

Seminario nacional de periodismo político. *Prensa, radio y T.V. en Mitaca 84*. Bogotá: Impresora Gráfica Ltda., 1984.

Sharpless, Richard E. *Gaitán of Colombia: A Political Biography*. Pittsburgh: University of Pittsburgh Press, 1978.

Sheahan, John. *Patterns of Development in Latin America: Poverty, Repression, and Economic Strategy*. Princeton: Princeton University Press, 1987.

Silva García, Germán. *El proceso de paz: un paso adelante, dos pasos atrás*. Bogotá: Comite de Solidaridad con los Presos Políticos y Fundación de Estudios Sociales y Investigaciónes Políticos, 1985.

Silva Lujan, Gabriel. *Política exterior: continuidad o ruptura?* Bogotá: Fondo Editorial CEREC, 1985.

Smith, T. Lynn. *Colombia: Social Structure and the Process of Development*. Gainesville: University of Florida Press, 1967.

Solaún, Mauricio, and Michael E. Quinn. *Sinners and Heretics: The Politics of Military Intervention in Latin America*. Urbana: University of Illinois Press, 1973.

Stepan, Alfred. *The State and Society; Peru in Comparative Perspective*. Princeton: Princeton University Press, 1978.

Strickon, Arnold, and Sidney M. Greenfield, eds. *Structure and Process in Latin America: Patronage, Clientelage, and Power Systems*. Albuquerque: University of New Mexico Press, 1972.

Tafur Galvis, Alvaro. *La constitución de 1991 y la modernización del estado colombiano*. Bogotá: Universidad Externado de Colombia, 1993.

Tirado, Thomas C. *Alfonso López Pumarejo, el conciliador: su contribución a la paz política en Colombia*. Bogotá: Espejo de Colombia, 1986.

Tirado Mejía, Alvaro. *Descentralización y centralismo en Colombia*. Bogotá: Editorial La Oveja Negra, Fundación Friedrich Naumann, 1983.

Tirado Mejía, Alvaro, and Magdalena Velásquez. *La reforma constituciónal de 1936*. Bogotá: Editorial Oveja Negra, Fundación Friedrich Naumann, 1982.

Torres Velasco, Javier. *Los partidos políticos en Colombia*. Bogotá: ANIF, 1979.

Turbay Ayala, Julio César. *Perspectivas colombianas*. Bogotá: Secretaria de Información y Prensa, Presidencia de la República, 1979.

————. *Memorias de un cuatrienio*. Bogotá: Editorial Presencia, 1983.

Ungar, Elizabeth, ed. *Gobernabilidad en Colombia: retos y desafíos*. Bogotá: Tercer Mundo Editores, UNIANDES, 1993.

Universidad Nacional, Instituto de Estudios Políticas y Relaciónes Internacionales. *Síntesis '94 Colombia*. Bogotá: Tercer Mundo Editores, 1994.

Urán, Carlos H. *Rojas y la manipulación del poder*. Bogotá: Carlos Valencia Editores, 1983.

Uribe Giraldo, Luz Elena. *El estado, las libertades individuales y el preámbulo de la constitución*. Bogotá: Pontificia Universidad Javeriana, 1984.

Uribe Rueda, Alvaro. *La quiebra de los partidos*. Bogotá: Escuela de Estudios Políticos Rafael Uribe Uribe, 1990.

Uribe Vargas, Diego. *La constitución de 1991 y el ideario liberal*. Bogotá: Universidad Nacional de Colombia, 1992.

Uribe Vargas, Diego et al. *Colombia: hacia una sociedad participante*. Bogotá: Fundación para la Democracia, 1973.

Uricoechea, Fernando. *Estado y burocracia en Colombia*. Bogotá: Universidad Nacional de Colombia, 1986.

Urrutia, Miguel. *The Development of the Colombian Labor Movement*. New Haven: Yale University Press, 1969.

————. *Los de arriba y los de abajo: la distribución del ingreso en Colombia en las últimas décadas*. Bogotá: Fedesarrollo—Fundo Editorial CEREC, 1984.

————. *Winners and Losers in Colombia's Economic Growth in the 1970s*. Oxford: Oxford University Press for the World Bank, 1985.

Urrutia, Miguel, y otros. *Ensayos sobre historia económica colombiano*. Bogotá: FEDESARROLLO, Editorial Presencia Bogotá, 1980.

Valencia Vargas, Margarita. *La predisposición al voto en los jovenes: hacia una investigación empírica sobre los procesos de socialización política en Colombia*. Bogotá: Pontificia Universidad Javeriana, M.A., 1984.

Valenzuela Ramírez, Jorge. *Producción arrocera y clientelismo*. Bogotá: CINEP, 1978.

Varios. *Juventud y política en Colombia*. Bogotá: FESCOL, 1984.

————. *Tregua y unión patriótica*. Bogotá: Centro de Estudios e Investigaciónes Sociales (CEIS), Editorial Colombia Nueva Ltda., 1985.

Vasco Montoya, Eloisa. *Clientelismo y minifundio*. Bogotá: CINEP, 1978.

Vásquez de Urrutia, Patricia. *La democracia en blanco y negro: Colombia en los años ochenta*. Bogotá: CEREC, 1989.

————, ed. *Colombia piensa la democracia: Iglesia, partidos políticos, medios de comunicación, escuela, gremios y sindicatos frente al sistema político colombiano*. Bogotá: CEREC, Ediciónes Uniandes, 1989.

Vázquez Carrizosa, Alfredo. *El poder presidencial en Colombia.* Bogotá: Sociedad Ediciónes Internacionales S.R.L., 1979.

———. *Amnistia: hacia una democracia mas ancha y profunda.* Bogotá: Oveja Negra, 1983.

———. *Las relaciónes de Colombia y Venezuela: la historia atormentada de dos naciónes.* Bogotá: Ediciónes Tercer Mundo, 1983.

———. *Betancur y la crisis nacional.* Bogotá: Ediciónes Aurora, 1986.

———. *Los No-alineados; una estrategía política para la paz en la era atomica.* Bogotá: Carlos Valencia, Editores, 1986.

———. *Historia crítica del Frente Nacional.* Bogotá: Ediciónes Foro Nacional por Colombia, 1992.

Vélez Bustillo, Eduardo, coordinator. *Juventud y política en Colombia.* Bogotá: Fundación Friedrich Ebert de Colombia (FESCOL), 1984.

Vellinga, Menno, and Dirk Kruijt. *Industrialization and Regional Development in Colombia.* Amsterdam: Centre for Latin American Research and Documentation, 1983.

Vidal Perdomo, Jaime. *La reforma constitucional de 1968 y los alcances jurídicos.* Bogotá: Presencia, 1970.

Villamil, José, ed. *Transnational Capitalism and National Development.* Brighton: University of Sussex, 1979.

Villamizar J., Rogelio. *Como nos gobiernan en Colombia.* Cali: Impresora FERIVA S.A., 1993.

Villar Borda, Luis. *Oposición, insurgencia y amnistía.* Bogotá: Ediciónes Nuevo Mundo, 1982.

———. *Democracia municipal: autonomía, planificación y desarrollo.* Bogotá: UEC, 1986.

Violich, Francis, in collaboration with Robert Daughters. *Urban Planning for Latin America; The Challenge of Metropolitan Growth.* Boston: Oelgeschlager, Gunn & Hain, for Lincoln Institute of Land Policy, 1987.

Wagley, Charles. *The Latin American Tradition.* New York: Columbia University Press, 1968.

Weiss, Anita. *Tendencias de la participación electoral en Colombia, 1935–1966.* Bogotá: Universidad Nacional de Colombia, 1968.

Whiteford, Andrew Hunter. *Twin Cities of Latin America: A Description of Social Classes.* Garden City: Anchor Books, Doubleday & Company, Inc., 1964.

Wilson, Thomas M. *Factionalism and Party Politics in Colombia.* Knoxville: University of Tennessee, Ph. D., 1979.

Zamosc, Leon. *The Agrarian Question and the Peasant Movement in Colombia: Struggles of the National Peasant Association 1967–1981.* Cambridge: Cambridge University Press, 1986.

Articles, Chapters, Papers

Athey, Lois E. "Democracy and Populism: Some Recent Studies." *Latin American Research Review* 20 (1984): 172–84.

Bagley, Bruce Michael. "Colombia: National Front and Economic Development." In *Politics, Policies, and Economic Development in Latin America,* edited by Robert Wesson, 124–60. Stanford: Hoover Institution Press, 1984.

———. "Colombian Politics: Crisis or Continuity?" *Current History* 86 (January 1987): 21–24, 40–41.

Bailey, John J. "Pluralist and Corporatist Dimensions of Interest Representation in Colombia." In *Authoritarianism and Corporatism in Latin America,* edited by James M. Malloy, 259–302. Pittsburgh: University of Pittsburgh Press, 1977.

Bergquist, Charles. "In the Name of History: A Disciplinary Critique of Orlando Fals Borda's *Historia doble de la costa.*" *Latin American Research Review* 25, no. 3 (1990): 156–76.

Campos, Judith de. "Las elecciónes de Mitaca de 1980 en Cali." *Boletin de Coyuntura Economica* 1 (mayo 1980): 29–45.

Chernick, Mark W. "Negotiated Settlement to Armed Conflict: Lessons from the Colombian Peace Process." *Journal of Inter-American Studies and World Affairs* 30, no. 4 (Winter 1988–1989): 53–89.

———, and Michael F. Jimenez. "Popular Liberalism, Radical Democracy, and Marxism: Leftist Politics in Contemporary Colombia, 1974–1991." In *The Latin American Left: From the Fall of Allende to Perestroika,* edited by Barry Carr and Steve Ellner, 61–81. Boulder: Westview Press, 1993.

Child, Jorge. "El Statuo Quo Colombiano." *Revista Javeriana* 512 (abril 1986): 195–207.

Craig, Richard B. "Colombian Narcotics and United States—Colombian Relations." *Journal of Inter-American Studies and World Affairs* 23 (August 1981): 243–70.

———. "Domestic Implications of Illicit Colombian Drug Production and Trafficking." *Journal of Inter-American Studies and World Affairs* 25 (August 1983).

Davíla L., Andres. "Una campaña de espaldas a la crisis." *Análisis Político* 8 (septiembre a diciembre de 1989): 79–84.

Deas, Malcolm. "Coalition in Colombia." *Current History* 354 (February 1971): 90–94, 117–18.

———. "Colombian Aprils." *Current History* 378 (February 1973): 77–80, 88.

Dix, Robert H. "The Colombian Presidency: Continuities and Changes." In *Presidential Power in Latin American Politics,* edited by Thomas V. DiBacco, 72–96. New York: Praeger, 1977.

————. "Non-Urban Oppositions in Latin America." *Inter-American Economic Affairs* 31 (Winter 1977), 75–91.

————. "The Varieties of Populism: The Case of Colombia." *Western Political Quarterly* 31 (September 1978), 334–51.

————. "Consociational Democracy: The Case of Colombia." *Comparative Politics* 12 (April 1980): 303–21.

————. "Populism: Authoritarianism and Democracy." *Latin American Research Review* 20 (1985): 29–53.

Eisenstadt, S.N., and Luis Roniger. "Patron-Client Relations as a Model of Structuring Social Exchange." *Comparative Studies in Society and History* (1980): 42–77.

Fals Borda, Orlando. "Violence and the Break-up of Tradition in Colombia." In *Obstacles to Change in Latin America,* edited by Claudio Veliz, 188–206. London: Oxford University Press, 1965.

Flinn, Peter. "Class, Clientelism, and Coercion; Some Mechanisms of Internal Dependency and Control." *The Journal of Commonwealth and Comparative Studies* 12 (July 1974): 133–57.

Foster, George M. "Interpersonal Relations in Peasant Society." *Human Organization* 19 (1960–61): 174–78.

————. "The Dyadic Contract: A Model for the Social Structure of a Mexican Peasant Village." *American Anthropologist* 63 (1961): 1173–92.

————. "The Dyadic Contract in Tzintzuntzan II: Patron-Client Relationships." *American Anthropologist* 65 (1963): 1280–94.

Gaitán de Pombo, Pilar. "Gobernabilidad y descentralización política en Colombia: Elementos para una reflexión." *Conference Paper # 47,* Columbia University and New York University, 1990.

Gilbert, Alan. "Bogotá: Politics, Planning, and the Crisis of Lost Opportunities." In *Latin American Urban Research, vol. 6: Metropolitan Latin America: The Challenge and the Response,* edited by Wayne A. Cornelius and Robert V. Kemper, 87–127. Beverly Hills: Sage Públications, 1978.

Gillin, John P. "Some Signposts for Policy." In *Social Change in Latin America Today,* edited by the Council on Foreign Relations, 14–63. New York: Council on Foreign Relations, 1960.

González G., Fernan E. "Clientelismo y democratización: La alternativa liberal." *Controversia* (1976): 95–243.

————. "Clientelismo y administración pública." *Enfoques colombianos* 14 (1980): 67–106.

Graziano, Luigi. "Patron-Client Relations in Southern Italy." *European Journal of Political Research* 1 (April 1973): 3–34.

Hartlyn, Jonathan. "Colombia: Old Problems, New Opportunities." *Current History* 431 (February 1983): 62–65, 83.

————. "Military Governments and the Transition to Civilian Rule: The Colombian Experience of 1957–58." *Journal of Interamerican Studies and World Affairs* 26 (May 1984): 245–81.

————. "The Impact of Patterns of Industrialization and of Popular Sector Incorporation on Political Regime Type: A Case Study of Colombia." *Studies in Comparative International Development* 19 (Spring 1984): 29–60.

————. "Producer Associations, the Political Regime and Policy Processes in Contemporary Colombia." *Latin American Research Review* 20 (1985): 111–39.

————. "Civil Violence and Conflict Resolution: The Case of Colombia." In *Stopping the Killing: How Civil Wars End,* edited by Roy Licklider, 37–61. New York: New York University Press, 1993.

Heinz, Wolfgang S. "Guerrillas, Political Violence, and the Peace Process in Colombia." *Latin American Research Review* 24 (1989): 249–59.

Helguera, J. Leon. "The Changing Role of the Military in Colombia." *Journal of Interamerican Studies* 3 (July 1961): 351–58.

Hoskin, Gary W. "Belief Systems of Colombian Political Party Activists." *Journal of Interamericn Studies and World Affairs* 21 (November 1979): 481–504.

Human Rights Watch/Americas. *State of War: Political Violence and Counterinsurgency in Colombia.* New York: HRW, 1993.

Johnson, Kenneth. "Political Radicalism in Colombia: Electoral Dynamics." *Journal of Interamerican Studies* 7 (January 1965): 15–26.

Junguito, Roberto. "The Colombian Debt Problem." In *International Money and Debt; Challenges for the World Economy,* edited by Rudiger Dornbusch and Steve Marcus, 61–77. San Francisco: ICS Press, 1991.

Kalmanovitz, Salomon. "Violencia y Narcotráfico en Colombia." *Conference Paper No. 44,* Columbia University, New York University, 1990.

Kaufman, Robert R. "The Patron-Client Concept and Macro-Politics: Prospects and Problems." *Comparative Studies in Society and History* 16 (1974): 284–309.

Kline, Harvey F. "Interest Groups in the Colombian Congress." *Journal of Interamerican Studies and World Affairs* 16 (August 1974): 274–300.

————. "The National Front: Historical Perspective and Overview." In *Politics of Compromise: Coalition Government in Colombia,* edited by Ronald Hellman and Mauricio Solaún, 59–87. New Brunswick: Transaction Publishers, 1980.

————. "New Directions in Colombia?" *Current History* 499 (February 1985): 65–68, 83.

Lande, Carl H. "The Dyadic Basis of Clientelism." In *Friends, Followers, and Factions: A Reader in Political Clientelism,* edited by Steffen Schmidt et al., xiii–xxxvii. Berkeley: University of California Press, 1977.

Leal Buitrago, Francisco. "El sistema político del clientelismo." *Analisis Político* 8 (septiembre-diciembre de 1989): 8–33.

———. "Modernización del estado y crisis política." *Conference Paper No. 39,* for Columbia University and New York University Consortium, 1990.

Lemarchand, Rene, and Keith Legg. "Political Clientelism and Development." *Comparative Politics* 4 (1972): 149–78.

Lemoine A., Carlos. "Leccións y tareas deducidas del 9 de marzo." *Revista Javeriana* 523 (abril 1986): 207–15.

López-Alves, Fernando. "Explaining Confederation: Colombian Unions in the 1980s." *Latin American Research Review* 25 (1990): 115–34.

Losada Lora, Rodrigo, and Miles W. Williams. "Análisis de la votación presidencial en Bogotá, 1970." In *Colombia política,* edited by DANE, 1–55. Bogotá: DANE, 1972.

Lupsha, Peter A. "Drug Trafficking: Mexico and Colombia in Comparative Perspective." *Journal of International Affairs* 35 (Spring-Summer 1981): 94–110.

Martz, John D. "Colombia at the Crossroads." *Current History* 553 (February 1991): 69–73, 80.

———. "Party Elites and Leadership in Colombia and Venezuela." *Journal of Latin American Studies* 24 (1992): 87–121.

———. "Contemporary Colombian Politics: The Struggle Over Democratization." In *The Colombian Economy: Issues of Trade and Development,* edited by Alvin Cohen and Frank R. Gunter, 21–47. Boulder: Westview Press, 1992.

———. "Colombia: Democracy, Development, and Drugs." *Current History* 581 (March 1994): 134–38.

Medard, Jean Francois. "Le rapport de clientele." *Revue Française de Science Politique 26* (February 1976): 103–32.

———. "Political Clientelism in France: The Center-Periphery Nexus Reexamined." In *Political Clientelism, Patronage and Development,* edited by S.N. Eisenstadt and Rene Lemarchand, 125–71. Beverly Hills: Sage Publications, 1981.

———. "The Underdeveloped State in Tropical Africa: Political Clientelism or Neo-Patrimonialism." In *Private Patronage and Public Power: Political Clientelism in the Modern States,* edited by Christopher Clapham, 162–92. London: Frances Pinter, 1982.

Mintz, Sidney W., and Eric R. Wolfe. "An Analysis of Ritual Co-Parenthood (Compadrazgo)." *Southwestern Journal of Anthropology* 6 (1950): 341–68.

Muñoz, Gloria. "Alvaro Gómez: Pensamiento y Propuestas." *Revista Javeriana* 523 (abril 1986): 169–80.

Oquist, Paul W. "Las eleccións presidenciales 1930–1970." *Boletín Mensual de Estadística* 268–69 (1973): 63–79.

Payne, James J. "The Oligarchy Muddle." *World Politics* 20 (1968): 439–53.

Peeler, John. "Colombian Parties and Political Development: A Reassesment." *Journal of Interamerican Studies and World Affairs* 17 (May 1976): 203–25.

Pínzon de Lewin, Patricia. "Tendencias electorales colombianas 1930–1926." *Revista Cámara de Comercio de Bogotá* 28 (1977): 89–107.

Pizarro, Eduardo. "Insurgencia Crónica, Movimiento Guerrillero y Proceso de Paz en Colombia." *Conference Paper No. 45,* Columbia University-New York University Consortium, 1990.

Pollock, John C. "Violence, Politics and Elite Performance: The Political Sociology of La Violencia in Colombia." *Studies in Comparative International Development* 10 (Summer 1975): 22–50.

Powell, John Duncan. "Peasant Society and Clientelistic Politics." *American Political Science Review* 64 (June 1970): 411–25.

Pulgarin M., Sergio. "El Partido Liberal y los Resultados Electorales de Bogotá y Cundinamarca." *Revista Javeriana* 523 (abril 1986): 223–33.

Revéiz, Edgar, and María José Pérez. "Colombia: Moderate Economic Growth, Political Stability and Social Welfare." In *Latin American Political Economy: Financial Crisis and Political Change,* edited by Jonathan Hartlyn and Samuel A. Morley, 265–92. Boulder: Westview Press, 1986).

Reyes Posada, Alejandro. "Paramilitares en Colombia: Contexto, Aliados y Consecuencias." *Conference Paper No. 46,* for Columbia University-New York University Consortium, 1990.

Roninger, Luis. "Caciquismo y Coronelismo: Contextual Dimensions of Patron Brokerage in Mexico and Brazil." *Latin American Research Review* 22 (1987): 71–101.

Rothlisberger, Dora, and Paul Ocquist. "Algunos aspectos de la abstención electoral." *Boletín Mensual de Estadística,* no. 268–69 (noviembre/diciembre 1973): 80–99.

Rozo Acuña, Eduardo. "El clientelismo político." *Revista de la Universidad Externado de Colombia* 19 (1978): 37–48.

Ruhl, J. Mark. "Party System in Crisis? An Analysis of Colombia's 1978 Elections." *Journal of Inter-American Economic Affairs* 32 (Winter 1978): 29–45.

———. "The Military." In *Politics of Compromise: Coalition Government in Colombia,* edited by Albert Berry, Ronald Hellman, and Mauricio Solaún. New Brunswick: Transaction Publishers, 1980.

———. "Civil-Military Relations in Colombia: A Societal Explanation." *Journal of Interamerican Studies and World Affairs* 23 (1981): 123–46.

Sánchez, Ricardo. "El presidencialismo y la Reforma Constituciónal." *Foro* (October 1990).

Sánchez David, Rubén, and Patricia Pinzón de Lewin. "Elecciónes y democracia en Colombia." In *Una tarea inconclusa: elecciónes y democracia en América Latina, 1988–1991,* edited by Rodolfo Cerdas-Cruz, Juan Rial, and Daniel Zovatto, 287–311. San José: IIDH/CAPEL, 1992.

Schmidt, Steffen W. "Bureaucrats as Modernizing Brokers: Clientelism in Colombia." *Comparative Politics* 6 (April 1974): 425–50.

———. *"La Violencia* Revisited: The Clientelist Bases of Political Violence in Colombia." *Journal of Latin American Studies* 6 (May 1974): 97–111.

———. "Patrons, Brokers and Clients in the Colombian System." In *Political Parties and Linkage,* edited by Kay Lawson, 266–88. New Haven: Yale University Press, 1980), pp. 266–88.

Scott, James C. "Corruption, Machine Politics and Political Change." *American Political Science Review* 63 (1969): 1142–58.

———. "Patron-Client Politics and Political Change in Southeast Asia." *American Political Science Review* 66 (1972): 91–113.

Silva Lujan, Gabriel. "Quien votó por quien en Bogotá." *Estrategía* (abril 1982).

———. "Las elecciónes parlamentarias por dentro." *Estrategía* (abril 1986).

Sloan, John W. "Regionalism, Political Parties and Public Policy in Colombia." *Inter-American Economic Affairs* 33 (Winter 1979): 25–47.

Sloan, John W., and Kent L. Tedin. "The Consequences of Regime Type for Public-Policy Outputs." *Comparative Political Studies* 20 (April 1987): 98–124.

Torres Restrepo, Camilo. "Social Change and Rural Violence in Colombia." In *Masses in Latin America,* edited by Irving Louis Horowitz, 503–47. New York: Oxford University Press, 1970.

Waterbury, John. "An Attempt to Put Patrons and Clients in Their Place." In *Patrons and Clients in Mediterranean Society,* edited by A. Gellner and John Waterbury, 329–42. London: Duckworth, 1977.

Weingrod, Alex. "Patrons, Patronage, and Political Parties." *Comparative Studies in Society and History* 10 (July 1968): 377–400.

———. "Patrons and Power." In *Patrons and Clients in Mediterranean Society,* edited by A. Gellner and John Waterbury, 41–52. London: Duckworth, 1977.

Wilde, Alexander. "Conversations among Gentlemen: Oligarchical Democracy in Colombia." In *The Breakdown of Democratic Regimes: Latin America,* edited by Juan Linz and Alfred Stepan, 28–82. Baltimore: The Johns Hopkins University Press, 1978.

Wolf, Eric. "Kinship, Friendship and Patron-Client Relations in Complex Societies." In *The Social Anthropology of Complex Societies,* edited by Michael Banton, 1–22. London: Tavistock, 1966.

Zamosc, Leon. "The Political Crisis and the Prospects for Rural Democracy in Colombia." *Journal of Development Studies* 26 (July 1990): 44–78.

Miscellaneous Documents and Publications

Inter-American Development Bank. *Latin America in Graphs: Demographic and Economic Trends.* Washington: IADB, 1993.
República de Colombia. Departamento Administrativo Nacional de Estadística [DANE]. *Colombia política: estadísticas, 1935–1970.* Bogotá: DANE, 1972.
———. Ministerio de Gobierno. *Legislación electoral: seis reformas estructurales al régimen político.* Bogotá: Ministerio de Gobierno, 1982.
———. Registraduría Nacional del Estado Civil. *Circunscripciónes electorales y división política-administrativa de Colombia.* Bogotá: Registraduría Nacional, 1983.
———. Departamento Administrativo Nacional de Estadística [DANE]. *Avance de Resultados preliminares.* Bogotá: DANE, 1986.
———. *Colombia estadística 1986.* Bogotá: Editorial Presencia Ltda., 1987.
———. *Indicadores de coyuntura: agosto 1987.* Bogotá: DANE, 1987.
———. Registraduría Nacional del Estado Civil. *Historia electoral colombiana.* Bogotá: Públicaciónes Reginat, 1988.
———. *Estadísticas electorales 1990: Presidente de la República, Congreso de la República.* Bogotá: Registraduría, 1990.
———. *Historia electoral colombiana, 1810–1988.* Bogotá: Imprenta Nacional de Colombia, 1991.
———. Senado. *La constitución política de Colombia y sus anexos 1991.* Bogotá: Congreso nacional, 1992.
World Bank. *Colombia: Economic Development and Policy under Changing Conditions.* Washington, D.C.: The World Bank, 1984.

Index

Adams, Richard, 28
Agricultural production and feudal clientelism, 15–17
 coffee exports, 99 and bananas enhancing conservative importance, 48–49, 75–76
Agudelo Villa, Hernando, 78, 176–77, 189, 195–96
Alianza Nacional Popular (ANAPO), 84, 93–94, 113, 115–16, 152–53, 155, 157, 174, 177, 190
Alliance for Progress, 80
Alzate Avendaño, Gilberto, 62, 87, 90–91, 102
Amaya Ramírez, Guillermo, 82–83
Arcos, Crescencio, 275
Arenas, Jacobo, 273
Arias de Grieff, Jorge, 148
Arnove, Robert, 76
Asamblea Nacional Constituyente (ANAC), 62, 64
Asociación Nacional de Instituciones Financieras (ANIF),
Asociación Nacional de Usuarios Campesinos(ANUC), 147–48, 191
Ayerbe Chaux, Gerardo, 110

Bagley, Bruce, 37–39, 147, 245
Balcázar Monzón, Gustavo, 173
Banco Central Hipotecario, 146
Banco Comercial Antioqueno, 212
Banco del Estado, 212
Banco Nacional, 212
Banco de la República, 103–4
Baquero Borda, Hernando, 227
Barco Vargas, Virgilio, 176, 197, 216, 233–35, 237–40, 292, 313, 316
 administrative policies, 245–48
 agrarian reforms, 247
 constitutional reform, 248

economic climate, 243–45
House of Nariño agreement, 248
industrial restructuring, 247–48
institutional decentralization, 248
International Monetary Fund, 244
national debt, 247
"National Plan of Struggle against Poverty and for Employment", 246
Plan Nacional de Rehabilitación (PNR), 249–50
policies of governance, 243–51
privatization of state managed banks, 247
"Rehabilitation, Reconciliation and Normalization", 249–50
social and political controls, 249–51
tax reform, 246
unemployment, 244–45
uniparty government, 251–62
Bateman Cayon, Jaime, 258
Bautista, Tulio, 60
Bejarano, Jesús, 277
Bernstein, Harry, 49
Betancourt de Liska, Regina, 238
Betancur, Belisario, 88, 114, 152–54, 175, 177, 180–81,196, 199, 203–4, 253, 256–57, 285, 291, 297, 311, 316
 administrative policies, 210–17
 biparty government politics, 229–40
 economic climate of state, 209–10
 income tax reform, 214
 International Monetary Fund, 214, 216
 low—cost housing, 211–12
 monetary controls, 213
 national debt, 210, 213, 216
 policies of governance, 209–10
 social and political controls, 217–29
 trade deficit, 213–14

20th century reform, 209–40
urbanization and changes, 209–10
Betancur, Jaime, 218–19
Betancur, Regina, 286
Biparty government, politics of, 229–40
   campaign and elections, 235–40
   candidate selection, 232–35
   competitiveness in, 229–32
Boissevain, Jeremy, 18–19
Bolívar, Simón, 42
Botero Zea, Fernando, 299, 301, 303
Botero Restrepo, Oscar, 277
Briceño Murillo, Luis Francisco, 227
Bureaucratization of political system, 65–71

Caballero, Antonio, 236
Caicedo Ferrer, Juan Martín, 256
Caicedo Ferrer, Manuel, 253–54
Caldera, Rafael, 270, 303
Camacho Leyva, Luis Carlos, 190–93, 195
Cano, Guillermo, 228
Castro, Fidel, 215–16, 218
Castro Castro, Jaime, 220, 222, 232, 239, 255, 281
Cepeda Ulloa, Fernando, 38–39, 65, 252, 302
Cepeda Vargas, Manuel, 299
Chalmers, Douglas, 26
Chernik, Mark W., 217
Clark, Robert, 9
Clientelism
   alternating presidential terms, 36
   brokerage and patrimonial clientelism, 8, 17–20
   bureaucratization of, 20–25
   characterizing Colombian politics, 35–41
   church, role in society, 43, 61. 64
   collapse and renewal of political controls, 57–65
      collective peasant activity and national political parties, 21–22, 24
   constitutionl government and re-shaping politics, 291–319
   corporate clientelism and bureau-cracy, 38

democracy and corporate clientel-ism—the political future, 304–319
evolution of, 7–31
feudal clientelism, 15–17, 41–54
   gamonales in power structure, 44–45, 47, 50
indentured labor in, 15–16
insurgence and disorder in system, 57–71
modernization and bureaucratization of, 28–31
necessity as function for political development, 305–19
nurturing democracy, 36
origin of, 12–15
paridad in elected and appointive offices, 36
patrimonialism in, 15–20, 35–54
political clientelism in Latin America, 25–31
power struggle of political bosses, 42
preserving social and political con-trol, 7–31
public disillusionment with reform, 292
status of citizen in state and clientel-istic economy, 7–31
traditional concept of, 12–15
universality of, 8–12
Coffee exports, 99
Colombia: *see* Nation of Colombia
Colombian clientelism of the 1990s and Democracy, 304–19
Comisión de Planeación, 104–5
Communism , 107, 12 and general strike, 170–71
Consejo Nacional de Política Econ-ómica y Planeación, 104–5
Cooper, Donald E., 167
Corporate clientelism and problems confronting constitutional reforms, 293
   democratization for civil and human rights, 295–96
   drug trafficking confronting, 292
   election of a General Prosecutor, 294
   guerilla activity and peace, 293
   holding multiple offices, 294

Indian tribal representation, 293
judicial reforms, 294
lawlessness, 291
legalization of civil divorce, 296
patronage and clientelism of democracy, 304–19
popular election of state governors, 295
presidential term limits, 294
publicly supported social programs, 298
recall of elected officials, 295
religions in, 293
two-party system, elimination of, 296
unauthorized foreign travel, 294
Corriente de Renovación Socialista (CRS), 274
Cuevas, Tulio, 171
Currie, Lauchlin, 145, 230

De la Calle, Lemos, 297
De la Calle Lombana, Humberto, 282–86, 294, 301–3
Democracy and Corporate Clientelism—the political future, 304–19
Departamento Administrativo de Seguridad (DAS), 149
Diego Jaramillo, Juan, 256
Dix, Robert H., 37, 39–40, 69, 76–77, 121
Drug trafficking, 193–94, 250–51, 255
income from, 188
perception of corruption, 185
underground activity, 210, 216, 225–26, 229
Duarte, José Napoleón, 215
Duplat, Carlos, 191
Duque Pérez, Jaime, 150
Durán, Eduardo Wiesner, 187
Durán, Hernando, 297
Durán, Maria Jimena, 36
Durán Dussan, Ernesto, 231
Durán Dussan, Hernando, 254–56

Echandía, Darío, 59, 86, 89, 91, 114, 154, 170, 191
Echandía Vicente, 59
Echaverry, Hernán, 155
Echeverri Mejía, Hernán, 173

Eisenstadt, S. N., 19–20; and Louis Roniger, 8
Ejército de Liberación Nacional (ELN), 107, 109–10, 149–51, 167, 190–92, 218–19, 273–74
Ejército Popular de Liberación (EPL), 150, 190, 221, 228, 273–74
Eliécer Gaitan, Jorge, 52–54, 201
Escobar, Andrés, 276
Escobar, Cristina, 312
Escobar, Pablo, 226–27, 271–72, 275, 313
Escabor Navia, Rodrigo, 230
Espinosa Vlderrama, Augusto, 176, 197–98, 231, 233

Fals Borda, Orlando, 44–45, 191
Fayad, Alvaro, 218, 220
Financiera Furatena, 212
Flinn, Peter, 14
Flores Vélez, Omar, 256
Foster, George M., 13
"Four Strategies" for consolidation and integration, 145, 161
Frechette, Myles, 300
Frente Nacional, 31
bureaucratization of political system, 65–71
campaign and elections, 93–95, 115–17, 137–40, 155–58, 179–81, 199–204 235–40, 258–60
candidate selection, 91–93, 113–15, 134–37, 153–55, 175–78, 196–99 232–35, 254–58
institutional revisions, 65–71
party competition, 86–91, 111–13, 131–34, 151–53, 172–75, 194–96, 229–32, 251–54
politics of, 86–91, 111–13, 131–40, 151–58, 172–75, 194–204
in post violencia period, 64–67, 70–71
seeking power base, 194–96
Frente Unido de Acción Guerrillera, 150
Fuerzas Armadas Revolucionarias Colombianas (FARC), 107, 110, 115, 149–51, 167, 190, 192, 218–19, 225, 228, 235, 249, 273–74, 299

Gaitán, Jorge Eliécer, 52–54, 201, la violencia

avenging his murder, 57–65
Gaitán de Valencia, Gloria, 87
Galán, Luis Carlos, 198–201, 203–4, 230–32, 234–35, 237–38, 246, 251, 253–55, 260–61, 297, 316
Gallón, Gustavo, 296
Gamer, Robert E., 9, 21
García Márquez, Gabriel, 168
Gaviria, César, 246, 255, 259–61, 292–93, 297, 313, 316
    decentralization and privatization, 265, 268–71
    economic climate, 265–67
    foreign debt, 266
    guerilla activity, 266, 273–74
    hope for peace, 265
    inflation, 266, 269
    internationalization of economy, 265, 267–71
    modernization and restructuring, 265–87
    "Peaceful Revolution", 269
    policies of administration, 267–71
    politics of governance, 265–76
    population growth and urbanization, 265–66
    power sharing politics, 276–87
    social and political controls, 271–76
    war against drug trafficking, 268, 271–76
    work stoppages, 269
Giraldo, Jaime, 277
Gómez, Alvaro, 196, 199, 201, 246, 250, 256–57, 259–60, 279, 281, 283, 285, 293
Gómez, Laureano, 52–54, 58–66, 77, 81–82, 87–89, 144, 309
Gómez Hurtado, Alvaro, 88, 135–36, 152–53, 155–57, 172, 175, 180, 231–32, 234, 237–38, 257, 259, 278
Gómez Martinez, Juan, 253
Gómez Pinzón, José 82
González, Andrés, 276
González Garcia, Rodolfo, 282
Governance in 20th Century
    Barco, Virgilio (1986–90), 243–62
    Betancur, Belisario (1982–86), 209–40
    Gaviria, César (1990–94),265–87

Lleras Camargo, Alberto (1958–62), 75–95
Lleras Restrepo, Carlos (1966–70), 119–40
López Michelsen, Alfonso (1974–78), 161–81
Pastrana Borrero, Misael (1970–74), 143–58
Turbay Ayala, Julio César (1978–82), 185–20
Valencia, Guillermo Leon (1962–66), 99–117
see also
    Barco Vargas, Virgilio
    Betancur, Belisario
    Gaviria, César
    Lleras Camargo, Alberto
    Lleras Restrepo, Carlos
    López Michelsen, Alfonso
    Pastrana Borrero, Misael
    Turbay Ayala, Julio César
    Valencia, Guillermo León
Grancolombiana de Promociones (PRONTA), 212
Grupo Colombia, 212
Grupo Santa Fé, 212
Guerrilla violence, 210–11, 214, 217–20, 229
Gunes-Ayata, Ayse, 307
Gutiérrez, Bernardo, 273

Hernández de Ospina Pérez. Bertha, 154, 169, 243, 252
Hirschman, Albert O., 79
Hobsbawm, Eric J., 58
Holguín, Carlos, 256
Holmes Trujillo, Carlos, 176
Holt, Pat M., 106
Hommes, Rudolf, 297
Hoskins, Gary, 204, 249, 311
Hoyos, Bernardo, 281
Hoyos Jiménez, Carlos Mauro, 250

Iberian heritage and tradition in political clientelism of Latin America, 25–28
Indentured labor, 15–17
Industrial development, emergence of, 49

Instituto Colombiano de Reforma Agraria (INCORA), 79, 105, 147

Jaguaribe, Helio, 21
Jaramillo, William, 255
Jaramillo Giraldo, José, 116
Jaramillo Ocampo, Hernán, 147, 153–54
Jaramillo Ossa, Bernardo, 251, 258–59, 273
Jiménez-Gómez, Carlos, 229
Johnson, Kenneth C., 7, 16
Junguito Bonnet, Roberto, 232
Juventudes del MRL, 112

Kennedy, John F., Alliance for Progress, 80
Key, V. O., 23
Kline, Harvey, 39, 48, 52, 66, 188, 213, 220, 296

Land tenure in clientelism, 15–16
Landazábal, Fernando, 217–19
Lande, Carl H., 21, 24
Lara Bonilla, Rodrigo, 224–25, 227, 230
Latorre, Mario, 46–47, 204
La Violencia, 106, the collapse and renewal of clientelism, 57–65
Leal Buitrago, Francisco, 39, 43, 63, 84, 105, 185, 194
Lehder, Carlos, 225–27, 99–117, 250
Lemarchand, Rene, 306
Lemos Simmonds, Carlos, 281–82, 285
Leupin, Eric, 167–68
Leyva, Alvaro, 256
Leyva, Jorge, 94–95
Leyva Durán, Alvaro, 232
Liphart, Arend, 36–37
Lleras Camargo, Alberto, 51–53, 65–66, 106–7, 114–15, 144, 153, 170, 178, 180, 186, 196–97, 309
  agrarian reforms, 78–79
  campaign and elections, 93–95
  candidate selection, 91–93
  and the National Front, 65–66, 86–95
  Pact of Sitges, 82
  policies of governance, 75–85
  social and political controls, 81–85
Lleras de la Fuente, Carlos, 282, 297

Lleras Restrepo, Carlos, 78, 80, 91–92, 112, 114–17, 144, 152–55, 162, 172–77, 179, 192–93, 196–97, 199–200, 214, 220,
  administrative policies, 121–28
  agricultural modernization, 121, 126–27
  bureaucratized clientelism, 122
  currency devaluation, 120
  economic climate of state, 119–21
  exports, drop in, 120–23,
  foreign trade, 123
  inflation, 120
  land reforms, 120
  National Front, 131–40
  party competition, 131–34
  price controls, 125
  social and political controls, 128–31
  trade deficit, 120
  urbanization, 119–20
Lloreda Caicedo, Rodrigo, 214–15, 256–57, 259–60
Londoño, Dario, 284
López Caballero, Felipe, 169
López Caballero, Juan Manuel, 169–70
López Gómez, Alfonso, 230–32
López Michelsen, Alfonso, 83, 86, 88, 91, 94–95, 12–16, 152–58, 161–81, 185–86, 195–98, 201–4, 279, 282, 291–92, 297, 311
  administrative policies, 162–66, 245–49
  charges of corruption, 169
  Communists and work stoppage, 170–71
  economic climate of nation, 161–62
  exports and drug trafficking, 164–66, 168, 171
  guerilla activism, 167
  peso, overvaluation of, 165
  policies of governance, 161–62
  population growth and unemployment, 161–62
  reform and modernization, 162–66
  social and political controls, 166–71
  technological backwardness, 165
  Tripartite Commission, 163
  unrest, protests and work stoppages, 164, 166–69, 170–71, 173–74

violencia, 168
López Pumarejo, Alfonso, 50–51, 65–66, 77, 162, 308
Losada, Rodrigo, 39

Mainwaring, Scott, 10
Malloy, James M., 28
"Mandato Claro", 162–63, 166, 172
Marín, Rodrigo, 257
Marino Ospina, Iván, 218
Márquez, Pompeyo, 303
Martínez, Guillén, 43
Marxism and internal unrest, 106
Matamoros, Gustavo, 218–19
Medard, Jean Francois, 8
Mejía, María Emma, 277
Mejía, Tirado, 42
Mestizo, status in political Clientelism, 25
Mintz, Sidney W. and Eric R. Wolf, 13
Mockus, Antanas, 302
Modernization and restructuring
   foundations for, 75–95
   politics of biparty government, 229–40
   reformist impulses, 209–40
Molina, Gerardo, 203
Morales Benítez, Otto, 231
Moreno Guerrero, Augusto, 228 173
Movimiento 19 de Abril(M-19), 191–94, 218–23, 229, 252, 258
Movimiento de Recuperación (MRL), 78, 86–91,93–95, 111–13, 116, 157, 162, 173
Muerte a Secuestradores (MAS), death to kidnappers, 226, 228

Nation of Colombia
   biparty government, 243–62
   breakdown and renewal of clientel-ism, 57–71
   claim to islands San Andrés and Providencia, 216
   clientelism, the individual and the State, 7–31
   conceptualization of politics, 2
   consolidation and erosion of clientelism, 143–58
   modernization, foundations for, 75–95

patrimonial state and clientelism, 35–54
   redistribution of goods and income, 161–81
   reformist developmentalism, 119–40, and impulses, 209–40
   urbanization and demographic changes, 99–117
National Front, see Frente Nacional
Navarro Ospina, Luis, 154
Navarro Wolff, Antonio, 258, 277–78, 280–81, 283–86, 293
Nuñez, Rafael, 46–47

Ochoa Vásquez, Fabio, 226, 272
Ochoa Vásquez, Jorge Luis, 226–27, 272
Olaya Herrera, Enrique, 48–49, 280
Orejuela, Raúl, 258
Orozco, Moisés, 303
Ortega, Daniel, 216
Ospina, Berta, 233
Ospina Pérez, Maria Eugenia, 64
Ospina Pérez, Mariano, 52–54, 58, 61–63, 65, 77, 87, 90–93, 113–14, 144, 152–53, 174–75, 211
Ossa Escobar, Carlos, 253

Pardo, Rafael, 258, 277
Pardo Leal, Jaime, 238
Parejo, Enrique, 275, 282
Pastrana, Andrés, 250, 281, 283, 297–98, 314
Pastrana Arango, Andrés, 253–54, 283–87
Pastrana Borrero, Misael, 114, 143–58, 211, 232–33, 239, 243, 252, 256–57, 259–60, 279–80, 292
   agrarian reform, 146
   bureaucratic centralism and erosion of clientelism, 144
   campaign and elections, 155–58
   candidate selection, 153–55
   consolidation and national integra-tion, 144–45
   distribution of national wealth, 145
   exports, promotion of, 145
   "Four Strategies" program, 145–47, 161
   guerrilla uprisings, 149

housing, stimulation of construction, 145
labor unrest, 143
National Front, politics of, 151–58
party in-fighting, 151–53
policies of administration, 144–48
public debt, 143
social and political controls, 148–51
social reformism, 145
state of economy, 143–44
student activism and academic autonomy, 148
Patron-Client relations in clientelism
historical developments in, 7–31
political relationships in post violencia period, 67
relevance in Colombian experience, 35–44
rural patron improving status, 9–13, 15–18, 23–24, 26
universality of clientelism, 8–12
Peeler, John A., 45–46, 70
Pérez, Manuel, 274, 284
Pérez, Maria José, 213
Pérez García, Juan David, 238
Pitt-Rivers, J. A., 17
Pizarro, Eduardo, 291, 296
Pizarro Leongómez, Carlos, 251, 258–59
Powell, John Duncan, 9, 22, 308, 312
Purcell, Susan Kaufman, 38

Ramírez Acuña, Luis Fernando, 286
Ramírez Ocampo, Augusto, 172, 231
Redistribution policies of Lopez Michelsen, 161–81
Reagan, Ronald, 215
Reno, Janet, 273
Restrepo, Luis Alberto, 210
Reveiz, Edgar, 213
Revolution Cuban-style, 167, 171
Rincon Quiñones, José Ramon, 168
Rodríguez Gacha, José, 226
Rojas de Moreno, María Eugenia, 155, 157, 180, 212
Rojas Pinilla, Gustavo, 61–64, 66, 315
return, trial and conviction, 84–85, 94–95, 101, 109, 113, 116, 153, 220
Romero, Carlos, 258

Roniger, Louis, see Eisenstadt, S.N.
Roniger, Luis, 305, 308
Rueda Hernández, Monseñor Héctor, 222
Ruiz Novoa, Alberto, 107–10, 157

Samper Pizano, Ernesto, 231, 253, 275, 277, 282–87, 294, 297, 313, 316–17
Sanchez, Julio Cesar, 277
Santa, Eduardo, 47
Santacruz Londoño, José, 273
Santofimio Botero, Alberto, 173, 196–98, 231, 255
Santos, Eduardo (ed. El Tiempo), 51, 309
Santos Calderón, Enrique, 293
Sanz de Santamaría, Carlos, 102–3
Schmidt, Steffen W., 39, 41, 69, 315
Scott, James C., 10, 14, 17–18
Seal, Barry, 227
Secretariado Nacional de Asistencia Social(SENDAS), 64
Serpa Uribe, Horacio, 293, 299
Silva Luján, Gabriel, 194
Silva, Miguel, 277
Sloan, John, 11
Sorauf, Frank, 23
State, see Nation of Colombia

Terrorism, guerilla activity, kidnapping and murder, 250–51
Thoumi, Francisco E., 100
Toledo Plaza, Carlos, 220
Torres, Camilo, 109–10
Turbay, Gabriel, 62–53
Turbay Ayala, Julio César. 14–15, 152, 154–55, 162, 172, 175–78, 180–81, 217, 222, 233, 254–55, 282
civil unrest and state of siege, 190
decentralization and regional development, 187
economic climate of state, 185–86
financing development, 187, 189
general strike of 1977, 190
guerilla activism, 190–93
inflation and problems of, 186–89
military rule, public unrest, state of siege, 190–92
mining and energy development, 187

monetary adjustments, 186–89
peace offerings of amnesty, 192–93
Plan de Integración Nacional (PIN),
187–88
policies of governance, 185–94
social and political controls, 187,
190–94
traditionalism and repression, 185–
204
Turbay, David, 282
Turbay de Uribe, Diana, 273

Unidades de Poder Adquisitivo Constante (UPAC), 146, 163
Unión Liberal Popular, 195–96
Unión Nacional coalition, 58, 77
Unión Patriótica (UP), 221, 224, 235,
239
Uniparty government
campaign and elections, 258–60
candidate selection, 254–58
loyal opposition to, 248–49, 252
toward constitutional reform, 260–
62
United States, Alliance for Progress, 80;
and military assistance for internal
security, 85
US Overseas Private Investment Corporation, 214
Urbanization, changing partisan domination, 185
Urdaneta Arbeláez, Roberto, 60–61
Uribe Díaz, 39, 43, 67
Uribe Rueda, Alvaro, 111–12

Valderrama, J. Emilio, 147, 154, 172,
191, 231, 233
Valdivieso, Alfonso, 300
Valencia, Guillermo León, 99–117, 250
aim for bureaucratic centralist state,
100
budget deficits, 100, 104
"Christian Social" revolution, 102

civilian supremacy challenged, 109
congressional policies affecting, 103
emergency powers requested, 103–
4
imports, restrictions on, 100
industrial growth, 100
internal party dissension, 111–17
International Monetary Fund assist-
ing, 103
monetary crisis, 103 and Junta
Monetaria (Monetary Board),
104
National Front, politics of, 111–13
nation-wide strike, 109
policies of administration, 101–6
relations with Congress, 103–4
self-defense and move for "independent republics". 107
social and political controls, 106–11
surtaxes, 104
United States loans, 100, 103
vacillation on economic policy, 106
Valencia, Hernando, 300
Valencia Tovar, Alvaro, 150, 166–67,
177, 181
Varón Valencia, Abraham, 167–68, 195
Vásques Cobo, Alfredo, 49
Vásquez Carrizosa, Alfredo, 172, 280
Vásquez Castaño, Fabio, 167
Veloso, Junco, 311
Villareal, Tiberio, 312
Villegas, Fabio, 277
Villegas Moreno, Alvaro, 278
Vives Echeverria, Ignacio, 153

Wagley, Charles, 26
Weingrod, Alex, 10, 23
Wolf, Eric A., 17 and Sidney W. Mintz,
13

Zamosc, Leon, 251
Zea Hernandez, Germán, 172, 189–90,
196–97